IDENTITIES, GROUPS AND SOCIAL ISSUES

EDITED BY MARGARET WETHERELL

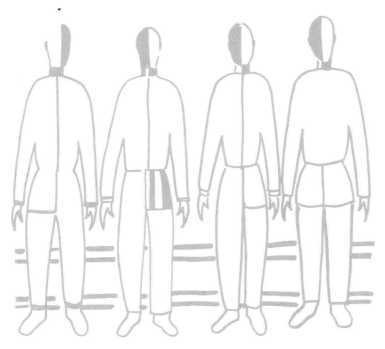

SAGE Publications
London • Thousand Oaks • New Delhi
In association with

The Open
University

105814

Cover illustration: Kasimir Malevich, *Sportsmen*, *c.*1928–32, oil on canvas, 142 × 164 cm., State Russian Museum, St Petersburg.

The Open University, Walton Hall, Milton Keynes MK7 6AA

SAGE Publications Ltd
6 Bonhill Street
London EC2A 4PU

SAGE Publications Inc
2455 Teller Road
Thousand Oaks
California 91320

Sage Publications India Pvt Ltd
32, M-Block Market
Greater Kailash - I
New Delhi 110 048

British Library Cataloguing in Publication data

A catalogue record for this book is available from the British Library

ISBN 0 7619 5037 0

ISBN 0 7619 5038 9 (pbk)

Library of Congress catalog record available

Edited, designed and typeset by the Open University.

Printed in Great Britain by Butler and Tanner Ltd, Frome.

This text forms part of an Open University course D317 *Social Psychology: Personal Lives, Social Worlds*. Details of this and other Open University courses can be obtained from the Course Reservations and Sales Centre, PO Box 724, The Open University, Milton Keynes, MK7 6ZS. For availability of other course components, contact Open University Worldwide, The Berrill Building, Walton Hall, Milton Keynes MK7 6AA.

16745C/d317b3i1.2

Contents

Social Psychology: Personal Lives, Social Worlds Course Team

Open University Staff

Dr Dorothy Miell (Course Team Chair, Senior Lecturer in Psychology)

Alison Bannister (Print Buying Co-ordinator)

Penny Bennett (Editor, Social Sciences)

Pam Berry (Compositor)

David Calderwood (Project Control)

Lene Connolly (Print Buying Controller)

Dr Troy Cooper (Staff Tutor)

Dr Rose Croghan (Research Fellow in Psychology)

Sarah Crompton (Graphic Designer)

Dr Rudi Dallos (Staff Tutor)

Jonathan Davies (Graphic Design Co-ordinator)

Jane Elliott (Producer, BBC)

Janis Gilbert (Graphic Artist)

Dr Sue Gregory (Senior Lecturer in Psychology)

Jonathan Hunt (Book Trade Department)

Tom Hunter (Editor, Social Sciences)

Carole Kershaw (Course Secretary)

Patti Langton (Producer, BBC)

Vic Lockwood (Senior Producer, BBC)

Dr Janet Maybin (Lecturer, School of Education)

Jeannette Murphy (Senior Lecturer in Health Informatics, University College London Medical School, co-opted on to team during course production)

Lynda Preston (Psychology Secretary)

Dr Roger Sapsford (Senior Lecturer in Research Methods)

Varrie Scott (Course Manager)

Brenda Smith (Staff Tutor)

Paul Smith (Media Librarian)

Richard Stevens (Senior Lecturer in Psychology)

Dr Kerry Thomas (Senior Lecturer in Psychology)

Dr Frederick Toates (Senior Lecturer in Biology)

Pat Vasiliou (Psychology Discipline Secretary)

Dr Diane Watson (Staff Tutor)

Dr Margaret Wetherell (Senior Lecturer in Psychology)

Kathy Wilson (Production Assistant, BBC)

Chris Wooldridge (Editor, Social Sciences)

External authors and tutor consultants

Dr Michael Argyle (Emeritus Reader in Social Psychology, University of Oxford)

Hedy Brown (Formerly Senior Lecturer in Social Psychology, Open University)

Dr David Devalle (OU Social Psychology Tutor)

Professor Robert Hinde (Retired, St John's College, Cambridge)

Dr Mansur Lalljee (Lecturer in Social Psychology and Fellow of Jesus College, University of Oxford)

Jackie Malone (OU Social Psychology Tutor)

Dr Patrick McGhee (Head of Psychology and School Director Teaching and Learning, University of Derby, OU Tutor Consultant)

Helen Morgan (Psychotherapist and Consultant)

Professor Jonathan Potter (Professor of Discourse Analysis, Loughborough University)

Dr Alan Radley (Reader in Health and Social Relations, Loughborough University)

Stephen Reicher (Reader in Social Psychology, University of St Andrews)

Dr Arthur Still (Part-time Senior Lecturer in Psychology, University of Durham, OU Social Psychology Tutor)

Dr Arlene Vetere (Lecturer in Family Psychology, Reading University)

External assessors

Professor Jerome Bruner (Research Professor of Psychology, New York University, Senior Research Fellow in Law, School of Law, New York University)

Professor Michael Billig (Professor of Social Sciences, Loughborough University)

Professor Steve Duck (Daniel and Amy Starch Distinguished Research Professor of Interpersonal Communication, and Adjunct Professor of Psychology, University of Iowa)

Professor Kenneth J. Gergen (Mustin Professor of Psychology, Swarthmore College, Pennsylvania)

Foreword

Studying social psychology and studying history are akin in one particularly interesting way. For either of them to matter much in your own life, you must end up making what you have learned your own. And the only way to do that is to explore different ways of framing or constructing the subject-matter at hand until you have found *your* way of making sense of it. For just as there is no *the* history, say, of the French Revolution, there is no *the* social psychology of the family. Both 'subjects' gain their meanings through the perspective one brings to bear on them. The French Revolution is a struggle for the rights of man, and it is a chapter in the story of mob tyranny. One studies it differently, even chooses one's facts differently, depending upon which of the two perspectives one has chosen as a focus. And so too the social psychology of the family – whether one wishes to look at family life in terms of 'systems theory', or in terms of the working out of the psychoanalytic Oedipus theme, or from the point of view of the phenomenologies of family members and how they are negotiated in dinner-table conversations.

This Open University social psychology course is a radical departure in teaching social psychology. Rather than insisting that there is a 'right and only' way to look at phenomena social psychologically – *the* social psychology of this or that – it takes the truth of perspective as its starting point. Its aim is to present a variety of perspectives on the standard 'topics' of social psychology, not only to give them depth but also to equip the student with the wherewithal for creating her or his *own* perspective. But it does this in such a way as to recognize not only the relativity of social knowledge, but also to honour the canons of good social science. For the relativity of perspective does not mean that 'anything goes'. Rather, it means that whatever perspective one brings to bear carries with it requirements of method. Has one gained sufficient information on the matter at hand, protected oneself against facile presuppositions, looked with sufficient care at the antecedents of the phenomenon one is studying, and so on? The course attempts to give as clear a view as possible of what constitutes good enquiry as conducted from the vantage-points of several crucial perspectives.

After studying the volumes in this series, the student should be prepared to evaluate different perspectives in social psychology and, as noted, to come up with one of his or her own, one that meets the standards of sound social science. In this sense, these books deliberately merge the conventional categories of teaching and research. The authors have succeeded in resisting the usual 'teacherly' approach of giving standard reviews of the existing literature on some narrow topics, and instead have provided abundant opportunities for the student to try his or her hand at creating original syntheses of several related topics that bear on each other. In doing so, they use the tools of research as a means of teaching in a most creative way.

There is one further feature of the series that needs special mention. Its emphasis upon the place of perspective in the legitimizing of 'facts' and the construction of theories inevitably leads to questions about the philosophy of knowledge – to puzzling issues in epistemology. Rather than simply tabling these and leaving them for some other course to discuss, this course tackles them head on. So in a way, it is a course not only about social psychology, but also, if I may use an odd term, about social epistemology. At times, then, the student will find himself or herself in a dialogue whose other members are not only psychologists and sociologists, but also philosophers and even literary theorists (for in a very deep sense, the 'data' of social psychology are texts of what people said about what they thought or felt, narrative texts at that).

The series crosses many disciplinary boundaries that are often regarded as either taboo or as too forbidding for students to cross. For social psychology is a field of study that grew out of two traditions that have often been regarded as antithetical – even at war with each other. One tradition is primarily societal or cultural, and looks at social interaction from the point of view of the roles and statuses that people occupy within a social structure, specifying the obligations and rights that activate and constrain those who fill these roles and statuses. This is 'sociological' social psychology – and a good part of social psychology as a disciplinary study is situated in sociology departments of universities. The other tradition is psychological, its emphasis squarely on the individual – his or her attitudes, values, reactions, and the like. And as psychological social psychology, this side of the discipline takes its methods from the different approaches that psychology has adopted over the century since its founding. It may emphasize a more strictly experimental approach, a more humanistic one, or one based on what has come to be called 'social constructionism' that sees the data and theories of psychology as situated in or deriving from the discourse of human beings in interaction. The volumes try to make a place for all of these approaches, treating them not as antagonistic to each other, but as complementary.

In tackling social psychology in so multifaceted a way, these books manage something that is rarely tried in the teaching of this subject. They bridge two traditions that rarely meet in the theatre of university instruction – a principally North American 'scientific' tradition based on the positivist ideal of objectivity, and a European tradition that is much more strongly interpretivist in spirit. And they manage to make as good a case as possible for both of them. Some critics of the books will doubtless say, I'm sure, that they give too much credence to one side, some to the other. And this is as it should be.

It is impossible to teach an honest course in social psychology in our times without taking into account the diversity of modern society. There is no such thing as a standard family or a standard work-place about which to make generalizations – whether they be statistical generalizations or interpretative ones. There are indeed families in Britain, for example, that meet the traditional criterion of being 'standard'. They are White, Anglo-Saxon, Protestant, Middle-class. They may fare better on the job market, but they are hardly 'standard' save in some possibly hegemonic sense. What holds for them does not hold for Jamaican families in Brixton, for immigrant Pakistani families in Bradford whose children are struggling to find an identity, and so on. So, again almost inevitably, social psychology needs to be sensitive not so much to 'society in general' but to the changing social patterns of our times. And I believe that this series achieves such sensitivity.

During the long preparation of these volumes, I have served in the role of what is called, in Open University terminology, the Course Assessor. The

Course Assessor quickly becomes a partner in dialogue with the course team. I have been such a partner 'from a distance' – geographically if not psychologically. We have been engaged for more than a year in a constant and busy exchange of chapter drafts, memoranda, and conversation – me in New York or in my writing hideaway in West County Cork, they in Milton Keynes. We have used every imaginable form of telecommunication – post, fax, e-mail, telephone. I have found it enormously rewarding, both psychologically and intellectually. For this series has been an adventure for those of us involved in constructing it, not only a scholarly one but, indeed, a moral one. For this is a series designed to teach people not just *about* social psychology, but how to *think* social psychology. And as with any such undertaking, it forced all of us to think hard about what a social psychologist *ought* to be. So I must close this foreword by thanking my friends at the Open University for what I can only describe as a 'consciousness raising trip'. And I rather suspect that the readers of this series will do the same when they're done with it.

Jerome Bruner, New York University

Preface

Identities, Groups and Social Issues is one of three books which form the core of the Open University course D317 *Social Psychology: Personal Lives, Social Worlds*. The others are *Understanding the Self* (edited by Richard Stevens) and *Social Interaction and Personal Relationships* (edited by Dorothy Miell and Rudi Dallos). Students of the Open University course receive supplementary material, including an opening 'trigger unit' which uses a discussion of health and illness to introduce key themes and topics within social psychology and, at the end of the course, a 'course review'. There is also a book on philosophical and methodological issues in social psychology, a set of projects, four television and eight radio programmes, and three audiocassettes which extend and develop the course material. The three volumes published in this series have been designed to be read independently of this supplementary material.

Taken as a whole, the books which make up this series present a trajectory through three central domains of analysis in social psychology – the individual, interpersonal relationships and, in this book, groups and collective life. We have tried to encompass a wide range of material, including the classics of social psychology, but have set these in the context of the overall philosophy developed by the course team in our discussions over many months. Key decisions were that this course should focus on theory, that it should take a multiple perspective approach, maintain an interdisciplinary focus, define social psychology broadly rather than narrowly, and try to describe the origins of ideas and the historical contexts in which they were developed. The goal was not to make life easy for students but, through the presentation of multiple perspectives, to emphasize choice, active learning and the importance of making up one's own mind. We wanted to try to develop a critical, comparative and evaluative orientation in the student, a sense of the different places in which it is possible to stand within social psychology and the implications of these different theoretical positions for people's involvement in social life.

Reflecting these general course-wide aims, this book explores three traditions of research on groups and collective life – experimental, social constructionist and psychodynamic. Due weight is given to the pioneers of group research in social psychology such as the Sherifs, Asch, Lewin, Festinger, Milgram and Adorno, and to the vibrant tradition of research which has emerged in recent decades within European social psychology stimulated by Henri Tajfel and Serge Moscovici among others. My aim in this book was also, however, to try to recreate some of the flavour of those excellent social psychology texts of the 1940s and 1950s. Looking back at these texts now, their breadth and scope are surprising. To be sure, they focus on experiments and on approaches which make up the main subject-matter of most modern textbooks, but they also range much more widely. The boundaries between psychology and sociology are not so strongly marked, the authors draw on anthropology, on ethnography, make literary references, are conversant with psychoanalysis, and move easily through discussions of contemporary social theory. Above all, the texts we wished to emulate are concerned with ideas, with provocative speculations about social life, and have a strongly practical and applied focus.

Like all Open University materials, *Identities, Groups and Social Issues* was the product of an intensive period of collaboration which involved the entire course team, the tutor panel and a number of external consultants (Hedy Brown, Helen Morgan and Jonathan Potter). I want particularly to note, however, the contribution of the Course Chair, Dorothy Miell, who somehow managed to find the time to comment extensively on three drafts of this book while also taking managerial and administrative responsibility for course production as a whole – a demanding task handled always with grace, flair and great skill. The book and my chapters in particular benefited greatly from Arthur Still's thoughtful comments and his extensive knowledge of the historical and philosophical bases of social psychology and, similarly, from the comments of Patrick McGhee, Jeannette Murphy, Kerry Thomas and Rudi Dallos. We were fortunate to be aided by an excellent Course Assessor, Jerome Bruner, and Book Assessor, Michael Billig, whose suggestions and comments were decisive in the organization of the book, and always apposite. Finally, my thanks must go to Carole Kershaw, a superb and very able Course Team secretary, to the Course Manager, Varrie Scott, to Chris Wooldridge and Penny Bennett for their very evident editorial skills, and to Sarah Crompton for her quality design work.

Margaret Wetherell
for the Course Team

INTRODUCTION

by Margaret Wetherell

As I was writing this Introduction, there were several stories which consistently featured in the newspapers and the television news – conflict in Bosnia, conflict over the peace process in Northern Ireland, the trial in the United States of the American football star O.J. Simpson, accounts of sleaze and turmoil in the British Conservative Party, and discussions of the absence of a 'feel-good factor' in the UK as short-term job contracts and redundancies bit into middle-class security. Some of these stories are more ephemeral than others. By the time you read this, O.J. Simpson, for instance, may be a distant memory, a difficult question on a Trivial Pursuit general knowledge card. The 'feel-good factor' will quite likely have given way to another neologism coined to capture the public mood. Turmoil and sleaze are likely to have been superseded by other political stories. I predict, however, that the questions these types of events raise for social psychologists will continue and will have a longer life.

The reporting of events in places such as Bosnia and Northern Ireland drew attention to the complicated group loyalties which underpin situations of conflict. It was a reminder of the strength of historically-based suspicions of those seen as 'other', and the intricate nature of judgements about self and group interests. Conflict, particularly when it is murderous and violent, raises questions about the *psychology* of social groups, as well as about economics and politics, and revives debates about 'human nature'. Is conflict between communities inevitable? It draws attention, also, to the asymmetries in people's constructions of situations so that acts which seem irrational, inexplicable and even crazy to one observer can seem obvious, strategic and entirely sensible to another. How does this variation arise?

One of the interesting things about the O.J. Simpson case in the USA was the illustration of the possibilities of 'mass culture'. These possibilities were initiated by the televising of O.J. Simpson's capture by the police which involved a dramatic (if slow motion) car chase through Los Angeles. For millions of people the trial became a hook for varied fantasies, fears, hopes and identifications. A global community was created who could argue the ins and outs of the evidence. The boundaries around what was 'real' and what was 'fiction', already difficult to distinguish, became further blurred as the obscure happenings on the night of the murder merged on the television screen with soap opera narrative and the genre of courtroom drama. This trial, like other high profile cases, rigorously questioned the rituals of justice. It was a reminder, as is the political and economic news in general, of how dependent social life is on organized institutions such as the law.

The central theme of this volume, *Identities, Groups and Social Issues*, is the social psychology of collective life. The focus will be on some of the *ordered* aspects of society – including groups (both large and small), social organizations and institutions, shared processes of sense-making, representations and discourse, social norms and social roles. Chapters 1 and 2 look at group process and ask how organized forms of social life emerge. What happens to people in groups? What is going on when aggregates of people start to act collectively? Chapter 3 considers research on attitudes, social representations and discourse. How do people form beliefs and opinions, and develop evaluations and assessments of the events which surround them? Chapter 4 focuses on intergroup relations, that is, on the relationships between groups, and the contribution social psychologists might make to the analysis of phenomena such as racism and ethnocentrism. Work, as a principal institution of our society, is the major theme of Chapter 5. Chapter 6 returns to the topic of identity and looks at the effects of social history upon individual life history, focusing specifically on gender and masculine identities. What is the personal significance of an individual's social positions?

The volume as a whole has a strong historical focus. We try to cover a broad canvas, looking at a range of thinking in social psychology from the 1920s onwards. Recent work is set in its historical context so that the conceptual development of the discipline over time can be seen. Indeed, the topics covered in this volume have been at the heart of social psychology since the discipline was established in the early decades of this century. In those early years, for example, one key debate concerned the presence and possibility of 'group minds'. McDougall (1920) developed this concept to express his sense that groups and collectivities, such as crowds, seem to have a mental life of their own (see also Le Bon, 1895; Freud, 1921 and Jung, 1936). McDougall argued that groups and crowds have a psychology over and above that of the individual. We often talk, for instance, of 'the crowd acting as one', of 'the sombre mood of the nation' and 'how the mob turned ugly'. As Turner (1987) notes, it is assumed that any significant group will have feelings, emotions, intentions, and desires of its own.

Does this notion of 'group mind' mesh in any way with your own experiences of organized crowd events such as sports spectating? What do you think might be going on when crowds begin to 'act as one'?

One of the main aims of the pioneers of experimental social psychological research on collective life, people such as Sherif (1936), Lewin (1948) and Asch (1952) whose work will be considered in Chapter 1, was to try and answer the questions raised by examples of collective action. These pioneers tried to clarify the *emergent properties* which groups seem to possess such as norms, roles, shared habits and patterns of response, and shared decision-making styles; the features which seem to develop out of the interaction of people with each other. Emergent properties also inter-

'The Mexican Wave' is a good example of 'crowds acting as one'

ested psychodynamic researchers such as Bion (1961) and continue to be a core topic for contemporary researchers working from a variety of perspectives.

The focus of this volume will be on the diverse ways in which social psychologists have theorized these and other features of collective life. As in the previous volumes in this series, our aim is not to close down debate but to indicate the plurality of knowledges in social psychology. In this volume, this will involve a discussion between three of the five perspectives that were introduced in *Understanding the Self*, the first volume of this series. We will look at the perspectives of experimental social psychology, psychodynamic theory and social constructionism (presented here as discursive psychology and discourse analysis). From time to time the voices of biologists and experiential social psychologists (the two other perspectives introduced in *Understanding the Self*) will also be presented, but to a minor extent as these have stimulated much less research on identities, groups and social issues.

By the end of the volume, the characteristic approach that each of our three main perspectives take to identities, groups and social issues should be clear – the kinds of questions asked, the conceptual vocabularies developed, and the sort of research engendered. In the remainder of this Introduction, to begin this process of explication, I want to briefly sketch out some of the main concerns of each perspective, beginning with experimental social psychology, the most prolific source of theories and research in this area over the last 70 or so years. The experimental perspective is defined in terms of its methodological prescriptions but, as we have tried to demonstrate in the two earlier volumes of the series, these prescriptions also encourage a particular set of angles on the nature of the individual and social life. This distinctive framework has been described as *psychological social psychology* and contrasted with *sociological social psychology.*

Experimental social psychologists argue that when faced with problems of understanding identities, groups and social issues, the best way to proceed is through painstaking empirical investigations of the variables which seem to be crucial. Usually, this will lead to the setting up of a controlled experiment in the laboratory or in the field where individuals can be presented with some social stimulus and their reactions can be closely observed. For example, Chapter 1 describes a famous study conducted by Asch (1952) on conformity which demonstrated that when presented with a set of unanimous, but obviously wrong, judgements, many experimental subjects conformed to others' views and denied the evidence of their own senses. In trying to explain these kinds of results, experimental social psychologists have developed hypotheses about the reasoning and motivational processes which might go on in an individual's mind as he or she conforms to or resists group pressures, as well as looking at individual differences in conformity.

As this volume will demonstrate, the best experimental work of this kind has tried to show how individual psychology is *transformed* in group situations so that individuals come to act in qualitatively different ways in collective situations (Turner, 1987). This research has focused on the emergent properties of collective life referred to earlier (social norms, roles, decision-making styles, group history). It has looked at the ways in which a group is *more than the sum of its parts* (the individuals which make it up). An institution like a school, for instance, in one sense is nothing but the people who go there every day, but it is also more than this aggregate of individuals since, collectively, through their interaction over time, social structures, rules, roles and shared understandings are created which in turn act on and shape individual responses. Experimental social psychologists have tried to demonstrate how these group properties affect individual thinking and feeling. These social psychologists, as Chapter 1 demonstrates, have tried to illustrate through their experiments the coordinated nature of social action and the moments when group properties appear.

Despite this emphasis on social influences, the focus in this work has remained firmly on the individual, largely because of the demands of experimental procedures. As Turner states, speaking on behalf of experimental social psychologists: 'it is a basic assumption of modern psychology that psychological processes reside only in individuals – in the most literal sense, at least, there is no such thing as a "group mind"' (1987, p. 4). The individual in this approach is seen as the most 'real', basic or core unit for social psychology. Furthermore, this individual has been seen as relatively self-contained, consistent and bounded rather than fragmented or contradictory. The main focus in explaining the social psychology of collective life has been on cognition (individual reasoning and thinking processes and how these are transformed in group situations) and on motivational states (how individual self-esteem and perceptions of self interest become locked into the group situation).

The psychodynamic tradition of research on groups and social life, which has an equally long history, takes a contrasting view of the participating individual and the way in which group properties emerge. Here the focus has been on natural groups rather than groups contrived within laboratories – on families, therapy groups, work groups within organizations, and so on. Research has been conducted by psychoanalysts who are often participants in these groups or are group leaders. They try to develop a narrative of what is occurring using their intuitions, their own emotional responses, and the detachment and concepts derived from their psychodynamic training. A further goal has been to refine and develop psychodynamic concepts to capture regular patterns in group processes found across many different kinds of group situations.

Concepts such as identification, projection and projective identification (Thomas, 1996a and 1996b) have been used to understand the emotional life of such groups, the development of recurrent patterns and roles, and to make sense of the ways in which anxiety is managed. The picture of the individual which emerges in this research stresses the role of unconscious motivations, irrationality, acts of semi-deliberate 'not knowing' and the complex and contradictory positions individuals can take up in groups. One of the most fascinating aspects of this work is the way in which it exemplifies McDougall's early notion of 'group mind' and to some extent rescues this concept from its dismissal by experimental social psychologists. Mental properties, such as fantasies and projections, are seen as dispersed and shared across group members so that the question of who owns what piece of psychological business becomes difficult to answer.

Social constructionist researchers share psychodynamic concerns about the constraints of the experimental method and the model of the individual and the interpreting self which results. In this perspective, the focus is not on the individual *per se* but on the *forms of life* and the *activities* which make up sociality. For example, if we take a workplace, such as a factory, the social constructionist would not begin with the cognitive processes of individual workers, but would start with the practices and narratives which characterize life in this place and would look at how identities emerge from these streams of activity and sense-making. To take an example from Chapter 5, the aim might be to discover what it is that makes a manager, and how being 'managerial' is negotiated in different kinds of corporations.

Similarly, Chapter 6 develops a feminist social constructionist analysis of the masculine identities found in different forms of life and looks at the ways in which these construct the possibilities for individual men. To be a working-class man, for instance, is to live out and inhabit a very different set of practices and narratives about what it means to be a 'real man' compared to, say, middle-class, professional or academic masculinity. An important focus in this perspective is on language and discourse as one medium of social activity. Thus *discursive psychology*, which is introduced in Chapter 3, has been concerned with the conversational activities of everyday life and the coordination of joint action through talk, studying the ordered, but often taken-for-granted, and pre-reflective basis of social life.

The social constructionist notion of a 'relational' and 'distributed' self (see Wetherell and Maybin, 1996) also encourages an interest in 'group minds' but from a rather different stance than the psychodynamic perspective. The researcher begins to focus on patterns in discourse and on the collective voices which become the internal dialogues making up the individual psyche. In this view, 'mind' is not so unambiguously and clearly located in individuals alone but is emergent from the collective socio-cultural and linguistic realm. The individual is seen as dispersed across, and emergent from, the streams of activity which make up social life.

The main aim of presenting a diversity of perspectives and theories is to encourage a *critical orientation*. Through comparing diverse vocabularies it becomes possible to evaluate the strengths and weaknesses of different theories and perspectives, to begin to make choices and to develop arguments for those choices. In this brief sketch of some of the broad theoretical perspectives developed in this volume, I have indicated the kinds of questions readers could usefully address to the studies, examples and theories encountered along the way. A good question to ask about any study or theory is – what conceptual language does this work with or presuppose? What is assumed about the nature of collective life? How are subjectivity, the person and the participants in collective life understood?

Discussion of the theoretical perspectives underpinning this book will be found at a number of points in the chapters that follow. Chapters 1 and 2, which look at small groups, concentrate on the experimental and psychodynamic perspectives respectively, and develop these two perspectives in detail. Chapters 3 and 4 take a more mixed approach. Chapter 3, for example, on attitudes, social representations and discursive psychology begins with experimental work on the development of beliefs and opinions and then looks at two more constructionist theories in this area. Chapter 4 on racism and intergroup relations compares and contrasts a variety of psychodynamic, experimental and social constructionist research, while Chapters 5 and 6 work mainly from a broadly social constructionist perspective noting also other developments. All in all, the story of *Identities, Groups and Social Issues* is a complicated one with many subtle variations in theory and method but it is also one with many rich and fascinating details along the way. We hope you enjoy it!

References

Asch, S. (1952) *Social Psychology*, Englewood Cliffs, Prentice-Hall.

Bion, W. (1961) *Experiences in Groups and Other Papers*, London, The Tavistock Institute.

Freud, S. (1921) *Group Psychology and the Analysis of the Ego*, London, Hogarth Press.

Jung, C. (1936, 1959) 'The concept of the collective unconscious', Vol. 9, Part One *Collected Works*, London, Routledge.

Le Bon, G. (1895, translated 1947), *The Crowd: A Study of the Popular Mind*, London, Ernest Benn.

Lewin, K. (1948) *Resolving Social Conflicts*, New York, Harper.

McDougall, W. (1920) *The Group Mind*, Cambridge, Cambridge University Press.

Sherif, M. (1936) *The Psychology of Social Norms*, New York, Harper.

Stevens, R. (ed.) (1996) *Understanding the Self*, London, Sage/ The Open University (Book 1 in this series).

Thomas, K. (1996a) 'The defensive self: a psychodynamic perspective', in Stevens, R. (ed.).

Thomas, K. (1996b), 'The psychodynamics of relating', in Miell, D. and Dallos, R. (eds.) (1996) *Social Interaction and Personal Relationships*, London, Sage/ The Open University (Book 2 in this series).

Turner, J. (1987) 'Introducing the problem: individual and group', in Turner, J., Hogg, M., Oakes, P., Reicher, S. and Wetherell, M. *Rediscovering the Social Group*, Oxford, Basil Blackwell.

Wetherell, M. and Maybin, J. (1996) 'The distributed self: a social constructionist perspective', in Stevens, R. (ed.).

CHAPTER 1

THEMES IN EXPERIMENTAL RESEARCH ON GROUPS FROM THE 1930s TO THE 1990s

by Hedy Brown

Contents

1   Introduction

Every time we turn on the television or read a newspaper we are confronted with examples of how group membership shapes human behaviour and attitudes. Several examples were presented in the Introduction to this book and no doubt other instances also occur to you now. You might remember items about religious sects, such as David Kuresh's influence on the members of his sect in Waco, Texas, or that of the Reverend Jim Jones on his followers in the isolation of their jungle settlement in Guyana. If these examples, though dramatic and memorable, are no longer part of general knowledge, you may recall discussions in the media about urban gangs, soccer hooligans or strife between ethnic and religious groups.

What strikes me about this list is that the instances I have cited all show the negative impact of group membership. One of the topics we will need to consider in this chapter, as we think about group influence and group processes, is whether group membership also leads to positive effects, bringing out the best in individuals, and what the relationship might be between the positive and negative aspects of group life.

ACTIVITY 1.1

To start you thinking about the influence of groups on their members, make a list of the various social groups to which you feel you belong; then compare your list with the following checklist.

Political group, sports club, religious group (church, temple or mosque), parents' association, trade union or professional association, residents' association, family, drama society, theatre group, film club, women's group, Automobile Association, Consumers' Association, Ramblers' Association, Youth Hostel Association, Students' Union, ethnic group, 'racial' group, work group, friends in local pub.

Are all these groups of the same kind, in your view?

Did your list include any of these? Are there any which are relevant but which you have omitted? If so, is this because you 'forgot' the category – does this imply that you would not ordinarily think of the category as a social group, or is it because the group is not terribly significant to you or so significant but unwelcome that you repress the thought of your membership?

What groups have you mentioned that I have missed? What does it say about me that I have left them out? On reflection, do you feel your social groups influence or control you?

The aim of this chapter and Chapter 2 is to look at the evidence concerning the effects on individuals of their group memberships. Chapter 2 develops a psychodynamic perspective on group processes, while this chapter focuses on the rich seam of knowledge about groups and group membership generated by *experimental* social psychologists from the 1930s onwards.

The term 'experimental', as the Introduction to this volume noted, describes a *general style* of social psychological investigation and theory building. The emphasis in this tradition of research is placed on measurement, reliability and objectivity, on developing hypotheses and then testing these in situations where the effects of different variables can be controlled. Experimental research is not confined to studies in the laboratory, of course. Variables can be controlled, outcomes carefully observed and quantified in a context beyond the laboratory, though such 'field' studies, as they are called, are sometimes more difficult to set up. As we shall see, this approach to the study of groups has led to an emphasis on the cognitive and motivational changes which occur within individuals when they become group members.

The study of groups from the experimental perspective has focused on many aspects of the relations between individuals and groups since the first controlled investigation of the psychological effects of the presence of others carried out by Triplett in 1897. A key emphasis from the beginning has been on the ways in which group membership may *inhibit* or *enhance* individual performance. Research has also focused on who is included in the group (and, therefore, is owed some consideration or assistance) and who is not part of the group and under what circumstances these membership criteria apply. Explanations of group influence and group processes have varied from those which look to the pre-existing psychology of individual group members to those which stress the transforming power of the social and group context. Why do we become so involved with other people? Why do we join groups? Why is group membership so important to people that they may be willing to 'bend towards group expectation' (Newcomb, 1952, p. 221).

As an example of an 'individual-based' explanation of group phenomena, sociobiological arguments (see Toates, 1996) suggest that in-group cohesion and out-group hostility were *adaptive* traits in early human history. Other theorists have suggested that there may be an inbuilt propensity, evident from the first days of life, to respond to other people, again an *adaptive* trait, given the dependence of the infant on caretakers. Childhood socialization depends on responding to cues from others and gaining rewards for doing so, and this is a two-way process as the discussion of 'first relationships' in Dallos (1996) demonstrates. In a different context, the sociologist Cooley (1902) argued that small spontaneously formed groups should be seen as the most basic *social* entity, meeting basic human needs for social relations. These kinds of explanations draw our attention to the interplay between individuals and their social contexts and suggest that adult behaviour in groups is the outcome of a long process of incorporation into social networks.

An important theme in this chapter will be how and to what extent we retain our individuality and to what extent we are changed by our group memberships. Stuart Hall, in Reading A of Chapter 6 of this volume, describes how 'our families shape us one way or another – positively because of what in them we identify with, negatively because of how we react against them' and 'we go on inventing ourselves anew and we take turnings which move us in different directions from the scripts which families write for us'. This chapter will be concerned with the process of 'reinvention' both in primary or face-to-face groups and in the wider groups which make up the public world.

Sections 2 to 4 of the chapter focus on the work of experimental social psychologists who have tried to understand the influence processes at work *within* groups. Sections 6 and 7, by contrast, are concerned with influence processes *directed* at groups and will explore topics such as group decision making, coercion and political indoctrination. Section 5 marks the transition: here you will be challenged to look at definitions of groups, an exploration which I have deliberately postponed until we have considered a range of studies, since definitions need anchoring in the research and theorizing which have given rise to them. As the examples you gave in response to Activity 1.1 may suggest, the word 'group' has been applied to many entities – small or large groups, informal or formal groups, groups which have a short life or those with a long-term existence. Groups differ in their functions, purposes, goals and history. Groups also need to be considered in the societal and cultural contexts in which they occur and whether these are relatively stable or are undergoing dramatic changes. As you go through this chapter, you might like to keep Activity 1.1 in mind and write down some definitions of your own, together with the reasons why you think these are appropriate and judge how well they fit the studies we will look at.

Aims of Chapter 1

The aims of this chapter are:

- To indicate the style of research on groups that has developed within experimental social psychology, focusing in particular on research on group influence.

- To review some of the classic studies from the 1930s onwards as well as recent developments such as research on minority influence, social identity and self-categorization.

- To indicate some of the implications for the study of groups in natural settings such as work groups, decision-making groups and the use of groups in political indoctrination.

2   Classic studies of conformity

We begin by looking at some of the classic research on social influence processes within groups, looking in later sections at how recent research and theorizing has asked new questions or produced new findings or explanations which may throw a fresh light or doubts on earlier studies.

2.1   The experimental creation of norms

One early classic study was conducted by Sherif in 1936. He used an optical illusion (the autokinetic effect in which a stationary point of light in a dark room appears to move) in order to place his subjects in situations which lacked any objective reality or external anchor points and to which no previous experience was relevant. He found that when individuals were put through the experimental situation on their own and asked to estimate the movement of the light, they quickly developed their own characteristic norms and ranges of estimates, a personal frame of reference, in fact. Individuals, when tested alone, made widely different estimates. When, however, two or three subjects were subsequently placed in this situation together, their estimates began to be similar. There was, however, no *averaging* of the estimates, and different sets of individuals, while converging in their judgements, arrived at distinct ranges and norms. This might suggest that some individuals expressed their estimates more forcefully or more quickly and hence, perhaps because they appeared more confident and knowledgeable, the developing norms veered towards their judgements. Sherif also placed some of his subjects first into the situation where two or three people, independently but in the presence of the others, made their estimates and only later placed them into this experimental situation on their own. What he found was that the norms and ranges developed in the 'group' situation were closely adhered to when the subject was alone. In other words, the frame of reference developed earlier persisted even in the absence of reinforcement by fellow subjects. This is a most remarkable demonstration of how people may come to coordinate their behaviour in social situations. What does this mean and what can we learn from this?

ACTIVITY 1.2

Can you think of any real life parallels to the processes described by Sherif? Instances which occur to me are the deliberations of a jury, decision making or voting by committee members and adolescent peer group pressures.

Whatever examples you think of, keep them in mind as you read through this chapter.

Although Sherif's study is one of the classics of social psychology, in some ways it seems to raise questions rather than provide answers. Here are some of the points which occur to me.

- Can we reasonably refer to Sherif's subjects as a group?
- Can similarity of response be considered an indication that group norms have emerged in this situation?
- Can we speak of group norms without any direct interaction taking place or subjects seeing themselves as engaged in a joint enterprise?
- Can we conclude that norms were 'internalized' simply because subjects kept to the same frame of reference when no longer in the group?

I would like to postpone suggesting answers to these questions since we need to look at them again in relation to subsequent research. But a few comments may provide insight into the *meanings* the subjects assigned to their experience. The subjects in post-experimental interviews all denied being influenced by the judgements made by other people (nor had they been instructed to come to an agreement) and all said they had struggled to arrive at the correct answers on their own. In other words, they did not consider themselves as members of a group (although there is always doubt about whether we can take subjects' reports about the motivation for their behaviour at face value). What the emergence of norms seems to do for the individual, whether alone in the experimental situation or in the presence of others, is to attest to the appropriateness and validity of the judgements made when no objective external frame of reference is available. Uniformity of response, then, may occur because of a need for an accurate picture of one's external world in an ambiguous situation, based as it may be on one's own subjective judgements or on the information provided by other people, as well as because accepted norms of behaviour facilitate social intercourse.

2.2   Group pressure towards conformity

Do you think the effects observed by Sherif were due, in part at any rate, to the ambiguity of the stimulus situation? Would the presence of others have been less influential if the task had been more clear-cut?

Asch (1952) set up a series of innovative experiments in which the stimulus, at any rate in the base-line experiments, was not ambiguous. These studies will be briefly reviewed here since they had a major impact on subsequent research and theorizing on group processes.

Asch's immediate objective was 'to study the social and personal conditions that induce individuals to resist or to yield to group pressures when the latter are perceived to be *contrary to fact*'. I continue this quotation to give you a flavour of his concerns:

The issues which this problem raises are of obvious consequence for society; it can be of decisive importance whether or not a group will, under certain conditions, submit to existing pressures. Equally direct are the consequences for individuals and our understanding of them, since it is a decisive fact about a person whether he [sic] possesses the freedom to act independently, or whether he characteristically submits to group pressures.

(Asch, 1952, p. 393)

BOX 1.1   An experiment on group pressure

Asch asked a group of male students to judge which of three unequal lines on a card matched a standard comparison line on another card. Is the standard line in Figure 1.1 the same as line A, B or C?

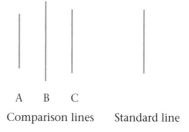

A   B   C

Comparison lines   Standard line

Figure 1.1   An example of the stimuli used by Asch (1955)

Each member of the group, in turn, was asked for and announced his judgement publicly; no discussion was allowed. In the initial series of experiments there were seven 'confederates' of the experimenter and one 'naïve' subject, that is, the one person in the group who did not know that the others had been instructed to give the same wrong answers after some initial trials when they would give the correct answers. The naïve subject, therefore, faced a situation in which he experienced a conflict between the evidence of his senses and the unanimous evidence of a peer group.

Subjects participating in Asch's experiments (the naïve subject is No. 6 while the remainder are confederates of the experimenter)

The technique employed permitted a simple quantitative measure of the influence of the confederates and the results were unambiguous: there was a marked movement towards the majority. One third of the judgements of the naïve subjects were identical with or in the direction of the (deliberately) distorted judgements of the majority. The significance of this finding becomes clear in the light of the virtual absence of errors in the control group who recorded their estimates in writing. Two points need to be emphasized.

1   Over twelve trials, nearly two-thirds of the responses were *correct* in spite of the pressure of the group.

2   There were extreme individual differences. One quarter of the subjects remained independent without exception; at the other extreme, one third of the subjects displaced their estimates towards the majority in half or more of the trials.

Post-experimental interviews revealed that the 'independent' subjects frequently experienced conflict, tension or doubt but were resilient in shaking off oppressive group pressures. Others were able to isolate themselves mentally from the group and hence were also able to stick with their own judgements. The interviews suggested that some of the 'yielding' subjects may have unconsciously distorted their perceptions – they said they actually 'saw' the lines in the way the confederates said they did. Most of the 'yielders', while correctly perceiving the lines, thought they must be misperceiving them and distorted their judgements to fit in with the group. Others yielded because of an overpowering need not to appear different from others.

Asch's experiments show that there are individual differences which lead some people to yield and others to remain independent. As always, the design features of the experiment may have influenced the outcome. What do you think would be the impact of varying the basic design?

In later variations of the experiment the difficulty of the task was increased by making the differences between the lines smaller. In these more confusing and ambiguous conditions *a greater proportion* of the subjects conformed to the group's judgements. When, in further experiments, a subject was joined by another genuine subject, resistance to the views expressed by the other members of the group increased, even though the two were still a minority in the group. (As we shall see later, the study of how a minority can not only *resist* a majority but *influence* it became a flourishing research topic.)

BOX 1.2 Some issues concerning the validity of experimental findings

Since much of the evidence we are discussing arises from experimental work we need to explore some of the difficulties associated with this methodology.

One point to note is that discrepancies in experimental outcomes may illustrate that the experimenters, as well as their subjects, may be affected by cultural changes and may expect more, or as the case may be, less conformity to occur. Even when the Asch set-up is apparently faithfully replicated, the experimenter may, unwittingly, convey to the subjects certain expectations as to the outcome of the experiment. Such unintended 'experimenter effects' are quite common and may present difficulties in interpreting the results. Double-blind trials (in which neither the person administering the drug, nor the patient, know whether the drug is the 'real thing' or a placebo) are, therefore, the rule in medical research when testing new drugs. Further, it is well-documented that the expectations a teacher has of the ability and likely progress of his or her pupils considerably affects their actual performance (see, for instance, Rosenthal and Jacobson, 1968). Psychological experimentation has inherent complexities, both because of 'the interdependence of the experimentally imposed conditions and the contribution of the individual personality' (Rosenzweig, 1933) and because of 'the biasing effects of subjects' compliance with the demand characteristics of the experimental situation' (Orne, 1962). Orne's contention was that the principal motives of research subjects, and perhaps particularly volunteer subjects, is to cooperate with the experimenter, be 'good' subjects and play out their perceived experimental roles guided by an altruistic wish to help science and human welfare in general. The implicit threats to the validity of outcomes from these sources are by now fairly well understood and, in consequence, experimenters may try to hide from subjects the true intention behind an experiment or other investigation by constructing a 'cover story' which should be sufficiently absorbing to make participants forget their concerns with how they come across to the experimenter or with being 'good' subjects. Such subterfuges, of course, raise ethical questions since deceived subjects are not in a position to give informed consent before participating. Even careful debriefing after the event, particularly where the experience has been stressful, does not quite meet this concern. A balance has to be struck between the danger of subjects distorting their reactions if they understood the exact substance of the study (and therefore reducing its validity and potential applicability) and compliance with 'good practice'. Most universities and other research organizations in consequence have ethics committees to which proposals must first be submitted for scrutiny.

Asch's experiments reveal that there are a number of variables which have a bearing on how individuals respond to this type of contrived group influence. The outcome was affected by:

- the characteristics of the stimulus situation (the ambiguity of the task)

- the group structure (whether the subject was the only apparent deviant or was partnered by another genuine subject)

- individual differences

- the cultural expectations of conformity participants bring to the experiment from their contemporary world.

Asch's studies were widely replicated since his easily reproducible experimental design presented a conflict situation in dramatic form, sharply highlighting the issues to be studied. The subjects were usually American college students and the results were fairly consistent and in accord with the original findings. A study by Larsen (1974), however, demonstrated significantly lower rates of conformity in American students than Asch had found. Larsen attributed this to the changed climate of opinion in the 1970s which encouraged independence of thought rather than conformity. Still more recently, Perrin and Spencer (1981), in a British study, found that in only one out of 396 trials did a subject join the erroneous majority, though, like Asch's subjects, they experienced tension and stress. The results, however, need not necessarily be attributed to a change in culture since these subjects were engineering, mathematics and chemistry students, people who might pride themselves on their ability to judge the length of lines and who would, therefore, be in a strong position to resist psychological pressures to agree with inaccurate judgements on this particular task. Perrin and Spencer in the same paper reported rates of conformity approaching those of Asch when their subjects were young offenders on probation and the experimenter's confederates were probation officers. In this study both the confederates and the experimenter were seen as figures of authority, a finding which links with the studies on obedience to authority discussed in section 2.3.

Clearly, these studies using Asch's experimental design suggest that there is no universal way in which individuals respond to group pressure when there is a discrepancy between their own perceptions and those of other group members. They show that participants will be affected by the *meaning* a situation has for them which itself may be influenced by *cultural* variables which have a bearing on how we relate to groups.

The fact that the *Zeitgeist* (literally the spirit of the time, the prevailing political or social mood of the period) may not only affect the choice of topic for research but may affect the outcomes of experiments raises questions about the status of psychological, and particularly social psychological research. If the same experiment can produce different results in different historical periods, are we to conclude that research, whether derived from experiments or field studies, is only valid in the context of the place and time where it was undertaken? The answer to this question must be a qualified 'yes'. It has to be recognized that all knowledge, including scientific knowledge, is embedded in a particular culture and history and thus reflects the biases and assumptions of the period. However, the fact that experimental social psychologists may not provide us with universal truths, as they first anticipated doing, does not make their work either unimportant or uninteresting. They help us understand our own times and our own place in it and, where a topic has been pursued over a period of time, they also document the changes which have taken place in society and in the expectations and attitudes of people. When we are trying to understand psychological *processes,* we may still arrive at valid and possibly long-lasting insights even though the *extent* to which such processes operate may vary from one historical period or one society to another and, indeed, from one individual to another.

2.3   Obedience to authority: compliance under pressure

Words such as conformity (literally: alignment) or compliance denote 'acceptance of influence'. A dramatic offshoot from Asch's work was the research of Milgram who, by focusing on obedience to authority, explored another area of 'acceptance of influence'. His experiments were carried out between 1960 and 1963 and later brought together in a book (Milgram, 1974). Milgram argued that there is a difference between obedience and conformity though he sees both as involving the abdication of personal responsibility. He viewed conformity as going along with one's peers in a group whilst obedience is accorded to a person in authority in a hierarchical situation. Influence of one person over another in this view arises from social power and status rather than from a psychological 'need' to be acceptable to others. Milgram used his experiments to vary the extent to which the experimenter would be seen as an authority figure by being close or at a distance from the subject or indeed by being absent from the room in which the experiments were carried out. The point to note here is that the experimenter is *part* of the group, one of the field of forces impinging on the participant.

The distinctions Milgram makes between conformity and obedience parallel those we make in everyday life. Conformity, if defined as going along with one's peers, is seen as to some extent under one's own control. Perhaps because of this a negative value judgement attaches to the word: people often deny that they conform while they may be quite willing to make excuses for themselves by saying they obeyed orders (though obeying orders is no excuse in law).

Milgram considered obedience a basic element in the structure of social life and a determinant of behaviour of particular relevance to the modern world. During the Second World War millions of people were murdered in concentration camps and, since then, we have seen extermination programmes of similar magnitude in the Killing Fields of Cambodia; 'ethnic cleansing' through killings and dispersal in the former Yugoslavia; genocide by the Hutus of the Tutsis in Rwanda and later revenge massacres by the Tutsis of the Hutus. The examples I have given all stem from pre-existing long-standing social tensions and 'racial', ethnic, religious or economic and class conflicts. The implication is that horrendous acts are not necessarily carried out by particularly evil men and women but stem from situational pressures. Such acts often depend on people obeying orders. Obedience, in Milgram's view, is the psychological mechanism that links individual action to political purpose.

While the moral question of whether one should obey when commands conflict with conscience has been argued over by philosophers and political scientists, Milgram wished to move from abstract discussion to the careful observation of concrete instances of the act of obeying and to this end he created a series of eighteen experiments in which he asked his subjects to act with increasing severity towards another person. The main question was how far the participants would comply with the experimenter's often relentless and extreme instructions before refusing to carry out the actions required of them.

BOX 1.3   Obedience to authority

Over a thousand people from all walks of life, recruited by advertisement, took part in Milgram's studies.

What happened in these experiments? Two people were invited into the psychology department, ostensibly to take part in a study on learning and memory which would assess the effect of punishment on learning. One was assigned the role of 'learner' (he was in fact a confederate of the experimenter), the other that of the 'teacher'; this person was the experimental subject. The 'teacher' then saw the 'learner' being strapped into a chair in the next room and an electrode attached to his wrist. The teacher subject was then seated before an impressive shock generator and told to administer the test and apply increasing levels of shock to the learner (up to levels clearly marked 'dangerous') when he made mistakes in learning a paired series of words. Each subject was given a sample of the kind of electric shock that was about to be administered to the learner. As the experiment proceeded, the learner's cries of anguish and pleas to stop could be heard. In actual fact the cries of the learner were pre-recorded and no electric shocks were administered.

The experiments were very realistically staged and created extreme levels of nervous tension, yet many subjects were, nevertheless, prepared to carry on and accept, or at any rate, act on the definition of the situation given by the experimenter, to obey him and ignore the 'victim' even when this person directly appealed to the subject to stop. In some of the experiments the 'victim' was in the same room as the subject, rather than merely heard from the adjacent room, and in these conditions fewer people were prepared to administer high levels of shock.

The shock generator used in the experiments. Fifteen of the thirty switches have already been depressed.

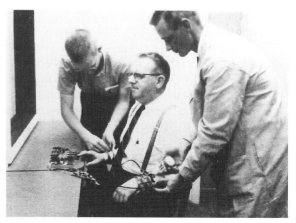

The learner is strapped into the chair and the electrodes are attached to his wrist. Electrode paste is applied by the experimenter. The learner provides answers by depressing switches that light up numbers on an answer box.

A subject receives a sample shock from the generator.

A subject breaks off the experiment.

Do you think you would have agreed to participate in such an experiment?

Most people when asked this question replied that they would not agree to participate, nor did they believe that other people would be willing to do so and, yet, many did participate and twenty-six out of forty male subjects in the original experiment administered the highest shock level on the generator. The other fourteen refused to continue at an earlier stage.

As a variation on the basic design Milgram set up further experiments. In one, the naïve subject, instead of being alone, was joined by other people. Two confederates of the experimenter participated with the subject but were instructed to defy the experimenter's authority and to refuse to punish the 'learner'. This experiment testifies to the powerful effect of group membership and allows us to observe the extent to which support from fellow group members can release the subject from authoritarian control. The effect of the 'peer rebellion', as Milgram called it, was very impressive – thirty-six out of forty subjects now defied the experimenter. Thus, in a situation where subjects have support from others, they can resist external pressures. We have already witnessed this in the Asch experiments: in the conditions where the subject was not the only naïve participant he was better able to resist pressures and to stick to his own perceptions and judgements. In the Milgram experiments, when operating as a member of a peer group, the male subject was able to oppose or as Milgram put it, to *liberate* himself from the experimenter's expectations and authority.

Milgram's experiments generated an unusual amount of controversy as to the ethics of carrying out research which puts stress on individuals. Milgram observed 'nothing is bleaker than the sight of a person striving yet not fully able to control his [sic] own behaviour in a situation of consequence to him [sic]' (*op. cit.* p. xiii). Furthermore, subjects had to live with the memory of their socially harmful behaviour. In defence of Milgram one might say that more often social psychologists are criticized for the trivial nature of their research and, at least, here was a series of experiments which tackled important issues. It is likely that the controversy was fuelled not simply by the methods employed but by the unpalatable results. As Aronson (1984) put it, there is a moral issue at stake in discovering unpleasant things (because the findings can be used to nefarious ends). The results were unpalatable because they demonstrated that it is the situations in which people find themselves (and that such situations can be very easily arranged) rather than their predispositions or character traits which lead them to act the way they do. In societies where emphasis is placed on people's responsibility for their own actions and where many psychological theories emphasize 'agency' and people's ability to initiate actions and control events (see Stevens, 1996), such findings are more disturbing than the thought that evil deeds are done by a few pathological people. It must be pointed out, however, that one strength of the experimental method is that it pinpoints the importance of the situational context. The experimenter can create diverse conditions to test whether, and to what extent, they affect the outcome.

2.4   Conformity: concepts and processes

ACTIVITY 1.3   Having looked at a number of key studies do you think that such studies give us insight into why and when individuals conform? Can you think of instances when you have felt under pressure to conform or yield? How did you deal with such situations and how did you feel about them?

The studies we have so far reviewed were created to explore psychological processes involved in real-life situations. While these studies tested hypotheses, they were not theory-led in the first instance. Are there theories which throw a light on the phenomena we have so far discussed? There is no one theory which encompasses all the observed processes but we can draw on several theoretical positions to help our understanding.

Lewin (1951) conceptualized the person as a point in a psychological space, constrained to move in certain directions by the field of contemporary environmental forces. This view of people contrasts with the idea that the person is a product of a long developmental history. Lewin's emphasis on environmental aspects lends itself to explore their influence through experimentation. We will discuss some of Lewin's studies in section 6: here we examine the work of some of his distinguished students who played a vital role in the development of social psychology. One of them, Festinger (1950), thought of small groups as systems tending towards equilibrium. In his view, disagreements are uncomfortable and disequilibrating and hence generate 'pressures towards uniformity'. Festinger (1954) developed this approach into his theory of *social comparison processes*. He proposed that, in many areas of judgement, reality cannot be measured by physical means (as we have seen in Sherif's experiments) and must be socially defined. When people disagree with others, they will be motivated to address the discrepancy in some way: they can change their mind, they can attempt to persuade others to do so, or decide that they are irrelevant for purposes of comparison. Festinger and his students spelled out the independent variables that they considered might affect the outcome and they conducted experiments on group cohesiveness (the attraction of the group to its members), issue relevance, degree of discrepancy and other aspects.

Subsequently, Deutsch and Gerrard (1955) distinguished between *informational* and *normative* influence. Normative influence results from the individual's need for social approval and acceptance, and the desire to avoid rejection by the group. Informational influence results from an individual accepting information as reliable evidence about objective reality; such influence is increased in ambiguous situations. The two influence processes can, of course, occur in tandem but they are analytically distinct. Thus normative influence (which arises from the desire to be accepted by others) is often proposed as the main explanation of Asch's results while informational influence is proposed as the main explanation of Sherif's findings in the autokinetic situation.

Look back at sections 2.1 and 2.2 and try to work out why this may be so.   ACTIVITY 1.4

You might well conclude that in Asch's basic experiment the situation was unambiguous, the confederates' judgements were a clear distortion of reality and, in this situation, influence pressures are more likely to be normative. In the Sherif experiment, by contrast, it was quite unclear what the right answer might be. When reality is ambiguous, informational pressures are likely to predominate.

Other conceptual distinctions have been made between *public compliance* (with the group norm, the majority opinion or the perceived expectations of the experimenter or leader) and *private agreement or change* (from a prior attitude or view). Again, public compliance is usually linked with normative pressures while private agreement is seen as characteristic of informational pressures. A number of researchers have stressed the importance of making such a distinction to alert us to the danger of taking too simplistic a view of the processes and outcomes occurring in conformity. When individuals are exposed to group pressure, they may publicly conform or not conform to the group. Regardless of this public response, they can privately agree or disagree with the group. Hence two ostensibly identical responses of public conformity may reflect two quite different psychological states and, similarly, public non-conformity may also represent two different private states. Thus, when with a group of friends who are Labour Party supporters, an individual may not reveal his or her private preference for the Conservative Party, even when directly asked. Similarly if asked for their voting intentions by a pollster, people may not reveal their private opinion but publicly voice support for the more popular party (and this contributes to the discrepancies between stated voting intentions and the actual votes cast).

The very words used by psychologists tend to reveal underlying value judgements. Asch certainly viewed conformity as deplorable and perhaps did not emphasize enough that in his experiments it was a minority response (though in Milgram's experiments obedience to the authority of the experimenter was a majority response). Asch describes conforming subjects as *yielding* when he might have referred to these subjects as *trusting* other people. Those who did not succumb to group pressure he refers to, approvingly, as *independent*. But these labels are relative. As has often been asked, do not so-called independent people also conform? They may continue to conform to the norms of *their* society according to which it is not acceptable or usual to defer to the opinions of the majority when these opinions differ from one's own judgements or views. A useful distinction to introduce here is that between *membership groups* and *reference groups*. The former refer to groups in which we are present, the latter to groups which we take as a reference point for our views or behaviour whether or not we are present in them or have any realistic expectations of joining them at any time. Hence we can think of the naïve subjects in the Asch situation as members of *temporary member-ship groups*. In this situation some people manage to maintain their links with their usual membership and reference groups outside the immediate situation, others do not. Could it be that all of us conform but the apparent resisters conform to other groups or standards? We may, of course, both resist and conform at one and the same time *within* the same situation. As we saw in Milgram's studies, subjects were better able to *resist* his authority when they had the opportunity to *conform* to the norms of resistance projected by his confederates.

Review of section 2

- Intra-group social influence processes may generate conformity to the majority view. The extent of conformity will depend on the interaction of various factors: task ambiguity, group structure, individual differences and cultural expectations.

- The concept of obedience to authority has been used to explain the abdication of personal responsibility for one's actions in a hierarchical context. The influence of peer group members on a subject's ability to withstand such pressures has been explored.

- Useful explanatory concepts developed by experimental social psychologists to make sense of their findings include normative and informational influence; membership and reference groups; differentiation between public and private acceptance.

3   Challenging conformity

This section explores a change of direction in research on conformity which reminds us that theories are never final statements, though you will see that many of the concepts and processes identified in the context of conformity research still play a role.

3.1   Minority influence

In reviewing work on conformity in section 2.2 we saw that a minority of two (as compared to a lone individual) is better placed to *resist* the influence of the majority in a group and remain independent. In the late 1960s, initially in France, the preoccupation of experimental social psychologists with conformity gave way to a new question: how and under what conditions can an individual or a minority not just resist the majority but *influence* it? This major shift in approach was based on the rejection of the idea that influence necessarily results in conformity.

For quite some time prior to his first experiments on minority influence, Moscovici in Paris had been interested in innovation and creativity and how, over a period of time, the novel ideas of original thinkers came to influence the thinking, vocabulary, cultural beliefs or images of the world of successive generations. He referred to a coherent set of *shared* cultural beliefs (whether newly emerging or longstanding) as *social representations* of the world. Such social representations were seen as providing a shared 'reality' and order for people, and enabled them to communicate with each other and make sense of their lives. This approach will be discussed in some detail in Chapter 3 of this volume.

Moscovici (1961) developed these ideas by following the spread of psychoanalytic concepts and ways of thinking from the world of psychologists and other professionals to their appearance in popular books, newspapers, television or films, and in the language and thought processes of 'ordinary' people who came to perceive and explain to themselves everyday phenomena in terms of psychoanalytic concepts such as the notion of repression or of unconscious motivation, or by explaining acts or utterances as 'Freudian mistakes'. People had made such terms, consciously or unconsciously, part of their world view. Moscovici's starting point was his interest in the diffusion of mould-breaking ideas and theories *over time*. Of necessity, when he initiated experimental studies on how groups react to members whose views differ from their own, he focused initially on the *short-term* influence of a minority in a laboratory group engaged in a simple task. Nevertheless, as you will see, the explanations evolved by him and other workers in this tradition took much more account of the cultural and societal factors impinging on the groups they studied than did some of the earlier workers whose research we have discussed.

BOX 1.4 Experiments on minority influence

Moscovici and his colleagues (Moscovici et al., 1969) conducted an experiment in which female subjects (with normal vision) were asked to indicate the colour of a slide they were shown and, as a diversion, to estimate its brightness on a five point scale. Six subjects estimated the colour and brightness in sequence and they were asked to make thirty-six judgements. Two of the six were paid confederates instructed to call the slides green on all trials. Thus they were a minority who said they saw green where everyone else saw blue and they were *consistent* throughout. The results were that the naïve subjects in this condition called the stimulus slides green in 8.42 per cent of the trials and 32 percent of the subjects reported having seen a green slide at least once. In the control condition, without confederates, the slides were referred to as green in only 0.25 per cent of the judgements made.

In a second condition, the confederates were *inconsistent*. They called the stimulus slides green twenty-four times and blue twelve times in random order. The effect on the naïve subjects in this condition was not statistically significant (1.25 per cent of the judgements).

How might one account for the effects produced by a consistent minority? Initially, the influence of the minority was explained as resulting from the minority first creating a conflict in the majority by challenging its norms and then providing a consistent alternative norm for them to consider (see also Moscovici, 1976). The minority, therefore, has to be *active,* rather than resemble the (allegedly) dependent, helpless, disorientated naïve subject at whom the majority targets its influence attempts in the typical conformity experiment. A consistent behavioural style was seen as crucial to the influence of an active minority since a consistent minority is seen as confident, competent, coherent and distinctive. However, subsequent studies came to the conclusion that consistency is a necessary, but not always a sufficient, condition for minority influence to occur. A very rigid style (of presenting arguments, repeating the same point again and again) makes the minority appear dogmatic. A large discrepancy between the position advocated by the minority and that of the target majority may also counteract the effects of consistency and affect the outcome.

Thus Mugny (1975), who used topics of contemporary concern for his group discussions, found that a flexible style of negotiation proved more effective when differences in opinion were large, whereas a rigid style of presentation proved more effective when the majority held a position close to that advocated by the minority. The degree to which the minority is effective may also be influenced by the wider context beyond the immediate group – that is, whether it advocates a position which is in accord with the spirit of the time. Paichler (1979) distinguishes between minorities which argue for or in advance of the social norms evolving in society and those opposing the direction of social change, the former being less threatening to the majority and the group's existence. Her research makes the important point that norms in a group on an issue (in her experiments the issue was attitudes towards the status of women) may differ from the norms in the wider society. A deviant or a minority point of view in a particular group, argued by the experimenter's confederates, may not be deviant in the wider society. In real life, too, minority groups are more effective when they press views that fit changing social conditions and are akin to views which are emerging more generally. Thus the 'Greens' have gained adherents in many countries in recent years.

Maass et al. (1982) coined the terms *single* and *double* minorities, a terminology subsequently used by other researchers. Single minorities are those who deviate from the majority in terms of their beliefs, whereas double minorities not only espouse different views but may be categorized as belonging to a broader *out-group* in society. For instance, during wartime, pacifists or conscientious objectors may be categorized as outgroups of this kind. Some experimental evidence suggests that double minorities are less effective since an out-group is less likely to be perceived as a valid reference group. Mugny (1982) has suggested that individuals perceive themselves and the source of influence as belonging to particular social categories and that they attribute certain stereotypical characteristics to these groups. The *psychological cost* of being influenced by an out-group minority is greater than the cost involved in being influenced by what is perceived as an *in-group* minority for the very good reason that adopting an out-group minority's point of view may involve attributing to oneself the (usually) negatively perceived characteristics of the out-group, in fact, it may involve redefining one's social identity.

What other theories and concepts have emerged to account for the minority's influence? Moscovici (1980) suggests that the influence of the minority may be at a *latent* (indirect) rather than at a *manifest* (direct) level. He describes the former as *conversion* and the latter as *compliance* (without inner conviction). If no change can be observed in response to a minority position on a direct, outward level, some alteration may nevertheless have taken place on an indirect, latent level and may become evident later. Thus when the blue/green slides experiment was followed by one in which ten of the sixteen slides shown were chosen to be ambiguous as to their colour, even without any influence attempts by the minority (subjects individually wrote down their judgements), *more* slides were seen as green. Remarkably, the answers demonstrated an enhanced and continuing influence from the previous experiment. Indeed, we observed the same phenomenon in Sherif's experiments (section 1.1) when his subjects also continued to be influenced in later sessions by the estimates given by the now absent original group members. The minority's views or actions may raise doubts which continue to work in the mind of the individual. In this way, Moscovici hypothesizes, the latent 'conversion' processes, initiated by the minority, may have a greater effect on a 'deeper' level than the overt, and possibly temporary, 'compliance' effects resulting from the influence of the majority.

Moscovici is arguing, therefore, that majorities and minorities achieve influence through different processes. The information coming from a minority source is likely to be processed more actively because it causes cognitive and social conflict, and generates more counter arguments. In particular, it has been suggested that minorities trigger more creative, original and divergent cognitive activity leading to the detection of novel solutions. Since people exposed to a minority are more likely to engage in issue-relevant thinking that goes well beyond the minority message, they will discover creative solutions rather than simply adopt the advocated viewpoint. Such active re-thinking of an issue, of course, requires motivation and ego-involvement.

So far we have seen that the majority and minority seem to exert influence in different ways. This view has been referred to as the *dual process* model. It has not remained unchallenged. Latané with various co-workers (e.g. Latané and Wolf, 1981) has proposed a *theory of social impact* which hypothesizes one common process to account for both majority and minority influence. Like Lewin whom we discussed in section 2.4, Latané thinks of a person as being in a field of social forces towards whom influence processes are directed by the other people in the field. Latané's theory of social impact views the majority and minority as separate sources of influence in the same social field, where each of these subgroups (or a single individual) is seen as a potential source of influence for the other. The *extent* of influence achieved will depend on potentially quantifiable aspects such as the number of individuals pressing a particular point of view, their status (which may change because of the position taken), their previous relationships with the target and such aspects as their 'immediacy' to the target, both in space and time. You have already seen an interplay of such factors in the Milgram experiments described in section 2.3. I mentioned that when Milgram was present (immediacy) his influence was greater than when he was in an adjacent room. When the subject was in the presence of peer group members, Milgram's authority was weakened as there were other influence forces in the subject's social field.

Unlike Moscovici's view, then, that the minority may have a greater effect on an initially latent level than the majority, the social impact model does not suggest that the minority's influence will be disproportional to its strength (as defined by size, status and other variables). Because of this, the social impact model predicts a decrease in minority influence in private as well as in public as the size of the majority increases. To tease out the extent of support for either model, experiments were set up in which the size of the majority and minority were systematically varied. One conclusion arrived at by Clark and Maass

(1990) is that the ratio of 2:4 between minority and majority group members, frequently recorded in the minority influence literature, may actually represent the optimal ratio for minority influence to occur. They suggest that, whereas higher minority to majority ratios may be unsuccessful in enhancing minority influence, a decrease in the minority to majority ratio would be detrimental to the minority's influence. There are, then, limitations on the extent to which social impact theory can explain observed phenomena (since they envisage both the majority's and the minority's influence to be *proportional* to their respective strengths). More generally, there is a lack of theoretical integration and neither the dual process model nor the social impact approach can explain all the facets of the interrelationships between minority and majority influence. The more one explores a topic, the more complexities one discovers which require a more differentiated vocabulary or theories which incorporate more aspects (such as the prevalence of views in the wider society in relation to the issue debated in the experimental session).

Can research on minority influence shed light on what goes on in the world around us? First, develop a list of active minority groups you are aware of from your own experience· and groups which feature in the media (e.g. the Green Party, feminist groups, animal rights activists, local pressure groups, religious groups, etc.).

ACTIVITY 1.5

Use your list to think through the definition of 'minority'. Can you find features that your groups have in common? Is a minority a matter of size? Have you included any examples of groups which are numerically large but which many regard as powerless (e.g. children, women)? Do the concepts of 'single' and 'double' minorities apply to some of the groups on your list? Think about how some of your minority groups advocate their message: can you identify different cognitive styles? Do they rigidly adhere to the same arguments or do they adopt a more flexible approach? Do broader social norms, along the lines proposed by Paichler, have an impact? Do the notions of 'dual-process' and 'social impact' cast a light on the influence process?

To wield influence, minorities need to build a power base, develop alliances, obtain access to communication networks and capture key positions from which to exercise influence. Does this apply to any of your groups? How often have you seen a documentary television programme clearly inspired by and based on material supplied by a campaigning group?

Consider also the reaction of the majority to the minority groups on your list. Do minority opinions become the majority's view? If so, is some of the original message lost? In other cases, has the majority fought back and promoted its own views? Can you think of contemporary examples?

Pressure groups in action: to gain influence, minorities need to organize themselves so as to put their views before a wider public

As we begin to think about contemporary examples, broader issues about ideology, persuasion and social control begin to come into view along with the role of language and discourse in how groups present themselves. Some of these issues will be taken up in Chapters 3 and 4 of this volume.

Review of section 3

- The extent to which a minority in a group can influence the majority depends on a number of factors such as the style of argument, whether the minority is considered part of the in-group or viewed as an out-group and whether the minority's opinions are currently gaining acceptance *outside* the group.

- Theoretical concepts which researchers have found helpful include a distinction between *latent* and *manifest* influence and *single* versus *double* minorities. The dual process model and social impact theory present competing analyses of minority influence findings.

4 A new approach to social influence

We have now considered a range of influence processes and how they have been explored in the laboratory. Explanations for *why* groups have these effects on individuals have been thinner on the ground. You might like to think back to section 2.4 and recall the kinds of explanations advanced there for these effects. Remember Festinger's point about social comparison processes and the distinction between normative and informational influence.

In this section I want to look at a new approach to why groups so strongly affect individuals. This approach was developed by Tajfel and Turner and their colleagues at the University of Bristol in the 1970s and 80s (Tajfel, 1981; Tajfel and Turner, 1979). Like Moscovici in Paris, this group was part of the resurgence of European social psychology during this period. Tajfel, himself a World War Two survivor of occupied France and of German prison camps, had plenty of experience of group conflict. He was particularly interested in the psychological processes involved in large-scale groups, such as ethnic and religious groups, and the consequences of conflict between groups. This work will be discussed in Chapter 4 of this volume. For the moment, I want to consider Tajfel and Turner's analysis of influence *within* groups.

4.1 Social identity and self-categorization theory

Tajfel and Turner were interested in what happens to people's identity (their sense of themselves) and then to their motivations, judgements and perceptions when they become members of groups. They argued that people's psychological processes are qualitatively transformed in group settings.

They suggested that, first of all, the bases for people's self-definition change in groups. *Personal identity* gives way to *social identity*. In many situations we react to others in terms of our identity as a unique individual with a particular personality, known likes and dislikes, skills and talents, attitudes and opinions. This definition of ourselves in terms of our personal characteristics can continue into a group situation and may be particularly salient when we strongly disagree with a group. But in groups there are also new identity possibilities – *we can perceive ourselves as a member of a social group and as someone with the characteristics of that group.*

This transition from personal identity to social identity is clearest when considering large-scale groupings but Tajfel and Turner argue that it also applies in small face-to-face groups, even in the notional groups developed in the laboratory. Instead of simply being a person with particular characteristics, we can begin to think of ourselves in terms of our group memberships and say about ourselves, for instance, I am a Catholic; I am a British citizen; I am a single parent; I am an OU student; I am a member of the Labour Party. As we label ourselves in this way (or are labelled by others) our sense of who we are and what we are like changes.

What does happen, psychologically, when a person begins to categorize him- or herself in group terms? First, the person's self-esteem becomes bound up with the fortunes of the group. According to Tajfel and Turner, to think well of themselves, people have to be able to take a positive view of their group. Second, Tajfel and Turner suggest that the bases of the kinds of comparison processes identified by Festinger, and discussed in section 2.4, change. Some people (out-group members – those who do not belong to the in-group) become less relevant sources of information and social pressure. For example, if you are a Catholic in a society where there is conflict between Catholics and Protestants, the latter's definition of social and political reality will not be so persuasive to you as the definitions of your own side. Section 3 demonstrated how minority influence theorists have built on these ideas.

Turner (1982) has also argued that when people identify with their group, they begin a process of what he calls *depersonalization* and *self-stereotyping*. We are used to the idea that we stereotype others, especially members of other groups, by focusing on only a few of their alleged characteristics and ignoring variations and diversity. Turner suggests that perhaps we stereotype *ourselves* when we think in terms of our social identities. In other words, collective images of what it means to be a man or a woman, a middle-manager or a senior citizen, for instance, may come to dominate our self-perceptions and, perhaps more import-antly, our understanding of how we should behave in situations where these group identities are relevant. Even if people have not previously had occasions to adopt a social identity, they can 'switch on' these ident-ities in appropriate situations, when they first become a parent, for instance, in response to images in their minds of appropriate behaviour for the membership of this new group. This process of self-stereotyping suggests that people may have very different responses to people at dif-ferent times. For example, we may respond to neighbours in terms of their and our personal identities and treat them as friends. But, on another occasion, when we think in group terms, in terms of social identity, the fact that we belong to very different social groups, such as different religions for example, may govern our actions and feelings.

What is the relevance of this approach for understanding influence pro-cesses? Turner (1991) suggests that we need to add a new kind of influ-ence to the normative and informational forms of influence we discussed in section 2.4. He calls this *referent informational influence*. This is the influence which occurs as people adjust their sense of identity, their thoughts and their behaviours to match the collectively defined attri-butes of their social groups. People take on the group characteristics and make these their own, at any rate for the time being, to a greater or lesser extent. Referent informational influence in itself, Turner argues, could produce conformity to group norms and it sets the conditions for the effectiveness of informational and normative influence.

Go back to the groups you listed for Activity 1.1. Think of your membership in some of these groups in the terms proposed by social identity/self-categorization theory. Was there a moment when you were aware that you categorized yourself as a member of a particular group? What effects did this have on you at the time? How did this affect your other group memberships?

Are you aware of the kind of switch Tajfel and Turner describe between social and personal identity? Are you aware of referent informational influence pressures operating either consciously as you aligned yourself with a group (possibly in cases of conflict with another group) or perhaps in a more tacit, semi-conscious way?

Chapter 2 of this volume will introduce a psychodynamic perspective on group processes and influence which depends on a very different model of the individual. What assumptions are Tajfel and Turner making about individual psychology? Can you relate their arguments about the nature of the person in the social world to any broader psychological perspectives on the nature of the self (see for example Stevens, 1996).

Finally, think back to the classic studies of conformity covered in section 2 and the work on minority influence in section 3. Can you apply the notion of *referent informational influence* to the analysis of these studies?

ACTIVITY 1.6

4.2 Group polarization

Social identity and self-categorization concepts have been applied to a number of areas of group research such as group formation and group cohesion, and to crowd behaviour (see, for instance, Turner et al., 1987). Here I want to look at a phenomenon called group polarization which has been studied extensively in the laboratory and which has attracted competing explanations including that of referent informational influence.

What happens in a typical polarization experiment? A group is convened and presented with a 'choice dilemma' (that is, a situation which has no one correct answer and where different people will make different choices). Individuals then make their choices in private. After discussion they are expected to reach a joint decision on the dilemma.

Group polarization is said to occur when the final group decision, after discussion in the group, is more *extreme* than the individual judgements but in the same *direction* as those individual judgements. Polarization refers to the group-produced *enhancement* or *strengthening* of prevailing individual tendencies in the group. The average group score (as compared to the initial individual scores) tends to be amplified by discussion in the same direction in which the group was initially heading as indicated by the average of their private judgements. For instance, in the first example in Figure 1.2, group discussion polarizes individual opinion so that, after discussion, individuals become *even more positive* about a course of action.

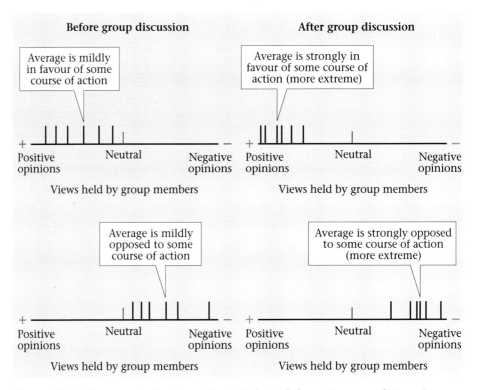

Figure 1.2 Group polarization effects (adapted from Baron and Byrne)

Polarization effects have been studied since the 1960s and various theories have been put forward which are no longer considered valid. (For a history of research in this field to the 1980s see Brown, 1986.) While the phenomenon has been observed in many laboratory studies, its explanation has proved more difficult. Social identity theorists took issue with two of the theories that are still current – social comparison and informational influence – and endeavoured to show that, while they had a role in understanding group polarization, they did not provide a sufficient explanation. They argued that the process of self-categorization as a group member and the subsequent self-stereotyping produced the polarization effect. We shall first look at the social comparison and informational influence explanations.

Engaging in social comparison processes in this context means that, when the choices of others are known or become apparent in discussion, individuals compare their own position to that of the others. The choice dilemmas used initially in most of this research area allowed one to make a cautious or a risky decision, for instance in advising someone in business on what options to take. If a person values caution, he or she may become more cautious than others in the group in order to emphasize and express this attitude and, similarly, when the person values risk-taking, his or her choices may become more risky in relation to the risky choices made by others in the group. People in a group may be thought of as being in competition with each other to take up the socially valued position. When the positions taken by others become known, group members move beyond them through a process of social comparison and self-presentation. The reasoning might be, if risk (or caution) is good, then I will be more risky (or cautious) than you. In that way the entire group shifts or polarizes. Indeed, one can demonstrate polarization effects occurring *without* discussion, simply by informing participants of the positions taken by others (Myers, 1982). This seems to be enough to stimulate participants to display opinions even more in line with what seems to be the socially desirable position. Social comparison theorists, therefore, argue that polarization can be explained as an outcome of the process of comparing oneself with others and wanting to be in tune with social values.

Persuasive arguments (informational influence) in relation to choice dilemmas are thought to work as follows. People make an initial choice, before discussion, based on arguments or views with which they are familiar. During discussion other relevant arguments emerge. If, for instance, the mean of individual choices was, in the first place, favouring risk, then more arguments in favour of risk will be voiced and the joint decision will move in that direction as people become persuaded by the new information and arguments they hear. This approach suggests that there is a polarization of opinion towards one extreme or other on the basis of the pool of opinions in the group and the balance of information held by the group. If this were always so, the American practice of allowing both the prosecution and the defence to challenge jurors (and have them substituted by others) makes sense since it allows each side to attempt to pack the jury with people who have views conducive to their own side which they would presumably express during the jury's deliberations and hence produce a decision shift.

The above discussion suggests that social comparisons and persuasive arguments can work in the same direction and both processes may operate together. At first sight they seem to provide a reasonable account. What new explanations have social identity theorists added to our understanding of group polarization?

BOX 1.5 Social identity and group polarization

Wetherell (1987) set up an experiment in which the student subjects did not debate the issues but listened to a tape recording of a group discussion after they had made their own initial choices on the issue. They were led to believe that the group they were listening to was one of the following:

1   an in-group similar to themselves
2   an in-group dissimilar to themselves
3   an out-group similar to themselves
4   an out-group dissimilar to themselves.

The students were allocated randomly to these four different social identification situations but all listened to the same discussion. After listening to the tape, they again gave their opinions on the issue. Because the same tape was used in the four conditions it was possible to examine whether identical arguments are differentially effective in different group settings. *If* informational influence theories could account for the outcome, the opinion shifts in all four groups should be similar (since the same arguments were presented). *If* social comparison theory could account for the effects, one would expect the opinion shift to be towards the similar groups since people tend to compare themselves to, and take their cue concerning social values from, similar rather than dissimilar people. The results, however, showed that the subjects were more likely to shift closer to the group when it was presented as an in-group (and hence, one may presume in the terms of this theory, that they self-categorized themselves as members or potential members) rather than an out-group. They tended also to shift more when they believed the group was similar to themselves rather than dissimilar. Thus the in-group similar condition showed the most shift, the out-group dissimilar the least.

The results suggest that people evaluate a *source* of information and may trust a source which is similar to themselves in some relevant respects. This and later studies of polarization demonstrate that the interactions in a group (or, as in this case, how the group is presented to the listeners) influence the perception of what is or is not a persuasive argument; an argument is seen as persuasive to the extent that it is seen as relating to the group norm (and this norm is more strikingly experienced if it can be compared to the norms of an out-group).

Interestingly, too, as in some studies on minority influence, it was found that groups were more persuasive when arguing for a position that was in the same direction as the subjects' initial judgements before listening to the tape, in contrast to cases where they argued in the opposite direction. According to social identity theory, this process of evaluation and identification with the group (self-categorization) is more potent in bringing about opinion shifts than social comparison or informational influence processes. More generally, identification with a group will elicit a tendency to conform to the in-group norm, a process referred to, as we have seen, as referent informational influence. This norm is not necessarily the actual average of individual opinions before discussion but rather the position which the group member *thinks* is *prototypical* of the group. The group member will conform to the position he or she perceives as *most representative* of group members and *most distinguishable* from the position of relevant out-groups. In other words, group members conform to an *exaggerated stereotype* of what they think their group position is and so conformity to this stereotype alone will bring about a shift in opinion and make groups more extreme and polarized.

The emphasis in this formulation on distinguishing one's own group from out-groups links with our earlier discussion of minority influence and how this influence depends, in part, on whether or not the minority is perceived as an out-group. Later research by social identity theorists (see, for instance, Van Knippenberg et al., 1994) has shown that in-group messages have their greater effects not just on the basis of recipients identifying with the group but because this perception of group belonging leads to (or is accompanied by) more cognitive elaboration and more attitude change. The focus on cognitive processing allies these studies to some of the thinking of those who studied minority influence.

Group polarization has been of interest to social psychologists in part because it is a non-obvious phenomenon. It does not always occur, however, even in the laboratory; other processes may operate. The spread of opinion may be too great for people to wish to compare themselves to others or adopt a common identity. Further, problems to be discussed in such laboratory situations need to be fairly innocuous so that people are not motivated to hold on to the views of their normal reference groups. Much research in social psychology on group decision making also shows that the *structure* of groups and modes of communication between members affect how messages are perceived and evaluated, quite apart from the original opinion pool in the group.

Perhaps we should also reflect on whether the experimental demonstration of polarization effects in group discussions accords with our own experience. I think polarization can often be observed in social groups when a 'discussion runs away with itself'. However, formal decision-making groups or committees do not usually exhibit such tendencies. There are several reasons for this: committees have a chairperson who directs the meeting, influences the discussions, sticks to the agenda, and so on. Also, group members may well be aware of each member's idiosyncrasies ('he always exaggerates' or 'she always brings this issue up'). They may, therefore, evaluate the arguments put in an *inter-personal* way while *ad hoc* groups in the laboratory lack this personal awareness of each other and (the imposed or manipulated) group identification may be stronger. More important in stifling any tendency towards polarization is another factor: if you are a member of, say, a management group who discuss an issue, you will be aware that you and your colleagues will have to implement the decisions taken and you are unlikely to wish to go to unmanageable extremes. You may like to consider, however, how polarization effects might operate in crowds, such as those moments, considered in the Introduction to this volume, where crowds begin 'to act as one'.

4.3   Some reflections on social identity theory

What social identity/self-categorization theory has achieved is to establish links between hitherto separate areas of research. Self-categorization, social identity, group membership and conformity can now be seen as addressing related issues. Social identity theory highlights the social dimension in social psychology. It looks on the group not as something external to the individual but as part of the person's self-concept.

Social identity theory is a very active research area which may continue to produce much interesting theoretical and empirical work. However, some unresolved issues remain, such as the distinction between social identity and personal identity. This is an important analytic distinction for social identity theorists but can the boundary lines between the two forms of identity be so neatly separated in real life?

Inevitably, social identities are not wholly divorced from one's personal identity; one's experience of a social identity (say that of being a member of a profession or sect) will affect personality and character and one's identity as a unique individual. One's personal identity, conversely, will have contributed to one's choice of social identities or the personal way in which a social identity is acted out. Of course, there is not always a choice: one does not *choose* to become a hostage or a conscripted soldier but how one performs these roles, or how one behaves in such predicaments, will have something to do with one's personal identity, as well as with how 'role models' have conducted themselves in the past and with the perceived demands, pressures or sanctions operating in the situation.

In practice, behaviour is likely to result from a complex intermixture of personal influences and the current group identity as well as previous and co-existing group identities. Social identity theory, however, comes across very much as an all-or-nothing conceptualization. Little attention is paid to individual differences and hence social identity theory would not appear to be capable of explaining individual variations in conformity such as occur in Asch-type experiments. Why do some people yield while others remain independent? As we have already discussed in section 2.4 one may describe (though perhaps not explain) these differences by conceptualizing the 'yielders' as taking the experimental group as both their membership and reference group, while the 'independents' remain anchored in reference groups outside the immediate situation. Social identity theorists might reformulate this explanation, suggesting that choosing which group to identify with sets the conditions for influence to occur – though this way of putting it does not offer, in itself, an explanation of which group is chosen as a point of reference in a particular situation.

Many of the social identity arguments apply most clearly when the examples used are of large-scale social categories such as gender, ethnic or religious groups. In these cases there are clear collective images of group members and identification can often occur in the abstract or become more relevant, for instance, in times of crisis. It is impossible to know all the other members of one's social categories and we might act in terms of a category membership without interacting with other category members. Small face-to-face groups may emerge out of wider social category membership, for instance when members of one ethnic group come together to form a pressure group or when workers, feeling threatened by changes in their workplace, 'activate' their social identity as union members so as to act in concert. As was pointed out in section 1, the small primary or face-to-face group can be shown to be psychologically important to people and such groups may form even when there is no objective reason for people being together. Thus groups may evolve over a period of time through acquaintance, friendship or proximity and it is a moot point when and if they will develop, self-consciously, a social identity.

Social identity theory does not allow for gradations in identifying with a group or the strength of convictions with which a social identity is adhered to. This stance makes it difficult to reconcile the theory with other formulations in social psychology. For instance, we saw in section 3.1 that deviant minorities within a group can exert influence on the majority members by stimulating new conceptualizations. Social identity theory, however, does not allow for change which might come about simply through exposure to new arguments and new positions. Nor do social identity theorists explore the role of leadership in creating a group identity and yet leaders can have a strong influence on group members.

I do not think that it is possible to decide finally on the status of any one of the different explanatory concepts so far introduced in this chapter nor is this necessary: theories should have an explanation for observed facts and the concepts they use should be capable of scientific testing as well as illuminating our experience. However, this is not necessarily the view of many social identity theorists who think of their position as providing a comprehensive theory which supersedes other approaches (see, for instance, Turner, 1991; Abrams and Hogg, 1990).

One further point needs to be made. While this theory is called 'social identity theory' you will find as you work through this volume, and especially when you come to Chapter 6, that there are other approaches to conceptualizing how social identity is constructed or developed.

Review of section 4

- Social identity theory focuses on the process of identification with groups and the cognitive and affective consequences of that identification.

- When identified with groups, people are thought to *stereotype* themselves and, in the process of assigning group characteristics to themselves, become open to a form of influence termed *referent informational influence.*

- Three contrasting explanations of group polarization were compared: social comparison (normative influence), persuasive arguments (informational influence) and group identification (referent informational influence).

5   What, then, is a group?

ACTIVITY 1.7

Look back at the questions in section 2.1 (p. 14) and also at your own definitions of groups. Would you like to revise these now? What questions have been raised in your mind by following the exposition of ideas in this chapter? How do the theories I have presented differ in their likely definitions of the group?

Do family relationships (e.g. Dallos, 1996) lend themselves to analysis by the concepts evolved here? Or are primary groups, such as the family or friendship groups in which interaction is prolonged and members have an emotional investment in interpersonal ties, so different from *ad hoc* laboratory groups that the analysis given here is inappropriate?

We have explored various social influence processes operating within groups. We have seen that the presence of others may have an effect on judgements (Sherif) that can be carried over to later situations. Then we saw that the majority may be in a position to sway a minority (Asch). Later we were able to show that group membership may shield the individual from demands and pressures emanating from the experimenter/ leader (Milgram). In yet other circumstances the minority can influence the majority (Moscovici and others). Finally, we saw that group membership may lead individuals to re-categorize themselves and adopt what they see as a relevant social identity (Tajfel, Turner and others) and how these processes of identification and self-categorization may account for polarization effects (where they occur).

Throughout we have also explored the concepts and theories offered as accounting for these processes. We have further seen that the outcome of influence processes may depend on what the targets of the influence process consider to be a relevant group for themselves. For instance, the influence of a minority on the majority may depend on whether or not the minority is perceived as an out-group rather than a disagreeing in-group.

I avoided giving you some definitions of groups at the beginning of our exploration since I thought that it would be more meaningful to attempt this after our discussion. However, our explorations may have suggested to you that it is still not possible to provide a definition in any simple or straightforward way. In everyday life we have no difficulty in *using* words such as 'individual' and 'group'. In psychology we may have problems limiting and *defining* both since their interaction and interfaces are some-what blurred and multi-faceted and one cannot be imagined without the other.

Has the word 'group' a particular meaning or could I have used the word 'social context' throughout? I think that in using the word 'group' social psychologists are looking at a specific context, one in which it seems more appropriate to say 'we' rather than 'I and they', and one in which members can be shown to have psychological effects on each other. Of course, the word 'member' itself is problematic as is the nature of the influence process and its depth and persistence. You do not need to be physically present to relate psychologically to a reference group or social category or, indeed, to ever meet any members of your reference groups. People's imaginative capacities enable them to identify with or have sympathy for those they have never met, even those who lived in pre-vious centuries. The power of the written word or images can bond us with others. Nations, religions or ideology may unite people and create a sense of belongingness but at the same time they may create dissensions with other groups.

Groups can be of any duration and of deep or superficial meaning to those involved in the relationship. Furthermore, as we have seen in the Sherif and Asch experiments, you need not be consciously aware that you are being influenced by your group membership. Cartwright and Zander (1968) in their influential collection of readings on the topic of groups and group dynamics have suggested that the term 'group' is not a definable entity: it merely describes an area of study whose boundaries are blurred. They cite many definitions, some sociological, others relating to various branches of psychology (behavioural, psychodynamic or cog-nitive). Each definition has its unique focus and may exclude from con-sideration aspects which form the core of other definitions.

Go back over you own definitions which you wrote down at the beginning of this chapter. Are some of them mutually exclusive? How well do the groups you belong to fit in with one or other of your definitions? What aspects did you stress – shared norms or goals, shared origins, shared experience, observable inter-personal relations, interdependence, or some other aspect?

ACTIVITY 1.8

Because our focus in this chapter has been on influence processes within groups I would like to suggest that, for our purposes here, we define an aggregate of people as a group if we can discern two aspects. First, that individuals think of themselves as being group members ('we' rather than 'I' and 'they') who experience a sense of belongingness and a common sense of identity. Second, as I noted earlier, that the participants have psychological effects on each other. These psychological effects of groups upon members include affective aspects (positive feelings about others in the group); cognitive aspects (coming to think more sympathetically about others in the group and about issues of concern to the members) and behavioural aspects. Finally, then, in terms of our definition, the questions I posed in section 2.1 (p. 14) can and should all be answered positively.

6   Using groups to change people

ACTIVITY 1.9   Have you ever joined a group with a view to changing some aspect of your behaviour or outlook – groups such as encounter groups, Weight Watchers, Alcoholics Anonymous, a psychotherapeutic group or a smoking clinic? Why did you do this rather than struggle on your own to achieve your aims? What were your experiences? Did they match your expectations? How were these groups run? Was there a leader or facilitator? Did members learn by role-playing? Think about your experiences whilst reading the following sections.

Our discussion so far has shown that we are affected by those with whom we interact and this has, almost inevitably, led to the use of group situations as potent forms of social control and change. You may well have joined one or other of the above self-help groups on your own initiative (or did you feel subtly pushed by family or societal expectations?) By contrast, our focus here will be on situations where the participants are not usually volunteers and where group membership is used to influence the participants in predetermined directions (though the psychological processes and outcomes may be similar whether a group is joined voluntarily or not).

Think of the vocabulary we use in everyday life to describe influence attempts – words such as socialization, education, persuasion, leadership, conversion, seduction, agitation, manipulation, propaganda, subversion, indoctrination and coercion. All attempts to influence people raise moral questions, though clearly the processes listed here differ in the extent to which psychological and physical pressures are applied, in the relationship between change-agent and the target and in the expected outcomes. We shall see that while influence attempts by change-agents can be (and are) directed at individuals, the manipulation of group membership very often aids the process and maintenance of the intended change in outlook or behaviour.

As I have emphasized before, many social psychologists are attracted to the discipline because of their interest in solving social problems and because of their concern with issues in the wider world. In this part of the chapter we will explore two of the influence processes mentioned in the last paragraph. First, we will focus on aspects of leadership and group dynamics, and their impact on managements' relationships with work groups, and second, in section 7, we will look at the more sinister end of the spectrum: indoctrination and coercion.

6.1   Lewin and group dynamics

Lewin was a strongly anti-fascist German-born psychologist who emigrated to the United States in the early 1930s. His particular interest was psychological research which might make a contribution to social reform and social policy and to the resolution of conflicts (Lewin, 1948). He was interested in finding out how to change behaviour – in particular, how to make fascists into democrats and Americans more tolerant of minorities.

One of Lewin's earliest studies in the United States experimented with contrasting leadership styles and their effect on the atmosphere in the group, the members' satisfaction and their output.

BOX 1.6   Research on leadership style

Lewin and his colleagues (Lewin et al., 1939) set up three parallel well-matched groups of boys and girls to engage in after-school activities. One group was led by a 'democratic' leader who got the children to discuss what they wanted to do and how to achieve their aims. Their choice of making masks was imposed on the two other groups. The second group was led by an 'autocratic' leader who issued orders. The third group worked with a 'laissez-faire' leader who was present but did not initiate any action. The leaders of these groups were instructed to act in these various leadership styles; they were not an expression of their personalities or habitual ways of conducting themselves. In fact, in a later phase the leaders were asked to change styles and it was again the style that affected the outcomes. What were the results? Lewin found that the 'productivity' of the autocratic and democratic groups was quite comparable but the children in the autocratic group were very dissatisfied and some of them became aggressive (to each other rather than the leader) and resentful, while others retreated into apathy. In the democratic group there was a good deal of cooperation among the children and they enjoyed the group. The laissez-faire group was neither very productive nor particularly satisfied.

What are we to make of these findings? Lewin was keen to demonstrate the superiority of democratic ways but the results must be understood in the context of their time and place; it is quite possible that if Lewin had conducted the research in Nazi Germany the children would have been more at ease in the autocratic group since their treatment in the group might have corresponded more closely to their experiences in the family or the wider society. While these studies may not be valid across cultures – in another society or context a different style could prove to be more appropriate – these experiments show that a leader can be instructed to adopt a particular approach and this implies that managers, officers or other leaders can be helped, through training, to adopt behaviour which approximates to the expectations of their group members and to the ethos of the wider society. I will return to these issues below but first I would like to consider another well-known study carried out by Lewin which utilized the ideas on leadership he had arrived at through this research and in his theoretical writings in the 1930s.

6.2   Decision making in groups

BOX 1.7   Group decision and social change

In the early 1940s the US government was anxious to get housewives to serve less popular cuts of meat to their families. Lewin (1947) set up a study to explore effective ways of getting people to change their dietary habits. Two methods were used. Three groups of between thirteen and seventeen Red Cross volunteer housewives attended interesting lectures which linked the problem of nutrition with the war effort, emphasized the vitamin and mineral content of offal (such meat products as kidneys and liver) and stressed health aspects and cost savings. The preparation of dishes was described and recipes distributed but the women's views were not elicited nor their cooperation asked for.

In three comparable groups a nutrition expert introduced the same topic and then let the group members discuss the issues. In these discussions, the expert helped the group with factual information but refrained from telling people what they should do, or think, or how to overcome their dislike of offal. At the end of the discussion period, members were asked if they would serve offal during the following week and the same recipes were distributed.

What were the results? A follow-up showed that only 3 percent of the women who had attended the lectures served one of the meats never served before, whereas 32 per cent of those in the discussion groups served at least one such meal.

How can one explain these markedly different outcomes? One possible explanation is that people dislike being lectured at and resist what they perceive as authoritarian pressures, but are willing to accept new ideas from their peers. Perhaps the 'to and fro' of discussion allows people to test the appropriateness of various ideas and gives them the feeling that they have made their own decisions. This process can generate considerable involvement in contrast to listening passively to a lecture. Some of the intra-group influence processes we discussed earlier are very likely to have been in play: a minority stimulating a re-appraisal or polarization processes influencing the decision.

A second reason for the more ready acceptance of new ideas in the discussion groups in these experiments may be the fact that in these groups each member was asked to make a *decision* about her own intentions. Later research by Pelz (1958) demonstrated that two factors were instrumental in bringing about the changed perceptions and intentions of the members of discussion groups:

1   a new *shared group norm* (a new group prototype) evolved during the discussions and became *apparent* to the participants

2   the act of *making a decision* of one's own choice, whether privately or publicly, led to the commitment to carry it out.

Making a decision may convert something external – the proposal of the discussion leader who is possibly viewed as an outsider, akin to an out-group member – into something internal to the individual, a conscious choice. With no decision, the leader's suggestion or the views emerging during discussion, are likely to remain external. Making a decision should lead to stronger commitment and the setting of definite goals for action.

We may or may not agree that it is a good thing that housewives can be led to convince themselves in group discussions that they can contribute to their country's war effort by changing the dietary habits of their families. Lewin was concerned with wider issues and thought of group discussions as an exercise in reason. He equated reasoning and democracy because 'it grants to the reasoning partners a status of equality' (Lewin, 1948, p. 83). And yet, we need to remember that the scene in these discussions was set by the group leader and the 'ideal' outcome was pre-defined by him; any equality was a temporary stratagem or illusion. The aims of such group discussions, as they have become widely adopted, have tended to be to effect changes in the direction desired by the leader or management and to make the change acceptable to the participants. Group discussions and group decision making are an attempt at social control (or 'social engineering' as Lewin called it approvingly, though since his time these words have acquired sinister overtones). This may be preferable to issuing and enforcing orders but the process is not normally one of according equal status to the participants.

Lewin was well aware of the paradox inherent in his ideas, particularly when he thought about building a post-war world of peace that would require the cultural reconstruction of Germany. He thought in that particular context 'the democratic leader has to be in power and has to use his power for active re-education' (*ibid*. p. 50) until new democratic ideas became rooted. Thus while democracy, by definition, should not be imposed, changing from autocracy to democracy may require a leader who actively leads. Indeed Lewin was faced with the same paradox in his leadership style experiments. In an experimental change, for instance from individualistic freedom (laissez-faire) to democracy, the incoming democratic leader could not tell the group members exactly what they should do because that would lead to autocracy: 'Still some manipulations of the situation had to be made to lead the group into the direction of democracy. A similarly difficult problem arose when the autocratic group was to be transformed into a democratic one. Relaxing the rules frequently led first to a period of aggressive anarchy' (*ibid.* p. 39).

ACTIVITY 1.10   Thinking back over the last section and using the psychological insights you have gained, what aspects would you take into account if you were asked to set up a health promotion campaign, for instance, to encourage people to have their children vaccinated?

6.3   Social psychology, management and the work group

Lewin's work is a good entry point for looking at the influence on management practices of psychological research, because his ideas on leadership styles and group-based methods of change have been very influential and were soon applied to organizational problems by several of his students, for instance Coch and French (1948). The latter particularly stressed that resistance to change can be reduced by allowing those affected by change to participate in the decision-making process, for example, in setting production targets.

We have seen that Lewin's work suggests that people can be more easily led to accept changes if they do so in a group setting and when directed by a more or less democratic management style. Some of these ideas have a long history. Mayo, a psychologist and management consultant, had shown in the 1920s and 1930s in his famous Hawthorne studies that working groups can resist management inducements and limit their output but, when consulted, may cooperate with management's aims (Roethlisberger and Dickson, 1939). This may not sound very surprising to us but we need to look at these findings in their historical context. In the 1920s, psychology, as applied in the workplace, focused on individuals rather than groups. Proponents of 'scientific' management such as Taylor (1911, reprinted in 1967), for example, placed exclusive emphasis on selecting and training individual workers and applying individual incentives to encourage or enforce performance. These management consultants were aware that workers could cooperate with each other to resist increases in the rate of output, for example, but they endeavoured to frustrate this tendency. Mayo showed it was possible to harness the group to achieve beneficial outcomes from the point of view of the management as well as the workers. What we need to add here is that this is possible only where *no* fundamental economic or ideological differences exist between the workers and the management. Where both management and workers desire the *same* ends, for instance increased productivity through the adoption of new technology and work practices, or better adherence to safety measures, then group discussions and a democratic leadership style may well facilitate a mutually beneficial outcome. Such techniques are useful where resistance is based on *unfounded* fears whereas fears of job losses in the wake of technological change are not necessarily unfounded. One may consider this approach 'manipulative' since, in fostering conditions in which the workgroup may identify with the objectives of an organization and participate in the decision-making process, managerial control is strengthened as it will also be supported by peer group pressures. Lewinians such as Coch and French (1948) clearly understood this and showed that, in cohesive groups, attitudes are a group and not an individual phenomenon and changing attitudes requires the participation of the group as a whole. Lewinians can be said to have provided managements with an 'acceptable' leadership style, being more in line with cultural expectations.

Later studies on leadership also centred on the notion that a leadership style and the leader have to suit the requirements of a situation. This approach can be contrasted with attempts to identify those qualities in leaders which will guarantee success in any organization. This has proved not to be a particularly useful enterprise, not because personal qualities are unimportant, but because it has been impossible to identify such generalized leadership characteristics even within a given sphere of activity such as the military, politics or management. Nor do such lists of qualities distinguish between good and evil leaders.

A more fruitful approach than a focus on personality attributes alone has been to view leadership and the pertinent qualities of the leader as *contingent on the situation*. The main contribution of contingency theorists such as Fiedler (1967) was to highlight the interdependence of the leader, those who are led and the requirements of the situation. Fiedler even proposed that, at times, situations should be arranged to suit a particular leader since, unlike Lewin, he considered leadership style a relatively stable personality attribute. Fiedler demonstrated in numerous studies that situational factors – such as the complexity of the task; the degree of power the leader has (a variable often neglected) and the quality of the leader–member relationship (for instance, whether the leader has the confidence of the group) – affect what form of leadership ('permissive' or 'autocratic', 'people-centred' or 'task-centred') is likely to be effective and acceptable.

Other writers have also pointed to situational determinants of appropriate management styles. Thus, among other post-Second World War writers, Woodward (1965) pointed out that production systems influence the structure of the firm, for example the centralization (or otherwise) of decision making, and this, in turn, profoundly affects the relationships between managers, supervisors and workers.

Socio-technical approaches, pioneered by the Tavistock Institute of Human Relations in London, go beyond analysing situational aspects to find an appropriate organizational structure and leadership style. What Trist and his fellow workers (Trist et al., 1963) demonstrated was that a technological system of production need not be taken as 'given' in a situation from which then flow certain organizational consequences and effects on relationships. When a new technological system of coalmining (the 'longwall' method) was introduced without achieving the hoped-for benefits in output, Trist and his colleagues were able, in consultation with work groups, to design work practices which did not disrupt the strong group cohesion (which is a feature of mining work) and which gave a degree of autonomy to workers to exercise their judgement. Taking heed of social and psychological as well as technological aspects achieved superior economic results.

More recent writers (for instance, Heller, 1995) on organizational development (a term embodying a broader focus than that on leadership and work groups alone) argue in favour of participative methods of management, ranging from information-sharing, to consultations with an individual or group, to setting up formal organizational structures for joint management/union decision making. This last procedure has been part of industrial law in Germany since the 1950s and is now embodied in the Social Chapter of the European Union's Maastricht Treaty. This range of alternatives sees participative decision making as an ideal towards which organizations should aim, both to achieve effectiveness and to realize the expectations of people in a democratic society. To what extent such approaches can be seen as a real devolution of power rather than as a means to achieve consensus and reduce resistance to change (though these are valid aims in their own right) is highly debatable even where structural changes, such as the decentralization of decision making or the formation of semi-autonomous groups, takes place.

The extent to which management has taken the work group, as opposed to the individual, as a focus for attention has also fluctuated in line with economic conditions. When worker power peaked, as evidenced by strikes and full employment, democratic and group-oriented methods were advocated; when worker power declined, more authoritarian approaches prevailed (Bramel and Friend, 1987).

Whether or not techniques of consultation, power-sharing or democratic leadership produce desired results may, however, depend on aspects extraneous to the organization. Technological, economic and political factors influence the fortunes of firms – well-led firms (including those with good personnel policies and/or utilizing socio-technical approaches) can collapse because of changing economic conditions outside the firm. Thus, while in this section we have seen how social psychology has influenced management theorists and the practice of management, the ultimate impetus for organizational change may not arise from an appreciation of the findings of the social sciences but through the pressures of external circumstances (Heller, 1995). Nevertheless, in times of turbulence one may well conclude that firms need an even greater understanding of how to develop their human resources.

Chapter 5 will return to some of these issues and, using work as an example, will explore motivation and the role of organizational culture.

Review of section 6

- Lewin's work in the 1930s and 1940s demonstrated the importance for influence of leadership style and group participation.

- This work has been extended to management and the work group, leading to a focus on worker participation, group structure and socio-technical factors such as the relationship between management style and production systems.

- Although Lewin saw his work as supporting the development of democracy, it is clear that research of this kind may carry mixed political messages.

7   Stepping up the pressure: manipulating group membership

I pointed out that deliberate influence attempts can range from relatively innocuous or even benign influence processes to those, such as coercion or indoctrination, which pose more of a threat to the individual. While the dividing line between 'acceptable' and 'unacceptable' influence attempts may, at times, be blurred, coercion and related techniques can be distinguished from education or persuasion or leadership, or even pressures towards conformity, chiefly in terms of the amount and type of force exerted, the extent to which the environment can be controlled and the intentions of the influence agent. Behaviour under extreme conditions, such as during captivity, interrogation, 'brainwashing' or torture, has been a topic which has long exercised popular imagination since it raises the question whether we all have a breaking point. We all fear being controlled by others with the consequent loss of autonomy that many see as fundamental to our self-image. The questions we need to reflect on concern the effects of the techniques adopted. Are they short- or long-term? Do they affect superficially held opinions or can they induce a change in more pervasive attitudes and world views? Is the apparent conformity opportunistic or does it represent real change? Can influence attempts be resisted even in extreme conditions? The sections that follow explore these questions.

7.1 Thought reform

The term 'thought reform' is a translation of the Chinese word which describes the psychological techniques used by the Chinese communists to effect changes in political views and self-concept. These techniques date back to the early days of the Chinese communist movement (the 1920s) when a scheme of education and propaganda was founded which was designed to modify 'the whole human being by giving him [sic] a totally new view of the world and awakening in him a range of feelings, reactions, thoughts, and attitudes entirely different from those to which he was accustomed' (Ellul, 1965, p. 304). These techniques were initially applied by Chinese communists to their own nationals to integrate them into a new political order and to detach them from their former groups by weakening strong family ties and by removing them from their traditional village organizations. The aim was to create a quite different world view. We know about this approach from a variety of sources such as autobiographical accounts, for instance the story of three generations told by Jung Chang in *Wild Swans* (1991) which, quite apart from the personal dramas portrayed, is a history of the Chinese revolution in the twentieth century and how it affected individuals and families. Other sources include authors like Dr. R.J. Lifton, an American psychiatrist who in the mid-1950s interviewed twenty-five western nationals and fifteen Chinese intellectuals who had been expelled from China or who had fled from there after undergoing various attempts at thought reform. Some of them had been imprisoned for many years and during this time had been subjected to leniency alternating with exceptional harshness, depending on how appropriate their confessions appeared and the extent to which they seemed to be able to re-cast themselves in the desired mould. The methods involved in these re-education processes are interesting from a psychological point of view because they go beyond normal influence attempts such as persuasion, social pressure, exhortation or ethical appeals. As Lifton points out, it is the extraordinary 'combination of external force or coercion with an appeal to inner enthusiasm through evangelistic exhortation which gave thought reform its emotional scope and power' (Lifton, 1961, p. 13).

Lifton (1957) also discusses the 'revolutionary colleges' set up all over China in the late 1940s and the techniques developed there for reforming the political views of their students who were mainly Chinese intellectuals and officials. Some were there as the result of thinly veiled threats but most were genuine volunteers eager to equip themselves for an important role in the new communist China. Students usually attended for about six months and Lifton distinguished three stages (see Box 1.8 below) 'which represent the successive psychological climates to which the student is exposed as he [sic] is guided along the path of his symbolic death and rebirth; the Great Togetherness, the closing of the Milieu, and Submission and Rebirth' (Lifton, 1957, p. 7).

> **BOX 1.8**   Thought reform in the revolutionary colleges
>
> During the first stage of thought reform the student became a member of a ten person *study group* in which the participants discussed their experiences and their hatred of the old régime. These group experiences were complemented by lectures on the new ideologies and purposes. Then, after four to six weeks, a change began to develop in the atmosphere – there was a shift in emphasis from the intellectual and ideological to the personal and emotional. Students began to realize that *they,* rather than communist doctrine, were the object of study. Their views and attitudes came under scrutiny and the leader and other members of their primary membership group exerted pressures on them to adopt the 'correct' views. Constant criticism of others and self-criticism leading to confessions and reform were required of the student. 'Backward' students with suspicious backgrounds or whose confessions were not sufficiently critical of others were singled out, relentlessly badgered, threatened and publicly humiliated. No one in these circumstances could avoid the fear of being considered reactionary. The last stage of this programme of thought reform was the student's final confession – a document of between five and twenty-five thousand words which was prepared over a period of weeks and which was read to the group where it was subjected to painful discussion and revision. When at last this confession was approved the student typically experienced great emotional relief. Confession was the symbolic submission to the group and at the same time the person's rebirth into the communist community.

Is thought reform effective? Obviously not in every case, since Lifton interviewed students from these colleges who had left China as dissidents. Nevertheless, there are many reasons for assuming that this programme did have wide-ranging effects. It was the control of the students' environment (which Lifton calls 'milieu control') which makes the programme potentially so awesome and effective. He writes: '[the student's] environment is so mobilised that it will psychologically support him [sic] only if he meets its standards, and will quickly and thoroughly undermine him when he fails to do so. More and more there is a blending of external and internal milieux, as his own attitudes and beliefs become identical with those of his outer environment' (*ibid.* p.13).

In addition, the student experiences: 'the emotional catharsis of personal confession, the relief of saying the unsaid, of holding nothing back. He attains the rewards of self-surrender, of giving up his individual struggles, merging with an all-powerful force, and thereby sharing its strength' (*ibid.* p. 18).

Thought reform is effective, not necessarily because students emerge intellectually convinced of the validity of the new information, dogmas or ideologies, but because, as we have seen all along in this chapter, they need to identify with fellow group members and their wider society to have a meaningful existence.

Thought reform (which preceded the Cultural Revolution of the 1960s and 1970s and its much more coercive programme) was directed at China's own population who, on the whole, participated willingly in this process. But now we turn to what happens when these techniques are applied to a captive audience of western prisoners.

7.2   Political indoctrination of prisoners of war: effects of disorientation and captivity

Chinese approaches to indoctrination became a major focus of interest in the West when the Chinese tried to indoctrinate United Nations prisoners (about 21,000 men) held by them during the Korean war in the early 1950s. Western government and army authorities were unprepared for and shocked by these attempts at mass indoctrination – the Chinese did not merely contain the men, as is usual with prisoners of war, but they tried to *convert* these prisoners to their own view of the world.

The conditions and experiences of the prisoners of war in Korea are of particular interest to *social* psychologists since such success as the Chinese had depended on their ability to undermine the prisoners' normal social relationships in the camps and setting men off against each other. They also interrupted contacts with their families and the outside world by withholding mail and news. The prisoners were surprised that they were expected to think of themselves as students of politics under the tutelage of their guards. They soon learned, however, that their treatment, and therefore their survival, depended on how far their political convictions pleased their captors. As in the revolutionary colleges, psychological pressures and inducements to 'progressive' students alternated with 'physical torture, revolting to the humane mind' (Ministry of Defence, 1955).

We have detailed accounts, debriefings and evaluations from contemporary sources (for instance, Ministry of Defence, 1955; Schein, 1956; Kinkead, 1959). From these we gain some understanding of the extent to which the pressures applied to the prisoners produced effects either in terms of *collaboration* (broadcasting for the enemy, falsely admitting to participating in germ warfare, informing on other prisoners, and so on) or in terms of a *change in political beliefs*. As to collaboration, it is estimated that the majority of prisoners resorted to this strategy for their survival at least on some occasions and a small percentage did so persistently – a fact which is perhaps not so surprising considering the physical and psychological hardships the soldiers experienced but which deeply disturbed the American army authorities, who subsequently developed a new code of behaviour for American soldiers in order to increase their ability to withstand mental as well as physical pressures in captivity.

While collaboration can be viewed, by and large, as a strategy for survival, the really intriguing question is: were many prisoners converted to communism and by what criteria should we assess the extent of influence? Only a handful of prisoners refused repatriation (and these may not necessarily have been converts but may have stayed behind for other reasons). Potentially the Chinese efforts should have been very successful. The prisoners endured a very harsh 'total milieu' for several years, cut off from the normal supports to their identity and convictions, and subject to relentless harassment and attempts at indoctrination. It would not be surprising if people yielded to such onslaughts since we know that all of us can be easily swayed in much less harrowing circumstances. Thus we saw in the Milgram experiments that a high proportion of subjects could not withstand the short-term psychological pressures he created (and particularly so when bereft of social support from fellow subjects). In other circumstances people may succumb to the transient pressures of a religious revivalist meeting. Indeed, the methods employed by the Chinese, while they shocked western observers at the time, are not really new nor are they peculiarly Chinese, except in their application to such a large number of people. Such techniques have been employed by religious bodies and mass movements throughout history. The Inquisition used coercion; confession and self-criticism are not just part of the Catholic religion but are also important to some Protestant revivalist groups and some modern cults.

Whatever short-term effects the indoctrination programme had, how likely was it that prisoners, once returned to their own society, would maintain any new-found beliefs? As always in considering change one has to assess three interlocking aspects:

1   people's initial values, attitudes, knowledge and their susceptibility to succumb to pressure

2   the techniques employed by the change agent, the extremity of the situation in which people find themselves, and the length of time during which a person is isolated from counterbalancing, outside influences

3   the society into which the recipient of influence processes emerges – will he or she be supported in their newly adopted views?

As to the first point, interviews by psychologists with soldiers during their long voyage home on board ship showed personality characteristics mattered and that, for instance, normally 'bloody-minded' and obstreperous soldiers were capable of defying their captors. Strong convictions were also important: one of Lifton's cases was a Catholic priest with strongly held religious beliefs which could not be shaken. In the case of the soldiers, many had been ill-prepared by their own side as to the reasons why they found themselves in Korea, not even fighting for their own country but for a fairly nebulous entity such as the (then) only recently established United Nations. They could not, therefore, rehearse to themselves counter-arguments to the information they were given. As to the second point, I discussed the extremity of the situation and the techniques adopted earlier in this section. As to the third point, it is not surprising that the Chinese students of the revolutionary colleges maintained their newly adopted views since they returned to a society which supported (and rewarded) these views. Returning United Nations soldiers, by contrast, re-entered a society which, on the whole, did not support any communist beliefs they might have adopted and hence, unless they took active steps to seek out like-minded associates, their new beliefs were unlikely to last.

The above schema of the influence process applies to most situations in which change is fostered or expected, such as, to choose a more everyday example, successful socialization into a professional role. What makes 'coercion' different is the extremity of the measures employed, particularly the isolation of the individual from his or her previous group memberships. Nevertheless, as Lifton (1961) has shown in his case studies, though individuals react to and cope with 're-education' in terms of their own personality and fundamental beliefs, they are unlikely to emerge unchanged given the intensive challenges to their thoughts and the self-questioning this provokes. They may be stronger, having undergone extreme physical and psychological pain and come out of their experiences with some degree of self-respect. (This is a point which emerges also from several of the books published by the western hostages in Lebanon in the 1980s, for instance in the moving account written by Brian Keenan, 1992, about his experiences as a prisoner of the Hezbollah.) At times, however, the insights gained into repressed and previously unknowable aspects of the mind which become conscious through the experience of 're-education' may leave people shaken and disturbed. Indeed, to a limited extent, the same could be said of Milgram's subjects who needed careful 'debriefing' to adjust to their disturbing experiences.

The Chinese indoctrination programmes as employed against Allied prisoners of war aroused great anxiety in the West and raised questions about the nature of loyalty and treason and the preparation of soldiers for captivity. For this reason, the returning prisoners of war were extensively studied by the military, psychologists and psychiatrists in several countries, and research, much of it in laboratory conditions, was subsequently undertaken, often financed by military authorities. For instance, Hebb (Hebb et al., 1952) studied the disorientating effects of sensory and sleep deprivation for the Defence Research Board in Canada, and Zimbardo (1973), supported by the US Office of Naval Research, set up a fake prison to study the effects of imprisonment. Zimbardo's study, among others, pinpointed the need for people to create and sustain cohesive groups so that they are not overwhelmed by the situations they find themselves in. It is salutary to remind ourselves that while the lessons to be learnt from such research can undoubtedly be used to prepare people to withstand pressures in the event they are taken prisoner, the very same research, of course, also identifies how to carry out effective interrogations, how to disorientate prisoners and weaken their resistance. Such methods, unfortunately, seem to be used in many countries.

Review of section 7

- Everyday influence processes can be distinguished from more intensive forms of thought reform and coercion in terms of the extremity of the situation, the techniques adopted and the extent to which the environment can be controlled.

- Research on thought reform and indoctrination emphasizes once again the role of social support and external validation for one's views, group identification and the importance of individual factors.

8 Conclusions

This chapter has posed many questions about group dynamics. Our initial focus was on influence processes within small groups and the theories which might account for them. Then we explored attempts to influence people deliberately through their group memberships, at times by divorcing them from previous memberships and/or putting them into new groupings. We also assessed the conditions under which any new-found views might be maintained. Implicit in our discussion was the question of how far people have a stable and meaningful existence outside the groups which provide and support their conceptions of themselves.

We reviewed laboratory experiments as well as studies based on interviews and naturalistic observations. Such diversity of research designs raises questions of validity. What is acceptable as evidence? Are different approaches required to investigate different problems? Are there methods of research (or mixtures of methods such as combining experimental data with post-experimental interviews or personality tests) which are likely to be impartial and value-free in a given context? You might like to compare, for instance, the more ethnographic style of investigation adopted by Lifton in his research on thought reform with Milgram's controlled procedures in his studies on obedience. The former allows considerable *ecological validity* while the latter makes it possible to identify different variables as principal causes of obedience.

I have discussed other methodological issues as they arose in relation to the specific material presented. Thus I mentioned that the design features of an experiment influence outcomes (Asch); that the cultural context affects outcomes (again Asch but also much of the work on minority influence and leadership style); that the experimenter, teacher or leader is part of the field of forces impinging on the individual, though it is not always taken into account (the variations in leadership style in Lewin's experiments and the way Milgram used his authority were, of course, part of the design); the need for control groups (as demonstrated, for instance, in the work of Asch). Thinking about methodology leads us also to consider the ethical issues involved in carrying out research and implementing the findings. I have mentioned the problem of obtaining the informed consent of the participants in a study involving deception (section 2.2) and the misgivings expressed by some critics about the stress caused to Milgram's subjects (section 2.3).

I have also pointed out in various places (in relation to Sherif and Moscovici, for example) that the *meaning* a situation has for the participants in a study needs to be explored and hence the analysis of experimental or other outcomes should also be 'grounded' in subjective self-reports and the experiences of the participating individuals. In general, validity is *always* an issue if only because of the questions which have *not* been asked and because results need interpreting in their cultural, historical and social contexts. This chapter has mainly focused on the internal validity of research and theories, that is, whether the conclusions follow from the research, rather than on external (ecological) validity, that is, whether the research reflects the world out there. The world, of course, keeps changing as well as being re-constructed and re-interpreted in people's minds. It is perhaps useful to remind ourselves, given the current emphasis in social psychological theory on social and mental construction, that such constructions are built on real events: wars, racism, industrial conflicts, redundancy, or personal experiences of childhood, love, family life, bereavement and other situations in which we have participated. Mourning may be displayed in different ways in different cultures – loud wailing at the grave side or presenting a stoical 'stiff upper lip' during the funeral service – but I would suggest that the experience of loss and bereavement are likely to be similar. What may change as social psychology evolves and advances are the questions we ask and the interpretations we offer. Yet sometimes psychologists are too conservative and lack a spirit of intellectual adventure: their questions tend to arise from what is there rather than what might be or ought to be.

Looking back over the studies reviewed in this chapter, do you come away with the impression that social psychologists are scientifically innovative, politically radical and provide knowledge useful to social reform? Or do you feel that, through their choice of topics for research and theorizing, they are more likely to be seen to be upholders of the status quo?

In addition to questions of methodology and ethics there is the fascinating topic of the *application* of the knowledge gained. If you wanted to develop strategies for changing attitudes or behaviour, how would you proceed? Would it be sensible to change *individuals* (through education, persuasion or more coercive measures); to change the *structure* and tone of an interaction (such as when an industrial dispute is switched to arbitration, or when a patient joins group psychotherapy from individual analysis); to change the *group* as a whole; or, finally, to change the *societal context*, for instance, through new legislation intended to provide new standards and a new moral framework for alleviating racism or engendering religious tolerance?

Further reading

This chapter has explored social influence in different contexts – from laboratory studies to prison camps. It is, therefore, difficult to suggest just a few books to extend the argument. If you have access to an academic library you might like to follow up some of the references given in areas that are of particular interest to you. I have also mentioned readily available books, many in paperback editions.

Here are some books not mentioned in the text which build on the arguments presented:

On the impact of institutions on self-concept and how to resist such pressures

Goffman, E. (1986) *Asylums,* Harmondsworth, Penguin Books.

Mandela, N. (1995) *Long Walk to Freedom,* London, Abacus.

On the 'banality of evil'

Arendt, H.(1963, 1994) *Eichman in Jerusalem,* Harmondsworth, Penguin Books.

On aspects of change in management

Handy, C. (1993) *The Empty Raincoat,* London, Hutchinson

Pugh, D.S. and Hickson, D.J. (1996) *Writers on Organizations,* (5th edition) Harmondsworth, Penguin Books.

On reactions to minority opinion

Dunant, S. (ed.) (1994) *The War of the Words: the Political Correctness Debate,* London, Virago Press.

On 'mind control'

Brown, J.A.C. (1963) *Techniques of Persuasion,* Harmondsworth, Penguin Books.

Watson, P. (1980) *War on the Mind: the Military Uses and Abuses of Psychology,* Harmondsworth, Penguin Books.

References

Abrams, D. and Hogg, M.A. (1990) 'Social identification, self-categorization and social influence' in Stroebe, W. and Hewstone, M. (eds.) *European Review of Social Psychology,* vol. 1, Chichester, John Wiley.

Allport, F.H. (1924) *Social Psychology,* Boston, Houghton Mifflin.

Allport, G.W. (1968) 'The historical background of modern social psychology' in Lindzey, G. and Aronson, E. (eds.) *The Handbook of Social Psychology* (2nd edition), vol. 1, Reading; Mass, Addison-Wesley.

Aronson, E. (1984) *The Social Animal* (4th edition), New York, W.H. Freeman and Company.

Asch, S.E. (1955) 'Opinions and social pressures', *Scientific American*, vol. 193, November, pp. 31–55.

Asch, S.E. (1952) 'Effects of group pressure upon modification and distortion of judgements' in Swanson, G.E., Newcomb, T.M. and Hartley, E.L. (eds.) *Readings in Social Psychology*, New York, Holt, Rinehart and Winston.

Baron, R.A. and Byrne, D. (1981) *Social Psychology: Understanding Human Interaction*, Boston, Allyn and Bacon.

Bramal, D. and Friend, R. (1987) 'The work group and its vicissitudes in social and industrial psychology', *Journal of Applied Behavioural Science*, 23, 2, pp. 233–53.

Brown, R. (1986) *Social Psychology: The Second Edition*, New York, The Free Press.

Cartwright, D. and Zander, A. (eds.) (1968) *Group Dynamics: Research and Theory*, (3rd edition), London, The Tavistock Institute.

Chang, J. (1991) *Wild Swans*, London, HarperCollins.

Clark III, R.D. and Maass, A. (1990) 'The effects of majority size on minority influence', *European Journal of Social Psychology*, 20, pp. 99–117.

Coch, L. and French, J.R.P. (1948) 'Overcoming resistance to change', *Human Relations*, vol. 1, pp. 512–32.

Cooley, C.H. (1902) *Human Nature and the Social Order*, New York, Schocken.

Dallos, R. (1996) 'Creating relationships: patterns of actions and beliefs' in Miell, D. and Dallos, R. (eds.).

Deutsch, M. and Gerard, H.B. (1955) 'A study of normative and informational social influences upon individual judgement', *Journal of Abnormal and Social Psychology*, 51, pp. 629–36.

Ellul, J. (1965) *Propaganda: the Formation of Men's Attitudes*, New York, Vintage Books.

Festinger, L. (1950) 'Informal social communication', *Psychological Review*, vol. 57, pp. 271–82.

Festinger, L. (1954) 'A theory of social comparison processes', *Human Relations, 7*, pp. 117–40.

Fiedler, F.E. (1967) *A Theory of Leadership Effectiveness*, New York, McGraw-Hill.

Hebb, D.O. *et al.* (1952) 'The effects of isolation upon attitudes, motivation and thought', *Fourth Symposium, Military Medicine*, Defense Research Board, Canada.

Heller, F. (1995) *The Levers of Organizational Change: Facilitators and Inhibitors*, London, The Tavistock Institute.

Keenan, B. (1992) *An Evil Cradling*, London, Vintage.

Kinkead, E. (1959) *Why They Collaborated*, London, Longman.

Larsen, K. (1974) 'Conformity in the Asch experiment', *Journal of Social Psychology*, vol. 94, pp. 303–4.

Latané, B. and Wolf, S. (1981) 'The social impact of majorities and minorities', *Psychological Review*, vol. 88, No. 5, pp. 438–53.

Lewin, K. (1947) 'Group decision and social change' in Newcomb, T.M. and Hartley, E.L. (eds.) Readings in Rinehart and Winston, *Social Psychology*, New York, Holt.

Lewin, K. (1948) *Resolving Social Conflicts: Selected Papers on Group Dynamics*, New York, Harper and Brothers.

Lewin, K. (1951) *Field Theory in Social Science*, (edited by D. Cartwright), New York, Harper & Bros.

Lewin, K., Lippitt, R. and White, R. (1939) 'Patterns of aggressive behaviour in experimentally created "social climates"', *Journal of Social Psychology*, vol. 10, pp. 271–99.

Lifton, R.J. (1957) 'Thought reform of Chinese intellectuals', *Journal of Social Issues*, vol. 13, pp. 5–20.

Lifton, R.J. (1961) *Thought Reform and the Psychology of Totalism: A Study of 'Brainwashing' in China*, London, Gollancz.

Maass, A., Clark III, R.D. and Habercorn, G. (1982) 'The effects of differential ascribed category membership and norm on minority influence', *European Journal of Social Psychology*, vol. 12, pp. 89–104.

Miell, D. and Dallos, R. (eds.) (1996) *Social Interaction and Personal Relationships*, London, Sage/The Open University (Book 2 in this series).

Myers, D.G. (1982) 'Polarizing effects of social interaction' in Brandstatter, M., Davis, J.H. and Stocker-Kreicgauer, G. (eds.) *Group Decision Making*, London, Academic Press, pp. 125–61.

Milgram, S. (1974) *Obedience to Authority*, London, The Tavistock Institute.

Ministry of Defence (1955) *Treatment of British Prisoners of War in Korea*, London, HMSO.

Moscovici, S. (1961) *La Psychoanalyse, son Image et son Public* (2nd edition, 1976) London, Academic Press.

Moscovici, S. (1976) *Social Influence and Social Change*, London, Academic Press.

Moscovici, S. (1980) 'Towards a theory of conversion behaviour' in Berkowitz, L. (ed.) *Advances in Experimental Social Psychology*, vol. 13, New York, Academic Press.

Moscovici, S., Lage, E. and Naffrechoux, M. (1969) 'Influence of a consistent minority on the response of a majority in a color perception task', *Sociometry*, vol. 32, pp. 365–80.

Mugny, G. (1975) 'Negotiations, image of the other and the process of minority influence', *European Journal of Social Psychology*, 5, pp. 209–29.

Mugny, G. (1982) *The Power of Minorities*, London, Academic Press.

Newcomb, T.M. (1952) 'Attitude development as a function of reference groups: the Bennington study' in Swanson, G.E., Newcomb, T.M. and Hartley, E.L. (eds.) *Readings in Social Psychology*, New York, Holt, Rinehart and Winston.

Orne, M.T. (1962) 'On the social psychology of the psychological experiment', *American Psychologist*, vol. 17, no. 11, pp. 776–83.

Paichler, G. (1979) 'Polarization of attitudes in homogeneous and heterogeneous groups', *European Journal of Social Psychology*, vol. 9, pp. 85–96.

Pelz, E.B. (1958) 'Some factors in group decision' in Maccoby, E.E., Newcomb, T.M. and Hartley, E.L. (eds.) *Readings in Social Psychology* (3rd edition), New York, Holt, Rinehart and Winston.

Perrin, S. and Spencer, C. (1981) 'Independence or conformity in the Asch experiment as a reflection of cultural and situational factors', *British Journal of Social Psychology*, vol. 20, pp. 205–9.

Roethlisberger, F.J. and Dickson, W.J. (1939) *Management and the Worker*, Cambridge; Mass., Harvard University Press.

Rosenthal, R. and Jacobson, L.F. (1968) 'Teacher expectations for the disadvantaged', *Scientific American*, vol. 218, no. 4, pp. 19–23.

Rosenzweig, S. (1933) 'The experimental situation as a psychological problem', *Psychological Review*, vol. 40, pp. 337–345.

Schein, E.H. (1956) 'The Chinese indoctrination program for prisoners of war', *Psychiatry,* vol. 19, pp. 149–73.

Sherif, M. (1936) *The Psychology of Social Norms*, New York, Harper and Row.

Stevens, R. (ed.) (1996) *Understanding the Self*, London, Sage/The Open University (Book 1 in this series).

Tajfel, H. (1981) *Human Groups and Social Categories*, Cambridge, Cambridge University Press.

Tajfel, H. and Turner, J. (1979) 'An integrative theory of intergroup conflict' in Austin, G.W. and Worchel, S. (eds.) *The Social Psychology of Intergroup Relations*, Monterey; California, Brooks/Cole.

Taylor, F.W. (1967) *The Principles of Scientific Management*, New York, Norton, (first published in 1911).

Toates, F. (1996) 'A biological perspective' in Stevens, R. (ed.).

Triplett, N. (1897) 'The dynamogenic factors in pacemaking and competition', *American Journal of Psychology*, vol. 9, pp. 503–33.

Trist, E.L., Higgins, G.W., Murray, H. and Pollock, A.B. (1963) *Organizational Choice*, London, The Tavistock Institute.

Turner, J.C. (1982) 'Towards a cognitive redefinition of the social group' in Tajfel, H. (ed.) (1982).

Turner, J.C. (1991) *Social Influence*, Milton Keynes, Open University Press.

Turner, J.C., Hogg. M., Oakes. P., Reicher, S. and Wetherell, M. (1987) *Rediscovering the Social Group: A Self-Categorization Theory*, Oxford, Blackwell.

Van Knippenberg, D., Lossie, N. and Wilke, H. (1994) 'In-group prototypicality and persuasion: determinants of heuristic and the systematic message processing', *British Journal of Social Psychology*, vol. 3, pp. 289–300

Wetherell, M. (1987) 'Social identity and group polarization' in Turner, J. C. *et al.* (1987).

Woodward, J. (1965) *Industrial Organization: Theory and Practice*, Oxford, Oxford University Press.

Zimbardo, P.G., Banks, W.C., Craig, H. and Jaffe, D. (1973) 'A Pirandellian prison: the mind is a formidable jailer', *New York Times Magazine*, 8 April 1973, pp. 38–60.

CHAPTER 2

A PSYCHODYNAMIC PERSPECTIVE ON GROUP PROCESSES

By Helen Morgan and Kerry Thomas

Contents

1 Introduction

Chapter 1 presented a view of 'what happens in groups' from the perspective of experimental social psychology – the dominant viewpoint of the last few decades. This research was inspired by some of the strange and overpowering things that can happen in groups and crowds. Their translation into *experimental* social psychology has shown that being in a group and subject to group processes clearly does have an influence on individuals, sometimes changing their behaviour in quite unexpected ways (see, for example, Asch's conformity studies discussed in Chapter 1, section 2.2) even when the group is largely simulated rather than face to face, or simply a 'role play'. We have seen that groups, in themselves, can have emergent properties and in this sense are more than the sum of the individuals. The norms, roles, emotional climates and patterns of communication constructed by the group act back on individuals, often constraining them but sometimes liberating them and facilitating group tasks. Such *emergent* properties of groups frequently outlast the particular individuals so the group seems to possess its own character which it then confers on members. Group members are also validated by their groups and gain a social identity as a consequence of their membership (see Chapter 1, section 4.1).

Like Chapter 1, this chapter examines the power of groups to influence individuals' behaviour, their experience and their joint constructions of reality, and it also looks at those properties that seem to belong to groups in themselves. The psychodynamic approach, however, looks at the effects of group membership not just more deeply, but with a different set of assumptions about the psychological processes involved and about the nature of the individuals and their relation to groups. The present chapter sets out to show that in groups 'other people' and the 'group as a whole' produce many of their effects unconsciously and irrationally. This is a shift to a different discourse – a different kind of theorizing and method. The focus is no longer on cognitive information processing which is, by and large, conscious and accessible, but on unconscious motives, unconscious communications and the processes of identification and projection.

We shall find that the methods used in the psychodynamic tradition are very different from those of Chapter 1 where the focus was on objectivity and a search for truths in terms of causes and effects – the aims of traditional science. Such methods have both strengths and weaknesses. Variables can be operationally defined and manipulated, and behaviours observed and sometimes measured, but the emphasis on objectivity and control means that many of the kinds of interactions and happenings between people that are so characteristic of groups in everyday life cannot take place. The experimental method defines the kinds of phenomena that can be legitimately studied. For example, the experimental approach is limited to issues that can be examined in a laboratory setting or in relatively simple and short-term field studies. The groups created for the purpose of an experiment have no history. Often they are newly formed, often made up of strangers, and sometimes they are structured as 'virtual groups' in which people do not actually meet. Often the rationale for their existence is the accomplishment of artificial tasks and the possible patterns and modes of communication are usually very restricted. The experimental approach neglects subjective experiences and emotions. We would argue that a great deal of the meaningfulness of group life is outside the brief of the experimental approach to groups.

ACTIVITY 2.1	Look back to the studies of Sherif and Asch in Chapter 1, sections 2.1 and 2.2. These studies, and others conducted from the same perspective, are trying to find general laws of group processes, in this case about the emergence of group norms and conformity. What are usually reported are generalized findings based on behavioural data. But in many of these studies the subjects were also interviewed and their accounts recorded; these subjective reports are outlined in Chapter 1, sections 2.1 and 2.2. Try to focus on these subjective reports and then imagine that *you* are a subject in experiments of this kind. Write down what it would feel like to be sitting in the dark watching a light as in the Sherif study; then write down what it would feel like to be a 'naïve' member of an 'Asch group' being presented with the lines and hearing the other members making their responses. Now turn to section 2.3 of Chapter 1 and do the same for the Milgram study.

For each of these studies write down what you think you would have been conscious of trying to do. What emotions might you have had? Then, for each experiment, try to find an equivalent example of an experience in a group in real life, when you thought and felt in these ways. Keep your notes on these three thought experiments near you as you continue with this chapter. In activities later in the chapter we shall come back to some of the emotions and understandings that you might have had in these group settings, and you will be able to think about them in terms of what you read in the rest of this chapter.

The psychodynamic perspective on group processes will differ from Chapter 1 on several key dimensions.

1 *Ecological validity:* Psychodynamics is usually applied to groups that have continuity and are studied over time – even if they are newly formed at the start of a study. Often they are groups which have a history and a role in real life – such as families, work groups, teams, therapy groups, and organizations, and will, therefore, have more ecological validity than newly formed experimental groups. In ordinary life we do not very often 'dip into' new groups of strangers. Most of our experience of groups is from ongoing membership. We live in groups and are constantly influenced by them. We are surrounded by groups and in some sense are 'in' groups from very early

in life; and we move in and out of groups thereafter all the time. Even when not in the actual presence of others we are continuously engaged in some kind of *symbolic interaction* or *reference* to groups of others *represented in our internal worlds*.

Ordinary life in groups is extremely complex and full of subtle dynamics that change over time – in direct contrast to the groups that feature in experimental social psychology. When we join new groups we are not naïve, but well-practised group participants who *know* (unconsciously) how to use others to learn, to achieve joint goals and to be helped with our emotional states. The psychodynamic approach attempts to add understanding of the more subtle and unconscious kinds of learning, and the construction of realities and selfhoods.

2 *Focus on meanings and subjective experiences:* The psychodynamic perspective characteristically looks beneath the surface of what happens. It goes behind observable behaviours to understand group life in terms of meanings, and in terms of the subjective experiences and emotional states of group members. It focuses on unconscious motivations of individual members and unconscious communications between them, and on the collective unconscious dynamics of the group as an entity.

3 *Methods and evidence:* The psychodynamic method uses evidence that would not be acceptable to the experimental approach. The method requires the kind of participant observation that is associated with psychoanalysis, where those who study the groups are both part of what is happening, experiencing the pressures and unconscious communications, and separate. Being simultaneously in both these positions, the group analyst, facilitator, or 'leader' is able to observe and monitor what is happening in the ordinary sense, and to *observe their own observing and their own reactions to what is happening* and then make inferences about underlying meanings. All these observations are made over time, and often on many occasions, thus providing a dynamic view of the group and the fluctuations in processes (see Thomas, 1996b, for a discussion of the 'psychoanalytic method'). In therapeutic groups it is relatively clear that group analysts are working with and as part of their groups; the dual perspective of psychodynamic consultants doing action research in organizations and institutions is less easy to appreciate. These researchers are 'outside' the organization – with an outside perspective – but once they are invited inside the organization's boundaries they are simultaneously outside and 'inside and participating' in some sense. Both group therapists and organizational consultants *construct* their understanding of the group processes and the relationship between individuals and the larger collective by treating the behaviours, physiological reactions, speech and other communications of the members as surface forms of deeper, underlying, unconscious processes.

4   *Assumptions about people:* What are the assumptions about individuals, alone and in their collective life, that underpin the approach?

First, there is the primacy of unconscious motivation and the *defensive* nature of people's internal worlds. People are seen as not necessarily rational beings who pursue the truth and the whole truth about the situations and relationships they find themselves in. This is not a matter of whether or not they *construct* versions of the external world – as opposed to internally representing 'accurate snapshots' of what is out there. The constructed nature of the internal world is assumed. What is important is that, according to psychodynamics, these constructions are driven by unconscious motives which centre on avoiding pain, conflict and anxiety. This chapter also questions people's capacity to gain access to their motivations through conscious reflection on the validity of their reasoning and plans and intentions.

Second, there is the idea that our selves are not tightly demarcated but have relatively permeable boundaries with other selves. The research described in Chapter 1 assumed that all psychological phenomena are located inside individuals. The psychodynamic perspective challenges much of this by suggesting that individuals have permeable boundaries and a great deal of psychological business goes on 'in the spaces between people', belonging neither to this individual or that one, but somehow jointly owned. When people participate in groups their boundaries become even more permeable. In the group setting this relocation of psychological phenomena leads to the experience of being mixed up with others, and mixed up with the *group as group*. These ideas highlight the unconscious, communicative processes of identification and projection. By bringing these psychological processes to the centre of the stage we reveal the depth at which other people and group life are the sources and maintainers of the self.

According to the psychodynamic view of this chapter, when we are in groups and other collectivities we are even less demarcated as individuals and this arouses anxieties. Some of these anxieties are leftovers and transferences from childhood efforts to separate as individuals, especially our efforts to separate from the safety and 'fusion' of the mother/infant relationship. If one accepts the idea of permeability or mix ups between people as a possibility, as something that occurs in close relationships and is perhaps exaggerated by being in a group, then group processes take on a new significance.

5   *Group mind:* Psychodynamics provides a set of concepts with which to think about mix ups between individuals. It also provides conceptual tools with which to think about how it is possible, in a group, to arrive (unconsciously) at collective sense-making and collective action – something approaching a revival of the notion of group mind. This idea, used by McDougall and Le Bon, was rejected by the experimentalists of Chapter 1: '...it is a basic assumption of modern psychology that psychological processes reside only in individuals –

in the most literal sense, at least, there is no such thing as a "group mind"' (Turner, 1984, p. 4). We shall reconsider this debate and begin to see that perhaps it is not too fanciful to talk of a group mind.

Section 2 of the chapter provides an orientation to group psychodynamics showing its origins in the work of Lewin (1947) and Bion (1961) in particular. It will demonstrate how assumptions and concepts deriving from individual psychodynamics and one-to-one psychoanalysis have been extended to the psychodynamics of groups. Section 3 will present and discuss case material of small groups in the light of the concepts introduced in section 2 and the group psychodynamic paradigm. Section 4 will extend this kind of discussion into work groups and the organizational setting.

Section 5 returns to the contribution of Bion, and his demonstrations of the conflict between the real world demands of group tasks and unconscious emotional assumptions about group life that drive the behaviour of group members. His ideas encourage us to think about the term 'group mind'. Then we shall outline how his work was influenced by Klein, leading to a new way of thinking about group life.

In section 6 we shall review some of the controversial issues that are raised by the psychodynamic approach to collective life.

Aims of Chapter 2

The aims of this chapter are:

- To outline the origins of the psychodynamic approach to groups, its assumptions and methods.

- To present and discuss case material illustrating processes of group psychodynamics in real life small groups and in organizations.

- To consider the contribution made by Bion to group psychology.

- To reconsider the concept of group mind.

- To present the idea of groups as containers for aspects of the self and explore the permeability and fluidity of the boundaries between individuals and groups, and the implications of these ideas for social psychology.

- To discuss aspects of the psychoanalytic method in relation to group processes.

2   The origins of group psychodynamics

Psychodynamics is most commonly associated with the psychoanalytic treatment of individuals. But it has another aspect – that of *group* psychodynamics. Group psychodynamics uses many of the concepts of individual psychoanalysis, together with the same methods of participant observation. Evidence is collected from observations, from transference and countertransference material, and from the effects of interpretations through which group members are helped to think about the processes in which they are unconsciously participating. Group psychodynamics, as a domain of study, includes group psychoanalysis and therapeutic communities, but it also has a strong research tradition in the workplace and in organizational settings; its origins were in practical attempts to solve problems in real life groups.

This section outlines the beginnings of group psychodyamics and the assumptions about people, taken from individual psychodynamics, on which it is based.

2.1   Focusing on the group: Bion's early contribution

The psychodynamic perspective on groups grew out of a combination of group dynamics in the tradition of Lewin (see Chapter 1, section 6), psychoanalytic theory and the practical needs of war-time psychiatry. An outline of this history is given in Box 2.1. Much of the early work centred on the ideas of Bion, a psychiatrist who worked with the army during the Second World War, and who later became an influential psychoanalyst in the individual psychoanalytic tradition. Bion and others combined basic research on group processes with the use of group processes to raise morale, to treat psychiatric casualties of war, to improve officer selection procedures and to increase the effectiveness of work groups.

After the Second World War, the productiveness of this research led to the growth of social psychiatry – a form of policy science whose goal was to study and implement interventions in large-scale social problems – and the development of therapeutic communities where patients live together and their psychiatric treatment occurs in groups. Tavistock-inspired research in industry and organizations emerged as a characteristic amalgam of psychology, systems theory and psychodynamics, an action research tradition that continues today (see Chapter 1, section 6.3).

BOX 2.1 The history of group psychodyamics

The history of group psychodynamics is very much associated with the Tavistock Clinic and its psychoanalysts, notably Melanie Klein, and with the Tavistock Institute for Human Relations. The dynamics and psychodynamics of groups became a recognized area of research and a means for 'doing' therapy in the 1940s in Britain. During the Second World War the British Government feared a loss of morale amongst the military, public panic and widespread psychiatric breakdown. They believed there was an urgent need to understand matters of morale, conflict, leadership and group behaviour. The traditional views of psychiatry and social organization theorists were felt to be unequal to the task. In 1939, J.R. Rees, the Director of the Tavistock Clinic was appointed as head of the army psychiatric service, supported by many colleagues from the Tavistock Clinic. This independent group was given a free hand to conduct extensive research into the behaviour of individuals in groups, and the finance and authority to support their work. It was a radical move that brought together military psychiatrists, psychoanalysts and social scientists working in the tradition of Lewin – people in a position to formulate new concepts of social dynamics, independent of those of the Establishment. Bion and Rickman were notable amongst these; their research was re-published much later by Bion in an influential book called *Experiences in Groups* (1961).

Trist, a clinical psychologist, has poignantly described the start of his collaboration with Bion and the start of the group psychodynamic movement.

> My first encounter with him [Bion], as an influence, was in 1940, when I was a clinical psychologist … housed in the premises of Mill Hill School as a neurosis centre in the Emergency Medical Service … I felt very dissatisfied and undertook an anthropological survey of all the activities in the hospital in the hope of finding something that would give me a clue as to how the wider social environment might be used therapeutically. The last straw was meeting on my way to the occupational therapy workshops a large punch-drunk ex-boxer, now in the Guards, forlornly carrying an absurd peacock painted on glass. There had to be a better way.
>
> […]
>
> [I] heard that 'something' was going on at the Wharncliffe in Sheffield (a hospital similar to Mill Hill) started by a Dr John Rickman … a former analytic trainee of his [Rickman's] now in the army, a certain Wilfred Bion, had … prepared a document which became known as the Wharncliffe Memorandum. This document contained a prospectus

for a therapeutic community. In the sense of making systematic use of the happenings and relationships in a hospital, it was the first time the concept had been formulated ...'

(Trist, 1985, in Pines, 1992, pp. 5–6).

At that time, although Bion was in a training analysis and deeply influenced by psychoanalytic thought, he was specifically trying to do something different from individual psychoanalysis. What was crucial about Bion's initiative is that it focused on the group as an entity, the *group as group,* rather than on the psychologies and psychopathologies of the individuals who made up the group.

Not long after the Wharncliffe Memorandum, Bion had an opportunity to begin the famous Northfield experiments. He was posted to take charge of the Military Training and Rehabilitation Wing of the Northfield military psychiatric hospital, working with Rickman. This *action research* lasted for only six weeks, but has had a profound influence on psychological and psychoanalytic thinking about group processes. Bion set out to discover what happens in unstructured groups and how the processes can be used therapeutically, and more generally, to provide the participants with insights about their unconscious processes. He wrote:

... it was essential first to find out what was the ailment afflicting the community, as opposed to the individuals composing it, and next to give the community a common aim. In general all psychiatric hospitals have the same ailment and the same common aim – to escape from the batterings of neurotic disorder. Unfortunately the attempt to get this relief is nearly always by futile means – retreat. Without realizing it doctors and patients alike are running away from the complaint.

(Bion, 1946, quoted by Trist, 1985, in Pines, 1992, p. 14)

Bion arranged a daily, half-hour, unstructured meeting of the whole Training Wing (between 100 and 200 men). The apparent purpose was to discuss the organization of small voluntary groups in which the men could study topics and activities of their own choice. But what happened in the big group and the small ones was that they spontaneously became studies of their own intra-group tensions. This group-generated agenda was so clear that it became established explicitly as the main task of the big group and the small groups within it. The essence of the therapeutic effect and the starting point for Bion's theory is the idea that in groups there are two agendas.

- There is the overt and conscious purpose for the group's existence – its work task or primary task. Insofar as the group attends to this task it is functioning as a *work group.*

- There is also another, hidden agenda – one which the participants are usually not aware of. This concerns the life of the group itself – a spontaneous but unconscious concern with intra-group tensions, relationships and emotions.

In Bion's view it was as if another group, comprising the same individuals, was operating simultaneously, at the unconscious level. Bion called this level of activity the 'basic assumption group'. In section 5 we shall examine what this phrase implies; but for the moment we shall refer to this second underlying group as the *unconscious group*. It is important to be clear that this does not refer simply to what the individuals bring in terms of their individual unconscious motives; it refers to another, underlying group – operating unconsciously and collectively. While groups vary in the 'tightness' of the requirements of their work task and the 'space' they have for the unconscious group and its activities, Bion believed that in *all* kinds of group settings this unconscious group takes form and then functions to satisfy the unconscious needs of the members and as a defence against anxiety.

In the Northfield experiments, for example, the big group – operating as an unconscious group – reported a joint belief that 'the problem' lay in the 'fact' that 80 per cent of the men were malingerers and should be punished. The therapy consisted of 'thinking' work and self-study by the group as a whole of its own reactions and tensions that followed when the psychiatrist refused to accept this 'diagnosis' or the 'treatment' – the punishment. Moral indignation and its enactment had to be replaced by reflection and an understanding, by all the participants, of the processes in the group that wasted energy and produced unhappiness. The activities of the unconscious group had to be made conscious and thought about in the group.

Bion's involvement with group psychodynamics lasted through the 1940s. The force of his contribution was that he was trying to establish a focus at the level of the group itself without using the language of psychoanalysis. Later, after his own training as a psychoanalyst, which included his training analysis with Melanie Klein, he re-considered the findings of his early group research in Kleinian psychoanalytic terms, but still focusing at the group level. We shall examine this re-view in section 5.4

2.2   Underlying concepts of individual and group psychodynamics

We have seen that Bion began by avoiding the individualistic language of psychoanalytic concepts so as to emphasize the impact of the group as an entity and the force of group processes. Nevertheless, his notion of the unconscious group is predicated on concepts from individual psychoanalysis. Three clusters of concepts and assumptions about people common to the major schools of individual psychoanalysis are outlined below, with illustrations of how the ideas can be extended into group settings.

2.2.1   Unconscious motivation

The first assumption is that 'things are not as they seem', that human behaviour and consciousness is largely determined by unconscious motives which may give rise to seemingly irrational feelings and behaviour. One-to-one psychoanalysis has been important in bringing into ordinary discourse the idea of the unconscious as a factor in determining behaviour, even when such behaviour is contrary to the conscious intentions of the individual concerned. If this fundamental tenet is accepted, it follows that when individuals gather together in groups, for whatever reason, the behaviour of the group will be determined by unconscious as well as conscious factors. Powerful feelings can be generated in families, work groups, large groups and crowds, sometimes for no obvious reasons, and it is common experience that when people organize themselves within groups, institutions, societies and cultures they do so in ways that often appear irrational and strange. Because we do not usually have access to these unconscious forces (other than with the help of trained observers), it is difficult or impossible to reflect on what is happening and thence modify behaviour and adapt roles and structures.

An example of the operation of unconscious motivations in groups and organizations might be unconscious conflict between the requirements of the tasks that have to accomplished, together with the norms and work roles that this task entails, and the undercurrent of *unconscious needs of the individual members*. For example, in a committee with many vetting decisions to make (perhaps about applications for jobs), an individual member can affect decision making, slow the process down – for personal (unconscious) reasons. But other members may get involved, and what begins as accidental commonalities between members can lead to collusions, largely unconscious, which have long-term effects. Existing decision-making procedures may be modified, or new ones instituted. Thus a committee can become increasingly rigid and, over time, establish a quite clear (to outsiders at least) emotional climate of resistance and low productivity. It may be that the particular task of this committee attracts certain kinds of individuals, creating an almost inevitable increase in bureaucratic rigidity. In Bion's terms, however, we could think of the committee as two parallel groups, one properly attending to the primary task of the committee and the other – the unconscious group – being concerned with the emotional life of the group as a whole.

2.2.2 The persisting influence of infancy and childhood: transferences, regressions and primitive emotions

The second cluster of assumptions concerns the continuing (and continuous) influence of very early life and experience through into adulthood. In this view, early experience leads to the formation of lasting internal worlds which are emotionally charged constructions of the external world and experience in it, rather than straightforward mappings. Internal worlds are created very early in life and provide a constructed basis from which life proceeds – a psychic reality.

Internalized (introjected) versions of other people and their relationships, particularly from early life, are central features of internal worlds. In object relations theories, identifications with these introjections are seen as the source of the self – a self as 'made up of other people'. Not only are people as individuals or couples introjected; but 'people in groups' are internalized. All these combinations of internal objects and internal object relations are potentially available for us to identify with, to use to build our selves, and as templates for re-enactments through the unconscious processes of transference. The idea of an 'internalized group' provides a new way of thinking about the impact of group membership; it is a step towards narrowing the divide between individuals and other members of groups.

In all cultures, the earliest group experiences take place within some form of family or close kinship system. According to psychodynamics, these experiences of families and close kin relationships survive as building blocks for the way we experience, behave and use others in group settings through the rest of life. Therefore, being a member of a group can evoke the early anxieties of relating and being in family groups. Group membership in our adult life can make us feel somewhat lost and childlike again, or lead to a more pronounced regression. We can enact early versions of people or relationships, use primitive defences and perhaps feel fragmented. This is more likely to happen when we are ill or stressed, or faced with repeats (or apparent repeats) of early conflictual configurations, such as finding ourselves in a group where the other members feel like siblings or parents. Anxiety can be aroused in groups by unconsciously re-experiencing sibling behaviours such as rivalries, envy, bullying, or not being able to make oneself heard. Or anxieties can follow transferences of feelings and conflicts about parental figures – often re-located as anxieties to do with feeling pressured, unappreciated (or singled out as special) by the more influential group members or by the group leader. Group members commonly identify with powerful leaders – in groups or crowds or, longer term, in a society or in political settings.

2.2.3 Controlling anxiety: irrationality and defence mechanisms

The third cluster of assumptions concerns psychological defences against anxiety. According to all schools of psychodynamics, consciousness and our internal versions of the world — established in infancy – are systematically distorted so as to avoid anxiety. Psychological defences are directed at creating internally a version of the world that reduces anxiety and makes life more tolerable. What we are talking about here is not objective anxiety about physical dangers, but signal anxiety i.e. an early warning of psychological pain. Because defence mechanisms keep certain conflicts and feelings out of consciousness, behaviour will be influenced in ways we may not understand. In other words, many of our seemingly irrational behaviours and irrational beliefs about the world and what is going on are the result of psychological defences.

We have seen that being in groups can arouse anxieties which are residues of early emotions and conflicts, sometimes transferred directly from our original families or other early experiences of relationships and groups. One of the most important sources of anxiety in groups is the reoccurrence of our original struggle to differentiate our selves from other people and then maintain a sense of identity. Defences in groups are often directed, unconsciously, at maintaining a sense of self and autonomy. Because group membership arouses anxieties, defence mechanisms can play a large part in the way we behave in groups and experience group life.

What happens when the concepts of individual psychoanalysis are applied to groups? Is it possible to understand group processes by using ideas that derive from a focus on individuals? These questions are addressed in the next section.

Review of section 2

- Group psychodynamics began as a response to practical problems concerning group morale, productivity, leadership and the need for new therapeutic techniques to help war-time psychiatric casualties.

- Although grounded in the concepts of individual psychoanalysis, the early work on group psychodynamics attempted to focus on the group as a whole rather than on the psychodynamics of the individual members.

- Bion worked with unstructured groups. He typically observed and experienced in these groups the emergence of two parallel agendas, that of the conscious work group and that of the unconscious group. The unconscious group is concerned with the emotional needs of the group.

- Individual psychoanalytic concepts that are central to group life are:
  - unconscious motivation
  - the persistence into group life of primitive emotions, especially those associated with the first experiences of groups, usually in families, and the transference of these emotions and early ways of relating into adult collective life
  - the ever-present psychological defences against anxiety; anxiety is often exacerbated by group membership and the recurrence of childhood attempts to differentiate self from others.

3   Using the concepts of unconscious motivation, anxiety and defence mechanisms to understand group processes

Group psychodynamics, like the experimental approach, needs to address phenomena that occur at the level of the individual, what individuals have already prior to group interactions and bring with them into the group, *and* the phenomena that seem to belong to the group itself. But psychodyamics, in contrast to the experimental approach, takes the notion of 'properties of groups' a little beyond the idea of emergent patterns of communication, norms and role structures. Psychodynamics is prepared to think about the group as if it were itself an organism – the group as group. The psychodynamic perspective on groups, therefore, tries to address three different domains or systems that make up *the group psychodynamic paradigm.*

3.1   Working with the group psychodynamic paradigm

In the examples that follow, the phenomena being examined or the problems in the groups may seem to centre on difficulties within individuals; but often it is the 'location' of the difficulty that *is* the difficulty. Working with the group psychodynamic paradigm means trying to understand what is happening and trying to find helpful interventions *in terms of the web of inter-relationships between individuals and the group,* rather than reducing the group to explanations in terms of individuals' motivations.

As you read the examples and case illustrations in this section, try to keep a list of the cases and of the domains that you can discern in each – using the following scheme (adapted from Ashbach and Schermer, 1994, pp. 14 and 15).

System 1: Internal/intrapsychic systems of each individual in the group, including internal psychodynamics and unconscious motivations.

System 2: Systems of communication, both conscious and unconscious, verbal and non-verbal, between two or more individuals.

System 3: The group as group.

ACTIVITY 2.2

Think about what group as group might mean and this notion of thinking about the group as if it were an organism in itself. Use the idea of Bion's work group and unconscious group outlined in section 2.1. See if you can find any phenomena in the case illustrations that are easier to understand when you use the idea of group mind. We shall return to group as group in more detail in section 5.1.

Try to compare the three domains (systems) of the group psychodynamic paradigm with the experimental approach of Chapter 1. Can you articulate any differences between what individuals bring to groups and how they are transformed in groups across the two approaches? Are the emergent group properties of the same kind? What differences can you list in the methods, evidence and process of drawing conclusions across the two paradigms?

Many forms of unconscious defence can be observed in group settings. The anxieties may be essentially located within individuals, although individuals' attempts to control or dissipate anxiety may have an impact on the patterns of communication between individuals or across the group, and sometimes lead to the emergence of roles. For example, an individual who is using the defence of *denial* rejects all difficulties by denying their existence. While other group members may engage in discussions about their feelings about being in the group, the person who is *denying* remains cut off from her or his own troubled feelings. She or he may offer concern for others' anxieties but remains unaware of her or his own. Because these anxieties are not expressed or acknowledged they may lead, unconsciously, to irrational solutions called acting out – such as lateness, illness or absenteeism. The denial may lead to *cynicism* where the individual responds with contempt to the concerns of the other group members, the group leader, or the task of the group, becoming a deviant and perhaps being rejected by the group. Sometimes an individual will deal with anxiety by withdrawing from the emotional life of the group. Such individuals may distance themselves through silence or other means and may leave the group altogether.

Although the anxiety may originate in one person, it can be communicated to others, consciously and/or unconsciously. This can create an emotional climate *as if* by contagion. When similar anxieties are present in several or all group members, they seem to collude unconsciously in their defences so that group defence mechanisms come into play. There is a sense of alignment as if the group is acting as one. This apparent contagion of an emotional state followed by common action is the kind of mechanism that has been used to explain some features of crowd behaviour. A less dramatic example of a group defence might be where group members, each similarly pre-occupied by anxieties, engage in *competition* with each other or perhaps with the group leader, creating a competitive atmosphere in the whole group. By feeling superior to others, the anxiety of feeling inadequate is avoided. *Intellectualism* is another group defence in which members can collude. For those who are relatively secure in their mental capabilities compared with their capacity to manage their own and others' emotions, intellectual debate can be a way of avoiding disturbing feelings. For example, an 'interesting' and rather abstract discussion might develop about the meaning of group membership that is safe and reassuring, while the personal emotions remain hidden. Casework illustrations of such defences are given in Box 2.2.

BOX 2.2   Casework examples of defence mechanisms operating in a group setting

Denial

A management team met to discuss the considerable changes in their organization, changes which were likely to lead to redundancies and alterations in work patterns – some for the managers themselves. Early in the group Jenny talked about how worried she was for her own future and for those of the people in her team. David showed some sympathy for her and then began to tell her how best to manage it – citing examples of what he was doing. He spoke in a rather lecturing manner 'solving' each of Jenny's problems in turn. As he spoke Jenny became increasingly agitated. Eventually another member of the group became angry with David, telling him to shut up. David missed the following group sending a message saying he had an urgent appointment.

In this example David is only able to deal with his anxiety by focusing on Jenny who has overtly expressed her distress. Instead of staying with this and talking about his own feelings, he concentrates on finding practical solutions to Jenny's difficulties which are, presumably, no different from his own. In this way he denies his own anxiety and projects it into Jenny. Jenny becomes the 'problem' which he then tries to treat. He was no doubt confused by the challenge to him which he then dealt with (defensively) by absenting himself from the following session.

Cynicism

Following on from the example above, David was talking to a colleague later in the week and the events of the group were raised. David told his friend that, while he realized things were difficult, it was their job to get on with effecting the changes and he couldn't see the point of this 'feely-touchy' business. He said he felt sorry for Jenny but he had never thought she was up to the job and what she had said in the group showed how she let her emotions get in the way of doing the work.

Intellectualization and competition

A group of trainee counsellors met fortnightly with a supervisor as part of their course to discuss their work. This process of talking

---

about how they worked often felt exposing and created considerable anxiety. One member frequently quoted from theoretical papers. Sometimes the points were relevant, but often it would seem that the aim was to impress the others with her knowledge and to catch the supervisor out by seeing whether she knew the paper mentioned. When an academic point was introduced in this way, the other members joined in the discussion, often quoting from papers themselves. A competitive, point-scoring atmosphere quickly developed. The difficult emotions aroused by the work with clients, the uncertainties of the trainee role and fear of inadequacy were defended against by the group members through a combination of intellectualization and competition. When this was pointed out by the supervisor, the group at first became angry and sullen. Gradually, however, members began to talk about their anxieties and fears and were able to return to the task of the group.

(Source: Morgan, private casework)

ACTIVITY 2.3

Try to think of occasions when you were in a group and these sorts of defences might have been operating. Are you now able to recognize any behaviours or feelings or ways of dealing with the work in hand that might have been irrational and defensive? Can you perhaps recognize defences other than those already discussed here? Use these real life examples from your own experience to try to distinguish between individual defences, defences which involved several group members and those which might have been defences of the group as a whole.

3.2   Primitive defences in groups

Anxieties and defence mechanisms observed in a group may be located in individuals, or they may, in some sense, be the joint property of several members, or of the group as a whole. In general, those defensive processes which most often seem to belong to the collective rather than to individuals tend to be versions of anxieties and defences that first arise very early in life. These primitive defences involve unconscious communications of mental states and mix ups between people.

The various schools of psychodynamics emphasize different sources of anxiety and different kinds of defence mechanisms, and place the first appearance of the defences at different ages. Freud, for example, focused on a need to defend against conflicts between instinctual urges (especially sexuality) and the rules and taboos of family and society. He believed that this internal battle reaches a peak at around age five and that victory requires a strong ego. In healthy children, ego strength gradually develops and is bolstered by ego defence mechanisms such as the repression of desires and conflicts into the unconscious. Denial and intellectualization are typical ego defences that operate in older children and adults who have the benefit of language.

In contrast with classical Freudian theory, Kleinians and object relations theorists emphasize anxieties and defence mechanisms that are thought to appear much earlier in life, before language, evoked by the powerful emotions of infancy. The intensity of very early experiences, such as infants' conflict between love and hate for those who care for them, require what are called *primitive defences*. For example, in the defence called *splitting*, versions of the people who surround the infant are introjected in split forms that make life less anxiety-provoking because the painful aspects of the external world are kept separate from the good aspects. For instance, two versions of mother — a good, loving mother and a bad, frustrating mother – might be introjected and mentally kept apart as if this were not the same person. In later life, splitting continues to be used by individuals and groups as a way of avoiding the conflict of managing ambivalences. Another example might be when certain people or groups of people are seen as difficult, troubled or problematic while others will be idealized as capable, confident and knowledgeable.

Splitting keeps the good and loving parts of experience separate from the bad and hateful ones, but it is often followed by a second defence – *projection*. Infants may be unable to tolerate the strength of the bad feelings and may defend themselves 'by getting rid of' or projecting the pain and the conflict. Adults also use projection, especially under stress or in situations that evoke the same relational configurations and feelings as early life, for instance when other group members are experienced like siblings and/or the leaders like parents. In groups, adults may, as individuals, resort to projection. They place those feelings or aspects of themselves that they find too difficult to own into other group members (in phantasy) and these others are then experienced as exhibiting the unwanted traits.

In the example of denial given in Box 2.2, David projects his anxiety into Jenny – not recognizing it in himself. In this particular example, Jenny was likely to have been anxious anyway – being in the same organizational dilemma. This would make her a good target for projection as she would readily respond to his communications. Individuals can project into other group members singly, or into the group, or into another group – an out-group. In all these instances, however, the unwanted feelings or parts of the self may then appear to 'come back' from the other or others into which they have been projected, creating persecutory anxieties.

We have already seen that the group setting can mobilize defences in individuals and also in the group as a whole; splitting and projection are most commonly used as a *group defence*. When used collectively, the combined nature of these two mechanisms can be powerful and absorbing. An example taken from a therapeutic community is given in Box 2.3 overleaf.

BOX 2.3 Group defence of splitting and projection in combination

This example of collective projection (taken from Hinshelwood, 1987) happens in a meeting of staff working in a therapeutic community with clients who have mental health difficulties.

A half-hour staff meeting, which followed a tense community meeting, began in an unpromising way. For five minutes or so a number of separate conversations seemed to be going on simultaneously, each appearing to be animated, excited and involving. Coffee was being poured out for everyone from a table in the centre of the room and there was a good deal of moving about. The general impression of disorder and tension was intense. In the course of pouring out coffee one of the members of the team, Rose, had to go to the kitchen for some more milk. On returning she complained that the kitchen staff had been disobliging and unorganised! Sheila then recalled that it was not the only case of this happening recently. Thelma said that she knew that one of the domestic staff in the kitchen was leaving at the end of the week. By this time the character of the staff meeting had changed completely. There was a unified concentration on the topic of the kitchen. A concerned discussion about what was going wrong in the kitchen began in earnest. Soon there was the suggestion that the administrative officer (who was officially responsible for the kitchen staff) should be asked to come to join the meeting for the benefit of the present discussion. This was agreed quickly and decisively and one of the group was dispatched to invite him. The efficiency of the group could hardly have been greater. Possible tensions and difficulties which might have beset the kitchen staff were isolated and discussed, and sensible practical solutions were suggested. The administrative officer arrived. In fact he did make it his business to know what was bothering the kitchen staff and he was well aware of their mood. It turned out that the explanations that the staff meeting had chewed over were wholly surmise and largely incorrect. It seemed unlikely that there was anything seriously 'going wrong' in the kitchen. However the enthusiasm of the staff meeting was unabashed and the helpful solutions continued to be put forward. Hardly anyone noticed that they were solutions to non-existent problems.

(Hinshelwood, 1987, pp. 68–9)

In his consideration of these events, Hinshelwood points out that:

The group dealt collectively with the 'bad experience' the members had just suffered in the community meeting. Their method was projection – what went wrong was in another group, in fact quite incidental to the problem and elsewhere in the hospital. It was a happy chance that produced this other troubled group. Once found, the staff group exploited it very effectively for their own comfort. Having projected the trouble into the kitchen, the staff meeting did not leave it alone but identified with it, discussing it, thinking how the domestics might be feeling, what was troubling them. And this was sustained in spite of the reality.

(ibid., 1987, pp. 69–70, emphasis added)

The example in Box 2.3 illustrates a collective way of avoiding conflict *within* a group. When this happens, all the 'bad' may be split off into others in order that the group can feel more comfortable. In this example the group projection is into another group. This is a frequent dynamic in inter-agency work where another professional group is seen as failing and useless while 'our' group is seen as doing well. Sometimes this group defence can work the other way around in the sense that the other group is endowed with the 'power to rescue' or some other form of idealization. Here strength and expertise is being projected while the original group is felt to be depleted of all resources.

This example also illustrates projection into another group *in phantasy* – there is no *actual* communication to the kitchen staff. The defensive function of the projection does not require that the kitchen staff are *made to feel the impact of the projection*. Nor are they made to identify with the projection and become a troubled group – no unconscious communication is necessary. In real life, however, such projections are commonly made where a 'hook' exists, that is, where the out-group already has some small measure of the failings that are to be projected. Whether the recipient group has the feature or is made to feel and identify with the projection (in phantasy), the outcome of the projection may still affect the relationship between the two groups. For example, a group of managers and a group of workers may each see the other as being difficult, ineffective or troubled while their own group is seen as honourable, effective and at ease within itself. This can lead to considerable conflict and failure to communicate as each group is attempting to communicate with a phantasized image of the other group which is based on projections rather than on reality. Eventually there may be some degree of identification with the projections – as a result of the communication failures.

3.3   Unconscious communication of mental states in groups or between groups

The defence of projection can be taken a step further. By all manner of unconscious, subtle, verbal and non-verbal means, the projector (an individual) or the projecting group can *force* the recipients of the projection (other people in the group or another group) to *feel* and *experience* and thus subsequently identify with the particular bad feelings – the state of mind – that is being projected. This is called *communicative projective identification* and is the unconscious mechanism through which mix ups occur between individuals and through which boundaries between identities begin to break down, (see Thomas, 1996b, for a more detailed discussion). An example of this complex defence splitting, involving projection *and* communicative projective identification between two groups is given in Box 2.4.

BOX 2.4   Communicative projective identification between groups

Students on a psychodynamically oriented management course complained that the tutors treated them in a harsh, uncaring and disrespectful way. The tutors found this frustrating and hurtful. They continually tried different ways of teaching, but it seemed to them that whatever they did was misinterpreted and distorted. It was puzzling, too, since in their other work contexts, even as tutors on other courses, they were regarded as supportive and helpful. They suspected that the students' perceptions of them were based on their [the students'] experiences of managers at work whom they regularly described in identical terms. Since this was a psychodynamic course, the tutors shared this hypothesis with the students. This proved quite unhelpful; indeed the students claimed this was but further evidence of the tutors' refusal to attend to their point of view, and of using their knowledge 'to put us down' rather than to be helpful.

Over time, the tutors began to notice they were discussing the students with each other in increasingly disparaging and judgmental tones. Whereas before they had been clear that something 'not me' was being projected, they now found themselves behaving and feeling in the very ways the students described. It was as if they had become the harsh, punitive managers they had been accused of being. At first the tutors rationalized this as a natural reaction to the students' seeming resistance to learning, but as they recognized the intensity of their punitive feelings towards the students, they realized they had been caught up in the process of projective identification. Only after they had acknowledged their own part in this process, how they actually were being unreasonable in their expectations of the students, did the climate of the course begin to shift in a way that allowed the students to learn again.

(Obholzer and Roberts, 1994, pp. 135–6)

Communicative projective identification can carry a massive emotive force: both projectors and recipients may feel confused and the recipients may feel confused and abused. This can be particularly unpleasant when the splitting and projections are made collectively, either inside a group leading to schisms and subgroupings, or between groups. In either case, where membership of groups and/or subgroups is defined by such characteristics as 'race', class or gender, projection and splitting can have a powerful and destructive effect.

> There are many examples of this kind of splitting and projection at a societal level. The war in Bosnia provided a dramatic example of the fragmentation of an entity into highly polarized subgroups which served as the recipients of powerful negative feelings, keeping the in-group idealized and 'pure'. And there are many examples of the destructive effect of projections into external groups already set apart by such socially defined characteristics as 'race' or class. In making this assertion, I am not suggesting that internal psychodynamics are the only source of societal divisions and the breaking up of entities into smaller groupings. Power structures, reinforced by economic inequalities, may be triggers for defining out-groups which then serve a psychological function; and certainly these social variables reinforce – after the event – any psychological mechanisms that might be in place. But it is also possible, and endorsed by some, that the fragmented and conflicted internal structure of the mind and its tendencies to split and project might be actively, if unconsciously, mirrored time and again in our external worlds. This topic is discussed from other perspectives in Chapter 4 of this book.

3.4   Unconscious communication and the differentiation of roles within groups

Processes of splitting, projection and projective identification within groups, whether essentially intrapsychic or communicative, can lead to the differentiation of hierarchy and roles in the group. This does not refer to the formalized, conscious roles such as Chair or minute taker, nor roles that follow from the existing hierarchy (manager, deputy etc.) but those created by unconscious processes in the group. For example, if it is difficult for the majority of group members to experience and own certain emotions, such as anger or anxiety, they may unconsciously choose one individual to hold this emotion for the whole group. This individual will then take on the role of 'the angry one' for the whole group.

> Are we talking here about 'roles' or about 'being', that is, being identified with something that has been projected into another person and is affecting identity at a deeper level? We need to think about how easy it is for the projectors and for the recipients to test the reality of what is happening. Is reality testing possible at all? Is there

enough history, information and conscious awareness for the projectors to withdraw their projections if necessary? Can a mismatch be
recognized?

In *benign projection*, the members of the group are able to engage in
reality testing – the checking of the projection against the reality of the
individual's experience. Should there be a mismatch between the
assumptions made about the person being projected into and the reality
of that person, the projections can be withdrawn and owned by all members of the group. But when no reality testing takes place, a *malign projection* persists, regardless of the actual experience of the person being
projected into. The recipient is unable to disidentify from the projection
and becomes depersonalized; he or she may take on the behaviour that
befits what is being projected. Those projecting, on the other hand,
become and remain depleted of those aspects of themselves they have
'got rid of' into that individual.

A crucial variable in this reality testing is the size of the group. So far
in this chapter most references have been to small groups, a term
used without definition. One useful distinction between small and
large groups is the kind of interactive constraint that size imposes.
When the group is too big for face-to-face interactions, whether verbal or non-verbal, when visual cues and 'reading' of signals between
the individuals is not possible, then the opportunities for reality testing are dramatically reduced. There is a point of discontinuity, often
at around 20 members, when the physical size of the group makes
reality testing very difficult. Other factors will play a part as well –
such as whether the group is new, whether the people are known to
each other already, the nature of the tasks they are engaged in, the
formal organization of the group, the physical arrangement of people
and the group's previous history. But large groups, where reality testing is not possible, are particularly prone to anxieties and group
defences of splitting and projection. These can snowball into quite
persecutory states and feelings of depersonalization (see Kreeger,
1975).

A common example of a malign projection is where one member *exhibits*
signs of anxiety; others may also be anxious but instead of feeling this
for themselves, they project their anxiety into the designated member.
She or he may then receive a lot of concern and care by the rest of the
group. As the anxiety is projected, he or she becomes increasingly distressed while the other group members become increasingly calm. In
extreme cases the individual may have to leave the group. For a while
the general anxiety can be perceived as having been 'got rid of' and
those remaining will continue to worry consciously about the other, per-
sisting in talking about her or him as if that person is still carrying the
anxiety for all. Eventually this will be unsustainable. The anxiety will
return to the group and either all members will own their own disturbed
feelings or another recipient has to be found. This kind of 'assigning a
role' can involve other attributes – such as 'victim', 'ill person' or 'crazy
person'.

Some of the systems theory work on groups, especially family groups, starts from this point. One member is identified by all as being the 'patient'. But later it can be seen that this individual is fulfilling an emotional function for the whole group (see Dallos, 1996).

Probably the most widely known of these forced roles is that of the *scapegoat*. Owning attributes such as weakness, vulnerability and uselessness can be very painful; group members unconsciously get rid of them by projecting them into one person who becomes the 'victim'. Once seen in this light, this person is victimized further, subjected to ridicule, bullying and made 'useless'. This unconscious communication of 'weakness' by communicative projective identification forces the scapegoat to *become* weak. These kinds of psychological defence processes in groups can be so powerful that they emerge even when people are role playing their allegiances and concerns.

Processes of splitting and projection can have a more positive side and can lead to the emergence of helpful leadership roles. If a member exhibits attributes or qualities that signal ability or strength in some way, then the others, in their anxiety about their own capacities to accomplish a task or become leaders themselves, may project the abilities and strengths that they do have into this other person. Insofar as the projection is accepted, then that person's abilities may be encouraged and elaborated, and a leader is created. An example of positive projection with a good outcome in given in Box 2.5.

BOX 2.5 'Positive' projection and the emergence of a leader

In an in-patient group one man, Don, was both older than any of the others and had more status, having been a lawyer in outside life. During a period early in the group where the members were expecting but not getting guidance from the two therapists, they did not challenge the therapists but turned to Don for advice. He was very ready to provide it. Even when the group moved on from this stage, Don continued to occupy this 'expert' role. He spoke very little, but was ready to come in when the group asked for his advice. Apart from his readiness to be an expert, Don remained unknown in this group.

(Whitaker, 1985, p. 345)

Conversely, there may be an absence of reality testing and a leader can be created through these projective processes who is quite inappropriate and incapable or worse. Unfortunately, as the leader is idealized and imbued with ego ideal attributes, the other members of the group may feel protected by the figure they have created. They may also feel weakened – as if they have lost their own strengths and capacity to think and judge.

Review of section 3

- According to the group psychodynamic paradigm, inter-relationships between three systems need to be taken into account. These are:
  - systems of internal worlds and unconscious motivations
  - systems of communications: conscious and unconscious, verbal and non-verbal, between two or more members of the group
  - the system of the group as an entity.
- Group psychodynamics emphasizes unconscious defences against anxiety as important forces underlying group dynamics. These may be individual defences or defences of the group as a whole.
- Groups can generate considerable anxiety that mobilizes primitive defences of a kind originating in infancy – splitting, projection and projective identification.
- These primitive defences, together with unconscious communications, lead to the dispersion and distribution of emotional states and confusions of identity.
- Group defences can confer roles on members, can lead to splintering of the group and can account for intergroup phenomena, especially those of a stereotypic and hostile kind.

4   The functioning of social systems in organizations as a defence against anxiety

In this section we move from small, face-to-face groups to organizations. Again the central hypothesis is that beneath the surface of the organization and the seemingly rational social systems that are set up to deal with the primary task, another kind of unconscious group life is operating. In any group of individuals that gather together for a stated purpose there will exist a conscious, task-oriented group and an underlying, unconscious group; the functioning of this underlying group may be in conflict with the requirements of the task. This is not to say that work groups never function. We meet in groups for a variety of reasons – for work, politics, interest and leisure – and for the most part we manage to perform the tasks we meet to achieve. However, performance may be inhibited by anxieties of which we may not be aware and by processes that develop in the group in order to alleviate this anxiety. Where the task itself contains a degree of anxiety – such as in very competitive hierarchies, or where the primary task is inherently stressful or dangerous, the anxiety may lead to dynamics within the group that seriously undermine its work.

One of the most important psychodynamic studies of organizational life was originally published in 1959 by Isabel Menzies Lyth (then Isabel Menzies) and has been re-printed many time since (see Menzies Lyth, 1988). She studied the way in which the anxieties generated by the primary task of a general hospital led to collective defences that became institutionalized as social systems and work practices. The study was initiated by the management of a general teaching hospital in London. Of the 700 nursing staff, about 150 were fully trained and the remainder were students undertaking the four year course. The trained nursing staff worked in administrative, teaching and supervisory roles so that it was the student nurses who were directly involved in patient care and their training needs took second place. There was increasing conflict between these two sets of needs and senior staff were concerned that the system might break down.

Menzies Lyth and her team began their work by conducting a series of formal interviews with nurses and senior staff, both individually and in groups:

> ... our attention was repeatedly drawn to the high level of tension, distress and anxiety among the nurses. We found it hard to understand how nurses could tolerate so much anxiety and, indeed, we found much evidence that they could not. In one form or another, withdrawal from duty was common. About one-third of student nurses did not complete their training. The majority of these left at their own request, and not because of failure in examinations or practical training. Senior staff changed their jobs appreciably more frequently than workers at similar levels in other professions and were unusually prone to seek postgraduate training. Sickness rates were high, especially for minor illnesses requiring only a few days 'absence from duty'.
>
> *(Menzies Lyth, 1988, pp. 45–6)*

The primary task of a hospital is the medical care of those who cannot be cared for in their own homes. This work generates high levels of anxiety and the nurses are continuously in contact with this stress.

> Nurses are in constant contact with people who are physically ill or injured, often seriously. The recovery of patients is not certain and will not always be complete. Nursing patients who have incurable diseases is one of the nurse's most distressing tasks. Nurses are confronted with the threat and the reality of suffering and death as few lay people are. Their work involves carrying out tasks which, by ordinary

standards, are distasteful, disgusting and frightening. Intimate physical contact with patients arouses strong libidinal and erotic wishes and impulses that may be difficult to control. The work situation arouses very strong and mixed feelings in the nurse: pity, compassion and love; guilt and anxiety; hatred and resentment of the patients who arouse these strong feelings; envy of the care given to the patient.

[…]

Patients and relatives have very complicated feelings towards the hospital, which are expressed particularly and most directly to the nurses, and often puzzle and distress them. Patients and relatives show appreciation, gratitude, affection, respect; a touching relief that the hospital copes; helpfulness and concern for the nurses in their difficult task. But patients often resent their dependence; accept grudgingly the discipline imposed by treatment and hospital routine; envy nurses their health and skills; are demanding, possessive and jealous. Patients, like nurses, find strong libidinal and erotic feelings stimulated by nursing care, and sometimes behave in ways that increase the nurses' difficulties: for example by unnecessary physical exposure. Relatives may also be demanding and critical, the more so because they resent the feeling that hospitalization implies inadequacies in themselves. They envy nurses their skill and jealously resent the nurse's intimate contact with 'their' patient.

(ibid., 1988, p. 46 and p. 48)

The force of the Menzies Lyth study is its demonstration, by empirical means, of the way that the organization is used by those who work within it to create social structures that will mitigate the anxieties; these social structures appear as parts of the structure, culture and practices of the organization. *Institutionalized defences* serve as 'objective', collective externalizations of individual psychological defences. They provide an example of how individual psychic systems interrelate with emergent structures in the organization – patterns of communication, norms, and social practices such as job descriptions and roles – and the evolution of these practices through unconscious alignments between individuals and the organization as a whole. The practices, once evolved, thereafter constrain the fluidity and responsiveness of the organization and are seen as an external reality with which individuals new to the organization and with no direct input to the defensive structure, must nevertheless conform.

Menzies Lyth found evidence of a number of defence mechanisms within the nursing service of the hospital. Some of these are outlined below.

Splitting of the nurse–patient relationship: Given that the source of the nurse's anxiety lies in her relationship with the patient, the closer this relationship, the greater the anxiety. Menzies Lyth found that practices evolved that lessen nurses' contact with patients:

The total workload of a ward or department is broken down into lists of tasks, each of which is allocated to a particular nurse. She performs her patient-centred tasks for a large number of patients – perhaps as many as all the patients in the ward, often thirty or more. As a corollary, she performs only a few tasks for, and has restricted contact with, any one patient. This prevents her from coming effectively into contact with the totality of any one patient and his [sic] illness and offers some protection from the anxiety this arouses.

(ibid., 1988, p. 51)

Depersonalization, categorization and denial of the significance of the individual: Menzies Lyth found a ward culture in which patients were depersonalized, categorized according to their illnesses rather than their personalities: '... nurses often talk about patients, not by name, but by bed numbers or by their diseases or a diseased organ: "the liver in bed 10" or "the pneumonia in bed 15". Nurses themselves deprecate this practice, but it persists' (ibid., 1988, p. 52).

In the present NHS, as part of the Patients' Charter, each patient is allocated a named nurse or contact person on admission. According to the psychodynamic perspective, this change of practice might be expected to raise nurses' anxiety. Perhaps new defences have evolved. Many hospitals now provide support groups for nursing staff.

Detachment and denial of feelings: The ethos of detachment, while a necessary feature in professional work, was found to be advocated to the point of denial. It was reinforced by the movement of nurses around the hospital as if '... the student nurse will learn to be detached psychologically if she [sic] has sufficient experience of being detached literally and physically' (ibid., 1988, p. 53). Little training was available to help the nurses develop genuine and appropriate professional detachment: a nurse experiencing distress was more likely to receive a reprimand than support. This was despite the *private* expression of concern and compassion by the seniors towards the students: 'Kindly, sympathetic handling of emotional stress between staff and student nurses is, in any case, inconsistent with traditional nursing roles and relationships, which require repression, discipline, and reprimand from senior to junior' (ibid., 1988, p. 54).

The attempt to eliminate decisions by ritual task-performance: All decisions inevitably involve some uncertainty and, therefore, anxiety. When decisions sometimes really are about 'life-and-death' issues, the anxiety is high. Menzies Lyth found that the number of decisions to be made was minimized by providing strict instructions and procedures resulting in standardization of all tasks. A by-product was that student nurses were actively discouraged from using their initiative and discretion.

Collusive social redistribution of responsibility and irresponsibility: In order to manage the internal conflict between the wish to be responsible and the fear of too much responsibility, the nurses were involved in a process of splitting and projection. Here certain groups, usually those more junior to the speaker, were considered to be 'irresponsible', while more senior groups were seen as over-strict and imposing repressive discipline as if those junior to them had 'no sense of responsibility'. This view of those above and those below was consistent at all points of the nursing hierarchy.

This evidence is from the 1950s. Would the same anxieties be present today? Would the same defences operate and would they lead to the same social practices?

Over the decades what has emerged is that the operation of unconscious defences in collective life can have effects *other than* those (unconsciously) intended; the social practices that evolve can make things worse.

We saw that continuity – in various senses – is reduced in hospitals so as to limit anxiety. But in some organizational settings, especially in some technologies, this very procedure of restricting opportunities for 'seeing the whole picture' and dividing up responsibilities actually increases the dangers that are inherent in the work task. For example, Hirschhorn (1988) has discussed this potential spiral of 'primitive' anxieties and task-anxiety in the inherently hazardous environment of the nuclear power industry.

Another by-product of unconscious forces leading to defensive social practices in the work place is that the devices that reduce anxiety also reduce job satisfaction. Menzies Lyth noted in her work that, while the defensive systems were developed as an unconscious means of helping the nurses avoid the experience of anxiety, guilt, doubt and uncertainty, they were not, and could not be, fully successful: '... the social system frequently functions in such a way as to deprive nurses of necessary reassurances and satisfactions. In other words, the social defence system itself arouses a good deal of *secondary anxiety* as well as failing to alleviate primary anxiety' (Menzies Lyth, 1988, p. 65, emphasis added). She found that the splitting-off of nurses from patients and the detachment that follows meant that the nurses experienced minimal relationships with those they went into the profession to care for. The nurse was prevented from investing his or her whole personality in the work, from making a highly personal contribution and receiving the satisfaction that results.

Institutional defences have their effect, in part, by reducing opportunities for conscious reflection. One by-product of this is that it is often very difficult to modify the defensive social structures once they have been set in place. This restricts responsiveness in the organization and the capacity to think about and implement change. Change always implies uncertainty and, almost inevitably, it means an alteration in the established defence system. Change, therefore, tends to bring a 'double dose' of anxiety. Menzies Lyth found that in the hospital the existing systems and structures were held to, even when most people agreed that they were inappropriate. Changes tended to be initiated only when there was a crisis.

When new members join a group or organization in which the social defences are already formed they have to adapt to the social system and incorporate its defences. Those who are most successful in adapting to the existing defence system of any institution or organization are those whose individual defence systems best match those of the social system, or are best able to incorporate them. Where such defence systems are over-rigid and detrimental to carrying out the primary task (as is usually the case in unconscious defence mechanisms) those who stay and gain status within the institution are those most likely to continue its counter-productive practices. In her work in the hospital, Menzies Lyth found some evidence that the high drop-out rate of student nurses included many who were considered to be potentially good nurses and who themselves expressed distress and a feeling of dissatisfaction. It might be that their sense of unease could have effected change in the less helpful aspects of the institution they had tried to join.

Review of section 4

- In the late 1950s, Bion's theory that in any group there will be a potential conflict between the needs of the unconscious group and the requirements of the conscious, task-oriented group was tested in an organizational setting – a London teaching hospital – by Isabel Menzies Lyth.

- The central thesis of Menzies Lyth's study was that in organizations, social systems and work practices evolve as institutionalized defences against anxiety.

- She found that high levels of stress and anxiety are generated in the nursing staff by the primary task of caring for patients.

- The study showed how many features of job descriptions, work practices, roles and norms of the nursing staff operated as unconscious defence mechanisms.

- Institutionalized defences in organizations can lead to rigidity, low job satisfaction and resistance to change.

5   Return to Bion

The three levels or 'systems' that make up the group psychodynamic paradigm were described in Activity 2.2, at the beginning of section 3. In the examples and discussion so far there have been several illustrations in which it was relatively easy to dissect out System 1 – what the individuals bring to the group. Examples include David's anxiety about organizational change (Box 2.2); the anxieties and feelings of exposure that the trainee counsellors brought to their supervision group (also in Box 2.2) and the tension and bad feelings that the staff group brought from the community meeting into their staff meeting (Box 2.3). We can also see how predictable patterns of relating and communicating emerge (System 2) in each of these instances, triggered by what the individuals bring into the group and, in turn, having an effect on the individuals. These are all examples of quite transient structures and group properties; but more lasting ones could develop which then outlive the particular members, for instance, the vetting committee described in section 2.2.1 might, over time, have evolved rigid procedures and a norm of inflexibility.

ACTIVITY 2.4   Think about the examples of the trainee counsellors (Box 2.2), the staff group complaining about the kitchen staff (Box 2.3) and the management students' reaction to their tutors (Box 2.4). See if you can identify anything different that might be going on in these examples (or in some of them) compared with David's anxiety about organizational change (Box 2.2) and the vetting committee in section 2.2.1.

In this section we are going to look more closely at the properties of groups to see if psychodynamic concepts and language make it possible to think about System 3 – the group as group – in a different way from the emergent group properties considered in the experimental approach to group processes.

5.1   Group as group

In the casework examples (the supervision group, staff group and management tutorial group) what the individuals brought into their groups *already had some alignment of emotional state*, and it was this alignment or unanimity of feeling that seemed to drive the patterns and the broad content of the communications that followed. The trainee counsellors (Box 2.2) all felt exposed and anxious; the staff group (Box 2.3) had all just experienced an unpleasant community meeting and felt tense, and the students on the management training course (Box 2.4) had brought into their tutorial group their anger about the way their own managers treated them. I would argue that what happened in these three examples illustrate the third level of analysis or System 3 – *group as group*. In each casework example the group seemed spontaneously to begin to act as an entity.

Is that so surprising? People come into groups with broad commonalities of purpose, for instance when they enter a work group with a particular task. Often the commonalities go further. Sometimes there are alignments of attitudes, beliefs and ideology as well as purpose, as for example, in a pressure group intent on re-routing a motorway. People in groups discuss, argue, reach consensus and plan joint action. What, if anything, makes these three casework examples different from, say, a motorway re-routing group?

There are several dimensions of difference to consider. First there is the unconscious nature of the alignments in the three casework examples. In groups that plan work tasks or argue about a motorway and how to stop it, members are aware of their arguments, of each others' positions, the negotiations involved and the overall goals of the group. Their plans for joint action are overtly discussed and made explicit, and at least some of the persuasive processes are overt.

Persuasive processes always have a hidden and unconscious aspect. The unconscious impact of language and its implications for power relations can be understood from a psychodynamic perspective and/ or from that of discourse analysis (see Chapter 3 of this book). We shall return to this issue in section 6.2.

In the three casework examples, the group members did not discuss their feelings. They may have had some awareness of an unpleasant emotional state (or they might have, had they been asked) but they did not articulate this to each other and then plan what to do to feel better. In all three casework examples the source of the bad feelings, their significance, and possibly all experiences of them, were unconscious. What happened – the actual behaviours that constituted the group defence – were spontaneous. In the supervision group there was no conscious planning for a joint intellectual defence and a climate of competition; in the staff group there was no articulated tactic of 'getting rid' of the bad feelings and projecting them into another group – the kitchen staff. It is possible that, on other occasions, the trainee counsellors had already discussed their anxieties about revealing how they work. And since the defensive behaviour was begun by one member in particular, it could be argued that the others might have consciously copied rather than unconsciously colluded to produce the alignment of behaviour. But in the staff group and the tutorial group, *where the group defences depend on projections,* the group members seemed to have no conscious awareness of the psychological mechanisms they were using, and the collective behaviour was unplanned. What might have been happening?

The psychodynamic concepts of unconscious communication, identification and projective identification, through which people are forced by subtle and unconscious means to take on someone else's state of mind, all suggest mechanisms by which emotions can be quickly dispersed and distributed among group members so that it is not clear who owns which bits of psychological business (see Thomas, 1996b). Alignments can be unconsciously recognized, communicated and shared. From this point of view, what happened in the supervision group, the staff group and the management tutorial group seems to be a form of collective behaviour that is rather different from what might happen in the motorway pressure group.

Of course, unconscious group processes are likely to be going on in the motorway pressure group too. Remember Bion's idea that all groups operate at two levels – the work group and the unconscious group concerned with the emotional life of the group and its members.

Psychodynamic concepts make it easier to think about a level of analysis which is more than the individual and also more than the kinds of emergent group properties that were discussed in the experimental paradigm of Chapter 1. We can begin to push notions of emergent group structures and joint action into another level (System 3), the group as group. Now we are using a notion of *groupishness* (Bion's word) that approaches group mind. We can think about and study group mind by considering the emotional alignments and identifications between individuals that occur at a very profound, unconscious level, and that reduce the boundaries between individuals and bring together the group as a whole.

In the experimental approach to group research, where all psychological phenomena must be located inside – belong to – bounded individuals, the concept of group mind is thoroughly rejected. But psychodynamics can legitimately explore these phenomena – continuing the tradition of Le Bon, Freud, Jung and McDougall – because it works with a very different set of assumptions about what humans are like and what they do, consciously and unconsciously, in the course of collective life. The concepts of identification, projection and projective identification can be used to think about the permeability of individuals' boundaries in groups, about the phenomenological experience of confusion with others, of receiving projections of other people's states of mind and being unable to disidentify, either because the processes are unconscious, and/ or because the group setting makes reality testing almost impossible.

ACTIVITY 2.5   Check back to the discussion of social identity in Chapter 1, section 4.1 and try to list any similarities and differences between Turner's concept of social identity and the kinds of alignments that are explored in the present chapter. You could also look at the notes you made for Activity 2.1, your imagined participation in the Sherif, Asch and Milgram experiments. Do any of the concepts such as alignment, unconscious communication, and identification help you to understand what you (and the real subjects in the experiments) might have felt?

These ideas will be explored in the remainder of this section by returning to the work of Bion. Sections 5.2, 5.3 and 5.4 outline Bion's early work on groups, especially group mentality and the concept of basic assumption groups – yet another way of thinking about unconscious group alignments. In section 5.5 we examine Bion's later, Klein-inspired, view of group life.

5.2   Bion's work on unconscious alignments in groups: group mentality, group culture and basic assumptions

As described earlier, Bion's research on group processes began during the Second World War with unstructured groups of army personnel in the Northfield Military Psychiatric Hospital. He continued working with groups after the war, as a group therapist with small groups of patients at the Tavistock Clinic in London. His original intent was to study group processes at the level of the whole group, so that the focus was on the larger picture, the whole rather than the parts. Using this viewpoint, he observed over and again that unstructured groups have certain predict-able features.

Bion found that his groups created situations that were often heavily charged with emotion. This emotional climate had a powerful effect on the group members and considerable influence on the activities of the group – but the members did not appear to notice. The chaotic emotional climate was contributed to by all members, including the group leader at times. It was as if the group, as an entity in its own right, had a pathology of its own which acted upon the individual members despite their conscious intentions.

He also noticed that while individuals met together to perform particular tasks, the attitudes and methods they developed did not seem to be con-ducive to the original intention. Behaviour often appeared irrational. Critical judgement and intellectual debate about the task were frequently absent. Solutions that were proposed and often agreed seemed not to be based on the reality of the situation. Many of the activities seemed irrational and *prompted by a need to fulfil some other function*. This second set of activities often appeared to work against the stated task. As noted earlier, Bion came to believe that when any group of people met to carry out a task, two types of tendencies emerged from within the group: one directed towards the accomplishment of the task and another that seemed to oppose it. It was the discovery of these two agendas that underpinned Bion's work on group processes, the idea of a work group and another group – an unconscious group – operating in parallel.

Bion devised the terms 'group mentality' and 'group culture' to describe the *collective mental activity* that emerges when people get together in a group, even if the individual members do not intend it and are unaware of it. The group often begins to function as an entity, soon developing its own emotional climate or group mentality, formed by the unanimous, unconscious wishes or desires of the group at a certain moment. Each individual contributes both unconsciously and anonymously. The group mentality may be in conflict with the conscious desires, thoughts and opinions of the individuals and this conflict may produce discomfort, frustration or anger.

Bion defined group mentality as

> ... the unanimous expression of the will of the group, contributed to by the individual in ways of which he [sic] is unaware, influencing him disagreeably whenever he thinks or behaves in a manner at variance with the basic assumptions. It is thus a machinery of intercommunications that is designed to ensure that group life is in accordance with the basic assumptions.
>
> *(Bion, 1961, p. 65)*

Elsewhere he wrote:

> We shall have to examine the mental life of the group closely to see how the group provides a means for making these anonymous contributions. I shall postulate a group mentality as the pool to which the anonymous contributions are made, and through which the impulses and desires implicit in these contributions are gratified. Any contribution to this group mentality must enlist the support of, or be in conformity with, the other anonymous contributions of the group. I should expect the group mentality to be distinguished by a uniformity that contrasted with the diversity of thought in the mentality of the individuals who have contributed to its formation. I should expect that the group mentality ... would be opposed to the avowed aims of the individual members of the group.
>
> *(ibid., 1961, p. 50)*

Here Bion is not alluding to a conscious decision to make a contribution that is anonymous but a process of unconscious communication – anonymous to the sender as well as the receiver and thus leading to evasion and denial.

Bion wrote of group culture as '... the structure which the group achieves at any given moment, the occupations it pursues, and the organization it adopts' (ibid., 1961, p. 55).

An example of the kind of evidence that underlies Bion's thinking about group mentality and group culture is given in Extract 2.1 – where the group is a therapy group.

Extract 2.1

'The group consists of four women and four men, including myself. The ages of the patients are between thirty-five and forty. The prevailing atmosphere is one of good temper and helpfulness. The room is cheerfully lit by evening sunlight.

Mrs. X: I had a nasty turn last week. I was standing in a queue waiting for my turn to go into the cinema when I felt ever so queer. Really, I thought I should faint or something.

Mrs. Y: You're lucky to have been going to a cinema. If I thought I could go to a cinema I should feel I had nothing to complain of at all.

Mrs. Z: I know what Mrs. X means. I feel just like that myself, only I should have had to leave the queue.

Mr. A: Have you tried stooping down? That makes the blood come back to your head. I expect you were feeling faint.

Mrs. X: It's not really faint.

Mrs. Y: I always find it does a lot of good to try exercises. I don't know if that's what Mr. A means.

Mrs. Z: I think you have to use your will-power. That's what worries me – I haven't got any.

Mr. B: I had something similar happen to me last week, only I wasn't standing in a queue. I was just sitting at home quietly when …

Mr. C: You were lucky to be sitting at home quietly. If I was able to do that I shouldn't consider I had anything to grumble about.

Mrs. Z: I can sit at home quietly all right, but it's never being able to get out anywhere that bothers me. If you can't sit at home why don't you go to a cinema or something?

After listening for some time to this sort of talk, it becomes clear to me that anybody in this group who suffers from a neurotic complaint is going to be advised to do something which the speaker knows from his [sic] own experience to be absolutely futile. Furthermore, it is clear that nobody has the least patience with any neurotic symptom. A suspicion grows in my mind, until it becomes a certainty, that there is no hope whatever of expecting co-operation from this group. I am led to ask myself what else I expected from my experience as an individual therapist. I have always been quite familiar with the idea of a patient as a person whose capacity for co-operation is very slight. Why, then, should I feel disconcerted or aggrieved when a group of patients demonstrates precisely this quality? It occurs to me that perhaps this very fact will afford me an opportunity for getting a hearing for a more analytical approach. I reflect that from the way in which the group is going on its motto might be: 'Vendors of quack nostrums unite.' [Those who trade in quack remedies unite.] No sooner have I said this to myself than I realise that I am expressing my feeling, not of the group's disharmony, but of its unity. Furthermore, I very soon become aware that it is not accidentally that I have attributed this slogan to the group, for every attempt I make to get a hearing shows that I have a united group against me. The idea that neurotics cannot co-operate has to be modified.'

Source: Bion, 1961, pp. 51–2

In the group described in Extract 2.1, any attempt to describe a problem is met either by others insisting that their problem is greater, or by others offering 'solutions' which are beside the point or futile. Bion, observing this, first assumes that the individuals cannot or will not come together to work at a problem. Indeed, the group seems intent on refusing to allow any problems to exist in the group. Bion realizes that, in fact, the group *has* come together, not to work on problems but to work against problems entering the group in any helpful and sustainable way. He realizes that there is a very strong group unity where the individuals are cooperating on an unconscious level – the group mentality. Since this is a therapy group, the stated task of the group implies that the group will work together to help the individuals with problems. However, the members are united in ensuring that this will not happen. The group is unconsciously functioning as a unit working against its conscious task and ensuring its leader is powerless to bring it back to that task.

According to Bion, the work group functions in a similar manner to that of the ego as described by Freud. It is a mental state that implies contact with reality, the capacity to tolerate frustrations and the management of emotions. Completion of the stated task of the group is the paramount aim of the work group and it will employ rational means to achieve it. The leader will be chosen as the person best able to carry out this function and not because of emotional allegiance, competition or other potentially destructive forces. There will be plenty of verbal exchanges and space for new ideas, which will be acted on where appropriate. Differences between people will be tolerated and conflicts managed. If people in groups, organizations and in society were able to function only within the work group, there would be no need for group analysts or for the study of groups at all.

While the work group is getting on with the task in hand, an unconscious group is forming and working to satisfy the unconscious needs of its members and defend itself from anxiety. It is this underlying group that Bion calls the basic assumption group. He gave the underlying, unconscious group this name because he believed that it is motivated by intense and primitive (basic) emotions and because it seems to be acting *as if on the basis of an unconscious assumption* about what the group is providing or should be providing for its members. The (unconscious) basic assumption group attempts to provide gratification of the unconscious needs of members, needs that usually centre around reducing anxiety.

5.3 Bion's three basic assumption groups

Bion believed that in all kinds of groups, quite apart from the stated objectives of the group, there will be unconscious alignments or basic assumptions which create an emotional climate and raise shared topics. These alignments drive a predictable way of collectively behaving in order to satisfy unconscious needs and defend against anxiety. Bion thought, early on, that there would be a range of such basic assumptions. But he believed that his empirical findings revealed just three distinctive emotional states or domains of alignment from which three basic assumptions can be deduced. These assumptions concern dependence, fight/flight and (broadly) hope, that is, hope of rescue through the pairing of members, the pushing of current problems into the future.

5.3.1 Basic assumption: dependency

Here the group acts *as if* it has met to find a leader who will meet its needs and alleviate its anxiety. There is an unconscious irrational assumption or belief active within the group that they can find someone who will take control, care for and protect the group. Often this dependency is directed towards the formal leader. In therapy groups, such as those Bion worked in, the therapist is looked to as the person on whom the group can be dependent. She or he is then idealized and pressurized into providing solutions, speaking wisdom and making everyone well, while the others become passive and give up their capacity for critical judgement – for thinking. The group settles down into acting as if they were disciples before a guru. Should the leader fail to produce the expected wisdom (as she or he eventually will) or, instead, attempt to *interpret* what is going on – that is, tell the group about their irrational dependency assumption, there will be a strong sense of unease and frustration in the group. The group may then look to one of its own members to perform this role and engage in the process of counter-dependency towards the designated leader, ignoring or contradicting whatever she or he might say. The newly selected group leader will be set up as the hero who will take on the formal leader in this attack. Eventually, of course, even the new leader is bound to fail and another leader must be sought or the group moves into a different basic assumption. An illustration of the dependency assumption, taken from Bion's work, is given in Extract 2.2.

Extract 2.2

'Here is a description of a therapeutic group in which the dependent assumption, as I shall call it, is active.

Three women and two men were present. The group had on a previous occasion shown signs of work-group function directed towards curing the disability of one of its members; on this occasion they might be supposed to have reacted to this with despair, placing all their reliance on me to sort out their difficulties while they contented themselves with individually posing questions to which I was to provide the answers. One woman had brought some chocolate, which she diffidently invited her right-hand neighbour, another woman, to share. One man was eating a sandwich. A graduate in philosophy, who had in earlier sessions told the group that he had no belief in God, and no religion, sat silent, as indeed he often did, until one of the women with a touch of acerbity in her tone, remarked that he had asked no questions. He replied, "I do not need to talk because I know that I have come here long enough and all my questions will be answered without my having to do anything."

I then said that I had become a kind of group deity; that the questions were directed at me as one who knew the answers without need to resort to work, that the eating was part of a manipulation of the group to give substance to a belief they wished to preserve about me, and that the philosopher's reply indicated a belief in the efficacy of prayer but seemed to belie earlier statements he had made about his disbelief in God. When I began my interpretation I was not only convinced of its truth but felt no doubt that I could convince the others by confrontation with the mass of material – only some of which I can convey in this printed account. By the time I had finished speaking I felt I had committed some kind of gaffe; I was surrounded by blank looks; the evidence had disappeared. After a time, the man, who had finished his sandwich and placed the carefully folded paper in his pocket, looked around the room, eyebrows slightly raised, interrogation in his glance. A woman looked tensely at me, another with hands folded gazed meditatively at the floor. In me a conviction began to harden that I had been guilty of blasphemy in a group of true believers. The second man, with elbow draped over the back of his chair, played with his fingers. The woman who was eating hurriedly swallowed the last of her chocolate. I now interpreted that I had become a very bad person, casting doubts on the group deity, but this had been followed by a increase in anxiety and guilt as the group had failed to dissociate itself from the impiety.'

Source: Bion, 1961, pp. 147–8

Extract 2.2 brings us face to face with the kinds of evidence that Bion and other group psychoanalysts use. We can see that Bion is using the change in behaviour and topic from the previous session – using the history of the group. He is using the manifest content to reach the threads of unconscious meaning that he thinks he perceives beneath the surface and common to all the group members. He is also using his own conviction – its strength as well as its intellectual status in his theory. He is using what the group 'did' when he made his interpretation of their basic assumption. Their denial became stronger if anything – they could not let it go, but, nevertheless, seemed more anxious. They also seemed to be giving non-verbal cues of guilt and dissociating themselves from his 'outrageous' suggestion. Following this extract, Bion goes on to discuss his own reaction to the group and their use of him to express their basic assumption of dependence on him. He talks about his reactions, his countertransference:

> ... the analyst in the group is at the receiving end of ... projective identification ... Now the experience of countertransference appears to me to have quite a distinct quality that should enable the analyst to differentiate the occasion when he [sic] is the object of a projective identification from the occasion when he is not. The analyst feels he is being manipulated so as to be playing a part, no matter how difficult to recognize, in somebody else's phantasy.
>
> *(ibid., 1961, p. 149)*

5.3.2 Basic assumption: fight/flight

Here the group acts as if there is an enemy who must be attacked or avoided. This enemy may be within the group and all hostility is directed towards him or her. Should the group eventually succeed in ejecting this enemy from the group they may continue to talk about him or her for some time, thus maintaining the illusion of an enemy, or go on to seek out a new enemy from within its ranks. Often, however, it is as if there is an enemy *outside* the group. In its unconscious efforts to destroy or avoid this enemy, the group unites to do battle or to engage in evasive tactics. In this way, the anxiety that is within the group and within each individual can be defended against. One example of this might be the staff group versus the kitchen staff described in Box 2.3.

5.3.3 Basic assumption: pairing

Here the group acts as if it has met to produce a person or an idea which will rescue the group from its difficulties. The unconscious collective belief of the group in this basic assumption is that, whatever the problems or needs of the group may be in the present, there will exist something or somebody *in the future* who will solve it – a kind of hope. The group is then intent on bringing two of its group members together so that out of this pairing, a 'messiah' will be born. This may be a friendly pairing where the two concerned are seen to have a lot in common and engage in dialogue together, monopolizing the conversation while the rest of the group look on. Or it may be a hostile pairing whereby the two become enmeshed in battle. Other group members will manage to keep the hostility stirred up whenever resolution seems to be imminent. Should the discussion be in danger of losing the focus of the pair, others will bring it back to the conflict between the two. As war rages, the other group members will settle back to watch as if from ringside seats.

In Bion's theory, at any give time the behaviour of a group will be organized by just one basic assumption; sometimes the group remains in this particular emotional state for a long time. But groups can also move from one basic assumption to another quite quickly. For example, if a group is in a dependent mode and wants the leader to make decisions and 'solve' the dependent needs of the group, but the leader refuses to do this, the others will become apathetic and resentfully silent. If, in exasperation, the leader then takes a decision, the group might rebel and refuse to accept such 'dictatorship'. The group may then move into fight/flight mode, arguing with the leader and ignoring all of his or her attempts to exert any authority. Or the 'enemy' will be found outside the group, for example, when a decision becomes impossible because the resources are too limited, or when other competing groups or senior management are blamed for the difficulties. The group might then move into pairing mode with two members arguing over the decision, while the others sink into a watching passivity, only acting to keep the conflict stirred up should it be in danger of resolution. Two members might be delegated the task of resolving the problem – a move that could come from the work group. But if it originates in the basic assumption group, any resolution that the couple might reach will inevitably fail. So long as the debate is performing a function for the basic assumption group rather than the work group, it will continue without resolution; if the group does manage to make a decision, it will then find another 'problem' on which to centre.

It is a difficult matter for members of such a group to recognize what is happening and attend to the *process*. The point about unconscious group dynamics is that they are powerful and consuming and all become easily caught up in them. While engaged in the process, the real anxiety is held at bay and it is hard for the group to extricate itself from this defensive position and address its real difficulties.

5.4   Basic assumptions and group mind

The idea of group mind is both intriguing and disturbing. Like individual mind, group mind is a concept with non-material, emergent properties. It is a notion that conveys the apparent unity of some forms of collective behaviour – something that can be observed and experienced in groups and crowds. Group mind suggests the breakdown of boundaries between individuals. It also suggests a sense of purpose that is collectively held, albeit unconsciously, together with some broad idea of the means to achieve that purpose. In a small group, group mind might conjure up the idea of irrational, destructive alignments or harmony and creativity; in a crowd it more often suggests contagion of emotion and the possibility of powerful destructiveness. Perhaps it is the sense of immersion in the process, loss of individuality and control, and the lack of conscious awareness of what is driving the collectivity and an underlying possibility of raw biological determinism that makes group mind a frightening and, for some, politically incorrect concept.

We have already seen that the psychodynamic perspective can throw some light on group mind. First, alignments of emotions can arise very rapidly and be spread between people by unconscious communication, producing *what looks like* spontaneous collective behaviour. Second, the concepts of projection, identification and projective identification are processes which reduce the boundaries between individuals and create powerful unconscious persuasive effects, forcing people to take in and experience states of mind that originate in others. But now we have a third way to understand group mind. Bion's early work on groups raises the possibility that certain aspects of group behaviour are determined by basic emotional states and assumptions which are already present in all of us and activated whenever we enter groups. His idea is that there is a limited set of basic assumptions about group life (i.e. not just emotional states but fairly specific domains of social behaviour) that are universal and unconsciously drive group behaviour. Where might these emotional states and assumptions come from? Are they learned? Are they innate?

Is it possible that basic assumptions of the kind that Bion observed are joint constructions negotiated anew in each group? Is this possible given that they are rarely conscious and therefore not consciously negotiated constructions? Are they cultural constructions that we absorb from the social environment and our direct experiences of group life as part of our sociality, and subsequently bring with us into groups? Are they emotional states that are common to everyone and perhaps innate, that are triggered by the group setting but given specific content and meaning by cultural practices?

This last suggestion certainly fits with Bion's *early* descriptions of basic assumptions and the functioning of basic assumption groups. It is also close to the Jungian concept of the collective unconscious and the elaboration of simple, innate unconscious pre-conceptions (archetypes) through our experiences of the social and cultural world (Jung, 1934 and 1936/7). Thus the overt manifestations – the content – of which we can be conscious are the result of an interaction of innate and cultural influences.

Perhaps we are born with unconscious preconceptions of what groups can provide and what our groupishness entails. For example, Bion's basic assumption, dependency, might well be a universal need state, coupled with a predisposition to certain emotional states in groups – throughout life. This would be a parallel form of the idea that infants have dependency needs that lead to emotions and instinctual behaviour patterns – which are then elaborated socially. In this view, basic assumption dependency would have a biological substrate and universal features but would lead to a range of group behaviours and social organizations around leadership and power in different cultures and/or different historical times.

We would argue that the alignments that are empirically observed in groups are the outcome of both innate and social factors. What people in groups and crowds actually do, in detail, has to be learned in the social context and triggered by contextual cues – accidental or more socially significant. For example, the staff group (see Box 2.3) experienced something that mobilized a group defence of splitting and projection – in Bion's terms a basic assumption group in fight/flight mode. At that moment, they happened to hear about the kitchen staff and the involvement of this particular other group was fortuitous, although it may well be significant that the kitchen staff made up a less powerful group. In Bion's view, movement between basic assumption modes can be triggered by events in the external environment. Crowd behaviour can be driven by a fight/flight basic assumption that has been 'released' by social inequalities. And the details of the behaviours that follow will be imported from established social practices and norms – including the norm of over-turning norms. Some of these features of crowd behaviour are described by Reicher (1984) although his central explanatory concept is that of social identity and referent informational influence (discussed in Chapter 1, section 4) rather than the influence of a basic assumption.

The interplay of internal psychological (possibly innate) factors and external social conditions on intergroup behaviour is discussed in Chapter 4, sections 5.1, 5.2 and 5.3.

Nevertheless, the force of Bion's early work on basic assumption groups is that our groupishness is built into us from birth. Bion believed that we are group animals and remain so – to the extent that 'no individual, however isolated in time and space, should be regarded as outside a group or lacking in active manifestations of group behaviour' (Bion, 1961, p. 169). The three basic assumptions have what Thelen (1985) called a '... broad evolutionary sweep' and there are compelling parallels with the animal stress reflex (fight/flight), family/group protection for growing up (dependency) and the 'creation of new relationships and through them, new group capabilities' (pairing) (adapted from Thelen, 1985, in Pines, 1992, p. 123). Schermer, the object relations group theorist, made almost the same point, linking the basic assumptions to child rearing and bonding to the social group (dependency), reproduction of the species (pairing), and protection of the group from internal and external danger (fight/flight). 'Perhaps Bion ... was able to perceive in the unstructured group the fundamental and wired-in (instinctive) aspects of our group-ishness ... the biogenetic components inherent in group life' (Schermer, 1985, in Pines, 1992, p. 149).

5.5 The group as a container

Bion's training analysis with Klein in the late 1940s led him to re-cast his ideas on the unconscious life of the group in terms of repeats of infantile anxieties, emotional states and defence mechanisms. He thus 'reduced' his earlier idea of predictable group dynamics based on *adult* forms of dependency, fight/flight and pairing with sociobiological relevance for group life to group dynamics based upon a recapitulation of the phases of an infant's relationship with, and separation from, its mother. The main features of his re-view are dependency; the use of primitive defences that involve projection of bad feelings into the mother – and the experience of returning persecutory anxieties (fight/flight); and early concerns with sexuality, especially between parents (pairing).

Recapitulation of early life is not a new idea – all psychoanalytic thought stresses the continuing influence of early emotions (see Thomas, 1996a). The classical Freudian view was that of the family as the prototype for all groups. For Freud, family life, and thence group life, focused on the Oedipal conflict and the power of the father. Adults in groups were seen as regressing to sibling rivalry and identifications with the father/leader (Freud, 1921a and b). For Freud the central process was identification – which he saw as the most primitive form of affectional bond. However, Bion, following Jung and then Klein, placed his emphasis on projective processes and the continuing use of the early defence mechanisms of splitting and projection and projective identification to explain certain group phenomena – mix ups between people, problems in locating just where and in whom the 'psychological business' lies. Following Klein, Bion saw much of group life and group processes as reflecting and re-reflecting very early, pre-Oedipal life. The focus moved from issues about the father/leader to issues about the relationship with the mother/breast.

Bion thought of the group (as a whole) being experienced as if it has a maternal function with direct parallels between the holding and contain-ing function that he believed mothers serve for their infants and the function that the group has for its members. On the positive side, Bion described a maternal, containing function that allows the distressed infant to project its bad feelings into the mother who then holds them, digests them and returns them to her infant in a form that the infant can bear. Bion extended this directly to groups. In this view, groups pro-vide a place and a set of functions through which and in which the members can express primitive feelings, and make use of the group as a whole and parts of the group (other people) to help defend against anxi-eties. (The idea of the maternal container and its role in the develop-ment of the self is discussed in Thomas, 1996a). On the negative side, in Kleinian theory, the infant has powerful negative feelings to deal with and these are often feelings about the carer – such as feelings of helpless-ness, dependency, frustration, abandonment, envy, fear of mix up of identity with mother and fear of separation from her. Bion believed that the group can be experienced in the same way; that bad feelings are pro-jected into the group and felt as if they are coming from the group, lead-ing to persecutory anxieties. Thus the group is a source of anxiety as well as a container. The examples and discussion in section 3 illustrate the influence of these ideas on group psychodynamics.

5.5.1   Boundaries

When a group is thought of as a container, its boundaries become cru-cial. They demarcate that which is inside (the in-group) and that which is outside (the out-group). Sometimes this demarcation is exaggerated to assist the process of projection: anxieties and conflicts – bad feelings – can be got rid of by projection from the in-group into the out-group just as from the self into another (mother). Stereotyping of the categories which define groups is one way in which the boundaries of groups are exaggerated for defensive purposes. This can make the out-group 'worse', but also the in-group 'better', thus amplifying the effect on self-esteem of identification with the group.

Boundaries also 'hold in' and keep safe. Within the boundaries of the container, conflicts and primitive anxieties can be dealt with in ways that reduce the bad feelings for the individual member – just as the primary carer can take on and deal with bad feelings for the infant and return them in a more digested, less painful and less frightening form. This process is sometimes called detoxification. Within the container of the group, individuals can regress, experience a lessening of boundaries of their selfhood and make use of the other individuals and the group as a whole to boost self-esteem and to hold and perhaps enact parts of the self. For example, conflict within a group is sometimes an externalization of conflicting feelings that individuals are experiencing but have difficulty in containing within themselves. Their internal conflict may be 'dramatized' in the group – projected into other members who can then identify with positions and 'play the parts' that represent the opposing sides. Externalization of the arguing parts of the self can reduce tension for individuals and bring issues into awareness, clarifying the internal struggle. But without some insight, this process can also lead to tension and polarization of positions within the group – as the members' identification with 'sides' gathers force and group members move further away from the difficult position of balancing the conflicting feelings and staying with ambivalence.

ACTIVITY 2.6   Look back to Chapter 1, sections 4.1 and 4.2, on social identity and polarization in groups. The psychodynamic discussion in the current chapter uses very different language and concepts from those used in Chapter 1 to discuss and understand the same or similar phenomenon. Can you articulate any differences between the two explanations?

In adult life, while we are far more able to manage the world than the infant is, we still require a degree of containment. At times of stress and distress, such a need is even more paramount. But there is a paradox here: groups can provide containment, but they also, in themselves, create anxieties. Since being in a group can raise anxiety for all members, its holding function can become crucial. In practice – in everyday life and in the workplace – attention needs to be given to the boundaries that demarcate the edges of the group, both physical and temporal. Simple factors such as being clear when the group is to meet, how long for and where, will be important features in establishing clarity for members. Uncertainty about such matters, by having a start and finishing time but often starting late and always running over, or by the venue for the group constantly changing without adequate notice, can cause confusion and raise anxiety.

5.5.2 Membership

For group members there is a two-way pull between belonging and separateness that is a replay of infants' dependency on and attempts to separate from their primary carer. This is re-activated when an individual becomes a member of a group and the anxiety it evokes is prominent in the individual's negotiation of group membership. How can we belong and be accepted and yet remain sufficiently separate? Even when we have a clear, formal entitlement to be a member of a group, there are almost always concerns as to whether we will be liked and accepted or rejected. We may fear that all the others know and like each other, that they understand the 'rules' of the group and are confident and competent, whereas we always seem to be getting it wrong and making a fool of ourselves. Fitting in and belonging, especially at first, can be very difficult. At the same time, the individual is concerned to protect his or her autonomy and separateness. There may be a fear that a strong group ethos exists to which she or he will be expected to pledge allegiance, and differences and individuality will be ignored and subsumed by the group. For some, the fear of rejection is the most powerful and they will subsume their individuality and comply rather than risk loss of membership. For others, the fear of the loss of separateness will dominate and they will fight the group and leave if necessary, rather than give up their individuality.

Look again at the notes you made in Activity 2.1 on your conscious imaginings about being a subject in Sherif's, Asch's and Milgram's experiments. Does this discussion of boundaries and membership help you to understand your imagined feelings – and the empirical findings of the three studies? And what about the earlier discussion of basic assumptions in groups? Perhaps basic assumption dependency is operating in conformity experiments. What about in the Milgram study? Which basic assumptions could be organizing this kind of behaviour?

ACTIVITY 2.7

The struggle to find a balance is a difficult task that is managed with more or less success at different stages of group membership, at different stages in the formation of a group and with different kinds and sizes of groups. Anxieties are strongest when group structures are not already in place or when change occurs. This might be in the earliest history of the group, or at the beginning of an unstructured meeting, or in a large group, or where structure and leadership are unclear. Because of these unconscious preoccupations, issues of membership of a group become crucial.

In practice, membership is an important feature in establishing and facilitating boundaries for a group – being clear who belongs to it and who does not. Often groups where people can 'drop-in' when they wish can prosper, but this fluidity of membership can feel difficult. This is particularly the case in work groups where the members might expect to have to think about difficult issues and anxieties might be expected to be high. In such a group, for example in a staff team where membership is clear, it is important that all members are aware when a particular member is expected to be absent because of illness or holidays. Making strict rules of membership is a way of marking boundaries, and it can, of course, have negative effects – of exclusion and provision of a convenient out-group to take projections of hostility.

Review of section 5

- The group as group – as an entity – can be explored using the concepts of identification, projection and projective identification. These concepts suggest that the boundaries between individuals in a group can be permeable and that identity can be fluid.

- Emotional states can be communicated unconsciously very rapidly by means of identification, projection and projective identification, creating or amplifying emotional alignments and emphasizing the group as group, or suggesting group mind.

- Bion believed from his research that groups tend to operate with two simultaneous mentalities – that of the work group and that of the (unconscious) basic assumption group.

- Bion observed that the unconscious group seems to be organized around one of three basic assumptions – dependency, fight/flight or pairing. Groups may stay with one of these basic assumptions for a long time, or move between them. This idea of a predictable, pre-existing alignment is another way of thinking about group mind.

- When Bion first wrote about these basic assumptions they were given an innate aspect and sociobiological significance – bonding to the social group, protection of the group from internal and external dangers and reproduction of the species. Bion's post-Kleinian writing treats basic assumptions as re-occurrences of infantile states, although still universal and innate.

- Bion believed that groups could be thought of as having maternal functions for individuals. He thought of groups as containers for emotional states, and places where emotions can be enacted and needs met, and that group life parallels aspects of the infant's early relationship with its mother. This approach focuses on issues such as boundaries, membership criteria, and anxieties and defences associated with both belonging and separating.

6 Conclusions

What can psychodynamics contribute to the *social psychology* of collective life? Its language, methods and assumptions about human beings and the nature of the mind set it apart from all other approaches. Its central concepts of unconscious motivation and defensiveness place emotions, conflicts and a form of irrationality under the spotlight in a way that no other kind of social psychology even attempts. What the discourse of *modern* psychodynamics, especially Kleinian and object relations theory, can provide is a way to theorize about group life that liberates social psychology from bounded individuality, without losing the subjectivity of selfhood.

6.1 Individuals and groups – a hall of mirrors

Modern psychodynamics *is* a form of social psychology. It suggests a model in which the distinction between the individual and others begins to dissolve. The external social world of people, groups and relationships is seen as already inside each individual *comprising each person's selfhood*. And simultaneously – in reality and in phantasy – this internal collectivity gets projected back into the external social world to create material for new constructions of what is out there *and* to communicate and actually influence others. This spiral continues, reflecting and re-reflecting self and others, back and forth – with images that are variably distorted. It is a process that makes us into who we are; it also enables us to maintain our selves, express our selves, modify and move between versions of our selves and influence others.

Psychodynamics describes the kinds of unconscious psychological mechanisms that are involved – introjection, identification, projection and projective identification. These processes show how the external world of other people and the internal world of self can flow into each other. They suggest the permeability of boundaries between people. And suggest that we are fragmented – made up of lots of bits of others – and fluid, moving between different self-representations, becoming other people (or aspects of other people) fleetingly or for longer periods.

One implication of this view is that the theoretical distinction social psychologists make between personal identity and social identity begins to break down. For example, Chapter 1, section 4.1, outlined Tajfel and Turner's cognitive approach to personal and social identity and the relation between the two:

> ... the bases for people's self-definition change in groups. *Personal identity* gives way to *social identity* ... in groups there are ... new identity possibilities ... [people] can 'switch on' these identities in appropriate situations ... adjust their sense of identity, their thoughts

and their behaviours to match the collectively defined attributes of their social groups. People take on the group characteristics and make these their own, at any rate for the time being, to a greater or lesser extent.

(pp. 33 and 35, emphasis in original)

According to Turner (1987) this is a form of self-stereotyping. It is a conscious process of choosing and adopting a relatively straightforward set of attributes, usually of social significance, rather like role-taking. But there is a fine line between this and *becoming*, using deeper processes of introjecting the alignments that exist in the group via identifications with (aspects of) the other people. From the psychodynamic view of group life as a hall of mirrors, we would argue that there is no clear demarcation between personal identity and social identity.

Another implication of the psychodynamic perspective on group life concerns the functions that groups serve throughout life – apart from the practical business of shared tasks. We have seen that Bion, influenced by Klein, thought of the group as having an essentially maternal function for individuals. This kind of analysis of group processes treats the group *as if* it provides a container for bad feelings, a space in which conflicts and anxieties can be dealt with by primitive (and usually unconscious) means such as splitting, projection and forcing other people to take in and to feel and sometimes enact our pain and *be* the rejected parts of our selves. It is as if in a group we can be turned inside out; our interiority is placed outside our own boundaries and dealt with *through others* in the 'spaces between people', spaces that do not clearly belong to individuals but do belong within the boundaries of the group.

The influence of Klein and Bion is very clear in these concepts. However, much as we as *outsiders* try to pull the dynamics apart in an attempt to understand what is happening, often our subjective experience of being in a group (apart from the work task involved) is of immersion in a web of interrelationships. We are only faintly aware of the precarious holding together, a concern with boundaries, and of using the group as a dynamic whole, rather like a child whose potentially fragmented and fragile self is held and regulated in relation to the primary early other – usually his or her mother (see Thomas, 1996a and b). Here the prototype of group existence is the infant's relation to the mother. 'Entry to a group recreates the helplessness, the tendency to fragmentation, the overwhelming impulses, and the condition of need experienced in the first months of life' (Ashbach and Schermer, 1994, p. 6).

The object relations group theorists Ashbach and Schermer have also described this hall of mirrors as a form of social psychology:

… through human interaction the inner life becomes transformed into social experiences and systems and, conversely, group experience comes to be personally and internally represented. The two dimensions of inner and group life are linked by an interface, a network-system (perhaps epistemologically and developmentally prior to both person and group) consisting of verbal and non-verbal interactions linking members of a group.

(ibid., 1994, p. 13)

This quotation captures one of the major tensions of this chapter and of this book. In one way or another all the chapters in this book are about how to understand and theorize the dialectic between inner and outer life, and individual and social processes. What is the relation between the individual and the group? Which comes first, selfhood or sociality? If we need interactions with other people to create our selfhood, whether these interactions occur in dyads such as mother and infant, or in groups, is it possible to be individuals before we are group members? What role does our experience in the family play in group life thereafter? And how can we preserve a secure sense of identity and, at the same time, remain open to the profound influence of other people in relationships and groups? Does it matter for our subjective experience of life whether or not we have a sense of separateness, whether or not we live alone and in isolation?

6.2 Evaluating the psychodynamic account – what kind of story?

Freudian psychoanalysis began as a form of medical science, with attempts to understand the mind in terms of biological and developmental universals. It was presented – like any other science – as a search for truths, in this case truths that might eventually be reduced to biology. Very quickly it became clear that the psychoanalytic enterprise, given the nature of the data it uses, would have to be thought of as a very particular kind of science – based on meanings, subjectivity, transference and countertransference evidence and little in the way of replication (see Thomas, 1996b, for a discussion of the evidence generated in the psychoanalytic process). What, then, are we to make of the group psychodynamic theories discussed in this chapter?

Group psychodynamics faces the same difficulties as psychoanalysis. Can the ideas discussed in this chapter be evaluated, given the focus on subjectivity and psychic realities? How would it be possible to validate theories where the basic data are not only *meanings* of behaviours and communications, but where these surface forms represent something that is hidden or even disguised? What evidence there is, is only accessible *through* the presence, the *understandings* and translations, and the countertransference reactions of the analyst. How can we deal with the inevitable indirectness and inaccessibility of these data?

The theories discussed in this chapter try to find an explanatory system that captures reality, sets out predictable processes, and looks for universal truths, perhaps even a biological truth. They set out to describe in *realist* terms what it is in people's internal worlds and developmental history that determines group phenomena. According to the theories presented here, what people communicate in groups is driven by internal states even if the product is disguised. In the scientific tradition, the observer – the one who describes and theorizes – has special access to the truth. This 'truth' – the insight and the psychoanalytic interpretation in the light of theory – can then be given back to the group or the clients and its effect monitored – providing a form of validation. In all these respects group psychodynamic theory is like psychoanalytic theory – except perhaps that the theories are 'tested' in a wider practice – with clients outside the therapeutic encounter. In these situations it is more likely that understandings and interpretations, for example of work group dynamics or resistance to change in organizations, might be negotiated to some degree.

Modern psychoanalytic thought, in one-to-one and group settings, has moved somewhat from its realist origins. As a *theory* it still claims to be unique in its grasp of the truth about the mind, and retains some biological and developmental determinism. The theories are still based on internal, unconscious states as determinants of what people do – in the broadest sense. *But,* internal worlds are seen as constructions rather than truths. Revelations of internal worlds in behaviours and language, the raw materials of psychodynamic explanation, are now generally treated as constructions. They are thought of as mixtures of historical truths, conscious fantasies, unconscious phantasies and unconscious constructions, together taken as 'narrative truths'. In groups, what is said (and done) by the group members is heard and interpreted as if it is designed (unconsciously) to have an effect. In other words the raw materials of group dynamics are treated as discourse; and an assessment of their impact on other people is a central part of the process of understanding the group dynamic.

The earlier casework example of the staff group's group defence (see Box 2.3) involving projections into the kitchen staff provides a good example of the possible confusion of realist and constructionist thinking that is common in modern psychodynamics. There are three 'accounts' of what is happening. One is the staff groups' defensive construction of what was going on in the kitchen; another is the account of the kitchen and kitchen staff that is learned from the administrative officer; and a third is the group analyst's account in terms of projections.

From a realist's point of view – and thus the basic psychoanalytic understanding – the group analyst's account is seen as the true one or the more real one. It incorporates the administrative officer's version of what is really going on and explains the defensive distortion produced by the staff group.

From a more constructionist standpoint, however, we would be likely to see these three accounts as different versions produced in different contexts and serving different functions. Each has its own 'narrative truth' or 'reality' and plausibility for those offering the account. But from this perspective would we want to give the group analyst the final authority – the only one who knows what is really going on? If we take this more constructionist or relativist view then practical and pragmatic issues come into focus. Which is the more useful account for bringing about desired changes? We become interested in the group analyst's description as an account in itself. How is this discourse of description formed? What kind of reality is the analyst constructing for the group?

A great deal of the impact of language is unconscious – unconsciously determined on the part of the person who constructs the account and unconsciously received by others. Therefore, much of psychodynamic research on group processes could be carried out more formally from a constructionist position, using accounts and discourse analysis. But it would be very difficult to maintain a constructionist position given the fundamental determinist view of psychodynamic theory. If the inner and unconscious states determine what the group members do and say – their use of language – is it possible to give enough emphasis to the local context, to the ordinary flux and imperfections of conversations? In the discussion of Bion's basic assumptions we saw that the unconscious mentality might determine the topic of conversation and the end point hoped for. But the exact form and the detail of what is said and done is open. Ways of understanding what people say in groups is one of the topics of the next chapter – making sense of the social context using attitudes, social representations and discursive psychology.

Further reading

A good place to start is a short textbook written in the Tavistock tradition by Robert de Board, *The Psychoanalysis of Organizations* (1978) London, Tavistock Publications. This book outlines group behaviour and aspects of organizational life from the psychodynamic perspective, including Bion's work, and from other viewpoints such as systems theory.

Wilfred Bion's *Experiences in Groups and Other Papers* (1961) London, Tavistock Publications, is a classic psychodynamic study of small groups. It is very difficult to capture the flavour of Bion's writing and this book is certainly worth looking at, even if you don't read it all. Pines' collection, *Bion and Group Psychotherapy* (1992) London and New York, Tavistock/Routledge has some fascinating papers on group psychodynamics and on Bion's contribution, although some of the papers are quite specialized. Hinshelwood's *What Happens in Groups* (1987) London, Free Association Books, has become a modern Kleinian classic, focusing on therapeutic groups of various kinds. Whitaker's book, *Using Groups to Help People* (1985) London and New York, Routledge and Kegan Paul, is a very clear account of the practice of groupwork from a slightly different perspective

This chapter has given an outline of the Menzies Lyth study of social systems as defences but to get the full impact of this pivotal piece of research you should try to read the original paper – published in several places, with different dates – but the same intriguing work: Menzies Lyth, I. (1988), 'The functioning of social systems as a defence against anxiety' in *Containing Anxiety in Institutions, Selected Essays*, Vol. 1, London, Free Association Books. A clear and simple account of the psychodynamics of the workplace and organizations, which builds on Menzies' research and brings it into more recent industrial and organizational settings, using plenty of case examples, is provided by Hirschhorn, L. (1988) *The Workplace Within*, Cambridge; Mass: MIT Press. The basic, psychoanalytic account of social systems as defences is in a paper by Jaques, E. (1955) 'Social systems as a defence against persecutory and depressive anxiety', in Klein, M., Heimann, P., and Money-Kyrle, R.E. (eds.) (1955) *New Directions in Psycho-Analysis*, London, Tavistock.

A recent collection of papers, many of which are relevant to the psychodynamics of small group from the perspective of the Tavistock tradition can be found in Obholzer, A. and Roberts, V.Z. (eds.) (1994) *The Unconscious at Work: Individual and Organizational Stress in the Human Services*, London, Routledge. Also in the Tavistock tradition, Miller, E. (1993) *From Dependency to Autonomy: Studies in Organization and Change*, London, Free Association Books, demonstrates the links between the psychodynamic and the systems approach to organizations.

Ashbach and Schermer's book on the object relations approach to group life is written at a higher level, but is an important source book on small groups: Ashbach, C. and Schermer, V. (1987 and 1994) *Object Relations, the Self and the Group*, London, Routledge and Kegan Paul.

In this chapter we have not had room to discuss the processes that operate in larger groups, so a good complement to the chapter would be Kreeger, L. (1975) *The Large Group: Dynamics and Therapy*, London, Constable. This is a fascinating account of the powerful emotions that are aroused and defended against in larger collectives.

References

Ashbach, C. and Schermer, V. (1987 and 1994) *Object Relations, the Self and the Group*, London, Routledge and Kegan Paul.

Bion, W.R. (1961) *Experiences in Groups and Other Papers*, London, Tavistock Publications.

Dallos, R. (1996) 'Creating relationships: patterns of actions and beliefs', in Miell, D. and Dallos, R. (eds.).

Freud, S. (1921a) 'Totem and taboo', in Strachey, J. (ed.) (1955) *Standard Edition*, vol. 18, London, Hogarth Press and the Institute of Psycho-Analysis.

Freud, S.(1921b) 'Group psychology and the analysis of the ego', in Strachey, J. (ed.) (1955) *Standard Edition*, vol. 18, London, Hogarth Press and the Institute of Psycho-Analysis.

Hinshelwood, R.D. (1987) *What Happens in Groups*, London, Free Association Books.

Hirschhorn, L. (1988) *The Workplace Within*, Cambridge; Mass, MIT Press.

Jung, C.G. (1934) 'Archetypes of the collective unconscious', in *Collected Works*, vol. 9 (1959), London, Routledge.

Jung, C.G. (1936/7) 'The concept of the collective unconscious', in *Collected Works*, vol. 9 (1959), London, Routledge.

Kreeger, L. (1975) *The Large Group: Dynamics and Therapy,* London, Constable.

Lewin, K. (1947) 'Frontiers in group dynamics: concept, method and reality in social sciences; social equilibria and social change', *Human Relations,* vol.1, p. 541.

Miell, D. and Dallos, R. (eds.) (1996) *Social Interaction and Personal Relationships,* London, Sage/The Open University (Book 2 in this series).

Menzies, I. (1959) 'The functioning of social systems as a defence against anxiety; a report on a study of the nursing service of a general hospital', *Human Relations,* vol. 13, pp. 95–121.

Menzies Lyth, I. (1988) 'The functioning of social systems as a defence against anxiety', in *Containing Anxiety in Institutions, Selected Essays,* vol. 1, London, Free Association Books.

Obholzer, A. and Roberts, V.Z. (eds.) (1994) *The Unconscious at Work: Individual and Organizational Stress in the Human Services,* London, Routledge.

Pines, M. (ed.) (1992) *Bion and Group Psychotherapy,* London and New York, Tavistock/Routledge.

Reicher, S.D. (1984) 'St Pauls: a study in the limits of crowd behaviour', in Murphy, J., John, M. and Brown, H. (eds.) (1984) *Dialogues and Debates in Social Psychology,* London, Lawrence Erlbaum in association with the Open University.

Schermer, V.L. (1985) 'Beyond Bion: the basic assumption states revisited' in Pines, M. (ed.).

Stevens, R. (ed.) (1996) *Understanding the Self,* London, Sage/The Open University (Book 1 in this series).

Thelen, H. A. (1985) 'Research with Bion's concepts', in Pines, M. (ed.).

Thomas, K. (1996a) 'The defensive self', in Stevens, R. (ed.).

Thomas, K. (1996b) 'The psychodynamics of relating', in Miell, D. and Dallos, R. (eds.).

Trist, E. (1985) 'Working with Bion in the 1940s: the group decade', in Pines, M. (ed.).

Turner, J.C. (1984) 'Towards a cognitive redefinition of the social group' in Tajfel, H. (ed.) (1984) *Human Groups and Social Categories,* Cambridge, Cambridge University Press.

Turner, J. (1987) 'Introducing the problem: Individual and group', in Turner, J., Hogg, M., Oakes, P., Reicher, S. and Wetherell, M. (1987) *Rediscovering the Social Group,* Oxford, Basil Blackwell.

Whitaker, D.S. (1985) *Using Groups to Help People,* London, Routledge and Kegan Paul

CHAPTER 3

ATTITUDES, SOCIAL REPRESENTATIONS AND DISCURSIVE PSYCHOLOGY

Jonathan Potter

Contents

1   Introduction

So far, two very different perspectives on groups and processes within groups have been discussed. Chapter 1 concentrated on social influence processes from an experimental social psychological perspective, while Chapter 2 presented a psychodynamic alternative which stressed unconscious processes. This chapter will have a rather different focus. It will be less concerned with group processes than with the representations people make of their world, and the evaluations which go along with them. In social psychology, such things are often taken to be features of individuals and understood using notions such as attitudes, beliefs or stereotypes. The treatment here counters this individualistic perspective. This chapter will emphasize the dependence of people's evaluations on widely shared images of how the world operates, which are in turn generated through social interaction and sustained through the mass media. Judgements about the environmental policy of a political party, for example, are closely related to images of the environment and of pollution, concerns about global warming, beliefs about motor car emissions, and so on. And, as we start to study these representations, it becomes impossible to see them as standing outside of broader social and political processes. Representations are a potent part of the action in collective life; social and political disputes can often devolve into struggles over which picture of groups, persons and events is the right one. Are cars a threat to the lungs of young people or are they a central element in the good life provided by advanced capitalism? Instead of group influence processes, then, or unconscious dynamics, the importance of the constructions that people use to understand the world will be stressed, along with the actions that these social constructions allow.

The chapter starts with the idea of attitudes, which has been at the heart of social psychology for over half a century. For social psychologists, attitudes have been one of the things which make up what persons are, which make them unique and different from geraniums and soft drinks machines. For all its centrality to social psychology, however, attitude research has not made a glorious march of intellectual success through the pages of social psychology. Although there are some well-established findings about the sorts of communicator messages that lead to attitude change, exactly what an attitude *is*, and how it relates to other aspects of a person's life, has been a source of open dispute for almost as long as attitude research has been conducted. There was a time in the late 1960s when the so-called attitude and behaviour problem – the lack of relationship between how people filled in measures of attitudes and how they acted in other situations – threatened to sink the whole research enterprise. A variety of methodological and theoretical innovations have since kept the notion afloat as one aspect of work on social cognition, social perception and information processing conducted from an experimental perspective (cf. Lalljee, 1996). These rescue attempts and their success will provide the major topic for section 2 of this chapter.

In the 1980s and 1990s, with the rise of social constructionist alternatives to experimental research on social cognition (cf. Wetherell and Maybin, 1996), the attitude notion has been attacked from different directions. On the one hand, problems have been raised with the treatment of attitudes as personal possessions, and with the failure to address properly the organization of attitudes into clusters and systems. On the other, there is the failure to address the sorts of everyday practices involving evaluations and judgements which have been transformed by psychologists into the abstract world of attitudes. The recent approaches of social representations theory and discursive psychology attend to these two different areas.

The central idea of social representations theory, the subject of section 3 of this chapter, is that people come to understand their social world by way of images or social representations which are shared by members of a social group. These act like a map which makes a novel and baffling terrain familiar and passable and, in the process of making the terrain familiar, also provides evaluations which indicate which area is good and which bad. Social representations researchers retain the concept of attitudes, but consider attitudes to be secondary phenomena which are underpinned by social representations. Social representations theory is notable for its attempt to specify precisely what is collective about groups, and to provide a historical account of people's understanding of the world. The coverage here will focus on the main concepts of the theory, some of its major studies, and some of its limitations.

The central idea of discursive psychology, the topic of section 4, is that the main business of social life is to be found in interaction, whether it is a couple arguing about the failure of their relationship, a minister speaking to a party conference, or a defence lawyer cross-examining a rape victim in court. It emphasizes the practical dimension of social life. How does a husband produce a particular narrative of relationship breakdown to show that the problem is his wife's rather than his own? How does a government minister organize her talk to elicit agreement and applause? How is a rape victim presented as subtly at fault for the attack, and how might she resist such a presentation? In addressing questions of this kind by way of records of interaction – tape-recordings, transcripts and videos – discursive psychologists have found that they need to rework central social psychological notions such as attitudes.

Aims of Chapter 3

The aims of this chapter are:

- To introduce three alternative approaches to the study of people's representations and evaluations. One of these approaches takes an experimental perspective while the other two work from a broadly social constructionist perspective.

- To introduce the kinds of evidence and research methods used to support the different approaches and to highlight areas of disagreement and agreement.

- To indicate how work on representations and evaluations might help psychologists understand current social issues, such as the effectiveness of health education programmes, reactions to policies of community care, and accounts of political disputes.

2 Attitudes

2.1 What are attitudes?

One of the most striking things about attitudes is that, however small our exposure to formal social psychology, we already seem to know what they are.

ACTIVITY 3.1   Spend a few minutes listing some situations where the term 'attitudes', or similar terms such as 'opinions' or 'views', have been used. Think of the kinds of everyday conversation you have with others, stories in newspapers, TV programmes, films, music or literature. Try to generate a range of examples.

Look at the list you generated in Activity 3.1. I expect that you thought of the kind of gossip about preferences that we engage in every day: 'What is Jason's attitude to driving since the accident?'; 'I don't like Derek's attitude to drink.' You might have thought of those war films where the burly drill-sergeant squares up to the unruly recruit and snarls, 'Doberman, you've got an attitude problem.' An American rap group was called Niggaz with Attitude, and Jah Wobble sang 'I know these are platitudes, but don't adopt an attitude.' You probably gave as an example the sort of public opinion story that appears in the media on a daily basis: 'A new poll by MORI shows that the Government is still the most unpopular since World War II'; 'There has been a gradual softening of attitudes to capital punishment over the last decade.' You might also have thought of popular examples, such as television game shows. For instance, Bruce Forsyth's *Play Your Cards Right* was based around guessing the views of particular groups of people: 'We asked one hundred tax inspectors if they thought people caught evading tax should go to jail; what percentage said they should?'

The core idea of these examples is that of preference; they involve evaluation. Moreover, they are the sorts of preferences which can vary between people. One of the things which makes individuals what they are, and distinguishes them from others, is their sets of tastes. Attitude research can be seen as the attempt to specify and measure what we commonly think of as people's views or preferences. This is a useful starting point; however, let us pause a moment to see whether the simplicity and obviousness of this understanding of attitudes is not a little deceptive.

One way to get a broader perspective on attitudes is to look at the history of the notion, and also to look at how attitudes are expressed (or not) in other cultures. In English, the term 'attitude' only developed the sort of meaning evident in the examples above relatively recently. In the fifteenth and sixteenth centuries, the term was mainly used to describe how figures were arranged in paintings or in statues. However, during the next couple of centuries, it developed a further meaning of a posture of the body which implies a mental state or action. Thus, the phrase 'to strike an attitude' meant to take on a position, or expression, which displayed what the speaker was thinking. For example, in 1784, Boswell wrote of Dr Johnson, 'He had a great aversion to gesticulating in company. He called once to a gentleman who offended him in that point, "Don't attitudinize"' (OED). The more modern notion of an 'attitude of mind' – a person's positive or negative position on some topic or issue – did not emerge until the mid-nineteenth century. So what we may take for granted as an obvious, common-sense idea turns out to be somewhat newfangled.

One reason for the emergence of the notion of attitude in Euro-American societies in the last hundred years or so is the relationship of this notion to the social and political systems also emerging during the same period. The influential attitude researcher William McGuire (1985) has argued that elaborate notions of attitudes and persuasion are only needed in periods where democratic consent is a central part of the political system. He highlights four historical eras and locations in particular: fourth-century BC Athens, first-century BC Rome, the Italian Renaissance, and most places in the twentieth century. In these places and periods, ruling involved consent and popular support expressed through votes. It became important to think about attitudes and how they could be surveyed and manipulated, leading to the development of persuasive techniques.

Another feature which encourages the development of notions such as attitudes is an emphasis on individual consumption. Attitudes thrive in situations of choice where what we choose is bound up with who we are as a person. The Italian fashion designer Giorgio Armani has described the creation of identity as the most important industry of the twentieth century. Showing that one likes an Armani suit is a demonstration of who one is as a person. However, this is not universal. In some cultures, the emphasis is less on individual differences than on position in a social system of family, status or caste. In many places, an emphasis on preferences would not make sense because there is neither the disposable income nor the elaborate retail system which would allow such preferences to be meaningful. The Ethiopian smallholder in the midst of a lean year is not going to be losing sleep over whether to buy this year's Nike or Reebok trainers.

The point, then, is that our intuition that attitudes are simply a feature of human nature, comparable to walking upright or eating with the mouth, should be treated sceptically. It is unlikely that in even the most non-individualistic cultures, and under the most brutal of dictatorships, people could get by without some minimal notion of personal preference. However, it is only in societies with some form of democracy, and particularly those in which consumer capitalism flourishes, that the notion of attitude is intensively refined. In such societies, attitudes may come to be seen as relatively enduring views or preferences which distinguish one person from another and are important for guiding what they do with their lives. Attitudes go with individualism.

The activities of attitude researchers in academia also have an impact on people's everyday notions of attitudes. Look back at the list I generated in discussing Activity 3.1. Both news reports of opinion polls and *Play Your Cards Right* are examples where the technical language of attitude and opinion research has become part of wider discourse. Most of us are now familiar with basic opinion-polling ideas about sampling and margins of error. And, even rather abstruse notions such as response biases and social desirability have had a wide public airing following notorious failures of poll organizations to predict the outcomes of general elections.

BOX 3.1   The ironic opinion respondent

Imagine you are stopped in the street and asked about the current government's economic performance. You might think about your views, perhaps remembering an argument you had on that very topic the previous week. But you might also think about the message your attitudes might convey. Whatever your views on actual performance (and talking of actual views in the abstract may be too simple anyway, as we shall see in section 4 below), you might decide that it would be a good idea for the government to avoid complacency. A poor poll rating might make them try harder. The irony here is that when people become more knowledgeable about polls, and as polls become news in themselves, they become less clear-cut as measures of opinion.

What technical definition of attitudes do social psychologists use? This question is not as simple as it seems. One of the things which has characterized attitude research is considerable disagreement over the best way to define attitudes. One recent popular definition comes from Zanna and Rempel. They write, 'we regard an attitude as the categorization of a stimulus object along an evaluative dimension based upon, or generated from, three general classes of information: (1) cognitive information, (2) affective/emotional information, and/or (3) information concerning past behaviours or behavioural intentions' (1988, p. 319).

Let's try to unpack the different components of what at first sight seems to be a rather cumbersome definition.

Categorization

The point here is that if you are going to evaluate something you need to identify it as some particular thing; that is, you need to categorize it. To have a negative attitude to Mars bars or the Welfare State you must be able to perceive and identify those things.

Stimulus object

These are the things people have attitudes about. The term 'stimulus' is really a hangover from an older behaviourist language of stimulus and response. Here a stimulus object is something that can be seen, and perhaps acted upon: we might buy a Mars bar, or vote for a political party which intends to support the Welfare State.

Evaluative dimension

Zanna and Rempel's definition suggests that attitudes can evaluate things in different ways. Something can be good or bad, judged against an absolute standard: 'The Welfare State just is a good thing.' Or the judgement can be a comparative one: 'For all its flaws, the Welfare State prevents the suffering of free-market capitalism.' Attitude researchers often want to go beyond this and place attitudes on a numerical continuum: 'I would give Mars bars 6 out of 10, but give Snickers bars 8.'

Based upon, or generated from, information

Here Zanna and Rempel's definition is addressing the issue of where evaluations originate. What is the basis for a negative evaluation of Mars bars? The suggestion is that the evaluation will be produced from information of various kinds.

Cognitive information

This covers a wide range of ideas, beliefs, remembered events, and so on. For example, we may have read accounts of the hardship of patients in countries without a National Health Service; we may have spent a long time on an NHS waiting list, only to have the operation done more quickly in a private clinic. We may believe that private insurance schemes will work out to be more expensive, or that supporting the NHS is congruent with our other political views. All these bits of information may be involved in an evaluation.

Affective/emotional information

Evaluations are not just based on ideas; they are often based on feelings. We may simply feel good about the NHS: perhaps because we have grown up with it, without any particular thoughts about why; or the good feeling may supplement more intellectual arguments in favour.

Zanna and Rempel's definition of attitudes does not assume that cognitive and affective types of information are necessarily counter to one another. They can operate on their own or in combination.

Information concerning past behaviours or behavioural intentions

A number of attitude researchers, most notably Bem (1970), have claimed that a major determinant of attitudes is how one acted in the past. That is, we work out if we like Mars bars, not necessarily by cognitive or emotional judgements in the present, but by considering our recent behaviour. Did we buy a Mars bar last week, or did we go into a shop intending to buy one, but they had sold out?

Zanna and Rempel, then, have done more than merely provide a definition of attitudes. Their definition starts to suggest, if only in a loose way, the kinds of things researchers should look for if they want to understand how attitudes arise. Their definition also begins to suggest how attitudes may be modified: if you are attempting to persuade someone, you could work in the area of cognitive information, perhaps providing facts and arguments. Or, you could work in the affective arena, trying to associate something with warm emotions; or you could simply try to get people to do something, regardless of their attitude toward it, with the expectation that attitude change might follow.

ACTIVITY 3.2   Try to think of how you could change someone's attitude to the NHS, and to Mars bars, working with cognitive, affective and behavioural information in turn. Which kind of information seems easiest to work with? Which seems most likely to be effective? If you are having trouble with this activity, think about recent television advertisements, or other sales techniques you have experienced. If you found it easy, then you are all set for a lucrative career in advertising or politics!

2.2   Attitudes and behaviour

What is the point of doing attitude research which tries to find out people's preferences and values? It would be nice to think that attitude research develops through pure intellectual curiosity about people's psychological life. However, that is not the only motive driving investigation into what Shapiro calls, 'probably the most highly funded kind of object in the modern social sciences' (1988, p. 28). One of the most important reasons for studying attitudes is to improve techniques for changing them. Huge amounts of money (and we are talking long telephone numbers here!) are spent annually in attempts to shift attitudes; whether it is toward Pepsi and away from Coke (or vice versa), or toward the paraphernalia of 'safe sex'.

Recent health education campaigns concerning the dangers of AIDS are a good example of attempts to change attitudes

The bottom line in attitude campaigns of this kind is that people should change what they do; they should start buying Pepsi and, when the occasion arises, not forget to use a condom. It is no good if people say they prefer Pepsi but somehow always end up asking for a Coke; neither is it helpful if they can dutifully declare how important it is to use a condom but seem to forget in the heat of the moment. This is the nub of the so-called attitude–behaviour problem. It refers to the mismatch between what people say when confronted with pencil-and-paper meas-ures of attitudes, and what they do in practice. Problems of this kind have long been recognized by attitude researchers. The classic study was done by LaPiere (1934) in the United States during a period of consider-able racism against minority groups, including ethnic Chinese. In several long car trips, LaPiere visited over two hundred restaurants, cafés, hotels and auto camps with two people whom he describes as a 'personable and charming' Chinese couple. LaPiere tried to stay out of sight and surrep-titiously noted the treatment meted out to the couple. In fact, they were turned away from these various restaurants and hotels on only one occasion. LaPiere accounts for this relatively low frequency in terms of the couple's social skills and display of spoken English:

> It appeared that a genial smile was the most effective password to acceptance. My Chinese friends were skilful smilers, which may account in part for the fact that we received but one rebuff in all our experiences ... I was impressed with the fact that even where some tension developed due to the strangeness of the Chinese it would evaporate immediately when they spoke in unaccented English.
>
> (LaPiere, 1934, p.232)

What is important for the attitude–behaviour issue is LaPiere's next move. After some months had elapsed, he sent out a questionnaire asking the establishments if they would be willing to 'accept members of the Chinese race as guests'. Over half replied, and of those, 92 per cent said no; only one said yes.

There are many potential reasons for this mismatch. The hoteliers' stereotypes of Chinese people were probably very different from the smart middle-class couple who turned up. And, even if they were reluctant to accommodate them, the embarrassment of turning them away may have outweighed their reluctance. Nevertheless, this study graphically illustrates that what people say when their attitudes are being measured may be quite at odds with how they act in other situations.

This is just a single case. However, in the late 1960s, Wicker conducted a comprehensive review of various studies measuring individuals' attitudes using three stringent criteria: '(1) at least one attitudinal measure and one overt behavioural measure toward the same object must be obtained for each subject, (2) the attitude and the behaviour must be measured on separate occasions, and (3) the overt behavioural response must not be merely the subject's retrospective verbal report of his [*sic*] own behaviour' (1971, p. 142). The point was to find studies which could compare a standard written attitude measure with some direct observation or record of the person's actual behaviour.

"Look, how would you like to trudge round in the pouring rain trying to get sensible answers out of a crowd of semi-literate morons? Very much, wouldn't mind, or stuff it?"

BOX 3.2 Measuring attitudes

Social psychologists use a range of techniques for measuring attitudes. Most involve some kind of questionnaire, either administered in an interview or filled in by the respondent ticking boxes. One of the most common techniques involves what is known as the Likert scale. On a Likert scale, people are asked to place their attitudes on an issue on a continuum, registering agreement or disagreement by circling the point on the scale which best fits their view. For example:

The nuclear power industry is a threat to world peace.

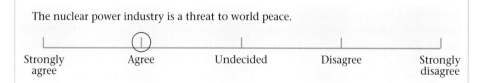

| Strongly agree | Agree | Undecided | Disagree | Strongly disagree |

The process of generating a set of items related to the topic which actually distinguish people with different views is a complex one (for more details, cf. Dawes et al., 1972). The goal is to generate a reasonably short list of opinion statements and a questionnaire which produces measurable scores.

A study by Corey (1937), which looked at students cheating in exams, should suffice to illustrate the sort of studies which Wicker drew on. A fiendish deception allowed Corey to identify and quantify cheating without the students' awareness; and he independently measured their attitudes to cheating with a questionnaire. When Corey compared the two measures of cheating, there was virtually no relationship between them, although there was a relationship with how poorly the students would have done in the exam. As he put it, 'whether or not a student cheated depended in much larger part upon how well he had prepared for the examination than upon any opinions he had stated about honesty in examinations' (Corey, 1937; cited in Wicker, 1971, p. 157).

Wicker was able to find 31 studies on various topics which met his criteria along with an earlier review of 15 further studies. This unusually wide sample of cases led his conclusions to be taken very seriously. The findings were summarized in terms of correlations between the attitude measure and the behavioural measure. The lack of correlation was striking – rarely above 0.3. Less than 10 per cent of the variation in the behavioural measures could be accounted for by the attitude measures. As Wicker put it, '[t]aken as a whole, these studies suggest that it is considerably more likely that attitudes will be unrelated or only slightly related to overt behaviours than that attitudes will be closely related to actions' (1971, p. 161).

This failure to predict behaviour was bad news for attitude researchers. It also suggested that there might be little point in spending enormous amounts of money in trying to change attitudes. Other ways of modifying what people do may be more cost-effective. If you are in charge of a government unit attempting to reduce the number of cancer deaths due to smoking, an expensive television campaign highlighting the risks might be replaced by a short conversation with a colleague in the Treasury suggesting that they increase the tax on cigarettes. People will buy less cigarettes as the cost goes up and fewer people will die of cancer. Everyone will be happy (apart from serious tobacco addicts and the companies that make money out of them!).

Since this low point at the end of the 1960s, attitude research has staged something of a recovery. The intervening years have seen a number of theoretical refinements and new lines of empirical work which promise more effective prediction of people's actions from their responses to attitude scales, as well as an improved understanding of when attitude measures will fail to predict. Myers (1993) neatly organizes this recent work into four themes. He suggests that attitudes can be used to make effective predictions about behaviour in the following conditions:

- When the influences on how people express attitudes are minimized.

- When influences on the attitude-related behaviour are minimized.

- When the attitude is specific to the behaviour.

- When the attitude is made salient.

ACTIVITY 3.3   Before I expand on these, spend some time considering each of these four conditions for the effective prediction of behaviour. Try to think of a concrete example for each point.

When the influences on how people express attitudes are minimized

One of the reasons why an attitude may not be any good for estimating what someone is going to do is that it actually may not be their attitude at all. This may sound like a rather obvious problem. However, it is absolutely crucial in attitude research. It is important to remember that attitude research is a form of social interaction between researcher and participant, and such interaction does not take place in a social psychological vacuum.

Social interaction has a number of features which have implications for attitude research. Say you have just been to a new movie with someone with whom you have just started a relationship. You are just about to complain about how awful it was, when he or she starts to tell you how much they enjoyed the film, how the script was great and the camera work stunning. What do you do? Well, you probably don't change to saying how fantastic the film was; but you probably don't start an argument about it either. You certainly modify what you were going to say, and probably soften your criticism of the film.

The situation in which attitude research is conducted is not too different. If people are answering questions from a social researcher, or even filling in a questionnaire, there is the potential for wondering what the researcher will think of them. You might well not want to appear racist to a liberal-seeming social researcher. You might downplay or disguise such feelings if you had them.

There are various ways of attempting to reduce this problem of influence. Some researchers have designed rather cumbersome deceptions which lead participants to think the researcher will spot them if they attempt to disguise their attitudes. Jones and Sigall (1971) produced a bit of fake apparatus looking like something from the Starship Enterprise and persuaded participants that it would be able to detect people who were not candid about their attitudes. Such techniques typically find higher levels of racism or sexism than more traditional attitude measures.

Other approaches stress anonymity. For example, after their embarrassing failure to predict the outcome of the 1992 UK elections, some poll organizations changed their approach. The exit polls – which were widely touted beforehand as highly reliable – predicted that there would be a hung parliament or possibly a small Labour majority. Yet in the event the Tories won relatively comfortably. People seem to have been sheepish about admitting they had voted for the Conservatives, because it made them appear selfish in supporting lower taxes at the expense of education and welfare. Poll organizations which recorded political feelings anonymously (participants posted their opinions into a box) found Labour support decreased and Tory support increased. It seems that the social influences on the expression of attitudes had been minimized.

When influences on the attitude-related behaviour are minimized

The point here is similar to the one about influences on expressed attitudes. There are all sorts of constraints and considerations which lead people away from following their preferences. For example, however much a young teenage smoker would like to buy a packet of cigarettes, when she is in a shop with her disapproving parents she will probably resist. One way of discounting the effect on any individual instance is simply to look at a lot of cases. We could follow this adolescent around and record her cigarette buying over a period of weeks. That might give a better picture.

When the attitude is specific to the behaviour

One of the features of many attitude questionnaires is that they ask rather general things measuring broad attitudes to 'race', health, or political parties. Some attitude researchers have argued that decisions are often related to rather specific attitudes. In a large review of studies of attitudes and behaviour, Azjen and Fishbein (1977) compared those studies which related general attitudes to behaviour with studies which related *specific* attitudes to behaviour. They found that the predictions were much more accurate in the latter cases. If you want to predict whether someone will protest against the building of a nuclear power station in their part of the country, you will be better off asking about their specific attitudes to a nuclear power station being built nearby rather than their general attitude to nuclear power *per se*.

When the attitude is made salient

A final situation in which attitudes are more likely to predict what people will do is when the attitude is made salient, when it is brought to mind. The explanation here is that much of the time we are acting out standard routines, or scripts. As Myers (1993) notes, when the waiter asks us if we liked the meal, we are likely to reply it was, 'Very nice, thank you' even if it was cold and poorly cooked. The standard script, and the social pressure not to make a fuss, encourage an immediate response which is out of line with what we actually felt about the meal. At these times, we may be much more attentive to features of the situation we are in than to our own values and attitudes and so the latter have no effect. It may be possible to overcome some of these scripted patterns, and the over-attention to things in the environment, by encouraging people to spend some time attending to their own attitudes before a task (Snyder and Swann, 1976) or to consider the way they acted in the past.

2.3   A theory of planned behaviour

Some researchers have tried to integrate the various features which might influence the relation between attitudes and behaviour into a general theoretical model. One of the most ambitious and successful of these is associated with Fishbein and Azjen (1975). Azjen (1988) dubbed a recent version of this model the 'theory of planned behaviour' because of the emphasis on the complex processes of planning and judgement guiding action. The model treats what people do as the outcome of considering their own views, the views and expectations of important others, and their own capacities. The various relations between the components of the model can be seen in Figure 3.1. Let's take a concrete example – the case of a prospective strike among the workers of a pharmaceuticals factory (cf. Smith, 1987). The model should be able to help us decide whether a particular worker – Jane Jones – will go on strike or not.

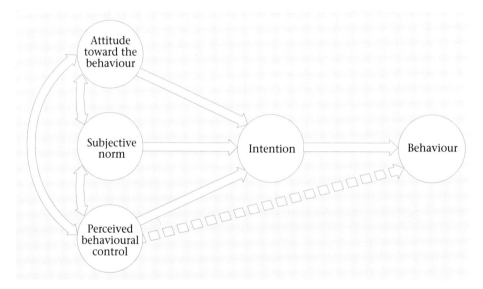

Figure 3.1   *Theory of planned behaviour (Source: based on Azjen, 1988, p. 133)*

The first thing to note is that the model treats Jane's *intention* to go on strike as more psychologically significant than her actual striking. The point here is that all sorts of things can intervene between the intention and the act – Jane might become ill, for example, or the factory might go into receivership. This would prevent the behaviour, but not because there is a problem with the model. Next, take the determinant labelled 'Attitude toward the behaviour'. Azjen wants to treat this rather differently from much conventional attitude research. As we have already seen, one of the problems identified with the working of attitudes is their lack of specificity. Here, Jane is not being asked her general views on the virtues of strikes or whether it is better to be rich than poor. She is being asked about her attitude to this *specific* strike. This attitude is one important determinant of whether she strikes or not – but not the only one.

The second determinant specified in the model is the 'Subjective norm'. The crucial thing here is Jane's view of other people's thoughts about her going on strike. Does she think her fellow-workers will approve and support her action? Does Jane care what they think? If she does care, and her understanding is that they strongly support her actions, then this will make her more likely to go on strike.

The third determinant of Jane's behaviour is 'Perceived behavioural control'. This involves Jane's considerations about whether she is able to go on strike. Does she think that she would find picketing difficult? Is she worried that she will not be able to manage on reduced pay during the stoppage? Azjen notes that, insofar as her judgements about her capabilities are accurate, they will have a bearing on whether she actually strikes or not over and above any intention. Hence the broken arrow running from 'Perceived behavioural control' to 'Behaviour'.

Look at Figure 3.1 again and note the bi-directional arrows which link the three major determinants of the 'Intention' component. Why are those there? Azjen stresses that these determinants are not always independent of one another; instead, there may be some complex interplay between them. For example, if Jane perceives that her fellow-workers are strongly in favour of the strike ('Subjective norm'), then that may influence both her own attitude toward going on strike ('Attitude toward the behaviour') and her perception that she will successfully be able to take part in it ('Perceived behavioural control').

Consider all the arrows in Figure 3.1. They are meant to show lines of influence. Some are bi-directional arrows indicating that influence can work in either direction. With some it is obvious why they are there; with others it is less clear. Go through each in turn and consider the kinds of influence the arrow is meant to represent.   ACTIVITY 3.4

So, does this model work? Does it enable better behavioural predictions than previous conceptualizations of attitudes? Azjen (1988) reports numerous studies conducted within the framework of the theory of planned behaviour, or earlier versions of the same theory, which provide better predictions of behaviours as diverse as slimming, voting and bottle-feeding than would be expected from the rather pessimistic picture painted by Wicker. See Box 3.3 for an example.

BOX 3.3   Support for Azjen's theory of planned behaviour

Work using Azjen's theory of planned behaviour can be quite complex. A recent and relatively simple study on blood donation was conducted by Giles and Cairns (1995). They gave over 140 undergraduates at the University of Ulster a questionnaire a week prior to the arrival of the blood donation service. The questionnaire included items related to the three variables in Azjen's theory: *attitudes* ('Is it going to hurt?'; 'Will it help others?'), *subjective norm* ('Do members of my family think I should donate blood?'), and *perceived behavioural control* ('I could easily donate blood if I wanted to'). After the donation service had left, they checked who had actually donated blood, and then analysed how well the answers to these different questionnaire items predicted this behaviour. They found that the three variables together could account for 61 per cent of the variance in blood donation. Put another way, although other things were affecting the donation, the theory explained nearly two-thirds of what was going on. This is much better than the bare 10 per cent typically found in the studies reviewed by Wicker and is strong support for Azjen's theory.

2.4   Problems and prospects

What are we to make of this history of criticism and response in attitude research? Do the reformulations of the last twenty years allow the attitude concept to be dusted off and given a central place on the mantelpiece of social psychology? The answer, I would argue, has to be 'no'. There are two reasons for my view. First, the resurrection of attitudes is only a limited one; they remain a ghost of their old self (which has not prevented the closely related notion of public opinion thriving largely untouched by these theoretical doubts). Secondly, a new set of difficulties has been raised by researchers working from a social constructionist perspective. Let me take these concerns in turn.

What made the attitude notion powerful originally was the claim that once you had measured a set of attitudes this would allow you to predict a wide range of actions. Moreover, the attitudes researchers were interested in were general ones. The hope was that by identifying a person's general attitude towards minority groups on a pencil-and-paper scale, for example, you would be able to predict who would act in a racist manner in particular situations. Once you start claiming that, before any prediction can be made, you also need to take into account a wide range of situational and normative factors, the usefulness of the attitude notion is undermined.

There is another more subtle, but potentially damaging, problem with newer models such as the theory of planned behaviour. Once it is necessary for the attitude to be entirely specific to the action, there is a danger that we no longer have an attitude leading to a behavioural intention (as expressed by the arrow on Figure 3.1). Instead, when people are expressing their specific attitude in research studies of this kind, they are merely stating their behavioural intention in a different way. The two measures simply capture different features of the same thing. It is not surprising that you can get a strong connection if there is a conceptual relationship of this kind. It would be a bit like relating eating to moving your mouth; you would find a strong relationship, but then it is hard to eat without chewing.

The second set of difficulties with the traditional attitude notion is raised by social constructionist approaches. There are a wide range of these objections; but for simplicity I will focus on four:

- atomism;
- individualism;
- variability with context;
- evaluations as actions.

Atomism

In traditional attitude research, attitudes are often assumed to be scattered around in people's heads, rather like currants in a fruitcake. Attitude theorists have not been blind to the patterned nature of attitudes. There have been some attempts to look at the way attitudes are related together. Theorists are not at all surprised when they hear someone who has just claimed that pollution is the main threat to human life go on to argue for massive investment in public transportation schemes, and then express concern about the conditions of animals in factory farms. Yet attitude theorists have not gone on to develop a successful theoretical account of these relationships. Why should such views hang together, even in a loose way?

Individualism

The second problem with mainstream attitude research is the idea that attitudes are individual possessions, so that the proper way to study attitudes is to look at individuals. Again, attitude researchers have not been blind to this issue. Attitude researchers, along with the rest of us, are well aware that there is nothing unique about people who express the view that pollution is the main threat to human life; many people share this view, and it is developed in widely available books, magazines and on popular television programmes. The researcher's problem is how to account for such shared views and to understand the relationship between collective views and individual attitudes. One approach which has attempted to address the problems of atomism and individualism is the theory of social representations, which will be the topic of section 3 of this chapter.

Variability with context

Another problem with the concept of attitudes is, superficially at least, similar to the traditional attitude and behaviour problem. When people's talk is examined closely, a surprising amount of variation is found in the evaluations that they make. For example, the same person may say both highly negative and highly positive things about the same minority group in different places in the same interview (Potter and Wetherell, 1995). Such variability makes it hard to sustain the idea that these evaluations are *expressions* of one consistent underlying attitude. We shall return to the topic of variability in section 4.

Evaluations as actions

The problem of evaluations varying with context leads to a further blind spot in attitude research. What are people doing with their evaluations? Could it be that variations in evaluations are produced by a whole different order of social psychological phenomena which has been invisible because of the particular theoretical and methodological stipulations of attitude research? Attitude theory has not encouraged researchers to look at how evaluative discourse (what they would call 'attitude expression') is used in natural situations such as complimenting your partner ('Great shoes') or arguing over who should load the dishwasher ('You always leave it for me'). Work exploring evaluations in natural settings will be discussed in section 4.2 below. The problems of variability and the role of evaluations as actions have been highlighted by the social constructionist perspective of discursive psychology.

Despite the problems identified above, attitude research continues to be a major research field in social psychology, particularly in North America. It draws on a well-established set of measurement techniques and, when used carefully, it can make impressive predictions about how people will act. In many applied areas, such as public health campaigns aimed at encouraging practices of safe sex, what matters is making the best prediction of the outcome, and the precise nature of the underlying psychological mechanisms is less important. In the future, ideas from social representations theory and discursive psychology may play an increasingly important role in these applied areas, but at the moment attitude research predominates.

Review of section 2

- Attitude research is based around the idea that people have within them sets of enduring evaluations of the world which encourage them to act in particular ways.

- The attitude–behaviour problem refers to the failure to find strong correlations between expressed attitudes and measures of how people act in different situations.

- Attempts to improve the predictive value of attitudes include minimizing potentially distorting influences on attitude expression and attitude-related behaviour, measuring attitudes which are specific to behaviour, and making attitudes salient.

- The theory of planned behaviour treats intentions to behave in particular ways as a consequence of three factors: the person's attitude, the normative expectations of appropriate people and groups, and the person's perceived control over his or her behaviour.

3 Social representations

Some years ago, a book was published under the title *Psychobabble* (Rosen, 1978). The details of the work are not relevant here, but the notion of psychobabble is an interesting one. The idea is that people are communicating with each other, particularly in areas of California, using a mish-mash of terms derived mainly from psychoanalytic and humanistic theories. In these areas the gossip would differ from that found in a typical British town. Instead of 'Jason is cheating on Ruth', 'Kylie's got a bit of a drink problem', it would be 'Bobby's getting really uptight; he's not externalizing his emotions enough' or 'Sherry and her dad are going through all that Oedipal stuff right now'. This is psychobabble – a new, patchwork language which mixes terms from encounter groups, meditation, psychological therapy and a range of what would now be called New-Age thinkers.

Psychobabble could be seen as a new form of common sense in the making. It may seem strange, unfamiliar or even laughable because most of us are outside of it. But could it be that our own common sense, our own ways for understanding ourselves and other people, and our own language of self and psychological processes are themselves merely more established forms of psychobabble? Perhaps Californian New-Age psychobabble seems so odd and contrived simply because of its unfamiliarity and because the process of 'sedimenting' from theory to everyday understanding is still fresh?

The theory of social representations suggests that our common sense is indeed a sediment from past theorizing about psychology and the self. Moscovici developed the notion from Durkheim's rather broader sociological notion of 'collective representation', and in the 1950s he carried out what is still one of the classic pieces of research on social representations (Moscovici, 1976). His interest was in psychoanalysis and particularly in how the ideas of psychoanalysis could be absorbed within a culture – in this case, post-war France. Moscovici looked at a wide range of materials, including women's magazines and church publications, as well as surveying people's views.

His conclusion was that psychoanalysis had trickled down from the analytic couch and scholarly journals into both 'high' culture and popular common sense. People 'think' with psychoanalysis, without it seeming as if they are doing anything theoretical at all. However, it would be wrong to say that in 1955 the general population of Paris were conversing with, and conversant with, psychoanalytic theory with all its complexities and different traditions. One of Moscovici's central arguments was that people were working with a simplified image of psychoanalysis; some of its concepts had filtered down into everyday use while others had not travelled out of the arcane scholarly world. The notion of repression, for example, had taken on a wide currency, yet the notion of libido – the sexual drive which Freud saw as the major motivation for behaviour – had not. The social representation of psychoanalysis is the simplified shared image drawn on in all sorts of everyday situations.

3.1　The theory of social representations

The theory of social representations is considerably more complicated and has a broader scope than many of the more familiar attitude theories. Moscovici's writings are not always consistent with one another, however, and there are divergent interpretations of the theory, with some researchers treating 'social representations' as meaning no more than a collection of beliefs. This exposition will stay close to Moscovici's own theoretical statements, particularly an extended overview (Moscovici, 1984).

Social representations theory is a constructionist theory. That is, rather than seeing people as simply perceiving (or misperceiving) their social worlds it treats those worlds as constructed. A social representation is a device for doing this construction. It allows someone to make sense of something that is potentially unfamiliar as well as evaluating it. For Moscovici, all thought and understanding is based on the working of social representations. Each social representation is made up of a mixture of concepts or ideas and images. And these are both in people's minds and circulating in society where they are carried by conversations and media texts.

Social representations have a specific structure: usually they are built around a figurative nucleus which is a core image or picture. Let me clarify this by making a contrast with attitude theory. Think of an opinion researcher who is attempting to find out people's opinions of the Labour Party. For attitude researchers, there are two relevant entities here. There is the actual Labour Party which is the object of the opinion, and then there is the opinion itself, which is about the Labour Party, and is the possession of the person who has been canvassed about their views (see Figure 3.2).

Figure 3.2

In contrast to this, social representations theory proposes a rather more complex, three-part model. This too invokes the actual Labour Party, and the person's attitude. However, it adds a new element that fits in between them; this is the social representation of the Labour Party (see Figure 3.3).

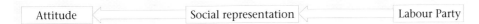

Figure 3.3

The social representation sits between the object and the attitude and its role is to make sense of the Labour Party. For a constructionist theory of this kind, sense is not simply there – lying around in the world to be seen and picked up – it has to be built. The social representation is the device that does the building. The attitude thus relates to the *image* of the party, rather than to its *actual* Members of Parliament, its grassroots, its offices and so on – and this is, of course, why political parties devote so much attention to press briefings and 'spin doctoring'.

So what might social representations of the Labour Party look like? There has not been a research project which answers this question, so the following examples are entirely hypothetical. Moscovici specifies that social representations will be partly composed of ideas and partly of images. For example, members of a pro-Marxist group at the margins of the Labour Party might represent it in terms of specific abstract elements (ideas such as 'a previously working-class, socialist party that been taken over by middle-class social democrats'), and concrete elements (an image perhaps of a group of 'true socialists' who have been marginalized by a resurgence of 'soft centrist' ideas). Note how neatly the metaphors here – marginalized, soft – allow a visual image to be formed of the party.

When a social representation is used to build a version of the Labour Party in this way it is not merely a neutral picture. The precise way in which this object is built will be the basis for evaluating it. A person with the representation discussed here might express an intention to vote Labour but combine this with critical comments on the Party's social and economic policies, and despair at the lack of a serious Marxist alternative. Moscovici's profound point, then, is that if we want to understand why a person has offered a specific opinion we need to understand their social representation of the object being considered. The representation guides the opinions. Of course, a fuller study of representations of the Labour Party would need a bit more than this; it might well want to include the person's representations of other political parties, the nature of the democratic process, the workings of the economy, the place of Britain in the world, and so on.

Go back to the Review of section 2 and spend a bit of time considering how social representations theory develops and supplements the notion of attitude.   ACTIVITY 3.5

So far, it might not seem obvious why the term 'social representation' is used. Why not just refer to them as representations and treat them as the unique possession of individuals? For Moscovici, there are at least three senses in which social representations are truly social.

Social representations are generated in communication

Social representations are intrinsic to effective communication. When people interact through gossip, argue with one another in pubs, discuss political scandals over breakfast, they are building up shared pictures of the world. As Moscovici puts it: 'social representations are the outcome of an unceasing babble and a permanent dialogue between individuals' (1985, p. 95). The theory places a lot of emphasis on the role of the media in sustaining, producing and circulating social representations. They are not reducible to images within people's heads.

Social representations provide a code for communication

One of the consequences of people sharing social representations is that this provides a common currency for communication. Individuals can clearly understand each other and have free-flowing conversations. The agreed representations provide stable versions of the world which can form a topic of conversation. The converse is also true; communication between people with different representations is likely to generate conflict. From this perspective, one of the roles of a mass circulation newspaper such as *The Sun* in the UK will be to invoke shared representations that facilitate communication between *Sun* readers on a range of different topics.

Social representations provide a way of distinguishing social groups

As we saw in Chapter 1, one of the great problems of the social sciences is what makes a group a group? For Moscovici, at least part of the answer is that a group is made up of people who share sets of social representations. Social representations provide a crucial homogenizing force for groups because they supply a conventional code for communication and because people who share representations agree in their understanding and evaluation of aspects of the world.

One of the classic studies of social representations was conducted by Herzlich (1973) and concerned the representations of health and illness in the French population. She used a set of intensive interviews with 80 people, the majority of whom lived in Paris, although a small group came from a rural village. The interviews were conversational – although they covered some set topics, they did not constrain responses as with the traditional opinion survey.

Herzlich found that this group of people's attitudes to health and illness, and their understanding of these notions, followed from a broadly shared underlying representation which developed an opposition between health and illness. Health was seen as residing within individuals as a pool or reservoir that could be tapped into but also used up. In contrast, illness was commonly seen as lying outside of individuals, generated by a particular way of life. In this representation, individuals are basically healthy, but health is a passive thing which can be undermined by lifestyle. For example, city life was viewed as toxic; it was seen as an illness-generator which actively attacks the individual. In contrast, country living was not seen to have toxic consequences; it allows people to be sustained by their pool of health.

If Herzlich's findings seem a bit abstract, think of the way health foods are marketed. Low-fat margarine and yoghurt are now manufactured in big plants that look like chemical factories. Yet what is pictured on the packaging? As often as not it is a rural scene of some kind: cows grazing or the sun going down over green fields. What you do not see is health food sold using scenes of urban life. And this is not because such scenes are unattractive, or do not appear in advertising generally – you will not have any trouble finding clothing, or perfume advertised against a backdrop of cars or skyscrapers. Herzlich's research shows up precisely the intuitions the advertisers are working with; that urban images conjure up a way of life which is toxic, and that is the last thing you want people to think about while buying a health product (however full of sugar and chemicals).

Even the advertisement of staples such as bread fits this pattern

Next time you are in a supermarket or large shop, take some time to look at the images on packets of different foods and other products. Look particularly at the packaging of 'health' products, and then compare these with images on perfume packaging or on sweet wrappers or look at television adverts for these products. Are there consistent differences? How do these differences relate to the social representations which advertisers and manufacturers are helping to construct and exploiting?

In addition to a general account of understanding, social representations theory provides a specific account of how people deal with new or unfamiliar experiences. Familiar experiences are simply handled via the person's store of social representations. Unfamiliar experiences are more problematic because there is no existing social representation to give them sense. Moscovici suggests that in these cases two processes go on: 'anchoring' and 'objectification'.

In anchoring, the novel experience is assigned to a category or element of an existing representation. In effect, it will be placed in the conceptual box which makes it seem most familiar. In objectification, the novel object is transformed into a concrete, possibly pictorial, element of the representation to which it is anchored. The old representation grows a new part, like a tree grows a new branch. At the same time, through the various processes of communication through which social representations circulate – the media, family arguments, and so on – this new representation will be diffused through the social group. What was previously novel and challenging now becomes, for this group, a familiar element in their reality.

Let us try to think about anchoring and objectification with the example of the Marxist Labour supporter we have been using. Say that person encounters a new left-wing political party. She reads about it in a left-of-centre newspaper, and chats to her friends about it. Her initial way of understanding the new party may involve anchoring it to her current representations of the Labour Party. Perhaps it shares a stress on public ownership, collective action and social responsibility, which are elements in her representation of essential features of the Labour Party. At the same time as it is being anchored in this way, the process of communication with like-minded friends might generate a concrete image of the new party – a representation linked to the original one of the Labour Party, but with some new elements. Anchoring and objectification are important to social representations theory because of its aim to account for change and show how attitudes, groups and representations become related together.

3.2 Social representations of madness

If anyone was asked to name the most dramatic change in British social policy over the last thirty years, a major contender would undoubtedly be the move to 'community care'. In the 1960s, there were many arguments about the ill-effects of life in long-stay mental hospitals, both for people with psychiatric illnesses and for people with learning difficulties. Since then, criticisms of such regimes have become enshrined in government policy to the extent that many hospitals and asylums were closed down throughout the 1980s. More recently, worries about the dehumanizing effect of living in total institutions, along with the difficulty of readjusting to everyday living, have been replaced by concerns about psychiatric patients ending up living in shop doorways, failing to take their medication, and even becoming a public risk. In many cases, small hostels created for people released from hospitals have generated strong local hostility.

BOX 3.4   'Care' in the community

(The Guardian, 4 March 1994)

(The Observer, 26 June 1994)

143

General support for community care combined with hostility towards particular care schemes in one's own community raises interesting and important questions – does it reflect something about the social representation of people with psychiatric problems? In one of the most ambitious pieces of research on social representations, Jodelet (1991) has attempted to provide a detailed description of the representations of mental illness shared in a particular community. Her work concentrated on a small French community called Ainay-le-Chateau. Here the policy of community care dates back from the turn of the century. Instead of being held in mental hospitals, patients lived with village people in their homes; they became lodgers in the homes of foster families.

Unusually for a social psychologist, Jodelet used a combination of research methods. Although she did conduct a large questionnaire survey characteristic of more traditional attitude research, the central part of her study involved an extended period of ethnographic observation. She lived in the community, attended cafés, church and village ceremonies, taking part, watching, and constantly trying to understand. This went hand in hand with intensive interviews with about 10 per cent of the families who had the 'mental patients' staying with them. In her difficult but fascinating book describing this research, Jodelet draws heavily on these interviews to illustrate arguments and justify claims. It is very important to hold in mind that Jodelet is not trying to find out what mentally ill people are really like – her topic is people's representations, which may be stereotyped and distorted in all kinds of potentially problematic ways.

One of the themes Jodelet found repeatedly emphasized by her participants concerned issues of cleanliness and contamination. There was much discussion, for example, about the lodgers (as they were called) wearing dirty clothes or being incontinent. She suggested that this kind of talk should not be taken as a simple description of a state of affairs but had a more complex motivation. A strong criticism of a lodger's dirtiness would often be coupled with a strong expression of loyalty. Why should this be? Jodelet's answer is that this representation provided a rationale for actions such as the family having separate meals from the lodgers. The separate eating could be presented, not as a result of prejudice or fear, but as a consequence of the family's concerns about taste and hygiene. In addition, and more subtly, she suggests that the construction of the patients as dirty was a psychological mechanism for containing more diffuse anxieties about their madness. As she put it:

> ... dirtiness seems to siphon off the major part of the negativity of insanity and is a less disturbing manifestation of the illness than others. Ultimately, it is reassuring. One then begins to understand the foster parent who declared, 'a bad lodger is a dirty lodger' and then told us of her oldest one, 'He's been with me for twenty-seven years. He's not bad at all. I'm not frightened of him.' Of course, 'He's dirty. I could kill him sometimes. Every day he goes in his trousers.' To have to wash a pair of trousers every day for twenty-seven years! But, 'He's not

wicked. That's what I'm afraid of. I would hate to change. I would prefer to put up with it.' Dirtiness which is due to illness is unthreatening. That alone makes it worth putting up with, whatever unpleasantness that entails, provided that it does not exceed a limit of revulsion which appears to be quite high.

(Jodelet, 1991, pp. 143–4)

Jodelet claims that her interviewees were reluctant to claim any special knowledge about mental illness: ' "Mental illness? I don't know about that." From the very start, all our interviewees forbade themselves any statement expressing knowledge of the subject' (1991, p. 149). Again, she interprets this as a strategy for managing the potential anxiety or threat posed by madness: 'It was as if by becoming the object of an explicit knowledge or formulation, the power of mental illness to generate anxiety would be released' (1991, p. 150). Nevertheless, Jodelet argues that the same participants who produced these professions of ignorance were, elsewhere in their interviews, able to produce elaborate conceptions of the nature of mental illness.

Jodelet suggests that the social representations of madness in this community involved a complicated lay theory of the origins of insanity in the person. Jodelet summarizes this lay theory as a structural model which captures what she calls the 'functional nucleus of the organism' (see Figure 3.4 overleaf); that is, people's representation of the different elements within the person – the brain, body and nerves – which regulate how they behave and which may be disrupted by mental illness. It is a complicated model which illustrates the ambition of the social representations approach and the type of explanation it is attempting. Jodelet is arguing that the residents of Ainay-le-Chateau used some kind of mental equivalent of this model to understand the nature and actions of the lodgers. You are not expected to fully grasp the model on just the brief exposition I have given here; in Jodelet's work it is backed up by many pages of discussion.

Jodelet's claim, then, is that this model faithfully captures the basic representation of insanity shared by the foster families she studied as well as indicating how these representations generated the different kinds of behaviour the families demonstrated towards the lodgers. The families used this model to make sense of different kinds of mental illness and to manage its different forms. For example, a maximum dysfunction of the brain could be the explanation for an almost complete lack of mental activity, while a major disturbance of the body might be seen as leading to a state close to bestiality involving a lack of control of biological functions and a blind satisfaction of needs. In these cases, the appropriate way for the foster families to manage the person was seen as involving training by threat of punishment with the objective of making the person submit to the basic rules of their placement. It remains to be seen how far this representation extends beyond the unique circumstances of the colony at Ainay-le-Chateau to the broader French population; and whether similar social representations could be identified in Britain.

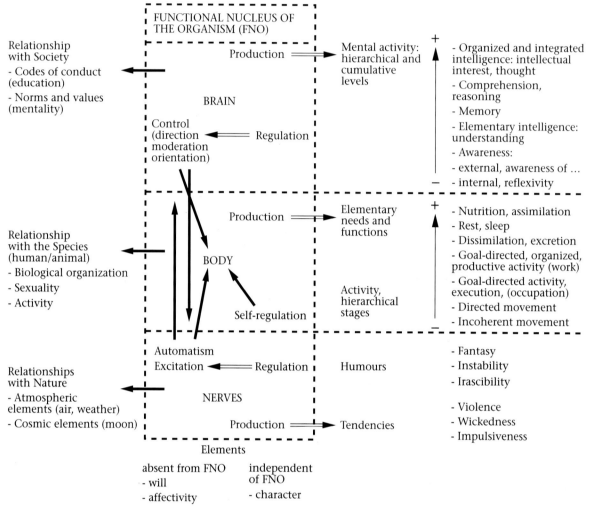

Figure 3.4 *Jodelet's structural model of the origins of insanity in terms of representations of the 'functional nucleus of the organism' (Source: based on Jodelet, 1991, p. 195)*

ACTIVITY 3.7   Spend some time considering the various parts of Jodelet's diagram. It is extremely complicated. Try taking one or two of the arrows and considering their roles in the representation. Consider also the basic relationship between the three parts of the organism: the brain, body and nerves. (Do not worry if this is unclear; just try to get a feel of what kind of model this is, and Jodelet's aims.) Now consider your own ideas about mental illness. Try to be concrete here: think of your experiences with friends, family or acquaintances who may have had psychiatric problems. Can you identify any similarities between your understanding of their problems and that identified by Jodelet in Ainay-le-Chateau?

3.3   Problems and prospects

As I noted at the beginning of section 3.1, social representations theory is rather more ambitious than the attitude theories discussed in section 2. It is also a much more social account than most attitude theories. If successful, social representations theory provides not simply an alternative account, but one which is much more comprehensive and able to explain aspects of attitudes (particularly their shared nature, and their organization) in a way that most attitude theories have failed to do. The specificity of the foster families' attitudes to their lodgers, for example, should be explicable, in part, by their shared representations of madness and the use of these to construct the lodger's problems. Moreover, this theory provides a corrective to the individualism and atomism of traditional attitude theories. It offers an account of how attitudes are systematically related together, and it stresses the way they are patterned by the membership of groups who share representations. In the period since the early 1980s, when social representations work was first published in English, research in this tradition has mushroomed, particularly in Europe, Australia and South America.

Before reading on, spend a bit of time thinking about the theory of social representations. What seems valuable about it to you? A number of criticisms have been directed against it over the last few years. Think about what these might be.

ACTIVITY 3.8

On the whole, the theory of social representations has been ignored by mainstream North American social psychologists in the experimental cognitive tradition. It may be that they find the ambiguities and complexities off-putting, or feel that the qualitative studies which are often the basis for the research are too open-ended to be reliable. Also, one of the characteristics of experimental social psychology is that it treats the identification of general laws and processes as the central aim of research. The goal is to capture some features of persuasion, group interaction, or whatever which would occur in all societies at all times in history. Social representations theory directly counters this by treating the specific content of a culture or group's representations as the main object of analysis. Jodelet's study, for example, attempts to show that attitudes to the lodgers of Ainay-le-Chateau were dependent on the specific social representations held by the families. With another group, or another culture, the representations might be different and the attitudes and reactions would differ as a consequence. Such an approach has profound implications for the way social psychology is conceptualized. It not only requires us to confront individual cultures in all their richness, but also opens up the possibility of a fruitful dialogue with other social sciences such as anthropology and linguistics.

Although social representations theory takes a broadly constructionist perspective, it has also been criticized by other social constructionist social psychologists such as discourse analysts (cf. Wetherell and Maybin, 1996, section 4). These critics have been sympathetic to some of the aims of the perspective while raising difficulties with the way it is put into practice, and with some of its individualistic tendencies (see Potter and Wetherell, 1987, pp. 142–6). The criticisms focus on:

- the relation of groups to representations;
- consensus and agreement in representations;
- the status of representations.

Let us take them in turn.

Groups and representations

In social representations theory, what defines a group is its possession of a set of shared representations. Empirical studies typically start with a relatively well-defined social group and then try to provide an account of its representations. There are two closely related difficulties with this strategy. First, it presupposes that representations mark group boundaries. This may give rise to a vicious circle whereby representations are identified from the group, and then representations are said to define the group. Secondly, there is the issue of how the researcher can identify social groups independently of participants' representations of those groups? The researcher ends up treating group categories as both a stable base for building research and as social representations produced by participants.

Take an example. Say we wish to study a protest movement which is split between 'hard-line militants' and 'moderates' (e.g. see di Giacomo, 1980). We might want to explore differences in the social representations held by these two groups; yet in taking 'hard-line militant' and 'moderate' as natural groupings we have already accepted one, potentially contentious, representation of the protest movement.

Consensus and agreement in representations

Social representations are taken to be shared across a social group. This is what makes them *social* representations rather than merely representations of the kind a cognitive psychologist might study. However, ascertaining consensus in practice is potentially very tricky. Often research techniques – both quantitative and qualitative – have been used which smooth over internal diversity. For example, Jodelet's research claims that there is a high degree of consensus among the foster families in their representations, yet with the kind of interpretative approach she uses it is hard to judge how far the consensus is a feature inherent in her materials or the product of her method of dealing with the materials which emphasizes agreement and downplays conflict.

The status of representations

Although social representations theory emphasizes the importance of conversation and interaction for the generation and transmission of representations, representations are none the less treated as mental entities. Indeed, social representations researchers have paid very little attention to discourse as such. For instance, Jodelet did not consider the talk which took place in her interviews as social interaction; its role was as a pathway to the participants' underlying representations. However, it is possible to consider the talk as much more interactionally determined.

Take the foster families' denial of knowledge about mental illness, noted above. Jodelet treats this as a psychological strategy for managing the potential anxiety which would be released by more explicit formulations about the lodgers' condition. But could such a denial be acting in a very different way, more oriented to the interaction with the researcher? After all, the issue of psychiatric knowledge might be a particularly delicate one when talking to a psychologist who is likely to be considered by the interviewees as an expert in this area. Denying knowledge could be an implicit way of saying 'don't hear me as posing as an expert on mental disorder'. Similar patterns of interaction have been observed where clearly knowledgeable parents talk to paediatricians about their children's illnesses (Silverman, 1987). Whether this particular interpretation is right or wrong, the point is that it is possible to consider another kind of analysis which focuses on the way the talk is a joint product of a particular interaction. This point leads us to discursive psychology, which is the topic of the final section of this chapter.

Review of section 3

- Social representations theorists argue that people understand the world by way of mental images and clusters of concepts which are widely shared across members of a social group and are one of the things which distinguish one group from another.

- Social representations originate and evolve in conversations between people and circulate in the mass media. They also provide a code for communication.

- New representations are developed mentally through processes of anchoring and objectification.

- Jodelet's work on representations of madness suggests that people make complex distinctions between different types of madness which involve largely unvoiced assumptions about cleanliness and contamination.

4 Discursive psychology

Every so often in British political life the news is dominated by the resignation of a government minister, sometimes with wide-reaching political consequences. The scandal associated with defence minister John Profumo in the early 1960s, for example, was widely seen as an important factor contributing to the Conservative failure at the following election. At the end of the 1980s, the resignations of Chancellor Lawson and Conservative Party Chairman Geoffrey Howe were thought to have played an important part in removing Margaret Thatcher from power.

It is tempting to view a political resignation as a clear-cut, objective event with clear-cut consequences. If a minister resigns in disgrace, for example, then his or her political future may be put in doubt; while a resignation over an issue of principle may prepare the way for a heroic comeback. But are resignations events where the sense is both determinate and open to perception? Social constructionists (cf. Wetherell and Maybin, 1996) argue that events in the social world are worked up through representation and argument. Sense is not a natural property but a social and cultural phenomenon. In the political arena, for example, we often witness conflicts over what really happened played out in newspapers and television interviews. Sometimes the issue is as fundamental as whether the event was a resignation at all, rather than a sacking, or a misunderstanding.

4.1 Basic elements of discursive psychology

Discursive psychology attempts to look at how events are constructed in the social and cultural arena along with the psychological implications for the study of people's evaluations and representations. This approach applies the broader perspective of discourse analysis (see Potter and Wetherell, 1987) to concepts at the heartland of mainstream psychology. Unlike attitude research and social representations theory, the focus is much more on everyday interaction, on talk and discourse, on the *activities* which people perform when they make sense of the social world and the *resources* (category systems, vocabularies, notions of persons, etc.) on which these activities depend. What do people *do* with their talk or writing? Discursive psychology shifts the emphasis away from the nature of the static individual to dynamic practices of interaction. I will focus on three basic elements of the theory and illustrate them using a study of Chancellor Lawson's resignation from Prime Minister Thatcher's Cabinet in 1989 (see Edwards and Potter, 1992, Chapter 6). The three basic elements are:

- construction;

- action;

- rhetoric.

You should read the extracts which follow carefully. All the protagonists have now retired from politics, but the issues have not gone away. You might think of more recent examples of resignations or similar controversies. I have not provided much context – but given the familiarity of material of this kind you should be able to imagine the furore surrounding this event.

The first extract comes from an exchange in parliament about Lawson's resignation.

Extract 3.1

Mr Kinnock: When the Prime Minister was asked why the Chancellor resigned, why did she not tell the truth?

The Prime Minister: If my right hon. Friend had wanted to resign on a point of policy, I could have understood that, policy is a matter for ministers. I find it totally incomprehensible that someone who has held the office of Chancellor with high standing, for six years, should want to resign over personality-

[*Interruption*]

Mr Speaker: Order.

The Prime Minister: Over personality, with such suddenness and haste.

Source: Hansard, 31 October, 1989, pp. 831–2

The second extract comes from a major television interview with the Chancellor after his resignation.

Extract 3.2

I explained to her that so long as Alan Walters remained as her personal adviser, conducting himself in the way he did, and indeed holding the views that he was known to hold, then my position as Chancellor (and it would have been the same for anybody else as Chancellor) was untenable.

Source: Chancellor Lawson speaking on *Weekend World*, 5 November 1989;
simplified transcript

Construction

Like social representations theory, discursive psychology is a social constructionist approach; but a different kind of constructionism is involved. Social representations theory is concerned with the way people make sense of their worlds through simplified representations, while discursive psychology is concerned with how people construct versions of the world in the course of their practical interactions, and the way these versions are established as solid, real and independent of the speaker.

Note the difference between the Chancellor's and the Prime Minister's version of his resignation. She constructs it as a baffling action done for personal reasons, while he constructs it as a principled resignation; something that any Chancellor would have been forced to do.

Action

Discursive psychology is concerned with action rather than cognition. It is not trying to move from the materials we can see in Extracts 3.1 and 3.2 to the underlying attitudes or representations of the protagonists. Discursive psychologists claim that in saying and writing things people are performing actions and that the nature of these actions can be revealed through a detailed study of the discourse. The Prime Minister's reply to Mr Kinnock, for example, is both an answer to his question, a defence of her handling of her cabinet, *and* a criticism of Chancellor Lawson.

One consequence of this emphasis is that discursive psychologists have based their research much more on 'naturalistic materials' such as recordings of conversations in everyday and institutional settings, and documents such as newspaper articles and television programmes. When open-ended interviews have been used, these have been studied as a form of interaction in their own right which will help reveal some of the resources that people may draw on in settings outside the interview.

Rhetoric

Discursive psychologists have argued that social psychologists have underestimated the centrality of *conflict* in social life, along with the importance people place on issues of stake and interest. An analysis of rhetoric highlights the point that people's versions of actions, features of the world, of their own mental life, are usually designed to counter real or potential alternatives and are part of ongoing arguments, debates and dialogues (Billig, 1987, 1992). Take the extract from Chancellor Lawson's television interview quoted above. This came a few days after the exchange in the Commons (along with other interviews and press briefings) where Prime Minister Thatcher developed the explanation that Lawson had resigned because of some kind of personal conflict. Note the way Lawson's account works to counter this version by emphasizing that the problem was specific to his role as Chancellor, and would have been so for any Chancellor.

In general, then, what discursive psychologists would claim about an event such as this is that people are *constructing* versions, in the performance of *actions*, and these actions relate to, and often *rhetorically* undermine, alternative constructions. In doing so, they are participating in and developing the collective and communal forms of life which make up their culture. Was Chancellor Lawson's motive for resigning honourable, or did he go because of a rather unseemly personality clash? For the people involved in this dispute the answer to this question is not a psychological one involving looking into Lawson's head; it involves

---

BOX 3.5 What is an individual in discursive psychology?

In the experimental research reviewed in Chapter 1, the individual is viewed as having a mind rather like a complex and rather inflexible computer which struggles to make sense of the social world. Much attitude theory shares this model, as does an important strand of research in the social representations tradition. Discursive psychology is a social constructionist theory which is attempting to shift the focus away from the person and on to the interaction – it moves to a more relational and distributed focus for social psychology (cf. Wetherell and Maybin, 1996). Thus, the question about the Chancellor's resignation is not whether he actually did, or did not, have a particular motive, nor even whether such things as motives exist in some inner psychological space, but rather how motives emerge from interaction and are constructed in the social and cultural realm.

---

much broader judgements about events. Was Alan Walters, the economic advisor, acting improperly? Did Prime Minister Thatcher have her own agenda for the economy?

Discursive psychologists suggest that recognizing this relation between versions of events in the world and versions of mental events has radical consequences. The process of establishing a version of events as correct involves both constructing and defending a believable version of the world and a believable version of the self. That is, people are simultaneously constructing versions of the 'outer stuff' of actions and events and the 'inner stuff' of motives and attitudes. Instead of making the traditional strong distinction between worldly events and psychological processes, discursive psychology treats the nature of both of these things as emergent in discourse.

Before reading on, take some recent newspapers and look at the reporting of some government initiative. Focus on the descriptions of the initiative by government members and opposition members. Look for variations in the way the initiative is characterized – these should not be hard to find! Then consider what activities these varied descriptions might be contributing to. Consider also the way they may be rhetorically designed to counter specific alternatives.   ACTIVITY 3.9

4.2   Attitudes, evaluations and conversation

This section will focus on some of the ways phenomena traditionally understood in terms of attitude theory are understood by workers from a discursive perspective. This should develop the contrast between discursive psychology and attitude theory in more concrete terms, as well as further illustrating the concern with construction, action and rhetoric found in discursive psychology. Unlike attitude theory, the goal is not to identify attitudes as individual mental possessions but to study the actual *practices* of evaluation found in social life, and to show how they throw light on situations involving persuasion.

Given the emphasis discursive psychologists place on action rather than static cognitive events, and particularly on action in natural settings, it is not surprising that researchers have not adopted the kinds of Likert scales used by attitude researchers which seek to tap into one underlying attitude measured out of context. For discursive psychology, the topic is actual evaluations made in particular settings. In fact, one of the best, and simplest, studies looking at attitudes as a feature of interaction was conducted not by a social psychologist but by a conversation analyst (Pomerantz, 1984). Conversation analysis combines aspects of linguistics with aspects of sociology to provide a distinctive approach to social interaction, studying the patterns found in transcripts of tape-recorded interactions (Sacks, 1992). It has been extensively used by discursive psychologists.

4.2.1 Everyday assessments

Pomerantz's study, at first sight anyway, was beautifully simple in design. She took a large number of careful transcripts of tape-recordings of everyday conversation and went through them looking for places where a speaker made an evaluative *assessment* of something; that is, described something as good or bad. She was not concerned with traditional attitude issues – did this assessment reflect a stable underlying disposition?; would it correlate with something the person said or did in another setting? – rather, she was interested in how assessments are part of interaction.

Pomerantz observed that there was a strong regularity in what happens straight after assessments. Overwhelmingly, after someone has made an assessment, the person they are speaking to follows it with their own assessment (e.g. see Extracts 3.3 and 3.4).

Extract 3.3

J: T's-it's a beautiful day out isn't it?

L: Yeah it's jus' gorgeous …

Source: Pomerantz, 1984, p. 65

Extract 3.4

A: (It) was too depre-ssing

B: -Ooooh it is terrible

Source: ibid., p. 67; transcription conventions simplified

Pomerantz further notes that there are some subtle, but very regular, differences between the patterning of second speakers' assessments according to whether they are offering agreement or disagreement. The examples above are of agreements. Agreeing second assessments typically follow with a minimum of delay, the agreement is made clear early in the turn, and the agreement is 'upgraded'. Thus, in Extract 3.3, there is no delay before L starts to speak, the turn is started with the agreement ('Yeah'), and the assessment is upgraded ('beautiful' is strengthened to 'gorgeous').

The pattern is rather different with disagreeing assessments. Here there is typically some delay before the second turn, the disagreeing component will be softened or qualified, and the disagreement will appear later in the turn. Indeed, disagreements are often prefaced by agreements. Extracts 3.5 and 3.6 illustrate some of these features.

Extract 3.5

A: ... You've really both basically honestly gone your own ways

B: Essentially except we've hadda good relationship at home

Source: ibid., p. 72

Extract 3.6

B: ... well a sense of humour, I think is something yer born with Bea.

A: yea. Or it's c- I have the- eh yes, I think a lotta people are, but then I think it can be developed, too.

Source: ibid., pp. 73–4; transcription conventions simplified

Note how in Extract 3.5 and 3.6 the disagreeing component is delayed until later in the turn, and is prefaced with an agreement.

You do not have to take Pomerantz's word for the generality of this pattern. Listen carefully to your next conversation with family or friends, and look out for evaluative assessments. See how many of the typical features you can identify in one conversation.   ACTIVITY 3.10

By treating attitudes (preferences and evaluative assessments) as features of interaction rather than as underlying cognitive entities Pomerantz was able to reveal a strikingly regular organization. These findings have been used to help make sense of a familiar public event: the political speech.

4.2.2   Assessments and oratory

Great oratory has, in the past, often been understood in terms of the special personality features of outstanding or charismatic orators. One of the insights of conversation analysts is that the situation of political oratory is in some important respects rather like a conversation between a speaker and the audience. Pomerantz shows that, in everyday conversation, when a speaker makes an assessment the person being talked to generally provides their own assessment. Now at a political rally, or in the hall of a political conference, the audience cannot simply talk back; they cannot say, 'Yes, the Labour policy on employment is disastrous', or 'Absolutely, we have got law and order cracked'. However, there are conventional and effective ways of producing evaluations in these contexts: people applaud, cheer, boo or, more rarely, heckle.

Researchers into oratory have found that clapping is by no means randomly distributed through a good speech; it is not that the speaker pauses every so often to allow the audience to let off a bit of steam with a clap. Applause regularly follows parts of speeches where the speaker is making an assessment; a claim of the form, 'Our party is brilliant', 'Our policy is great', 'Their party is awful' and so on (although generally a little more subtly put). Just as in an everyday conversation, then, when the speaker comes to an assessment, the audience will want to respond to it with their own assessment.

If this were all there was to effective oratory, anyone could get up on conference platforms and get almost continuous applause by simply stringing together lots of assessments. However, as we are all aware, this does not happen. We have all seen a boring delegate droning on in a way that suggests to the audience that this would be an excellent time to slip out to the toilet. Let's think about this from the point of view of someone sitting in the audience. You are listening to a politician who makes an assessment with which you agree. This puts you in a potentially very tricky situation. You can applaud. But what if you are the only one who does? What if 6,000 people turn to stare at you? Humiliation! You can't check what they are doing because the chances are your seat does not allow you a proper view of the rest of the audience. You could wait and see. But applause which starts late sounds half-hearted – you have got half a second at the absolute outside to start clapping. Given this dilemma, it is a wonder anyone ever applauds a public speaker.

Well, clap they do. The problem is, how is it coordinated so that people dare take part in such a risky activity? Conversation analysts such as Atkinson (1984) and Heritage and Greatbatch (1986) have been able to throw light on this question. They suggest we think of what is going on here in terms of a design problem. How can orators design their assessment in such a way that the audience knows, with plenty of warning, exactly when to start their own agreeing assessment? Everyday conversationalists face a similar problem in predicting when a speaker is going to end their turn of talk so that they can start their own turn seamlessly and without a gap (Nofsinger, 1991).

BOX 3.6 When should you not stop clapping?

Here is one vignette from those years as it actually occurred. A district Party conference was under way in Moscow Province. It was presided over by a new secretary of the District Party Committee, replacing one recently *arrested*. At the conclusion of the conference, a tribute to Comrade Stalin was called for. Of course, everyone stood up (just as everyone had leaped to his feet during the conference at every mention of his name). The small hall echoed with 'stormy applause, rising to an ovation.' For three minutes, four minutes, five minutes, the 'stormy applause, rising to an ovation,' continued. But palms were getting sore and raised arms were already aching. And the older people were panting from exhaustion. It was becoming insufferably silly even to those who really adored Stalin. However, who would dare be the *first* to stop? The secretary of the District Party Committee could have done it. He was standing on the platform, and it was he who had just called for the ovation. But he was a newcomer. He had taken the place of a man who'd been arrested. He was afraid! After all, NKVD men were standing in the hall applauding and watching to see *who* quit first! And in that obscure, small hall, unknown to the Leader, the applause went on – six, seven, eight minutes! They were done for! Their goose was cooked! They couldn't stop now till they collapsed with heart attacks! At the rear of the hall, which was crowded, they could of course cheat a bit, clap less frequently, less vigorously, not so eagerly – but up there with the presidium where everyone could see them? The director of the local paper factory, an independent and strong-minded man, stood with the presidium. Aware of all the falsity and all the impossibility of the situation, he still kept on applauding! Nine minutes! Ten! In anguish he watched the secretary of the District Party Committee, but the latter dared not stop. Insanity! To the last man! With make-believe enthusiasm on their faces, looking at each other with faint hope, the district leaders were just going to go on and on applauding till they fell where they stood, till they were carried out of the hall on stretchers! And even then those who were left would not falter … Then, after eleven minutes, the director of the paper factory assumed a businesslike expression and sat down in his seat. And, oh, a miracle took place! Where had the universal, uninhibited, indescribable enthusiasm gone? To a man, everyone else stopped dead and sat down. They had been saved! The squirrel had been smart enough to jump off his revolving wheel.

That, however, was how they discovered who the independent people were. And that was how they went about eliminating them. That same night the factory director was arrested. They easily pasted ten years on him on the pretext of something quite different. But after he had signed Form 206, the final document of the interrogation, his interrogator reminded him: 'Don't ever be the first to stop applauding!'.

(Solzhenitsyn, 1978, vol. 1, pp. 69–70)

The research done up to now suggests there are a rather limited set of designs for arranging the onset of applause effectively. In fact, Heritage and Greatbatch (1986), in a study of almost the entire set of speeches from the 1981 party conferences in Britain, identified six basic designs or, as they called them, rhetorical formats: contrasts; lists; puzzle-solutions; headline-punchline; position taking; and pursuit. All these formats provide information for the audience concerning precisely *when* applause is due. For example, with contrast structures – which are the most common format – the audience is readied to applaud in good time by the onset of the first part and are thus well prepared by the completion of the second.

In the example shown in Extract 3.7, from the 1994 Tory Party Conference, the Home Secretary, Michael Howard, is attacking Labour's law and order policy. He works up to the contrast (marked by the A and B arrows) with a very deliberate three-part list (marked by the arrows at 1, 2 and 3).

Extract 3.7

Howard: The moment the bill went into committee (.)

Labour showed their true colours (0.8)

Reforming the right to silence (.)

1 → they voted against it (0.2)

Curbing bail bandits (0.2)

2 → they voted against it (0.4)

Locking up young tearaways (0.2)

3 → they voted against it (.)

When it comes to the fight against crime

A → judge the opposition not by their words

B → but BY THEIR VOTES

Audience: [Applause 8 seconds]

(Numbers in brackets show pauses timed in tenths of a second; full stops in brackets show pauses which are hearable but too short to measure; capitals mark talk which is louder than the surrounding.)

In their study, Heritage and Greatbatch found that two-thirds of 1,588 sets of applause followed one or more of the six rhetorical formats they identified. Put another way, if you couch some evaluative statement in one of these rhetorical formats it is at least twice as likely to get applause, and in some situations may be nearly ten times as likely. Of course, that is not all there is to it. Speakers can use contrasts or lists in a

*Michael Howard in action at a
Tory Party Conference*

confused way, downgrading their effectiveness, or they can enhance their
effectiveness by combining formats (as in the example above) or by coordinating spoken oratory with suitable gestures (Atkinson, 1984).

If you have time and a video recorder, it is a relatively simple matter to   ACTIVITY 3.11
duplicate this research. Record the speech of a cabinet member (or a political
non-entity) and then run through the tape for the sections of speech just
before applause. If you want to get very sophisticated you can transcribe these
parts of the speech and even time the applause. Atkinson suggests that roughly
eight seconds is considered normal. Less than that sounds a bit lukewarm;
more than that sounds particularly enthusiastic. Look for the use of lists and
contrasts. Consider the way the gestures fit in with the speech.

If you do not have time or access to a video recorder, simply look at a recent
newspaper report of a political speech. Atkinson suggests that journalists often
use applause as a guide for what to quote, so the quotations in the papers are
often contrasts and three-part lists. Can you confirm this?

4.2.3   Construction, action and rhetoric revisited

The conversation-analytic work on assessments and oratory shows some
of the virtues of moving the focus away from events and processes in the
heads of individuals and considering instead the sorts of practices that
go on when people are using evaluations in social contexts. The theoretical ideas of discursive psychology further eat away at the assumptions of

traditional approaches to attitudes and highlight previously unnoticed or ignored features of people's evaluative practices. Let me illustrate this with the themes of action, construction and rhetoric.

The stress on action suggests the importance of considering not just the content of the assessment but what people are *doing* when they are making assessments or evaluating a product or a political policy. These things are activities in their own right, and organized as such. For example, Pomerantz's study of assessments allows us to compare the performance of this action with others, such as giving an invitation, say, or making an accusation. If we consider a research issue such as racism or sexism, our way of understanding what is going on becomes rather different. Instead of treating attitude expressions as an abstract way of diagnosing whether or not a person is prejudiced, evaluative assessments are understood as actions in their own right which may be blaming or hostile towards minority groups. Some of the implications of this reformulation are picked up in the next chapter.

The stress on construction highlights another issue. When people are offering evaluative assessments, they involve categorization and description of the 'attitude object'. Traditional attitude and public-opinion measures often use single words or short phrases that may at first sight seem to be transparent stand-ins for the objects themselves (cf. Box 3.2 and measuring attitudes to nuclear power). However, doubts immediately arise. First of all, there are a lot of difficulties in treating some words as standing for simple attitude objects; the use of descriptions such as 'coloured immigrants' in attitude surveys is an example where all sorts of technical and definitional (not to say political) issues are presupposed (Potter and Wetherell, 1987, pp. 43–56). Secondly, the way the attitude issue is constructed can have a major impact on how people respond to it. For example, during the controversy in the 1980s over the placing of Cruise Missiles in the UK, many surveys of public opinion were carried out. However, the results of these surveys varied widely according to how the question was worded. For example, people were less positive about Cruise Missiles when they were described as American Cruise Missiles on British soil, but they could be made more positive by describing them as Cruise Missiles based in Britain to counter the Soviet threat (see Potter, 1996). The point is that there is not a simple attitude object which people are responding to; such objects are always constructed in talk and discourse. While this remains a problem for traditional attitude and opinion research, it becomes a fascinating research area for discursive psychology.

The stress on rhetoric encourages us to consider how evaluative assessments are embedded in arguments. Billig expresses this as follows:

> ... attitudes are not to be viewed solely as individual evaluative responses towards a given stimulus object. Instead, attitudes are stances taken in matters of controversy: they are positions in arguments (Billig, 1987; 1992). Every attitude *in favour* of a position is also, implicitly but more often explicitly, also a stance *against* the

counter-position. Attitudinal justifications and criticisms are not to be seen as epiphenomena, tacked onto some more basic psychological predispositions, but are integral to attitudes qua attitudes.

(1991, p. 143)

This encouraged Billig to study, not abstract attitudes, but the discussions and arguments within which evaluations are made and 'strong views' expressed. The topic, then, becomes the arguments: the way they are developed in everyday contexts such as families or newspaper stories, and how they are organized around basic social and ideological dilemmas (Billig et al., 1988).

4.3   Representations in actions

Both discursive psychology and social representations theory treat representations as a crucial part of human life. However, they have a rather different conception of representation. As we saw in section 3, in social representations theory the place for representations is in the head. There they are used to help the person understand the world and can be a basis for evaluations and actions in talk. In discursive psychology the issue is rather different. How is a particular representation constructed to perform some action?

Let me flesh this out with a deceptively simple example (see Extract 3.8).

Extract 3.8

C: [referring to a club where the defendant and the victim met]

its where girls and fellas meet isn't it?

W: People go there.

Source: Drew, 1990, p. 45

ACTIVITY 3.12

Spend some time thinking about Extract 3.8 before going on to read the discussion. It comes from a court case. C is Counsel for the Defence and W is the (female) Witness. But can you identify the type of crime, and what might be going on in the case? Think about what C says, and what W replies. Speculate about why C might have said precisely what they did, and why W replies in precisely this way. Now read on to see how close your interpretation is to the one offered here.

The extract comes from a paper by Drew (1990), although the points are also developed in Wooffitt (1990, pp. 13–15). It comes, as you have probably guessed, from a rape trial. Counsel for the defence is examining the central prosecution witness, the victim of the alleged rape. The Counsel is referring to a club where the defendant and victim met. Wooffitt points out that both Counsel and the Witness produce versions of activities that take place in the club. These are not formally contradictory (girls and fellas are people, after all) – yet these versions can be the basis for different inferences on the part of the jury. The Counsel's description, 'it's where girls and fellas meet', gives an impression of the intentions and expectations the clientele might have of one another. People go to the club to pick up a partner for sex. The alternative description offered by the Witness, 'people go there', works to neutralize these implications.

A lot of the work is done by the categorizations: 'girls', 'fellas', 'people'. The Counsel's version, the categories 'girls' and 'fellas', not only establishes gender as a relevant concern, but implies a particular *style* of relationship. Constructing a sexual motive for the victim is the basis for an attack on her credibility. Alternative categorizations such as 'men and women', 'girls and boys' would not do the same job. The categorization 'people' used by the Witness, in contrast, is gender and age neutral. The general point I want to emphasize is the way the contest between Counsel and Witness is conducted here through alternative representations of events; the representations are performing the actions of blaming and defending.

Note also another characteristic feature of the kinds of analyses performed by discursive psychologists. Just as we saw (in the discussion in section 4.1) different versions of the events prior to Chancellor Lawson's resignation implicating different versions of his *motivation*, here the different descriptions of the club implicate different *intentions* on the part of the witness. Did she go to the club for a drink and a chat, or was she intending to have sex? One version implies the former; the other the latter. Building versions of the world has direct implications for the mental life of the participants. We might understand what is going on here as a dispute about the politics of mind.

One way to highlight the difference between social representations theory and discursive psychology is to show how the two approaches might deal with the same piece of data. The example in Extract 3.9 includes a passage of data from Jodelet's (1991) book *Madness and Social Representations* and her analysis of this material.

Extract 3.9

Whatever it does, the population never completely erases the silent and close menace of insanity from its consciousness:

> 'I get the impression some people are going to raise objections because they're afraid. Because you do see it, you know! I always wait for my little girl when she leaves school, in a square with a bus stop. I wait there along with lots of other mothers, in the car. Some of them come up to talk to you, to joke with you because you're a woman. All the same, I don't think some of them are very good for the community. Some of them you don't notice,

but there are others ... There's one of them, on the road up towards Saint-Mamet, one of them who I don't like one little bit. If I went out by bike I know I would meet him. Perhaps he's quite harmless. I don't know. It's just the way he looks. He makes an impression on me. He walks a bit like a dancer, and he's got a black face, and his eyes ... he stares at you. It's really dreadful and it scares me. There's something about him which frightens me. His face is ... I don't know how to describe it but it worries me. His eyes stare at you. He stares at you when he looks at you. That's all. I can't describe the effect it has on me. It upsets me.'

In the face of this multiform, incessant presence of insanity a subtle knowledge evolves, one which makes it possible to stifle the onset of this obscure apprehension, transformed into the terse *leitmotif* 'he frightens you', and which sometimes overwhelms its victim with a specific illness: the 'attack of fright'. Seen from this viewpoint, the smoothing away of emotional reasons seems to result from a collective technique of maintaining a calm, harmonious social façade.

Source: Jodelet, 1991, pp. 54–5

This is a complex quotation and analysis. However, some brief points are sufficient to show the differences between a discursive and social representational approach.

The stress on action in discursive psychology encourages us to consider what may be being *done* by the talk in this extract. We do not have available the question or point put by the interviewer, but from what is said right at the start the issue seems to be possible objections to the community care scheme. This may well be a sensitive topic; the speaker may be concerned not to present herself as prejudiced against mentally ill people. She does not directly align herself with the people who may raise objections, but she spends some time providing the kind of reason (fear) that could be used as the basis for raising objections. So here is a first point of contrast. Fear in Jodelet's analysis is something that shows through the extract; indeed, it is mainly *stifled* or *smoothed* away to lie below the surface. In my discourse analytic reading, the talk is seen as *highlighting* the fear, and it is highlighted precisely because it is needed to justify a reaction that might be heard as prejudiced. Indeed, a discourse analytic interpretation is not concerned with whether there is, or is not, fear; it is focused on what *a description of* fear is doing in the extract.

If we continue with the speculation that the speaker is addressing an issue which relates to prejudice, then we can understand some other features of the passage. Having introduced the issue of fear, the speaker immediately gives a description of something that is quite the opposite – she paints a brief picture of joking conversations she had with some of the lodgers while waiting for her daughter to come out of school. This is presumably one of the features of the extract that led Jodelet to write of the threatening 'multiform, incessant presence of insanity'. In a discourse analytic alternative, however, this brief description would be seen as doing something very different, but very important. It is showing that the speaker does not have a *general* prejudice against mentally ill people; rather, she is scared by some of them who look and act in frightening ways, but is happy to share a joke with others. And note how carefully this judgement is managed. She says that she could be wrong ('perhaps he's quite harmless' – this displays how reasonable she is) but provides quite a lot of detailed description to justify the fear. It is not a fear based on blind prejudice; she presents herself as an open-minded women who encounters some disturbing people. On this interpretation, the extract shares features with other kinds of discourse where there is a potential for being identified as prejudiced or racist (Van Dijk, 1992; Wetherell and Potter, 1992). This becomes a subtle version of the familiar phrase: some of my best friends are black (or gay, disabled, mentally ill ...).

It is impossible to provide more than a speculative alternative interpretation here. Only a small fragment of talk is available; it is presented in a cleaned up form which has wiped out many of the discourse features (intonation, delay, hesitations, etc.) that would be analytically helpful in a proper transcript; and there is no information about what went on before and after (crucially, the researcher's question). Nevertheless, the basic contrast should be clear. Jodelet's social representations analysis is trying to read *through* people's talk to possible underlying emotions and their repression. My discourse analytic interpretation is attempting to work with the talk as a piece of interaction in its own right, where each of its elements may be relevant to some current activity.

In the previous chapter, which presented a psychodynamic account of group process, examples were given of the kinds of conversations and exchanges which go on in groups. You might like to consider the way a discursive psychologist might approach these data and the different focus on the individual and the individual's psychology found in the discursive approach compared with the psychodynamic perspective.

4.4   Facts and the dilemma of stake

One of the features of interaction highlighted by researchers into discourse is that in everyday talk people and groups are commonly taken to be entities with desires, motives, institutional allegiances, and so on. They are taken to be entities with a personal or institutional *stake* in their actions. This sense of people as *interested* and the way interests are managed is something that is often absent in traditional social psychological research characterized by what Tajfel (1972) called 'experiments in a social vacuum'; where people are abstracted from the complex weave of interests and entitlements which characterize everyday life.

The referencing of someone's, or some group's, stake is one principal way of discounting the significance of an action. For example, an offer may be discounted as an attempt to influence; a blaming can be discounted as merely the product of spite. When the 'call girl' Mandy Rice-Davies was asked in court about a member of the aristocracy's denial that he had sex with her she famously replied, 'Well he would say that, wouldn't he?' Noting that the aristocratic gentleman has an interest in making such a denial is treated as sufficient to undermine it. For this reason, Edwards and Potter (1992) argue that people may be caught in a *dilemma of stake* where anything they say or do may be potentially discounted as a product of their interest in its outcome.

Edwards and Potter maintain that people will manage this dilemma in a variety of different ways, and that this management should be one of the topics for discourse analysis. The concern is with the way participants treat *each other* as interested, or fail to do so. Edwards and Potter are not suggesting that discursive psychologists should start researching people's *actual* stake or interest; rather, they want to look at regularities in the way *assumed* stake or interests become treated in interaction.

4.4.1   Stake inoculation

One line of research which interests me is the way in which people construct representations which are resistant to being discounted as mere products of stake (Potter, 1996). As I noted in section 4.3, representations of events and other people are often ways of performing actions. The action can be undermined by relating it to an interest. There are various ways of resisting such undermining; one of these can be called 'stake inoculation'. Just as flu inoculation is intended to prevent flu, a stake inoculation is intended to prevent a claim being undermined as a product of stake. Extract 3.10 is a simple example taken from a newspaper account of some research on madness and creativity.

Extract 3.10

Psychiatrist reveals the agony and the lunacy of great artists

The stereotype of the tortured genius suffering for his art and losing his mind in a sea of depression, sexual problems and drink turns out to be largely true, a psychiatrist says today.

While scientists, philosophers and politicians can all suffer from the odd personality defect, for real mental instability you need to look at writers and painters, says Felix Post.

Dr Post was initially sceptical, but having looked at the lives of nearly 300 famous men he believes exceptional creativity and psychiatric problems are intertwined. In some way, mental ill health may fuel some forms of creativity, he concludes.

Source: *The Guardian*, 30 June, 1994

What is interesting here is the description of Dr Post as 'initially scepti-cal' (see first line of final paragraph). Why put it this way? One clue is hinted at in the article itself – there is a familiar stereotype of the mad artist. Perhaps Dr Post has been influenced by this stereotype, setting out to find evidence for it. However, the extract is 'stake inoculated' against this way of undermining it by referencing the Doctor's initial scepticism. He was not looking for this link, it suggests; on the contrary, he expected to undermine it but was forced by the evidence to recognize its exist-ence. Note again, this analysis does not depend on whether Dr Post was, or was not, sceptical – what counts is how the description of him as sceptical works in the article.

BOX 3.7   A new social cognition?

The study of discourse and rhetoric has started to rework a range of concepts traditionally the province of cognitive psychology or social cognition. Discursive psychologists want to transform the study of attitudes into the study of evaluative assessments, and treat representations as constructions produced in discourse to perform particular actions. Similar reworking has been proposed for memory (e.g. Conway, 1992), causal attribution (e.g. Edwards and Potter, 1993), categorization (e.g. Potter and Wetherell, 1987, Chapter 6), scripts (Edwards, 1994), social identity (Widdicombe and Wooffitt, 1995), and even such apparently individual/biological notions as emotion (Buttny, 1993). This raises the possibility of a whole new style of social cognition which is concerned with the practical role of mentalistic language (cf. Coulter, 1989; Edwards, 1996).

Let me end with a second example of stake inoculation which illustrates the subtlety with which it can be managed. At the same time, this shows how attentive the discourse researcher has to be to features of discourse that might easily be overlooked as trivial. Sacks (1992) has stressed that every feature of interaction, including hesitations, pauses, corrections, is potentially relevant to the activities being done by the talk. Consider Extracts 3.11 and 3.12.

Extract 3.11

Jones: There have been a lot of ideas put, *what is it*, that the majority of rapes are committed by Islanders or Mäoris and ...

Source: Wetherell and Potter, 1992, p. 96

Extract 3.12

Jimmy: Connie had a short skirt on *I don't know*

Source: Potter, 1996, p. 131

The point I want to emphasize here is that both of these descriptions are particularly delicate ones, where the speaker's interest is likely to be of special concern. Extract 3.11 comes from a long passage of talk in which Jones makes a number of highly racist descriptions of minority groups living in New Zealand. Extract 3.12 is part of a dispute in a relationship-counselling session where Jimmy is accusing his partner of flirting with other men, but also dealing with the accusation that he is jealous. In each case, the speaker qualifies his description with an expression of uncertainty: *what is it* and *I don't know*. One thing that these expressions do is work against the suggestion, in Jones's case, that he is actively noting negative ideas about minority groups because of his racism or hostility, and, in Jimmy's case, that he is jealously inspecting his partner's appearance. These throw-away phrases, easily missed on the tape, are beautifully designed stake inoculations: displays of disinterestedness precisely at points where this could be a particular issue. These extracts show again what can be gained through close attention to the detail of interaction, and the virtues of studying natural interaction rather than starting with interviews or laboratory simulations.

4.5 Problems and prospects

Discursive psychology is the most recent of the three approaches discussed in this chapter and it focuses on rather different questions. As we have seen, rather than centre on the cognitive processes that underlie attitudes and representations, it is concerned with how versions of the world are constructed, and how those constructions are fitted to interaction. It is too early to say to what extent this will prove to be an alternative to other approaches and how far it will supplement them. On a more methodological level, discursive psychologists have attempted to develop a research approach which is both qualitative and rigorous by focusing on talk and texts themselves.

Discursive psychology has attracted a range of critical responses from psychologists who take a more traditional cognitive and experimental perspective (see Abrams and Hogg, 1990, and a range of papers discussed in Conway, 1992). For some of these critics, the problems with discursive psychology are methodological. They doubt that the analytic approach can be made rigorous without the discipline of significance tests and randomization, and they worry that it may open up an abyss of alternative interpretations of texts and transcripts with no possibility of choosing between them (a few of these critics simply see experiments as the only path towards reliable knowledge).

Consider the various criticisms of discursive psychology listed here. What responses can you imagine a discursive psychologist would make to them?   ACTIVITY 3.13

Table 3.1 A comparison of perspectives in terms of their theorizing of cognition, construction and action

	Cognition	Construction	Action
Attitude theory	Attitudes are overwhelmingly treated as cognitive entities of some kind	The issue of how the objects of attitudes are constructed is generally ignored	Attitudes are ways of understanding the world which influence action, but are not themselves parts of actions. Attitude theorists have not studied what people do with attitudinal evaluations
Social representations	Social representations are treated as cognitive entities and images circulating in conversation and the media. Anchoring and objectification are cognitive processes used to explain the development of social representations	Social representations is a constructionist theory. It emphasizes processes in conversation and the media as well as cognitive processes of anchoring and objectification	Social representations are ways of understanding the world which influence action, but are not themselves parts of actions. Social representations theorists have not studied what representations are used to do
Discursive psychology	Discursive psychology studies texts and talk for how they are constructed and what they do. It does not try to explain these things in terms of cognitive processes	Discursive psychology is a constructionist perspective. It emphasizes the way versions of actions and events are constructed in discourse	Discursive psychology takes the construction of versions of the world and of mental life to be part of the performance of actions. The focus of analysis is on how constructions enable particular actions

Other criticisms include concerns about the move away from studying psychology in terms of 'inner' processes and entities seen as located within unique, private and detached individuals. Since the widespread demise of behaviourist approaches, the cognitive approach has become central to psychology, and attempts to question and reformulate it are treated with suspicion or even incredulity. Likewise, discursive psychology is at odds with the kind of psychodynamic approach to social life developed in the previous chapter which also seeks to find causal entities below the 'surface', although there have been some notable attempts at integration (e.g. see Hollway, 1988). Whether discursive psychology can provide a systematic approach to psychology without traditional cognitive psychological assumptions is open to question, but it has certainly provoked some profound discussion of the topic (Edwards, 1996).

Social representations researchers have responded by stressing what they see as the limits of a language-centred approach to interaction (Moscovici, 1985, 1994). As Moscovici writes:

> The richness and originality of meanings, this is indeed what we try to communicate to one another. But in this communication linguistic forms are not enough to explain how the communicated message is received and then understood. Why? Because we perform many more practical operations on it before transmitting it or in order to receive it ... Too often the communication of a message does not coincide with linguistic communication properly speaking.
>
> *(1994, pp. 164–5)*

Moscovici argues in this paper that social representations are not what are communicated so much as the presuppositions for what is communicated. This has been an area of fruitful mutual dialogue between social representations researchers and discursive psychologists which looks set to continue (for a review see de Rosa, 1994).

A final set of difficulties with discursive psychology has been raised by psychologists involved with social criticism. For them, discursive psychology provides only a limited basis for criticizing current social organizations because of the tension between taking a more relativist social constructionist perspective and treating power, institutions and collectivities as real entities that can be the starting point for social analysis (Parker, 1992). This critique raises profound and difficult questions about the nature of knowledge, the status of analytic claims, realism and relativism, and the nature of the world which is being researched. Some of these issues will appear again in the next chapter, where a critical, discourse-oriented approach to the issue of racism is introduced.

Review of section 4

- Discursive psychology is concerned with people's talk and their texts as social practices in their own right. It is concerned with action, construction, rhetoric and the way building versions of the world is related to building versions of the self.

- Evaluative assessments appear in regular patterns depending whether they display agreement or disagreement. Applause at party political conferences, for example, can be seen as an agreeing assessment made by an audience which is coordinated by a range of rhetorical formats.

- Representations are used in the performance of actions. Analysis can reveal how specific elements in the representation contribute to the performance of the action.

- People are often caught in a dilemma of stake, which they may manage by constructing their versions as factual and independent of their own interests. Discursive psychologists study the devices people use for fact construction. Stake inoculation involves protecting discourse from being discounted as merely a product of interests.

Further reading

For a high-level and sophisticated overview of attitude research from a cognitive, experimental and North American perspective, see Fiske, S.T. and Taylor, S.E. (1991) *Social Cognition* (2nd edn), Reading, Mass., Addison-Wesley. It discusses different ways of theorizing attitudes and attitude change and reviews and integrates a large amount of research. You should focus particularly on Chapters 1 and 11.

There is no single clear introduction to social representations theory. Moscovici's own account is hard going, but rewards attention: Moscovici, S. (1984) 'The phenomenon of social representations', in Farr, R.M. and Moscovici, S. (eds) *Social Representations,* Cambridge, Cambridge University Press. For a more general study which is rich and interesting, although not always easy to follow, see Jodelet, D. (1991) *Madness and Social Representations*, Hemel Hempstead, Harvester Wheatsheaf.

For an overview of discursive psychology which illustrates its main features through a series of studies of political disputes, see Edwards, D. and Potter, J. (1992) *Discursive Psychology*, London, Sage. For a discursive approach to representation, see Potter, J. (1996) *Representing Reality: Discourse, Rhetoric and Social Construction*, London, Sage.

References

Abrams, D. and Hogg, M. (1990) 'The context of discourse: let's not throw out the baby with the bathwater', *Philosophical Psychology*, vol. 3, pp. 219–25.

Azjen, I. (1988) *Attitudes, Personality and Behaviour*, Buckingham, Open University Press.

Azjen, I. and Fishbein, M. (1977) 'Attitude-behavior relations: a theoretical analysis and review of empirical research', *Psychological Bulletin*, vol. 84, pp. 888–918.

Atkinson, J.A.M. (1984) *Our Master's Voices: The Language and Body Language of Politics*, London, Methuen.

Bem, D.J. (1970) *Beliefs, Attitudes and Human Affairs*. Belmont, Brooks/Cole.

Billig, M. (1987) *Arguing and Thinking: A Rhetorical Approach to Social Psychology*, Cambridge, Cambridge University Press.

Billig, M. (1991) *Ideologies and Opinions*, London, Sage.

Billig, M. (1992) *Talking of the Royal Family*, London, Routledge.

Billig, M., Condor, S., Edwards, D., Gane, M., Middleton, D.J. and Radley, A.R. (1988) *Ideological Dilemmas: A Social Psychology of Everyday Thinking*, London, Sage.

Buttny, R. (1993) *Social Accountability in Communication*, London, Sage.

Conway, M.A. (ed.)(1992) 'Developments and debates in the study of human memory', *The Psychologist*, vol. 5, pp. 439–55.

Corey, S.M. (1937) 'Professed attitude and actual behavior', *Journal of Educational Psychology*, vol. 28, pp. 271–80.

Coulter, J. (1989) *Mind In Action*, Oxford, Polity Press.

Dawes, R.M., Singer, D. and Lemons, F. (1972) 'An experimental analysis of the contrast effect and its implications for intergroup communication and the indirect assessment of attitudes', *Journal of Personality and Social Psychology*, vol. 21, pp. 281–95.

de Rosa, A.S. (1994) 'From theory to metatheory in social representations – the lines of argument of a theoretical methodological debate', *Social Science Information*, vol. 33, pp. 273–304.

di Giacomo, J.P. (1980) 'Intergroup alliances and rejections within a protest movement (analysis of social representations)', *European Journal of Social Psychology*, vol. 10, pp. 329–44.

Drew, P. (1990) 'Strategies in the contest between lawyers and witnesses', in Levi, J.N. and Walker, A.G. (eds) *Language in the Judicial Process*, New York, Plenum.

Edwards, D. (1994) 'Script formulations: an analysis of event descriptions in conversation', *Journal of Language and Social Psychology*, vol. 13, pp. 211–47.

Edwards, D. (1996) *Discourse and Cognition*, London, Sage.

Edwards, D. and Potter, J. (1992) *Discursive Psychology*, London, Sage.

Edwards, D. and Potter, J. (1993) 'Language and causation: a discursive action model of description and attribution', *Psychological Review*, vol. 100, pp. 23–41.

Fishbein, M. and I. Azjen (1975) *Belief, Attitude, Intention and Behaviour: An Introduction to Theory and Research*, Reading, Mass., Addison-Wesley.

Giles, M. and Cairns, E. (1995) 'Blood donation and Azjen's theory of planned behaviour: an examination of perceived behavioural control', *British Journal of Social Psychology*, vol. 34, pp. 173–88.

Heritage, J. and Greatbatch, D. (1986) 'Generating applause: a study of rhetoric and response at party political conferences', *American Journal of Sociology*, vol. 92, pp. 110–57.

Herzlich, C. (1973) *Health and Illness: A Social Psychological Analysis*, London, Academic Press.

Hollway, W. (1988) *Subjectivity and Method in Psychology: Gender, Meaning and Science*, London, Sage.

Jodelet, D. (1991) *Madness and Social Representations*, Hemel Hempstead, Harvester Wheatsheaf.

Jones, E.E. and Sigall, H. (1971) 'The bogus pipeline: a new paradigm for measuring affect and attitude', *Psychological Bulletin*, vol. 76, pp. 349–64.

Lalljee, M. (1996) 'The interpreting self: an experimentalist perspective', in Stevens, R. (ed.) *Understanding the Self*, London, Sage/The Open University (Book 1 in this series).

LaPiere, R.T. (1934) 'Attitudes vs actions', *Social Forces*, vol. 13, pp. 230–7.

McGuire, W.J. (1985) 'Attitudes and attitude measurement', in Lindzey, G. and Aronson, E. (eds) *The Handbook of Social Psychology*, vol. II, New York, Random House.

Moscovici, S. (1976) *La Psychoanalyse: Son Image et Son Public* (rev. edn), Paris, Presses Universitaires de France.

Moscovici, S. (1984) 'The phenomenon of social representations', in Farr, R.M. and Moscovici, S. (eds) *Social Representations*, Cambridge, Cambridge University Press.

Moscovici, S. (1985) 'Comment on Potter and Litton', *British Journal of Social Psychology*, vol. 24, pp. 91–3.

Moscovici, S. (1994) 'Social representations and pragmatic communication', *Social Science Information*, vol. 33, pp. 163–77.

Myers, D.G. (1993) *Social Psychology* (4th edn), New York, McGraw-Hill.

Nofsinger, R.E. (1991) *Everyday Conversation*, London, Sage.

Pomerantz, A. (1984) 'Agreeing and disagreeing with assessments: some features of preferred/dispreferred turn shapes', in Atkinson, J.M. and Heritage, J. (eds) *Structures of Social Action: Studies in Conversation Analysis*, Cambridge, Cambridge University Press.

Parker, I. (1992) *Discourse Dynamics: Critical Analysis for Social and Individual Psychology*, London, Routledge.

Potter, J. (1996) *Representing Reality: Discourse, Rhetoric and Social Construction*, London, Sage.

Potter, J. and Wetherell, M. (1987) *Discourse and Social Psychology: Beyond Attitudes and Behaviour*, London, Sage.

Potter, J. and Wetherell, M. (1995) 'Discourse analysis', in Smith, J., Harré, R. and Van Langenhove, L. (eds) *Rethinking Methods in Psychology*, London, Sage.

Rosen, R.D. (1978) *Psychobabble: Fast Talk and Quick Cure in the Era of Feeling*, London, Wildwood House.

Sacks, H. (1992) *Lectures on Conversation*, Oxford, Blackwell.

Shapiro, M. (1988) *The Politics of Representation: Writing Practices in Biography, Photography, and Policy Analysis*, Wisconsin, University of Wisconsin Press.

Silverman, D. (1987) *Communication and Medical Practice*, London, Sage.

Smith, J. (1987) 'Making people offers they can't refuse: a social psychological analysis of attitude change', in Hawthorn, J. (ed.) *Propaganda, Persuasion and Power*, London, Edward Arnold.

Snyder, M. and Swann, W.B. Jr (1976) 'When actions reflect attitudes: the politics of impression management', *Journal of Personality and Social Psychology*, vol. 34, pp. 1034–42.

Solzhenitsyn, A. (1978) *The Gulag Archipelago*, vol. 1, London, Collins.

Tajfel, H. (1972) 'Experiments in a vacuum', in Israel, J.A. and Tajfel, H. (eds) *The Context of Social Psychology*, London, Academic Press.

Van Dijk, T.A. (1992) 'Discourse and the denial of racism', *Discourse and Society*, vol. 3, pp. 87–118.

Wetherell, M. and Maybin, J. (1996) 'The distributed self: a social constructionist perspective', in Stevens, R. (ed.) *Understanding the Self*, London, Sage/The Open University (Book 1 in this series).

Wetherell, M. and Potter, J. (1992) *Mapping the Language of Racism: Discourse and the Legitimation of Exploitation*, Brighton, Harvester Wheatsheaf; New York, Columbia University Press.

Wicker, A.W. (1971) 'Attitudes versus actions: the relationship of overt and behavioural responses to attitude objects', in Thomas, K. (ed.) *Attitudes and Behaviour*, Harmondsworth, Penguin Books.

Widdicombe, S. and Wooffitt, R. (1995) *The Language of Youth Subcultures: Social Identity in Action*, London, Harvester Wheatsheaf.

Wooffitt, R. (1990) 'On the analysis of interaction: an introduction to conversation analysis', in Luff, P., Frohlich, D. and Gilbert, G.N. (eds) *Computers and Conversation*, New York, Academic Press.

Zanna, M.P. and Rempel, J.K. (1988) 'Attitudes: a new look at an old concept', in Bar-Tal, D. and Kruglanski, A.W. (eds) *The Social Psychology of Knowledge*, Cambridge, Cambridge University Press.

CHAPTER 4

GROUP CONFLICT AND THE SOCIAL PSYCHOLOGY OF RACISM

by Margaret Wetherell

Contents

1   Introduction

This chapter will explore a cluster of problems and issues which have preoccupied social psychologists at least since the Second World War. Events such as the persecution of the Jews in Nazi Germany in the 1930s and 1940s, the 'official' marginalization of black people in South Africa through apartheid policies, the history of response and counter-response in Northern Ireland, or any number of conflicts happening on a daily basis, push social psychological explanation to its limits. These events are often of global significance, with complex political, economic and social histories, involving large numbers of people. Yet, since they do involve people, acting individually and collectively, they raise important questions about the *psychology* of social conflict and what is known as the social psychology of *intergroup* relations.

The main intergroup situation we will be concerned with in this chapter will be issues of 'race' and racism. Most research on the social psychology of intergroup relations has concerned problems of discrimination, stereotyping and the relationship between majority groups and minority groups from different ethnic backgrounds. Perhaps because it has seemed more irrational than other forms of conflict, 'race' has been seen as a more appropriate topic for the psychologist than class conflict or conflict between religious and nationalist groups. The first section of the chapter will look at the issues involved in developing a social psychological analysis of racism. The remaining sections will look at the problems racism presents from several different theoretical perspectives – from the perspective of experimental social psychologists, psychodynamic researchers and social constructionists. The previous chapter of this volume looked at attitudes, social representations and discourse, while Chapters 1 and 2 examined group processes. In this chapter we will see how insights from these areas have been applied to make sense of larger-scale forms of human interaction.

Aims of Chapter 4

The aims of this chapter are:

- To review social psychological approaches to issues of 'race' and racism.

- To demonstrate how lines of research considered in previous chapters, such as social identity theory (Chapter 1), psychodynamic theory (Chapter 2) and discursive psychology (Chapter 3), have been applied to these issues.

- To compare and contrast social psychological theories of intergroup conflict in terms of the emphasis they place on 'human nature'.

2 Setting the scene

2.1 'Race' and racism in the UK

Racism is the process of marginalizing, excluding and discriminating against those defined as different on the basis of their skin colour or ethnic group membership. Racist practices have the effect of maintaining power inequalities between groups. The most vivid demonstration of racism comes in the form of violent physical attacks or harassment and a recent Home Office British Crime Survey estimated that there were 140,000 such incidents in 1992 in the UK, of which only 7–8,000 were reported to the police. Eight people died as a consequence of racist attacks during this period (Skellington, 1995).

Such attacks take place against the background of a climate of opinion among the white community in the UK which is fragmented and contradictory. On the one hand, there are many who find racism repugnant, who stress the importance of equal opportunities, and who call for new legislation to reinforce the civil powers of the laws against 'racial' discrimination introduced during the mid 1960s to the mid 1970s. On the other hand, there is the legacy of hostility to black immigration, evidence of continued and widespread discrimination in employment, housing and education, and some clear failures of political will.

A 1993 Gallup survey of white British opinion found that 25 per cent said they would object to living next door to non-white people, 10 per cent wanted anti-racism laws to be abolished, while three-quarters felt that 'race' relations in Britain were 'only fair' or 'poor' (Skellington, 1995). More positively, 40 per cent of the sample of 959 people questioned wanted the laws banning discriminatory practices strengthened. In many respects, this marks a considerable shift of opinion from the 1950s and 1960s when much immigration occurred. As Brown (1992) notes, until 1968, discrimination in employment on the grounds of 'race' was lawful and the preference of landlords and employers for white workers and tenants was seen by most as entirely natural and legitimate. Studies of covert discrimination in employment and housing conducted by the Political and Economic Planning Group in the 1970s demonstrated that discrimination continued well after the introduction of legislation (Smith, 1977). Research in London, Manchester and Birmingham in the 1980s, ten years on, demonstrated more or less exactly the same results as the research conducted in the 1970s. One third of private employers, for instance, still discriminated against Asian applicants, Afro-Caribbean applicants or both (Brown, 1992; Brown and Gay, 1985).

Anger as BNP chief walks free over race attack

THE ORGANISER of the British National Party, Richard Edmonds, yesterday received a three-month prison sentence for his part in a "cowardly" attack that left a black man scarred for life.

But Edmonds walked free from Southwark Crown Court because of the time he had already spent in custody awaiting trial.

Supporters of the Anti-Nazi League staged a noisy demonstration outside the court, insisting Edmonds should have been punished more severely.

Edmonds, 50, was largely credited for steering the BNP's Derek Beackon to his Tower Hamlets council by-election win last year.

The court had heard that days after that victory, Edmonds hurled a glass at Steven Browne outside the Ship pub in Bethnal Green, east London. Others then "glassed" Mr Browne in the face and punched and kicked him as he lay on the ground.

Edmonds, who lives above the heavily-fortified BNP bookshop in Upper Wickham Lane, Welling, south-east London, was convicted earlier this month of one offence of violent disorder.

Just before Edmonds was dealt with, a BNP supporter, Stephen O'Shea, 38, of Hill House, Purfleet, Essex, was jailed for 12 months for his part in the attack.

Judge Christopher Hardy told the unemployed plasterer that Mr Browne and his white girlfriend, Jenny Bone, were outnumbered by as many as 20 to one that day. O'Shea, who was also convicted of violent disorder, waded in after another man smashed a beer glass into Mr Browne's face.

Mr Beackon was inside the pub as Mr Browne and Ms Bone were having racial abuse and beer hurled at them and being spat on.

The attack came against a background of earlier clashes involving Asians and left- and right-wing extremists in nearby Brick Lane.

At the end of the trial, a BNP supporter, Simon Biggs, 28, from Penge, south-east London, who smashed the beer glass into Mr Browne's face causing deep wounds, was jailed for four and a half years.

An ANL spokesman, Rahul Patel, said it was "disgusting" that Edmonds should be allowed to walk free immediately. "It is an appallingly light sentence ... he is the main instigator behind the violence that the BNP perpetrates. He should have gone down for a long time."

BNP leader jailed for race attack

Paul Myers

A LEADING member of the British National Party was given a three-month jail sentence yesterday for his role in an attack which left a black man scarred for life.

Richard Edmonds, a party organiser credited with steering former BNP councillor Derek Beackon to his Tower Hamlets local election victory last September, was freed at Southwark crown court because he had already served the time in custody awaiting trial.

Two other BNP supporters were jailed for their part in the attack. Simon Biggs, aged 28, from Penge, south-east London, was sentenced to 4½ years after being found guilty of wounding with intent and violent disorder. Stephen O'Shea, aged 38, from Purfleet, Essex, was found guilty of violent disorder and jailed for 12 months.

Judge Christopher Hardy told Mr Edmonds: "When people associate themselves with extreme political organisations, whether on the right or the left, as officials they are to a certain extent riding a tiger. I suspect you like that ride because it gives you a sense of importance and power.

"There is no doubt from what I have heard in this case that people in the BNP respect you and look up to you. It is, however, a dangerous animal and when it is loose in the streets you must restrain it and not goad it."

Mr Edmonds's sentence was greeted with dismay last night by politicians and anti-fascist campaigners. David Winnick, Labour MP for Walsall North, said: "Unfortunately it gives totally the wrong signals. The court was dealing with a professional racist agitator. This thug should have been given a heavier sentence."

Rahul Patel, an Anti-Nazi League spokesman, said the sentence was disgusting. "He is the main instigator behind the violence that the BNP perpetrates."

Mr Edmonds, aged 50, of Welling, south-east London, had pleaded not guilty to violent disorder during the 3½-week trial.

The court was told that Steven Browne had been walking with his white girlfriend, Jenny Bone, past the Ship pub in Bethnal Green, east London, within days of Mr Beackon's election victory.

BNP supporters drinking on the pavement shouted racist abuse, threw beer and spat at them before Mr Edmonds threw a glass at Mr Browne.

Paul Dodgson, prosecuting, said that Mr Biggs hit Mr Browne in the face with an empty beer glass causing severe injuries. Mr O'Shea kicked and punched Mr Browne as he lay on the ground.

Anti-Jewish incidents rise by 20%

JASON BENNETTO
Home Affairs Correspondent

ANTI-JEWISH attacks in Britain have increased by about 20 per cent in the past year, according to a report published yesterday.

The number of reported incidents rose to 346 in 1993, with Jews having to endure assaults, threats, the desecration of cemeteries and synagogues and the widespread distribution of anti-Semitic literature.

Computer networks are also being used as worldwide links to spread anti-Semitic material, the report by the Institute of Jewish Affairs says. It feared the spread was going unchecked as the networks were almost inaccessible to law enforcement agencies. Anti-Semitic attacks have increased by 85 per cent in the past decade. Abusive behaviour accounted for about one-third of the incidents and damage to communal property about a fifth. There were about 40 assaults, including a very small number of life-threatening beatings. The publication of racist material made up about 15 per cent of the actions. The figures are almost certainly an underestimate because many incidents go unreported. The statistics represent single incidents, which may in the case of literature, affect thousands of people.

The threat posed by the far right, particularly the British National Party, and Combat 18, a clandestine group with links to the BNP, was seen as a major cause of concern.

□ Anti-Semitism World Report 1994; Institute of Jewish Affairs, 79 Wimpole Street, London W1M 7DD; £10.

Black migrants to the UK in the 1950s often faced a hostile and unfriendly welcome

Brown (1992) argues that discrimination plays a substantial role in reinforcing the structural inequalities and material disadvantage black people experience in the UK, evident in employment patterns and in the unemployment figures. For unemployment, for example, black people totalled more than twice the national average at the beginning of 1993; 25 per cent of black adults were classified as unemployed. Pakistani and Bangladeshi women and men were particularly badly hit by the economic recession in the early 1990s with more than three times the average unemployment rate. A survey conducted in 1989–91 demonstrated that 20 per cent of West Indian or Guyanese men and 28 per cent of Pakistani and Bangladeshi men held professional managerial positions compared to 36 per cent of white men (Skellington, 1995). Similarly, research on black women graduates in London in the 1980s found that they earned on average only 71 per cent as much a week as white women graduates (Bruegel, 1989).

The effects of racism in the UK can be seen, therefore, in three interrelated arenas. First, in violent physical attacks, second in terms of public opinion and the ideological and cultural expression of hostility, and third in economic inequalities and in access to material resources. At the ideological level, the concern is with the chains of association built up around 'race' and reinforced in the media and popular culture along with the nature of the 'moral panics' which sweep across public opinion. As cultural studies researchers have demonstrated, these concerned, first, black migration, then as a subsidiary concern, law and order and 'mugging', and, more recently, questions of the make-up of the nation, citizenship and patriotism (Centre for Contemporary Cultural Studies,

1982; Gilroy, 1987). Afro-Caribbean and Asian groups in the UK have not responded passively to this situation, however, and have organized forms of resistance, asserting their rights through direct action against harassment, through trade union activity, through developing autonomous cultural organizations, through campaigns for legislation, and through campaigns for better political representation on local councils and in government. As a result, a vibrant 'identity politics' has developed among these communities.

What do you understand by racism? Make some notes on your personal experiences in this area and on those of your community.   ACTIVITY 4.1

2.2   Making sense of the 'other'

According to the sociologist Miles (1989), at the heart of racism is a process of representing or making sense of the 'other', a set of processes through which communities are constructed and various forms of 'us' and 'them' are created. Representations of others can either lead to, and legitimate, acts of violence, discrimination and denigration, or produce a situation where there is no recognized 'race' problem. You will remember from Chapter 3, Moscovici's points about the transmission of social representations and their collective nature. Understanding the origins of European representations of its various 'others' (African, Asian, Oriental, Jewish, Irish) is a complex task, however. As Rattansi (1995) notes, we need to find out about the history of encounters between groups in relation to the cultural frameworks of the day, and also the economics and politics of different periods.

In his review of some of this history, Rattansi describes the images which set the scene as European contacts with non-Europeans increased in the sixteenth century. What merchant adventurers and explorers 'saw' was understood through the lens of already familiar representations of the 'alien', in particular through early representations of alleged 'Wild Men' and 'Wild Women' (referred to as 'Wodewose' in England) and ideas about 'monstrous' people circulating in Europe in the Medieval period. Linked to this was the strong negative connotation of 'black' in Christian colour symbolism of the period. Ideas about the nature of otherness, however, were not just anchored by already familiar understandings, they were also mobilized to justify courses of action and linked to complex economic and political interests.

Thus notions of black inferiority and savagery intensified in British public opinion in the eighteenth and nineteenth centuries to legitimate what Rattansi describes as the 'triangular trade' (Box 4.1 overleaf, see also Fryer, 1984).

BOX 4.1   The triangular trade

Ships sailed from Liverpool, Bristol and London carrying textiles, guns, cutlery, glass, beads, beer and other British manufactures. These were bartered for slaves on the African coast. Anything between twenty million and sixty million able-bodied Africans were crammed into these ships during the whole period of slavery, under the most oppressive and inhuman conditions, and transported across the Atlantic to Jamaica, Barbados and elsewhere. There they were exchanged for sugar, rum, tobacco and spices which in turn were brought back and sold in Britain (Fryer, 1984, pp. 14–15) ... Slavery generated enormous wealth for British traders and planters, and was crucial to the rapid growth of Bristol and Liverpool in the eighteenth and nineteenth centuries ... The rapid development of Britain's banking system owed much to the surpluses generated by the trade in sugar, slaves and cotton and many major present-day banking corporations can trace their origins to banks set up with funds originating in the triangular trade (Fryer, 1984, pp. 40ff).

(Rattansi, 1995, pp. 51–2)

As Rattansi notes, the slave trade and the money surpluses it generated gave a powerful impetus to claims about the supposed rights and superiorities of white people in relation to black people. The presumed natural inferiority of black people legitimated the oppressive conditions of slavery. (It is important to note, though, that from the sixteenth century to the present there have also been influential critics of the apologists for oppression, see, for instance, Pagden and Lawrance, 1991.) Images of other groups such as Jewish and Irish people, the subject peoples of the Empire and perceptions of Islam were similarly conditioned by European and British political and economic interests and by contemporary debates about the causes of 'otherness'.

During this period of conquest, expansion and slavery, such was the pressure to mark out the difference between European and 'others' that notions of humans divided like animals into different 'species' began to take hold. These ideas coalesced in the nineteenth century around popular scientific notions of different 'races' and 'racial types' and in this way a biology of 'race' emerged. Overt differences in physical appearance (such as skin colour) were seen as indications of profound biological and genetic divisions between human groups. Two people seen as belonging to different 'races' were regarded as belonging to fundamentally different types which could be ranked in terms of their qualities from more 'advanced' to 'less advanced'.

The sociologist Banton (1987) notes that this belief in 'racial types' reached its heyday in Victorian times and during the first half of the twentieth century. Scientists of this period became engaged in a flurry of measuring skull sizes, body types and facial characteristics to prove the existence of these fixed types, and arranged them in a hierarchy from 'superior' to 'inferior'. There was little agreement, however, between different groups of scientists on the ordering of these 'races', particularly the white European 'races'.

These early conceptions of human variation are a good example of how persistent themes in popular culture and the ideological pressures of the day become taken up and worked as science. The activities of scientists in establishing 'racial types' lent this method of understanding social groups considerable authority. These ideas, however, have been gradually discredited this century as modern genetics has developed (see Banton, 1987, for an account of changing conceptions of 'race' and Miles, 1989, Chapter 1, for a discussion of the scientific evidence). Darwin's theory of evolution, for example, suggested that there were no fixed or permanent biological types of the kind proposed by 'racial' theories. Population geneticists have pointed to the difficulty of neatly categorizing 'races' or rigidly separating one from another in terms of clear-cut genetic similarities. Indeed, biologists note the strong similarities between humans across the globe. Most genetic variation occurs between individuals in the same population rather than between populations.

> Of all human genetic variation ... 85 per cent turns out to be between individuals within the same local population, tribe, or nation. A further 8 per cent is between tribes and nations within a major 'race' and the remaining 7 per cent is between major 'races'. That means the genetic variation between one Spaniard and another, or between one Masai and another, is 85 per cent of all human genetic variation, while only 15 per cent is accounted for by breaking people up into groups. If everyone on earth became extinct except the Kikuyu of East Africa, about 85 per cent of all human variability would still be present in the reconstituted species. A few gene forms would be lost, like the FYb allele of the duffy blood group that is known only in American Indians, but little else would be changed.

[...]

> The result of the study of genetic variation is in sharp contrast with the everyday impression that major 'races' are well-differentiated. Clearly, those superficial differences in hair, form, skin colour, and facial features that are used to distinguish 'races' from each other are not typical of human genes in general. Any use of racial categories must take its justification from some source

other than biology. The remarkable feature of human evolution and history has been the very small degree of divergence between geographical populations as compared with the genetic variation between individuals.

(Lewontin, 1987, cited in Rattansi, 1995, p. 67)

Although talk about the innate characteristics of different 'races' and 'racial types' is still an important aspect of modern racism, and can still be heard across the dinner table and in the House of Commons, what modern biological research points to, as Rattansi notes, is the difficulty of founding *social* differences between groups, and *cultural* assumptions about the nature of those groups, upon *natural* differences. 'Race' is a social rather than a natural phenomenon, a process which gives significance to superficial physical differences, but where the construction of group divisions depends on the kind of economic, political and cultural processes sketched out in this section. For these reasons, many writers, such as Miles (1989), prefer to put quotation marks around the term 'race', a practice also followed in this volume to indicate that we are dealing with one possible social classification of people and groups rather than an established biological or genetic reality.

In this very brief review of some of the factors involved in the emergence of representations of social groups, I have tried to highlight some of the complexity of the social context surrounding racism. Any complete explanation of racism will need to work across the social sciences, analysing history, local and global economics, politics, the process of migration as well as patterns in popular culture and the ways in which these have been taken up by scientists and biologists. What can the social psychologist contribute?

2.3   Racism and social psychology

Intergroup situations such as social conflicts around 'race' present a number of psychological issues. The way groups are divided and how group categories are understood depends, as we have seen, on the social history of group interaction. But how do these categories and this history affect the ways in which people perceive and analyse their social world? What are the cognitive, emotional and motivational consequences of living in a social world divided in this way? Are there some typical features of the way people's minds work that might encourage differentiation and discrimination?

And what about individual differences? How important are they in predicting people's responses? Why does one white British employer, for instance, welcome and encourage black applicants while another states, when explaining his discriminatory actions to an industrial tribunal: 'I'm sorry but I'm completely prejudiced and there would be no point in him coming along because I would not employ him' (Guardian, 11.8.93, cited in Skellington, 1995)? Does this indicate different perceptions of material interests, different exposures to social norms of egalitarianism, or can these differences be put down to personality? In general terms, the challenge for the social psychologist lies in explaining how racist ideologies come to engage the individual and come to seem meaningful and 'reasonable'.

Most attention has been paid to explaining the actions of the perpetrators of racism (and this will also be the main focus in this chapter) but there are also important psychological issues here for Asian and Afro-Caribbean people and for other groups in the UK such as Jewish and Irish people who face discrimination on the basis of their group membership – questions about how to survive and resist a racist climate, how to claim a self in this context, and how to resist, too, what Fanon (1967) described as a 'colonized interior', or the development of a psychology of oppression. Much less time and effort has been expended on these topics, although a Journal of Black Psychology addressing these issues has recently been established in the United States.

At this point you should read Reading A from Fanon's book, *Black Skins, White Masks*, which can be found at the end of this chapter. Fanon was concerned with the effects of colonization upon the colonized and wrote from a black African perspective during the 1950s. A major focus in his work was the phenomenological and psychodynamic consequences of the extreme 'Negrophobia' displayed by colonial regimes of that period. He drew on his experiences as a psychiatrist, his experience of growing up in Martinique and on his observations of French controlled Algeria. His work tries to develop a liberatory and revolutionary politics for colonized people. In this reading, he is exploring white reactions to black bodies, the white sense of black as 'other', and how this influences the black man's embodiment and sense of himself as an object in space. Given the gender politics of the 1950s, and Fanon's autobiographical focus, the main focus throughout his work was on black *male* experience. For a modern account of the experience of black women in the UK you might like to look at Bryan, Dadzie and Scafe's (1985) book, *The Heart of the Race*.

ACTIVITY 4.2

Fanon's work indicates why developing an adequate social psychology of racist actions has seemed such an important project. Racist social relations construct the self and the identity of black and white protagonists, the colonizer as well as the colonized. As Fanon notes, in such social relations, 'the white man [sic] is sealed in his whiteness, just as the black man is sealed in his blackness' (1967, p. 9). Racism is a matter of psychological as well as physical violence and raises issues about human dignity and self-alienation, as well as the immediate ethical and political effects of domination.

Like other chapters in this volume, this chapter will take a historical perspective, considering a range of work from the 1920s to the 1990s. We will look at three broad social psychological perspectives and the different theories contained within these. It will become clear how each theory and perspective develops its own conceptual language and its own definition of the most basic issues in the social psychology of racism. Experimental social psychologists have looked mainly at the *cognitive processes* involved in racism and at the *effects of group membership*. We will be looking at their work in sections 3 and 5. Psychodynamic researchers have focused on *personality* and the *emotional dynamics* of racism. Their analyses are reviewed in section 4. Social constructionists have looked at *identity, discourse, history* and *culture* and we will be considering some of their work in section 3, but principally in section 6.

2.4   Debates about human nature

One persistent problem for researchers from all three perspectives has been relating *individual* attributes to the *social context* of racism discussed in section 2.1 and 2.2. A primary theme in this chapter will be the model of the individual and the social context informing the research reviewed. Studies can be placed on a continuum, with those which focus on presocial individual psychological processes at one end of the continuum and those which focus on the way that the social context constructs and determines individual psychology at the other end. Some researchers have argued that pre-social individual characteristics explain racism, others have seen a complex interaction between human nature and the social context, and yet others have argued that patterns in the social context entirely explain racist actions.

Figure 4.1   A theoretical continuum

The clearest example of an individual pre-social or 'human nature' theory can be found in sociobiological explanations of racism. While abandoning earlier biological theories of 'racial types' discussed in section 2.2, sociobiologists (Hamilton, 1975; Reynolds, 1986) and some sociologists (for example Van den Berghe, 1981) have explored the idea that ethnocentrism, or hostility towards others defined as different, might be an inherent or universal feature of human nature, built into us as a result of natural selection. The core argument is that survival at the level of genes is more likely if individuals act unselfishly and cooperatively, helping their kin or 'blood' relations to breed through sharing food and dwelling sites. The individual may not survive but, if their kin reproduce, then the genes held in common will continue. From there it is a short step to arguing that: 'during man's [sic] evolution in small hunting-gathering groups, natural selection would have favoured an ingroup/outgroup dichotomy in human thinking and human behaviour. Kin and, indeed, all neighbours able to reciprocate, would be favoured, whereas strangers would be viewed without warmth, indeed, at times of shortage, with hostility' (Reynolds, 1986, p. 379).

Reynolds goes on to note that such evolutionary tendencies could still underlie our actions today despite the fact that human behaviour is very obviously also a product of learning and cultural conditioning. Van den Berghe (1981), for instance, argues that modern ethnic groups can be seen as extensions of kin groups so, in multi-cultural situations, people generalize their feelings of kinship to other members of their ethnic group, producing an automatic hostility to those defined as outsiders.

One of the difficulties with this account is the assumption that a large modern ethnic group, often criss-crossed by internal conflicts, resembles in any sense the small kin groups on which the original theory is based. Theorists who have placed more emphasis on the social context as the determinant of group behaviour argue that these 'human nature' accounts cannot explain the variability of racism or the specific forms it takes. How might such an account explain the complicated social phenomena discussed in section 2.2. which seem to determine the way people become grouped and represented? Why has skin colour become such an important marker of identity? Why are some societies preoccupied with 'race' while it is a more minor issue in other multi-ethnic societies such as Brazil, Mexico, Barbados and Kenya? Biological explanations in terms of kin altruism cannot explain how human groups become constructed and divided and yet these processes of group formation seem to be the key to understanding racism and the forms group conflict assumes. In the course of this chapter we will encounter many similar debates about individual versus social determinants of behaviour in conflict situations.

At this point you could review some of the explanations you have ACTIVITY 4.3 encountered for the origins of racism inside and outside your academic studies. Do some of these seem more useful and convincing than others? To what extent do you think racism is a psychological issue rather than a sociological, economic, political or biological problem? As you read on, try and identify the model of the individual and the social contained in the different theories discussed in this chapter and try to place them on the continuum in Figure 4.1.

Review of section 2

- Racism in the UK is evident in the physical violence directed at black and Asian communities, in stereotypes and popular culture and in patterns of material disadvantage. This inequality has a long history with complex social and economic origins. It cannot be explained as the result of natural 'racial' differences.

- Although racism is a social, political, economic and historical phenomenon, there are also some important psychological issues at stake concerning individual differences, the development of perceptions and beliefs about others, motives for discrimination, the experience of racism and the relationship between individual psychology and collective forms of action.

- Social psychological theories of racism have focused on cognition and stereotypes, emotion and personality, the influence of group membership on individual behaviour, and on the relationship between identity and culture.

3 The nature of prejudiced judgement

As Milner (1981) notes, it was not until the 1920s that psychologists seriously began to consider 'race' and 'racial issues'. When racism gained a higher profile as a consequence of changing public opinion, the problem rapidly became framed as one of 'prejudice'. This term drew attention to the *cognitive* dimensions of racism and to its *irrational* nature. According to Allport (1954), prejudice is 'thinking ill of others without sufficient warrant' (p. 6). In Allport's view, prejudice was an antipathy to groups or individuals based on faulty and inflexible generalizations. It indicated a 'thinking error' and was illustrative of the ways in which a racist social climate might come to structure an individual's thought process. In this section, I want to look first at some representative research on stereotypes and social cognition (cognition about social objects) to give a flavour of the work on the cognitive dimensions of racism from an experimental social psychological perspective, I then want to look in more detail at models of the 'thinking individual' underlying this work.

3.1   Stereotypes and social cognition

The term 'stereotype' focuses attention on the kinds of judgements made about others which underlie the beliefs, discrimination and violent 'racial' attacks considered in section 2.1. A stereotype associates traits or attributes with groups of people. A common stereotype of the English, for instance, is that they 'keep a stiff upper lip' and display the attributes characteristic of the 'British bulldog'. A contrasting stereotype is evident in this Antipodean joke – how can you tell when a planeful of Poms has arrived at Auckland Airport? ... The whining noise continues even when the jet engines are shut off.

Whether it is the English as 'whining Poms' or the much more disturbing racist assessments Fanon was concerned with, stereotypes contain an evaluation. They are statements which denigrate out-groups or are used to glorify the in-group. In terms of Allport's criteria for prejudice, a stereotype is a selective over-generalization which *prejudges* any individual member of the group. Serious social scientific investigation of this prejudgement was initiated by Lippman in 1922, in his book *Public Opinion*. As Oakes et al. (1994) point out, Lippman's account was remarkably prescient. He identified a number of the themes which dominated stereotype research from the 1930s until the 1990s.

Lippman argued that the problem with stereotypes is their partial, biased and inadequate nature. He saw them as pictures or fictions people carry in their heads which distort or muddy their perception of reality. Stereotypes prevent a clear perception of people as they actually are. The white employer discussed in section 2.3 who refused even to contemplate the possibility of black employees might be said to be a victim of his stereotypes. Lippman contrasted stereotyping with ideal judgements that would respond flexibly, rationally and innocently (without preconceptions) to the unique characteristics of each individual and social situation with no mental shortcuts. But Lippman also speculated about the inevitability of such cognitive shortcuts. Perhaps the modern world is so complex that the economy of stereotypical thinking is necessary to get by.

Early research on stereotyping was largely concerned with recording the *content* of 'racial' and national stereotypes. What representations do white North American college students have of other groups such as Germans, Italians, English, Jews, Irish, 'Negros', and so on (see Katz and Braly, 1933)? What kinds of prejudgements do these display? Explanations of stereotyping focused on social norms and socialization and the ways in which people learn to reproduce stereotypes. Alternatively, researchers considered the psychodynamic factors which might encourage this style of thinking (see section 4). In the 1960s, however, social psychologists became much more interested again in the actual judgemental processes identified by Lippman and Allport which might be associated with prejudice and stereotyping.

This work was stimulated by an influential paper published by Tajfel in 1969 which was in turn stimulated by ideas from the 'New Look in Perception' developed by Bruner and his colleagues at Harvard University in the 1950s. It took a while for this line of investigation to take off but in the late 1970s and during the 1980s, social cognition research on stereotypes was a principal topic for North American experimental social psychology (see also Lalljee, 1996, for a general perspective on social cognition research). Literally hundreds, if not thousands, of experimental investigations of the cognitive bases of person perception have been conducted.

Tajfel's own work concerned the cognitive and perceptual consequences of categorization. What happens to people's thought processes, to their assessment of a situation when they are presented with group dichotomies, when the world is divided into A and B, into groups such as white, black, British, Asian, Afro-Caribbean in the UK context? How does this affect perceptions of the members of such groups?

ACTIVITY 4.4

One way of investigating this issue is to look at what happens to perceptions of the physical world. You might like to consider one experimental situation Tajfel and Wilkes (1963) set up and then try and second guess the outcome.

The subjects in this experiment were asked to judge the length of lines and were presented with eight lines which differed from each other by a constant ratio in one of three possible ways. As you can see, in Condition 1, the lines were arranged so that the shorter lines were labelled 'A' and the longer lines were labelled 'B'. In Condition 2, the lines were again arranged according to 'A' and 'B' but with no relation between the length of lines and the label, while in Condition 3, no labels were attached and the lines were arranged in random order.

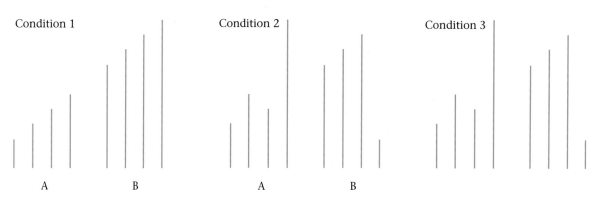

Figure 4.2 (adapted from Tajfel and Wilkes, 1963)

What effects do you think the process of labelling the lines 'A' and 'B' might have on people's perceptions of the length of the lines? What kind of mistakes might they be more likely to make in Condition 1 compared to Condition 3?

Tajfel and Wilkes found that subjects were more likely to exaggerate the differences between lines marked 'A' and 'B' when it was possible to form a stereotype, prediction or association between label and line length, compared to the lines of the same length arranged randomly, or where there was no association between the label and length of the lines. There was also some evidence that people would over-estimate the similarity of the lines to each other when they could be classified together as 'A' or 'B'. In technical terms, there was an accentuation of inter-category differences and an accentuation of intra-category similarities.

What might this have to do with the stereotypes which make up racist ideologies? Tajfel argued that, cognitively and perceptually, group labels like 'black', 'white', 'English', 'Afro-Caribbean', 'Australian' operate like the 'A' and 'B' attached to the lines except that in the social world, values and social histories are also attached. But the mere presence of social categories will lead to perceptual and cognitive biases – people will accentuate the differences between members of these social categories and exaggerate the similarities of people categorized as part of the same group.

In many respects, the experiment conducted by Tajfel and Wilkes simply refined and clarified the claims of earlier researchers about the over-generalizing nature of stereotypic thinking. Yet it was an important study because it raised the possibility that the stereotypes which are so characteristic of racist taunts might be a consequence of the way human minds are structured to process information. In other words, stereotypes may be like visual illusions, an unfortunate but inevitable by-product of the way human minds are designed to work. This pessimistic conclusion fuelled the next wave of research on stereotypes conducted in the late 1970s and 1980s.

Research on the cognitive bases of stereotyping has explored a number of avenues. Researchers have looked at how stereotypes are held in people's memories. Are they encoded as lists of attributes triggered off when the person encounters a member of the relevant group? Or, as seems more likely, following the work of the cognitive psychologist Rosch (1978), stereotypes may be organized around 'prototypes' or representative images of the typical group member (c.f. Lalljee, 1996). How do stereotypes affect the way people deal with and encode information? Do they affect what people notice and pay attention to and the items about another person which people miss or ignore? What about the interpretation of that information? Researchers have also examined how stereotypes form in the first place. We will look at three classic studies from the 1970s which illustrate some of these cognitive effects, beginning with effects of prototypes on memory.

Synder and Uranowitz (1978) argued that people are more likely to remember information about another person which is consistent with their stereotype of a social category, or more particularly, information which is consistent with their prototype of that category (their image of a typical category member). Their study concerned homophobic stereotypes but the same principles were thought to be characteristic of any stereotypic judgement. Subjects in their study were asked to read an extensive case history about a female character called Betty. This case history was like a typical psychiatric report in that it described Betty's childhood, her education, adult career, relationships with parents, social life, and so on. Subjects then returned a week later and were given a recognition memory test on various details of Betty's life but before this test was given, half the subjects were told that Betty was now living with another woman in a successful and happy lesbian relationship while the other half were told that she had formed a happy and successful heterosexual relationship. Synder and Uranowitz found that this incidental information had a significant effect on subjects' memory for the details of Betty's life. Their memories and recall of information became organized around their prototypes of 'lesbian' and 'heterosexual woman'. Category information, in other words, is used by people as a device for selectively interpreting and drawing on their memories.

Such retrospective effects are not too surprising. What is more disturbing are the results from a study conducted by Duncan (1976, and discussed in Lalljee, 1996). Duncan showed subjects a videotape of a discussion between two men. In the course of the videotape one of the men seemed to push or shove the other. There were four versions of the videotape. In one, the man shoving was white and the recipient of the shove was black. In another, these roles were reversed so that the man shoving was black and the recipient white. In the remaining two versions of the video both men were either black, or both white. Duncan found that the subjects (North American college students) selectively perceived and interpreted the ambiguous push according to 'race'. They were more likely, for example, to define the black actors as 'violent', while interpreting the white actors as 'fooling around'. This study and many similar investigations provide evidence that the ways in which people perceive situations and process information depends on their *prior* stereotypic schema.

The final study we will examine concerns the origins of stereotypes and is more contentious. Hamilton and Gifford (1976) were interested in the question of why stereotypes might form in the first place and whether cognitive biases might have something to do with this process. They argued that stereotypes are best understood as correlations. Stereotypes such as 'Italians are over-emotional and melodramatic' or 'academics are vague and impractical' typically correlate characteristics with group membership. Could these be 'illusory correlations', where the illusion depends on typical mistakes people make when correlating events, such as assuming a causal connection where there is none? Often, for example, when correlating events, people's perceptions become biased because they pay undue attention to vivid and statistically infrequent events. Mistaking one-off coincidences for general rules is a good example of this error. How might this cognitive shortcut relate to the illusory correlations of stereotypes?

Hamilton and Gifford's experiment presented subjects with descriptions of people's activities which took the following form – 'John, a member of Group A, goes to visit his mother in hospital'. There were 39 statements of this kind, the majority concerned Group A, while a small minority of statements concerned members of Group B. The majority of statements consisted of socially desirable behaviours (such as visiting your mother in hospital) while a small minority of statements concerned mildly undesirable behaviour (such as throwing litter). The ratio of different kinds of sentences was carefully arranged so that there was always the same ratio of desirable to undesirable behaviour for Group B as for Group A. Relative to their size, Group B engaged in the same proportion of undesirable acts as Group A. However, Hamilton and Gifford predicted that in *cognitive* terms, Group B would be seen as disproportionately bad. The most *distinctive* and most memorable events would be those in which members of Group B engaged in undesirable behaviour (since these were the most infrequent statements). Did the subjects form an illusory correlation between Group B and undesirability?

Hamilton and Gifford found that the subjects did develop what could be called a stereotype of Group B. What might this behaviour in an experimental laboratory have to do with the formation of stereotypes of real life social groups? Hamilton (1981) argued that sometimes people encounter social groups they know very little about. If they also happen to witness members of this group engaging in statistically infrequent behaviour, such as socially undesirable acts, then there is an analogue to the laboratory situation. He argued, too, that the subjects' experience in the laboratory may be similar to the experience of children from a majority group going to school and encountering children from a minority group for the first time. If the minority group children also engage in distinctive and unusual social practices then the combination of two kinds of distinctiveness sets the scene for illusory correlations to develop. Finally, Hamilton suggested that, in some cases, stereotypes might have a 'kernel of truth'. The image held by a majority group of a minority group may greatly exaggerate characteristics which were present in an occasional form in the minority group. This kind of stereotypic exaggeration could result from the operation of illusory correlations. These statements are controversial because they suggest that pernicious racist chains of association could simply be a consequence of cognitive biases and the normal ways in which our minds work. We will return to this point in the next section.

3.2 Mind in culture

What assumptions does the research we have just considered make about the nature of cognition and the relationship between individual minds and the social context?

The kind of cognitive research which prevailed in the 1970s and 1980s was dominated by what Taylor (1981) describes as a 'cognitive miser' model of the thinking individual. The key metaphor underlying this work was of the person as a kind of overworked bureaucrat whose filing system was not keeping up with all their paper work (Billig, 1985), and who, as a result, uses all manner of shortcuts to keep up with the flow of information.

In other words, research was dominated by notions of the *limited capacity* of human minds faced with the richness and diversity of the social environment. Social cognition researchers argued that we simply do not have the mental space for noting all this diversity, richness and individual difference. Social interaction and the perception of others have to be organized, ordered and simplified around a set of cognitive categories, stereotypes and their prototypes. One could argue that this theory of the nature of the human mind and information processing is not surprising as an outgrowth of post-industrial ideologies where 'information' comes to replace all other 'goods'.

Framed in this way, research on social cognition moves towards the left-hand end of the continuum identified in Figure 4.1 in section 2.4. Individual pre-social processes (in this case the way human minds organize information) become emphasized as the cause of the judgements associated with racism. Some theorists have argued, for example, that the cognitive biases associated with categorization are inevitable. They suggest these features are innate and 'built into' human minds, since these shortcuts were adaptive and useful features in evolutionary terms. There are three other features of this 'information processing' model of cognition which are worth stressing.

One is the emphasis on error. The concept of stereotypes as a type of bias, for example, suggests that it is possible to contrast true perception with mistaken perception. The stereotype is seen as an 'illusion' while responding to an individual in all their uniqueness is seen as the 'true' situation. The second and third features concern the emphasis on a solitary perceiver and the assumption of universalism. The guiding image in the information processing approach is of an independent individual contemplating his or her social world in a solitary way, applying cognitive strategies which are a product of this individual mind, but which are also universal and likely to be applied by any human brain in the same situation.

These assumptions about the nature of mind and thought have generated a great deal of important research but they are not the only possible premises. Recent social cognitive research, for example, has questioned the focus on error and the contrast between 'inaccurate' stereotypic judgement and 'true' judgement defined as responding to individuals as unique human beings. Oakes et al. (1994) have argued that cognition is better seen as a flexible and responsive system which responds dynamically to social reality. Categorization, selection and prior judgement occur at all levels, from judgements of other individuals *as individuals* to judgements of groups. Oakes et al. argue that stereotypes are not instances of cognitive pathology, therefore, or an indication of biased or faulty information processing. Rather, stereotypes are a response to the change in social reality which occurs when groups are introduced into the situation. It is not that people's minds have gone awry when they stereotype; they are responding to the group dimensions of the social situation. These responses may be partial, interested, hostile or pernicious but this partiality reflects the social situation and the nature of social conflict rather than any *inherent* bias in human information processing.

This work suggests a shift from a view of the solitary contemplative individual with limited intellectual capacity to a notion of *mind in culture*. In this perspective cognitive strategies and the kind of thought processes Fanon described, for example, are not seen as a *pre-existent* part of human nature but as reflecting the organization of material in the social domain. Lave (1988), following on from the work of Vygotsky (see Wetherell and Maybin, 1996), argues from a social constructionist perspective that ways of making sense and mental strategies are *socially distributed*, emerging from the collective engagement of people with their social world. Lave sees the study of cognition as part of the study of cultural psychology. Cognitive strategies, therefore, may prove to be specific to particular social settings so that the person learns skills of judgement, organization and perception in relation to particular social tasks and in relation to prevailing social practices and then acquires a quite other set of mental habits for a different social setting or form of life.

Cognition need not be seen as universal, or as a matter of cogs and wheels turning in the heads of individuals, but as highly situated, dynamic and patterned by social relationships. Discursive psychologists have similarly argued that stereotypic statements can only be understood in the rhetorical and social contexts in which they emerge (Wetherell and Potter, 1992). Stereotypes are part of ongoing interactions, conversations and public debates and the structure of these debates will channel what is said and how it is understood. This point is elaborated in section 6.

The concept of mind in culture leads to a less individualistic approach to stereotypic judgement. Tajfel, for example, looking back at the response to his research in the 1960s, argued in 1981 that social cognition investigators were in danger of neglecting the central point about stereotypes. Stereotypic images of other groups and prejudicial chains of association serve social and ideological functions for the groups concerned. As we have seen, negative stereotypes of African people played a major role in justifying the slave trade and conferring an aura of legitimacy, as did stereotypes of 'primitive peoples' in the process of annexation and colonization for the expansion of the British Empire.

The notion of illusory correlation as the basis of stereotype formation, when carried to the extreme, indicates some of the problems here. Not just any distinctive or statistically infrequent event becomes the basis of stereotypes, I would suggest, only those which play some argumentative or ideological role in intergroup conflicts. In other words, cognitive shortcuts cannot, in themselves, be the basis for stereotypes. We do not find, for example, white primary schoolchildren forming long-lasting socially relevant stereotypes about Afro-Caribbean children and unusual pets because, on their first day at school, they happen to encounter several Afro-Caribbean children who keep snakes. Any illusory correlation of this kind would not work as a stereotype unless it was collectively held and, more importantly, had some bearing on current dimensions of social comparison between groups.

Finally, some social psychologists have been concerned about the messages social cognition research seems to give to black audiences. Social cognitive work from an information processing perspective often suggests, for instance, that a change in stereotypes can only come about when the white stereotyper is presented with new, startling, vivid and disconfirming information (e.g. Rothbart, 1981). As contrary information accumulates, the stereotyper might begin to 'readjust their account books' and modify their prototypes and their stereotypic schema for social categories. This, along with the concept of stereotypes having a 'kernel of truth', seems to suggest that if only black communities would behave differently then white communities might be able to process information in a non-stereotypical way. As Henriques comments, in this way 'the black person becomes the cause of racism whereas the white person's prejudice is seen as a natural effect of their information processing mechanisms' (1984, p. 74). This message not only exonerates white racism but also removes the debate from the political arena of intergroup struggle to a psychological or even biological arena where stereotypes become considered for their 'adaptiveness'.

Review of section 3

- Social cognition research has been concerned with the judgements involved in racist reactions and responses and the ways in which people categorize and group stimuli together.

- Much of this research has adopted a 'cognitive miser' analysis of information processing. Errors and biases are seen to arise because of universal and otherwise adaptive aspects of the organization of human minds.

- An alternative approach argues that cognitive strategies are situated, flexible and dynamic, emerging from people's collective engagement with the social world. Mental process emerges from social process.

4   The inner world of the racist individual

The previous section considered social psychological research on the *cognitive* elements of racist reactions and responses. Much less research has been conducted on the *emotional* dynamics identified by theorists such as Fanon. As Frosh (1989) has noted, racism has come to be seen primarily as a problem of the mind rather than the heart. Yet, claims Frosh, for the racist individual, disparagement of others, negative stereotypes and ethnocentrism have a strong *subjective value*. They are intensely felt, saturated with emotion, symptomatic of a series of 'violent and desperate (internal) defensive manoeuvres' (1989, p. 226). Frosh argues that an adequate social psychology of racism must include a psychodynamic perspective. There have been few systematic applications of psychodynamic concepts to racism, however; perhaps because of the clinical and individual focus of this perspective. Section 4.1 looks at the best known psychodynamic study of racism while section 4.2 considers the general contribution a psychodynamic perspective might make.

4.1   The authoritarian personality

Research on the authoritarian personality conducted by Adorno, Frenkel-Brunswik, Levinson and Sanford in the late 1940s and published in 1950 is one of very few attempts, and certainly the most sophisticated, to develop a psychodynamics of prejudice. It was a piece of research sponsored by the American Jewish society and conducted in California by a group of scholars who were either refugees from Nazi Germany and former members of the Frankfurt School of Social Research or very much influenced by that intellectual tradition.

Adorno et al.'s account of their research begins with this question: 'Why do competing political ideologies have such differing degrees of appeal for different individuals?' (1950, p. 2). If we take something like fascism, for example, with its conspiracy theories, its profound anti-semitism, its hostility, certainly in recent UK manifestations, to black migrants, and its authoritarian approach to political life, what makes this ideology attractive to particular individuals? Adorno et al. argued that there was a personality type which was particularly drawn to this philosophy of life, a personality type which had its roots in childhood.

> ... a basically hierarchical, authoritarian, exploitative parent-child relationship is apt to carry over into a power-oriented, exploitatively dependent attitude towards one's sex partner and one's God and may well culminate in a political philosophy and social outlook which has no room for anything but a desperate clinging to what appears to be a strong and disdainful rejection of whatever is relegated to the bottom.
>
> *(Adorno et al., 1950, p. 971)*

Adorno et al. argued on the basis of their empirical research that the *authoritarian personality type* was much more likely than other personality types to express anti-semitism and strongly ethnocentric attitudes. In characterizations of the authoritarian personality the following descriptions recur: conventional; conformist; rigid; locked into stereotypical and categorical thinking; dislikes loose talk; respects strength, organization and obedience; defers to authority; advocates punishment and discipline; is intolerant of ambiguity.

In psychodynamic terms, the authoritarian personality is described as having both sadistic and masochistic trends. Strong, strict parents who are often inconsistent disciplinarians and fond of harsh punishment produce children who rapidly learn to submit to authority and who fear having to assert themselves. Such children become masochistic and cringing as they submit to their parents' disciplinary order. The parents' standards are almost completely internalized and thus a strong and punitive super-ego develops, a punishing conscience and a feeling that social norms must be rigidly followed. The importance of obedience and respect for conventions and authority are instilled in the child. This pattern will continue throughout life. Other authority figures come to substitute for the parents and an exaggerated respect will be shown for leaders who are as symbolically strong and punitive as the parents. Excessive deference, however, produces excessive resentment. Anger and hostility which could never be vented against the parents or other recognized authority figures is displaced and projected on to other targets. Specifically, those seen as inferior or weaker in contemporary political ideologies, such as minority ethnic groups, become the butt of punishing and aggressive impulses. This sadism directed outwards can be extreme and vicious. Adorno et al. argued that it is as if one part of the authoritarian's social world must be over-idealized, while another part, in compensation, must carry all the negativity.

In evaluating this analysis, it is important to note that Adorno et al. are *not* suggesting that personality and child-rearing cause authoritarian, racist and fascist ideologies. Rather, these ideologies, which reflect prevailing social and economic circumstances, become especially congenial to certain people because of their personality and upbringing. There is a mesh, in other words, between an individual's character and the philosophy of life she or he finds sympathetic among those on offer in a particular historical period.

Adorno et al. argued for a complex relationship between psychological factors and sociocultural conditions. They claimed that in societies at certain points, because of the economic and political climate, authoritarian child-rearing styles become popular. Fromm (1942) suggested that such societies, for example the German petit-bourgeoisie during the inter-war years, become potential breeding grounds for fascist regimes. Much else must happen for a society to become fascist, but Adorno et al. felt that prevailing attitudes and philosophies of life conditioned by child-rearing patterns must also contribute.

What psychological motives might underlie the insistence in Nazi Germany that Jews should wear a yellow star to mark their group membership?

What is impressive about this analysis and unusual for social psychology is the focus on ideology and the attempt to decipher how racist ideologies 'grab hold' of the individual, becoming psychologically real and motivating. In the end, however, the consensus among many social psychologists working in this field (for example Billig, 1978; Milner, 1981; Tajfel, 1981) is that this is a theory of racism with a limited explanatory range.

ACTIVITY 4.5

At this point you might like to anticipate the objections of these social psychologists. Read back through the account of the authoritarian personality, what are the limitations of this approach as an explanation of everyday racism?

The central problem for social psychological analyses of racism is explaining *collective* social action. While the authoritarian personality might explain the actions of some few individuals, critics suggest that it does not explain (and perhaps was not intended to explain) the racism displayed by the majority in a society. It is simply not feasible to suggest that an entire nation becomes swept by anti-semitism because of shared personality attributes. After the Second World War, the ordinary German citizen presumably retained the same character structure in psychodynamic terms, and yet may have gone through a sea change in philosophy of life and political opinions as a result of war-time experiences. The concept of the authoritarian personality may account for the Nazi elite in Germany during the Second World War (although some studies of the personalities of Nazi leaders question this assumption) but does not explain why fascist movements swept across Europe.

This point was demonstrated in Pettigrew's (1958) incisive study of South Africa and the southern states of the USA. Pettigrew found that university students born in South Africa were significantly more prejudiced than North American students but they were not correspondingly more authoritarian. Equally, significantly more prejudice was expressed by people living in the southern states of America than the northern states. Clearly social norms, rather than personality, play a crucial role in determining the mass expression of racism. However, Pettigrew did suggest that personality factors had a minor role to play, since there was some evidence that those who were more authoritarian in these contexts were also more prejudiced than the 'norm' for their community.

Billig (1978) arrived at similar conclusions in his detailed analysis of the social psychology of the fascist group, the National Front, in the 1970s in the UK. Billig's study was focused on the content of the Front's political ideology, the structure of its groups and included interviews with eleven National Front members. One of the National Front members interviewed did conform to Adorno et al.'s profile of the authoritarian personality and in this case there were logical connections between the man's character and his political concerns. This was not true, however, of other National Front members.

Billig argues that to understand the social psychology of an organization such as the National Front, a multi-layered approach is required along with concepts which can cope with contradictions in the presentation of the ideology, contradictions between National Front members, and within the personalities of particular individuals. Political allegiance is a highly complex matter and the concept of the authoritarian personality is too uni-dimensional to grapple with the personal and social history which leads to an individual espousing extreme racist views.

One of the dangers of this approach lies in neglecting the material interests which lead to racism and their role in maintaining power relations between groups. A general emphasis on the irrationality of racism also obscures the *specificity* of racist sentiments, their orientation to a particular social context and to the pressing political issues of the day. Crudely speaking, the same kind of basic explanation is offered for why the white male authoritarian doesn't get on with his mum as for why he discriminates against his black workmates. A theory which can be more responsive to subtle fluctuations in social conditions seems to be demanded.

4.2   Racism and 'unconscious pleasure'

One of the advantages of a psychodynamic account, however, is that it seems to explain some of the passion with which racism is invested and the primitive chains of associations that it seems to evoke. The psycho-analytic sociologist Rustin (1991) notes, for example, that excrement is often used in racist attacks – pushed through people's letter boxes, for instance. Rustin comments:

> Deep psychic confusion is revealed when faeces become such import-
> ant carriers of meaning as they have been in the mythology of race
> relations in Britain. It is clear that disgusting and degraded aspects of
> the self are here being dealt with by being either ascribed to, or liter-
> ally dumped on, the unwanted group. Anxieties about fecundity and
> sexual potency of other racial groups are an indication of another
> source of primitive disturbance … The connection between primitive
> oral phantasy and contemporary racism can be seen in the way emo-
> tions and anxieties about food suffuse racial prejudice today. *The
> Observer* of 22 November 1987 reported (among many other inci-
> dents) severe harassment and attacks on an Asian family in
> Thamesmead initiated when 'the next-door neighbour banged on the
> door and said: "Your curry is making the whole street stink"'. The pas-
> sions and disgusts thus evoked by food habits reveal deep preoccu-
> pations with, and probable confusions about, bodily functions and their
> inner meanings.
>
> *(1991, p. 67)*

Elliot (1992) argues that the passion with which some racist acts are per-formed indicates that, in his words, strong 'unconscious pleasure' is derived from denigrating and punishing others. This pleasure is often denied and presented as a virtue under the guise of just being a 'good citizen' or protecting 'our' way of life. A theorist like Melanie Klein, for example, would argue that 'unconscious pleasure' might derive from the relief of expelling painful, conflicting parts of the self by projecting them onto other people in the external world where they can be attacked with impunity. Klein, and some object relations psychoanalysts, might also think of 'unconscious pleasure' as unconscious identification with introjections of those who had controlled or inflicted pain and humiliation in childhood. So 'unconscious pleasure' would follow on from re-enactment of the humiliations of childhood with the power relations reversed.

Contemporary psychodynamic theorists would agree that the notion of one racist personality type suggested by Adorno et al. is too global and rigid. The concept of the authoritarian personality obscures the complex and multiple connections between the internal world of the individual and the external social world. It also links racism too narrowly to one form of child-rearing. These theorists would argue that psychodynamic concepts still have a part to play in understanding racism. This more recent work extends the reciprocal or dialectical (back and forth) relationship Adorno et al. see between the individual and society. Elliot, for example, argues that society provides the individual with deeply entrenched social divisions: groups, constructions of 'us' and 'them', of 'self' and 'other'. The way people process these divisions and manage them internally works to intensify racism, and helps to produce collective ideologies based on disgust, for example.

Elliot argues that the divisions characteristic of racism and the historically conditioned representations of otherness, described in section 2.2, are incorporated or 'introjected' into the internal psychic life of the individual to become part of people's mental and symbolic life. The individual then *externalizes* these 'imaginary representations' in their actions, thoughts and responses. In this process of externalization, however, racism becomes intensified since these notions of 'self' and 'other' have become bound up and worked through various psychodynamic mechanisms of the kind discussed in Chapter 2 – such as displacement and projection. Images of others have become imbued with phantasy and can become as a result 'phantastic' and grossly distorted.

This work stresses the contradictory and unintegrated nature of individual experience and the fact that this fragmented individual is also embedded in a contradictory social and symbolic world. An incomplete and always open sense of identity is managed in a world cross-cut by inconsistent value systems, evaluations of others and ideologies. Psychodynamic concepts such as projection (see Chapter 2, section 2) are seen, then, as a way of looking at how the individual makes emotional sense out of these fragments and how this sense-making reflects and sustains racist views of others. I will return to this theme of fragmented and shifting ideologies and identities in section 6.

Review of section 4

- Adorno et al. argue that people with authoritarian character structures, which result from certain child-rearing practices, are more likely to become caught up in racist and fascist movements. They suggest that personality is central in a person's acceptance of or resistance to racism.

- Critics of this research argue that explanations based on individual personality as the main cause of racism cannot explain shifts in the expression of racism across time and across countries.

- More recent psychodynamic work has argued that even if no single personality type is associated with racism, psychodynamic concepts can explain some of the passion with which racism is invested.

5   The effects of group membership

We have now covered two important themes in social psychological research on racism – cognitive processes and the role of emotions and personality. In this section, our focus shifts to the *group* domain of analysis and work within the experimental social perspective on this area. I want to return to some of the themes introduced in Chapter 1 of this volume and show how two sets of theorists first encountered in that chapter have applied their work to understanding relationships between groups. We will be looking, first, at the work of Muzafer Sherif and Carolyn Sherif and then at Tajfel and Turner's work on social identity.

The main argument these experimental researchers advance is that group membership *in itself* has profound effects upon the psychology of the individual, regardless of personality and individual differences. These effects are evident in the ways in which individuals come to understand themselves in groups and the ways in which they react to and develop relationships with others. To understand racism, they suggest, it is not sufficient to look at personality or cognitive process *per se,* we need to understand how the psychology of the individual is transformed in group situations.

5.1   Realistic group conflict theory

Sherif and Sherif (1969) dismissed explanations of intergroup conflict which adopt either biological or traditional psychological concepts. They firmly rejected, for example, analogies between human aggression directed toward out-groups and the aggression shown by animals in defending territory. Among animals it is rare to witness groups or associations of individuals acting aggressively in a coordinated or collective fashion and yet this is the essence of human social aggression. Sherif and Sherif argued that territorial aggression in animals is based on the relatively simple chemical, tactile and visual discriminations involved in detecting unfamiliar 'opponents' while for humans the concept of 'territory' depends on complex cultural symbolizations of property or 'homeland'. People, they pointed out, are quite capable of territorial loyalty without actually living in the territory itself. They concluded that a different level or order of explanation of human conflict is thus required.

Sherif and Sherif favoured a strongly environmentalist approach, arguing that the *immediate social situation* causes or brings about the psychological states involved in aggression, discrimination and intergroup conflict. More specifically, they suggested that the *objective* relationship between two groups (competition for scarce resources or cooperation between groups) causes the various *subjective* or psychological states characteristic of intergroup relations. People's perceptions of those who belong to their own group and to the other group, their emotions, identifications or lack of identification will fall into line with the state of relations between the groups. Because of this emphasis, the Sherifs' theory became known as 'realistic group conflict theory' (Campbell, 1965).

The Sherifs' analysis and their main hypotheses were dramatically illustrated in a famous series of field experiments conducted in boys' summer camps (see Box 4.2). Three studies, each with slight variations, were undertaken in 1949, 1953 and 1954 (see Sherif and Sherif, 1969). The common theme was the manipulation of the objective intergroup situation and the functional relationship between the groups along with measures of the psychological and behavioural effects of these manipulations.

BOX 4.2 The Summer Camp Experiments

The researchers involved in this large-scale project set up their own summer camp for a two week period (see Sherif and Sherif, 1969). As far as the boys who participated were concerned, this was a normal summer camp including all the sporting activities North American children of the time would expect to find. For the researchers this was a carefully structured experimental environment where they played double roles, not just as camp counsellors or activity leaders but also as trained observers, taking extensive recordings, and making detailed notes of events. Muzafer Sherif's role as project organizer was combined, for example, with a day job of camp handyman and janitor. In line with the rest of social psychology of the time, little is said in the accounts of this work about the ethics of this form of research. Presumably, the boys' parents volunteered their children as experimental subjects on the basis of informed consent, while the children remained unaware they were participating in research.

The boys involved were carefully selected for their 'mainstream' and 'super-normal' characteristics and did not know each other in advance. All were white and middle-class 11 to 12 year olds from families with no history of disturbance or emotional problems. Since the authoritarian personality research was an important point of contrast for the Sherifs (they saw their work as testing its central claims), it was vital that the results of their study could not be explained in terms of the personality characteristics of those participating. Over the course of the three experiments, four different social situations or stages in the experiment were engineered.

1   *Spontaneous friendship formation*: On arriving at camp the boys were allowed to mix and mingle as they pleased, entirely free to choose their partners for the various activities and as room-mates.

2   *In-group formation*: After some days the boys were split into two groups apparently arbitrarily but in fact carefully arranged so that the group allocation cut across all the pre-existing and spon-taneously chosen friendship patterns. The groups were then kept separate from each other and engaged in activities that required the group to work together. As expected, during this stage, the boys' friendship choices quickly reversed as each group developed a cohesive structure and they came to strongly prefer the members of their own group. Each group developed its own norms of behaviour, jokes, secret codes, and preferred places, coining names for themselves – the Bulldogs and the Red Devils, for instance, in one of the studies.

3   *Intergroup competition*: In this stage, the two groups were brought back together in situations of group competition. A tournament was announced, for example, in which the groups were to compete against each other for points which only one group could win. The points were kept artificially equal so that the groups were neck and neck. Initial norms of good sportsmanship quickly degenerated into overt group hostility and into minor acts of discrimination and aggression directed against members of the other group. Name-calling, stereotyping and other phenom-ena of prejudice such as glorification and over-estimation of the in-group's achievements and denigration and under-estimation of the out-group's achievements were rife. During this period, in-group loyalty, solidarity and cooperation was at its height. There was a match, in other words, between the strongly negative feelings expressed towards out-group members and the strong positive identification with the in-group.

The Summer Camp Experiments in action.

The tug-of-war was used in Stage 3 to establish competitive relations between the groups; the drawings and flags designed by the boys demonstrate the strong solidarity which emerged within the group, as well as the intergroup hostility

4   *Intergroup cooperation*: As a final stage, Sherif and his co-workers introduced a further manipulation of the intergroup situation and the functional or objective relationship between the groups. Mutual super-ordinate goals, that is, goals which both groups thought desirable but which could only be attained by both groups working together, were introduced. These included goals such as combining to solve a problem with the water supply to the camp, or getting a broken-down truck started. Other cooperative activities were introduced and, when repeated over time, were successful in alleviating intergroup hostility. The introduction of a third group (boys from a nearby camp) as a common enemy for both groups was also effective in reducing hostility. The situation in the camp returned to something resembling the first stage of spontaneous friendship formation, although group allegiance remained important for the boys in defining their relationships with each other until the end of the summer camp.

Real life intergroup situations such as those characteristic of racism involve, as Sherif and Sherif were quick to acknowledge, many more layers of complexity, including power, structural inequalities in access to resources, and histories of contact and dominance. Nonetheless, the Summer Camp Experiments are important since they seem to demonstrate a clear link between individual psychology and the group situation. As Sherif and Sherif (1969, p. 252) note, maladjusted, neurotic or unstable psychological tendencies were not necessary for the appearance of intergroup hostility. All that was required was an objective or functional relationship of competition (a clash in real vested interests) and all the mental paraphernalia of prejudice (stereotypes, negative perceptions, hostile emotions) followed along with the corresponding group ideologies (the sense of in-group solidarity, the specialness and superiority of the in-group, and justifications for the in-group's negative opinions of the out-group).

Some important moral and political points follow from the Sherifs' conclusions. Consider the difference between understanding racism as a psychopathological response and seeing stereotypes and discriminatory behaviour as a predictable, universal and even 'normal' response to a conflict of interests. What are the implications, in your view, for anti-racism and for personal accountability for one's actions?

Experimental research since the Summer Camp Experiments has supported Sherif and Sherif's conclusions (Tajfel and Turner, 1979), although the difficulties of alleviating hostility through mutual super-ordinate goals has become clearer. Some groups become even more pro in-group and anti out-group when forced to cooperate with other groups. It has also become clear that in-group formation, in itself, may bring about hostile attitudes even without the third step of intergroup competition. In their review of this research, Tajfel and Turner conclude that although competition and mutual super-ordinate goals are undoubtedly important factors, it seems likely that there may be some other psychological business also involved in the development of inter-group hostilities and intergroup cooperation.

5.2   The minimal group experiments

In following up the concerns of the Sherifs, Tajfel and his colleagues became interested in the processes involved in identification with in-groups and the psychological consequences of this identification (roughly the events occurring in the second stage of the Summer Camp Experiments during in-group formation). Like the Sherifs, Tajfel (1981) argued that something psychologically special occurs when people are placed in group situations. It is not sufficient, therefore, for social psychologists to generalize on the basis of their knowledge of how people make friends, develop relationships or relate together as individuals in general. The group context adds a whole different dimension to people's psychology.

Tajfel's concern was formalized as a distinction between two kinds of behaviour which could be placed on a continuum. At one end of the continuum there was 'interpersonal behaviour' and at the other end 'intergroup behaviour'. Brown (1988) describes these two possible kinds of behaviour as follows:

> For Tajfel, *interpersonal behaviour* meant acting *as an individual* with some idiosyncratic characteristics and a unique set of personal relationships with others (e.g. J. Smith of certain physical appearance, intelligence and personality, and with various friendships and animosities with a number of individuals). *Intergroup behaviour*, on the other hand, meant acting *as a group member* (e.g. behaving as a *police officer*, or as a *Liverpool supporter*). In the first case the various social categories one belongs to are less important than the constellation of individual and interpersonal dynamics. In the second case the reverse is true; who one is as a person is much less important than the uniform you are wearing or the colour of the scarf around your neck.

(Brown, 1988, p. 388)

The boys in the third (group competition) stage of the Summer Camp Experiments thus fall into the intergroup end of the continuum. In contrast, the boys spontaneously making friends in the first stage of the Summer Camp Experiments on the basis of personal preferences, similarities, shared likes and dislikes were responding on an interpersonal basis, reacting to each other as *individuals* rather than group members.

> Stop and consider for a moment your own behaviour. Does this distinction between responding to others as individuals and responding to them as group members ring true for you?

As Tajfel acknowledges, most behaviour is mixed or is in the middle of the continuum. Situations where one behaves purely in response to another's known group characteristics or purely in response to the individual personality are probably quite rare. It must also depend, too, on cultural factors and the concepts of the person held in a society. In highly collectivist and interdependent societies such as Japan (see Wetherell and Maybin, 1996), this separation between individual and group is likely to be understood very differently. The distinction, social identity theory researchers suggest, is nonetheless important as an analytic device for clarifying the psychological issues researchers should investigate.

Turner (1982) argues that the most important psychological difference in the two situations is that in intergroup behaviour people tend to 'depersonalize' and stereotype themselves and other people (see Chapter 1, section 4). Ignoring individual diversities and individual differences, people in intergroup situations focus on the similarities between themselves and other members of their group for the relevant group attributes. The out-group also comes to be seen as homogeneous rather than being made up of individuals with different personal characteristics and idiosyncrasies.

Tajfel's interest in the process of identification with groups received a strong impetus from a series of studies conducted in the early 1970s which have come to be known as the minimal group experiments (see Tajfel, 1981 and Box 4.3 overleaf). These studies were exciting and provocative because they seemed to suggest that something more basic was involved in intergroup hostility than the conflict of group interests investigated by the Sherifs and their colleagues. Tajfel's experiments set up the most minimal group situation possible – the mere recognition of two groups. There was no history to the group membership, certainly none of the compelling logic which shared interests give to identification with a group, no interaction between group members, and personal rewards or outcomes were not dependent upon behaviour to other group members. Yet, as Box 4.3 demonstrates, subjects in this situation showed clear signs of in-group favouritism and discrimination against those seen as the out-group.

BOX 4.3   The minimal group situation

The minimal group experiments were usually conducted with adolescents or younger schoolchildren. A typical procedure would involve first showing the students a series of abstract paintings said to have been done by painters such as Klee and Kandinsky and asking them to indicate which ones they liked best. After the results of this 'preference test' had been supposedly scored, the students were told that they had been assigned to one of two groups, they were either in the Klee group or the Kandinsky group. In fact, students were randomly assigned to the two groups. Group membership was anonymous, and for the rest of the experiment the students worked individually in cubicles. As far as they knew their best friends could have been assigned to the other group. In some variations of the experiment, group assignment was done on an even more minimal basis. Subjects were assigned to groups on the basis of a simple coin toss or told that they were either in the blue group or the red group.

Students were then asked to divide points worth money between the two groups using matrices like the ones in Table 4.1. Their task, however, was always to allocate points to other people in the two groups identified by code numbers. At no point would they be awarding money to themselves. The matrices set up a number of possible strategies including:

- fairness

- maximum joint profit

- maximum in-group profit

- maximum difference.

Looking at Table 4.1, then, subjects in the Klee group who wanted to go for *fairness* could choose those options in the matrices which divided the points equally between the in-group and the out-group (options such as 13/13 from Matrix 1 or 17/17 in Matrix 2). The strategy of *maximum joint profit* involved choosing the maximum number of points available in the matrix to obtain the most money out of the experimenter regardless of which group actually got most (choices such as 11/29 on Matrix 2 or 23/29 on Matrix 4). The strategy of *maximum in-group profit* involved picking the largest number of points possible for the in-group regardless of the gain to the out-group (choosing, for instance, 19/25 when a member of the Klee group was presented with Matrix 3). Finally, the strategy of *maximum difference* involved choosing options which maximized the difference between the two groups in favour of one's own group even if this meant the in-group getting less points on the matrix than was possible (e.g. the Klee group choosing 7/1 when presented with Matrix 3 or 11/5 when presented with Matrix 4).

Table 4.1   Matrices used in the experiment (adapted from Tajfel, 1981, p. 269)

Matrix 1	Klee Group	19	18	17	16	15	14	13	12	11	10	9	8	7
	Kandinsky Group	1	3	5	7	9	11	13	15	17	19	21	23	25
Matrix 2	Klee Group	23	22	21	20	19	18	17	16	15	14	13	12	11
	Kandinsky Group	5	7	9	11	13	15	17	19	21	23	25	27	29
Matrix 3	Klee Group	7	8	9	10	11	12	13	14	15	16	17	18	19
	Kandinsky Group	1	3	5	7	9	11	13	15	17	19	21	23	25
Matrix 4	Klee Group	11	12	13	14	15	16	17	18	19	20	21	22	23
	Kandinsky Group	5	7	9	11	13	15	17	19	21	23	25	27	29

Typically, British and North American subjects ignored the maximum joint profit strategy and went instead for maximum in-group profit and maximum difference. Fairness was usually also quite a significant strategy. In situations where maximum in-group profit was combined on a matrix with maximum joint profit, which meant the out-group getting more than the in-group (e.g. a choice by a member of the Klee group for 23/29 on Matrix 4), then subjects tended to prefer the maximum difference response (e.g. 11/5 on Matrix 4). In other words, the results suggest that people will discriminate against the out-group even when group membership is anonymous, no contact is made between group members and there is no obvious self-interest involved.

Before continuing, consider again the results from the minimal group studies.   ACTIVITY 4.6
This result has been repeated many times with North American and British subjects. How would you explain what is going on? How would you behave if placed in this situation? Consider again, too, Tajfel's notion of a continuum of psychological responses from interpersonal to intergroup behaviour. How might this be applied to make sense of the minimal group results?

5.3   Social identity theory

Tajfel and Turner's social identity theory which seeks to explain the minimal group findings proposes a three stage psychological process linking an individual's desire for a positive self-image to discriminatory intergroup strategies. It also takes some of the earlier research on the cognitive dimensions of prejudice reviewed in section 3.1 and puts that work in a new light. The three stages in their theory are as follows.

Social categorization

The first effect of a group division, like the one engineered in the minimal group experiment, is to provide a new cognitive scheme with which to view the world. Two categories, such as the blue group and the red group, or the Klee and Kandinsky groups, are superimposed on a continuous and otherwise undifferentiated school class or other sample of subjects. The subjects' perceptions of themselves and other people participating in the experiment will begin to be organized around these cognitive labels.

Tajfel and Turner argue that exactly the same process happens in everyday life, outside the experimental context. The social or group categories of daily life, such as those of class, gender, 'race', community or nationality or, on the smaller scale, the categorizations of football supporting and other leisure activities found in school life and at work, act like a template for making sense of society and for organizing perceptions of self and other. The categories we use in everyday life do not arise spontaneously, however. They are not idiosyncratic but consensual, conventional and socially constructed. Tajfel and Turner see these categories as the product of human activity in specific historical contexts. Thus black and white are important not because of the colour difference *per se* but because of the social histories attached to this distinction.

Tajfel argues that one consequence of this process of categorization for cognition and people's judgements of themselves and others may well be the kind of 'perceptual illusions' discussed in section 3.1 – an accentuation of intergroup differences and intragroup similarity along some relevant dimension. One cognitive or mental effect may be to push the two groups apart perceptually and judgementally while pulling all the members within each group together. People may see members of their own group as more similar to each other than they really are while over-accentuating the differences between the groups.

Social identification

Social categories not only organize and order cognitive impressions, they also create social identities. Tajfel and Turner argue that social categorizations change self-definitions and create a value system. The minute a categorization is effected and you are identified as belonging to one group rather than another, you take up an *identity* in your own eyes and in the eyes of others. The template provided by social categories for making sense of the social world not only gives a sense of order but also defines people's positions and one's own position in the social network.

Tajfel defines social identification as the knowledge that one belongs to a group along with the emotional and value significance attached to that membership. He argues that in an important sense a person's social identities, or their group memberships, come to determine their value or status as a person. Social identity is an important basis of self-esteem and vital in self-evaluation. In many social situations the answer to the question 'What particular groups do I belong to and how are these valued?' will be crucial for sorting out the evaluation you put on yourself and other people.

Social comparison

In most situations where social identities or group memberships are functioning, self-esteem, according to this logic, will be tied to the position of one's groups *vis à vis* other groups. To think well of ourselves, therefore, it is necessary to think well of our groups. Tajfel and Turner maintain that this link between thinking well of oneself (individual self-esteem) and group self-esteem is crucial for understanding intergroup discrimination and hostility.

Groups are almost constantly forced into rounds of intergroup comparisons. Comparison is the only means towards group evaluation and thus will lead inevitably to intergroup competition as each group struggles to establish a value difference between itself and another group. Each group member who desires a positive social identity and positive self-esteem is thus encouraged to maximize the difference between in-group and out-group on the dimension of comparison.

Applied to the minimal group situation, it is clear how this sequence might explain subjects' choice of maximum difference and maximum in-group profit. Tajfel and Turner argue that it is only these choices that allow people to set up the comparison between groups in a way which enhances the differences between groups in favour of the in-group. If self-esteem is tied to group performance, the maximum difference and maximum in-group profit strategies are the most obvious route for enhancing one group's advantage in relation to the other group, and hence the identity of the members of that group.

Look back at the matrices presented in Table 4.1 in Box 4.3 and consider why   ACTIVITY 4.7
this might be so. Compare the maximum difference options, for instance, with
the maximum joint profit choices.

To summarize, the Sherifs suggest that groups come into conflict and phenomena, such as racism, develop because of competition for resources and as a result of the state of the objective relationship between group interests. Tajfel and Turner claim that self-evaluation and the desire for positive self-esteem in intergroup situations are equally important factors. The two theories make different predictions. Sherif and Sherif suggest that conflict, discrimination and negative stereotypes only come about when there is a goal which only one group can attain, whereas Tajfel and Turner maintain that groups will compete even when there is no 'objective' reason for doing so, and where the only aim is a positive social identity. The minimal group experiments seem to support this interpretation since they are an example of discrimination as a consequence of group categorization without competition for scarce resources. Tajfel and Turner thus seem to have demonstrated intergroup discrimination in the equivalent of the second stage of the Summer Camp Experiments without the necessity for the third stage of competition for resources which only one group can attain.

Tajfel and Turner conclude that competition for a scarce resource will cause conflict and the psychology which goes along with intergroup hostility, but, equally, competition to establish a value difference between groups will also cause conflict. Economic competition or competition over goals is only part, therefore, of a general process of *social competition* to establish value differentials based on social comparison between groups. The positive outcome of such a comparison can also be seen as a scarce resource. Individual group members will struggle against members of other groups because their own self-worth is tied to the group's wider standing.

5.4   Intergroup strategies

As Sherif and Sherif pointed out in the 1960s, to study intergroup relations in the pure situation of the experimental laboratory or in a field experiment is one thing, it is another to apply that understanding to complicated existing group divisions. One feature of real-life group divisions, such as those based on 'race', is that they are often characterized by long-standing relations of dominance and oppression where one group has been consistently in a position to maintain power, control resources and enforce inequalities. What happens to the social competition identified by Tajfel and Turner in these situations? What is the experience of members of minority groups confronting majority groups either in a situation of struggle or in situations where the status inequalities are stable, entrenched and apparently unchanging?

Tajfel (1981) described a number of 'cognitive alternatives' open to such groups. He saw the problem, in part, as one of developing strategies to cope with the negative social identities which might result from continually taking 'second place' in intergroup comparisons. One possible response is for the minority group member to accept the negative identity and perceive subordination as legitimate, determined by the actual inferior characteristics of their group. The psychological result would be to interiorize a sense of stigma and inferiority. This outcome is most likely when the majority group is so dominant and its ideologies of superiority are so pervasive, as in the situations Frantz Fanon (1967) studied for example, that there may be no other basis for group-linked self-evaluations (see Reading A).

Some have argued that this was the situation for many Afro-Americans in the USA before the civil rights and other resistance movements. This point was developed by two Afro-American social psychologists, Kenneth and Mamie Clark, in their work in the 1940s.

> Human beings who are forced to live under ghetto conditions and whose daily experience tells them that almost nowhere in society are they respected and granted the ordinary dignity and courtesy accorded to others will, as a matter of course, begin to doubt their own worth. Since every human being depends on his [sic] cumulative experiences with others for clues as to how he should view and value himself, children who are consistently rejected understandably begin to question and doubt whether they, their family and their group really deserve no more respect from the larger society than they receive. These doubts become the seeds of a pernicious self- and group-hatred, the Negro's complex and debilitating prejudice against himself.
>
> *(Kenneth Clark, cited in Tajfel, 1981, p. 324)*

The Clarks' case was built on disturbing results from their own studies with Afro-American children in the 1940s. Their methodology was simple and involved presenting children with a pair of dolls, one black and one white, and then asking, 'which one looks most like you?' Typically, as many as a third of the Afro-American children replied that the white doll resembled them most closely. Clark and Clark (1947) presented evidence that this was not a mistake on the children's part or due to genuine confusion, rather it was interpreted as a strong pro-white bias. The children were expressing the wish that they would rather be white, and the fantasy that they were white, because of the highly negative connotations attached to being black in a strongly racist society.

The Clarks' results and their testimony in 1954 to the American Supreme Court were decisive in the legal battle to overturn the segregation laws. Research using the doll methodology continued through until the 1970s and became an important marker for social change. As Milner (1981) comments in his review of this research, by the early 1970s, it was evident that there was a complete reversal in black children's preferences and the virtual disappearance of white identification. Some studies demonstrated higher self-esteem among black children than white. With this has come a reconsideration of the earlier findings and the meaning of the earlier misidentifications (see Milner, 1981). Was the misidentification really a sign of low group self-esteem? The link was often assumed rather than demonstrated. To what extent were children responding in terms of their assumptions about the preferences of the researchers and broader society?

Tajfel notes that the children's responses hint at another strategy open to minority group members. Members may leave or aspire to leave their group and seek to 'pass' as members of groups with more economic and political options. There is, Tajfel argues, such a thing as a 'social mobility belief structure' where the individual's goal is to improve their own position independently of the group. The psychology of the socially mobile involves thinking in interpersonal rather than intergroup terms in relation to the continuum of behaviour (interpersonal to intergroup) identified in section 2.4. People may deliberately distance themselves from other members of the group. Women, for example, in societies where sexism operates, may regard themselves as sharing masculine traits, and being as good as, if not better than, most men, while at the same time denigrating other women and femininity as a whole.

An important moment occurs, Tajfel argues, in the life of a minority group or minority group member when the transition is made from a social mobility belief structure to what he calls a 'social change belief structure'. It is at this moment that questions of 'voice' or efforts for change for the group as a whole come to predominate over questions of 'exit' from the group, or how to achieve social mobility as an individual. Psychologically, Tajfel claims, this transition mirrors the shift along the continuum from interpersonal to intergroup behaviour discussed earlier. Group members begin to mobilize as a group. One consequence might be a struggle to redefine the parameters of social competition, to carve out new criteria for intergroup evaluation. The second wave of feminism for example, beginning in the late 1960s, sought to actively re-evaluate femininity and masculinity and develop new understandings of what it means to be human. Similarly the 'black is beautiful' movements of the same period and the popularity of what were known as 'Afro haircuts' sought to redefine concepts of style and the basis of popular culture (a strategy successfully continued by black youth in the modern UK and USA around rap and other musical forms).

This 'social creativity' around the bases for self and group evaluation is one kind of social change activity with its own psychological dynamics. The social change belief structure described by Tajfel is also present whenever groups struggle directly to change inequalities, for material resources, and compete for power. In this case social mobility has given way to revolution.

5.5   Evaluating social identity theory

Social identity theory is perhaps the best known attempt to explain the social psychological basis of group conflict. It is a complex account which, as we have seen, tries to describe what happens to people's emotions, their motivations and their self-understandings in group situations. The theory places a great deal of emphasis on the social context as a cause of conflict, but it also emphasizes the role of individual psychology. Intergroup conflicts based on skin colour develop as a result of social history but they acquire their force, Tajfel and Turner argue, because of a psychological process of categorization, identification and comparison followed by differentiation and competition to maintain self-esteem which is seemingly built into people. Psychology and the social context thus combine.

Where would you place this theory on the continuum outlined in section 2.4?

Tajfel and Turner's work emphasizes the 'ordinariness' of racism and its continuity with other forms of group behaviour. Intergroup conflict is not seen as a psychopathology or as the result of irrational prejudice but as a form of behaviour involving complex psychological states which are also at the heart of more positive group actions such as developing a sense of solidarity with others, group loyalty, group cohesiveness and national belonging. These are processes which might underlie any form of collective action such as crowd behaviour. Tajfel and Turner are arguing that racism is only inevitable given a particular social context where 'racial' categories become significant and acquire meaning as group divisions. These categories are not natural but become powerful as a result of social history.

Tajfel and Turner, however, paint a more pessimistic picture of the possibilities for 'race relations' than that provided by realistic group conflict theory, for example. Social identity theory claims that conflict will be triggered whenever social categories and group divisions are present (as in the minimal group situation) because of the inexorable logic of the process of identification, comparison and group differentiation to maximize self-esteem. Muzafer and Carolyn Sherif state that conflict depends on the normative climate (recognized codes of conduct) along with the goal relationship between the groups. Are the groups in competition for a scarce resource or are they working together for a superordinate goal? Indeed, among the approaches we have considered so far, realistic group conflict theory places most emphasis on the social determination of individual reactions in group situations.

Those who are sceptical about social identity theory have questioned whether it is the case that there is one universal psychological process associated with group conflict. Cross-cultural research with the minimal group experiment suggests that children from other cultural backgrounds do not automatically discriminate between groups in the same way as British and North American children (Wetherell, 1982). This research with young Pacific Island, Maori and white European New Zealand children supports a normative or social constructionist interpretation of the minimal group results. Whereas white European New Zealand children showed the same pattern of behaviour as British and North American children, Pacific Island children repeatedly chose to maximize the *joint* profit of both groups even when the choice of this strategy would mean their group getting substantially *less* than the out-group (see Box 4.3 for a definition of maximum joint profit). This behaviour makes sense in terms of the cultural and social frameworks of Polynesian societies and the emphasis these societies place on generosity to others as a marker of high status.

Results like these suggest that what determines behaviour in the minimal group situation may not be an automatic psychological link between group identification and competition. What may be more crucial is the way in which group members interpret and give meaning to the intergroup situation in line with the collective frameworks of their culture and community. This sense-making will determine the consequences of group identification – whether it leads to in-group favouritism and out-group discrimination or to some other outcome. It also will determine how a positive group identity is understood. Individual self-esteem, feeling good about one's group and one's self, may not be necessarily linked to being able to maximize the difference between in-group and out-group in favour of one's own group. Such a view is, perhaps, most likely to predominate in cultures where there is a strong emphasis on the independent individual and where societies and their economic systems are organized on a competitive basis. A more flexible set of psychological reactions might be at the root of intergroup behaviour than the sequence Tajfel and Turner suggest. But, nonetheless, their work raises important questions about the process of group identification and its consequences.

Review of section 5

- The Sherifs and social identity theorists argue that everyone has the potential to behave in a discriminatory fashion. In their view it is not a question of personality, instinct or the limitations of human cognition but a result of the influence of group situations upon individual psychology.

- The Sherifs' Summer Camp Experiments suggest that the key determinant of ethnocentric and discriminatory behaviour is the objective relationship between groups. If groups are in competition for scarce resources, hostility, negative stereotypes and aggression will result. If groups are working together for a superordinate goal, more positive and cooperative behaviour emerges.

- Social identity theorists argue that although group competition is important, the minimal group studies demonstrate an even more basic effect of group belongingness. Group members will compete in the absence of any rational reason simply because their self-esteem is linked to the position of their group.

- Tajfel describes a number of 'cognitive alternatives' open to members of minority groups including a social mobility belief structure and a social change belief structure.

6   Discourse, identity and culture

In this chapter I have introduced a number of different conceptual vocabularies for making sense of racism. Compare, for example, concepts of the 'authoritarian personality', 'projection', 'sado-masochistic character structure' with 'functional relationship between groups', 'mutual superordinate goals', 'social comparison', 'social mobility belief structure', and so on. Each of these vocabularies has focused on different phenomena and has placed racism in a different light. In this final section I want to develop a social constructionist perspective which looks at discourse, the development of shared meanings and the emergence of identity from the sociocultural field. This orientation will develop a new perspective on the acts of categorization, discrimination and identification which seem to be at the heart of racism.

6.1   Racist discourse

One of the problems social constructionists identify with experimental research is the tendency to remove phenomena from their context. The complex patterns of communication and everyday talk which sustain racism are reduced, for example, to one feature, the stereotype, and to statements such as individuals in Group A have x, y and z characteristics. But what does racist talk actually look like? How are group categories used in practice?

Take a look at Extract 4.1 which comes from a study conducted by Cashmore (1987) in the West Midlands. The speaker is a white, middle-class company director and in this part of the interview he is developing his view of immigration policies. His account fits the definition of racism to the extent that he seeks to marginalize and exclude people on the basis of their ethnic group membership. It is a statement from a person who is a member of a powerful group and is an attempt to rationalize and exert that power over others constructed as subordinate.

Extract 4.1

We gave them hell in the Empire; but just because they had no freedom then doesn't mean they can have freedom in a different way now. They've become members of the Commonwealth, and all we should have done is have people who really wanted to get education, educated them and then said, 'Right, now go back to your own country and implement those things we've taught you. And if you don't like it, fine; go to Moscow, or the States, or wherever you like. Don't expect to come here and enjoy ours because it's very serious and we don't want you here'. The politicians were blinded. 'They are part of the Commonwealth;

they fought for us in two world wars,' they said. Of course they did, but I still wouldn't have given them full rights. I would have allowed in people who'd shown educational ability, the people who want to become doctors, civil servants and so on, given them three or five years training and then sent them back. It's hindsight, I know, but even in those early days, we at the Rotary Club were saying, 'These people have got to stop coming in', and people turned their backs on it. The people who were coming over here were straight from the cane fields.

We've always said, 'Anybody who's a member of our colonies is free to come into this country.' Undoubtedly there's a lot who come in just to draw the dole. I personally think we'd be much better off if nobody could draw national assistance until they'd been in a job for six months. They come here and, within a month, they're living off the state, whether they're black, yellow or any other colour. I think that's wrong. I've got two Indian friends. One's a doctor and the other's a business associate, and they're always amazed at the number of Indians and West Indians floating around. Where do they all come from? Whereas they came in with nothing, they're now starting to climb the business ladder and very shortly, if we don't watch it, they'll be getting ahead of us.

Source: Cashmore, 1987, pp. 166–7

It is unusual in racist talk to find examples of direct stereotypic statements of the classic 'Italians are over-emotional' form. Rather, as in Extract 4.1, highly offensive descriptions of groups are embedded in arguments and in complex and shifting webs of categorizations. It is also the case that most racist talk is not necessarily about 'race' *per se* but works through broader discussions of 'England', 'us', 'them', the nation, cultural difference and discussions of seemingly broader social, economic and political issues.

ACTIVITY 4.8   As an exercise, you might like to list all the different group categorizations you can find in this extract. Take a look, too, at the use of 'we' and 'they', and chart the shifts in who seems to be referred to in each case.

In section 4 of the previous chapter, Jonathan Potter argued for a discursive psychology which would analyse the kinds of statements found in Extract 4.1 as *activities* constructed in interaction as opposed to attitudes or schema fixed in people's heads. In this view the derogatory categorizations and group descriptions which form the substance of racist talk are best seen as rhetorical and communicative acts rather than as primarily perceptual or cognitive phenomena. The speaker in Extract 4.1 is not describing the nature of the world and giving his reactions to it, but is constructing a world. The sense he finds is not a natural property of the world but is worked up through representation and argument and is an attempt to persuade the person listening to him. The speaker is trying to present an account in a way which seems coherent and logical (however it might seem to us). He is not describing the objects of his perception in the way a person might be asked to recall an array of objects laid out on a table in a memory experiment.

When the speaker, for instance, makes a distinction between 'people straight from the cane field' and 'educated people' he is not, I would suggest, reporting on a set of ordered categories derived from his observations over time or describing prototypes held as permanent schema in his mind, rather he is constructing a categorization which temporarily furthers his argument. At other times in his talk, migrants become categorized differently, simply as a homogeneous 'they', for example, contrasted to a 'we', described as 'members of the Commonwealth', or as 'black, yellow, or any other colour'. In this way we can see the thrust of claims introduced in section 3.2 about 'mind in culture'. The categorization, perception and ordering of social groups is a process which is very sensitive to social factors and emerges from narrative, discourse, dialogue and social practices.

Group descriptions and stereotypes are not, in this view, like visual illusions and thus indicative of errors, biases and shortcuts in people's information processing. Rather, group descriptions are developed as part of stories and accounts which are *ideological* in nature. The term 'ideological' suggests that this discursive work needs to be understood in terms of the patterning of social relations, power and inequalities within a society. To understand the forms group descriptions and categorizations take, the social psychologist should look first to the nature of the broader patterns of communication in which group categorizations are embedded rather than to the structure and modes of operation of the human mind (Wetherell and Potter, 1992).

Another salient and typical feature of Extract 4.1 is the speaker's inconsistency. When we look at everyday talk and interaction, as the previous chapter stressed, the variability in the way people talk about issues is quickly apparent. Black migrants are caught in a double-bind in Extract 4.1. On the one hand, the speaker stresses that migrants should work and try to become educated, on the other hand, if they make their way 'up the business ladder', they are also a threat and unwelcome. This is a no-win situation for black communities, and it is worth thinking about the psychological impact of double binds of this kind on members of minority groups over time.

It is clear, too, that just as the group categorizations shift throughout this extract according to the ebb and flow of the argument, the speaker's own identity also shifts and is thus multiple rather than singular. At one moment he speaks, seemingly, as a British national with an exclusive sense of who else belongs in the UK, at another point he speaks as someone with Indian friends, or as a member of a supposedly prescient group within the Rotary Club who saw problems coming before the politicians.

The speaker is not only continually casting and recasting other people as he talks, his own identity is also being continually constructed and reconstructed. In developing a version of the social world, the speaker is also positioning himself as he constructs his account. The process of identification which the social psychologist needs to understand to make sense of racism seems to be more flexible and moment-to-moment than social identity theory, for example, implies.

I will come back shortly to this point about identity and multiplicity. A further feature about this extract is that like talk in general it is oriented towards a listener or an audience and has to be seen as one side of an argument. Billig (1987) has noted that contrary to a common view of people reproducing the ideologies of their culture in set speeches, like robots or 'social dopes' trotting out clichés, most talk, especially around political and social issues, is argumentative in form. It is part of an on-going dialogue and debate within communities.

In Extract 4.1 the speaker is trying to put his best case forward as he sees it. He is aware of counter arguments and perhaps is aware, too, that he might well be perceived as a racist. The reference to Indian friends is a device often found in contemporary racist talk (van Dijk, 1984; Wetherell and Potter, 1992), as are disclaimer structures more generally (e.g. 'I'm not prejudiced but ...' or 'some of my best friends are black but ...'). The speakers in such cases are orienting to the likely reception of their remarks. They are constituting their descriptions within a broader argumentative field. In Extract 4.1, the interviewee seems to be trying to add to his own credentials and the credentials of his argument. The subtext seems to be that he is someone with Indian friends and, moreover, if they are concerned about the numbers of migrants then his own concern is justified.

Finally, it is possible to see in Extract 4.1 echoes of other voices. The speaker spends much time reporting speech, constructing his own and others' talk ('they fought for us in two world wars', 'these people have got to stop coming in'). As theorists such as Vygotsky and Bakhtin would stress (see Wetherell and Maybin, 1996) this is a *communal* text. This communal and collective aspect is evident not just in the moments where the speaker deliberately quotes the voices of others but throughout the text. The speaker is speaking in tune with his in-group and this collective aspect is typical of ideology along with the way in which this talk protects vested interests and tries to maintain power relations and the status quo.

In Said's terms, we might say that 'communities of interpretation' are involved here.

> ... what we are dealing with here are in the very widest sense communities of interpretation, many of them at odds with one another, prepared in many instances literally to go to war with one another, all of them creating and revealing themselves and their interpretations as very central features of their existence. No one lives in direct contact

with reality. Each of us lives in a world actually made by human beings, in which such things as the 'nation' or 'Christianity' or 'Islam' are the result of agreed-upon convention, of historical processes, and above all, of willed human labor expended to give those things an identity we can recognize.

(Said, 1981, pp. 41–2)

A social constructionist social psychology of racism is concerned, therefore, with the human labour of interpretation which Said identifies. The aim is to *describe* patterns in contemporary ideologies, to understand the social and psychological implications of certain ways of talking, especially for people's definitions of their own and others' identities, and the way in which interpretations become bound in with patterns of action. This description is seen as a central part of the explanation of racism. If we can understand how representations of self and other emerge as collective phenomena and become meaningful for individuals and groups, then we have gone a long way to understanding the perpetration of racism. There is a new interest in understanding the *content* of racist cultures and communications and in the shifts which take place in these over time as a way of combating racism.

In the UK, for example, there have been profound movements in the ideologies and chains of association surrounding 'race' in recent years with important consequences for people's sense of identity. As anti-racist groups, for example, develop and circulate new forms of argument, and public opinion changes, new ways of justifying inequalities also evolve. Similarly, as material circumstances change, new patterns arise and must be incorporated into the collective common sense.

Many commentators across the western world have noted how forms of racism, based on the biological claims about 'inferiority', and 'advanced and primitive races' discussed in section 2.2, are gradually disappearing from political and public life. These commentators argue, however, that this does not mean that racism is diminishing, rather, new kinds of discourse and forms of talk now legitimate social divisions and inequalities. In the UK, the chains of association around 'race' have moved increasingly from discussion of biological differences, 'natural' capacities and questions of 'purity and pollution' to links with talk of 'nation', 'inner cities' and 'law and order'. Condor (1988) notes, for example, how in the 1987 Conservative Party manifesto, 'race' appeared subsumed under the general heading 'Freedom, Law and Responsibility' where other subsections under this heading included 'the fight against crime' and 'tackling drug abuse'. This discursive linking can become so well established that the step from 'black' to 'mugger' becomes automatic. Current ideological struggles concern just who becomes defined as 'one of us', and the nature of being British in a time of anxiety over European integration. As Gilroy (1987) points out, for the black British person the experience has always been one of being defined as some kind of problem but the grounds for this 'problem identity' are not constant and have changed substantially over the years.

6.2 Shifting identities

The view which is developing in this section suggests that group and individual identities emerge from the social context and stresses the role discourse and language play in this process. The developmental theories of Mead and Vygotsky (reviewed in Wetherell and Maybin, 1996) are relevant here, too. Both Mead and Vygotsky argue that thought or individual mental life consists of internalized social dialogues. Indeed, it is easy to hear the speaker in Extract 4.1 externalizing these dialogues. Individuals incorporate the narratives of their culture and their incorporation of these narratives construct their self-understanding – external cultural narratives become a set of personalized voices and positions.

This process of internalizing dialogues, voices and narratives, and creative work with these, can be seen most vividly in children's discourse around 'race'. Children are not naturally oriented to 'race' but have to be taught that skin colour is an important social division while height, for instance, does not have the same salience. Children have to be taught how to notice and respond to differences, and narrative plays an important part in this process. Milner (1981) notes that the echoes of parental voices can be very sharp and vivid. Thus one small child commented in a study in which white children looked at photos of minority children, 'If I have to sit next to one of them, I'll have a nervous breakdown'. Here, in echoing racist adult statements, the child is also learning a particular construction of intergroup relations.

To talk at all is to construct an identity. The point being made here is that these constructions are shifting rather than stable and draw upon the multiple voices of an entire culture. Social psychologists have often assumed that people have one fixed identity and that this identity prompts them to talk in a certain way – their words represent what they are, their intrinsic being, whether this is as an 'authoritarian personality' or as a 'tolerant individual'. Discourse analysts and social constructionists suggest that identity is constructed in a more partial way and is more flexible, multiple and inconsistent. Identity is accomplished as people speak. And, of course, because the process of speaking has a long history for each individual, which is rooted in childhood, individual human minds become built up from the accretion of voices spoken over the years (Wetherell and Maybin, 1996). It is this long-term incorporation which accounts for individual differences in the expression of racism tied to different individuals' social positions and interests, while the multiplicity and inconsistency make social change possible. Psychodynamic researchers, of course, would wonder whether this sufficiently accounts for the depth of the emotions associated with racism, while social identity theorists might argue that this emphasis on the social causes of racism ignores the contribution of independent and universal cognitive and psychological processes.

As a reader of this chapter connected to one or more of the many ethnic groups in the UK, you might like to consider how you are positioned by social psychological research on racism.

For instance, I noted in section 2.3 that this chapter, following the main trend in social psychology, focuses on the perpetrators of racism and the action of majority groups. One of the dangers of this emphasis is that, once again, black people and black communities can disappear from view and become seen as passive victims rather than active agents, as reactive rather than creative, determined rather than determining. The sense of 'otherness' or 'outsiderness', which is the essence of racism, can be reinforced.

Similarly, the white reader (and author) of writings on racism is often assumed to be beyond racism – to be considering the actions of other people who are different from us. The social constructionist perspective questions any such simple construction of identity – that we are either all 'good' or 'bad', 'liberal' or 'illiberal', 'racist' or 'anti-racist'. It is important to ask about *all* the internal dialogues and cultural narratives from which identities are constructed, and the effects of privilege and disadvantage on these possible identities (see Frankenberg, 1993). Chapter 6 will return to this issue of the relationship between identity and social position.

Another, perhaps more positive, way of putting the argument about identity developing in recent social constructionist work on racism is to note, following Hall, that identity is always in production. It is a *continuing process* rather than an already accomplished fact.

> Cultural identity … is a matter of 'becoming' as well as of 'being'. It belongs to the future as much as to the past. It is not something which already exists, transcending place, time, history and culture. Cultural identities come from somewhere, have histories. But, like everything which is historical, they undergo constant transformation. Far from being eternally fixed in some essentialized past, they are subject to the continuous 'play' of history, culture and power. Far from being grounded in a mere 'recovery' of the past, which is waiting to be found, and which, when found, will secure our sense of ourselves into eternity, identities are the names we give to the different ways we are positioned by, and position ourselves within, the narratives of the past.

> *(Hall, 1990, p. 225)*

Hall's concern here is with the identity strategies developed by Afro-Caribbean and Asian migrants for dealing with their sense of displacement. Is there some authentic Afro-Caribbean cultural identity or even black African identity which a British Afro-Caribbean community, for instance, could refer back to? Hall argues that cultural identities, in all cases, have to be actively created and constructed. Cultural identity, whether Jamaican, white British, or black British, involves a struggle over representation and narrative, it is not a reflection of some identity which is already present and determining. As Hall notes, power is involved in this struggle. Some groups such as the British in the history of Jamaica, or India for that matter, have had a disproportionate influence on the narratives and stories by which a people come to understand themselves. You may recall the words of Fanon at this point and his record of an internal psychological struggle against identities imposed and constructed by other powerful groups in Martinique and Algeria.

Over the years, the Notting Hill Carnival has become symbolic of the struggle for space, voice and identity in the UK

Along with the acknowledgement of the shifting narratives and voices which make up the identities involved in social conflicts has come an awareness, too, of the diversity of people's social positions. 'Race' is an important marker and studied as a topic by social psychologists in its own right. But, of course, 'race' intersects with other identities such as gender, class and sexuality. Each of these involves other complicated communities of interpretations. As social psychologists have become more interested in studying ideological fields and the identities, emotions and motives constructed within those fields, so the dividing lines between the study of gender, 'race' and class have become more blurred. These distinctions are important ones because each is massively socially significant, yet it is also clear that identity is more complicated than 'race' or ethnic group membership *per se*.

Review of section 6

- Social constructionists argue that people's emotions, understandings, and beliefs in intergroup situations will reflect the social and ideological situation in which they are placed.

- The categories which make up 'us' and 'them' are not seen as natural phenomena, there to be observed by any perceiver, but are seen as human constructions tied to ideologies and mobilized in rhetoric and argument.

- Research on discourse around 'race' suggests that such discourse is fragmented, contradictory and 'dilemmatic' in form, built up from a patchwork of interpretative resources and multiple voices.

- Identities, therefore, are also fragmented and changing rather than fixed and essential, constructed through group narratives and struggles over representation which are linked to conflicts of interest and power inequalities.

7   Conclusion

We have covered a large amount of ground in this chapter, examining research from the 1920s, the 1950s and the 1970s as well as some of the most recent developments in social psychology. We have seen continuities in the concerns of social psychologists as well as some key contrasts in the conceptual languages social psychologists have developed for making sense of racism. What conclusions can we reach? Is there any consensus emerging in the social psychology of racism?

ACTIVITY 4.9   Consider a particular conflict, perhaps between anti-racist demonstrators and National Front members marching in the East End of London as has happened on a number of occasions in the last fifteen years, controversies over racist chanting directed at black players on British football fields or a hypothetical dispute between black communities and estate agencies over, for instance, covert discrimination in house rentals.

Make some notes on how each of the approaches considered in this chapter would investigate the *psychology* of these situations. What would be the main themes in the explanations offered by sociobiologists, social cognition researchers, psychodynamic theorists, realistic group conflict theorists, social identity theorists and social constructionists?

In many respects, the concerns of different theorists complement each other. Social identity theorists, social cognition researchers and social constructionists, for instance, are all concerned with the group categorizations which are salient in 'race' situations. Social cognition researchers would be interested in the formal nature of this process – what does the process of grouping indicate about the nature of the human mind? And, how does the existence of these categories result in misperceptions, biases and misjudgements? As the term 'bias' suggests, this line of inquiry has generally, but not always, assumed that it is possible to get outside the group situation and have an unbiased view of the nature of those involved.

Social identity theorists and social constructionists would be more interested in questions of content. How are 'we', 'you', 'us', 'them', 'in-group' and 'out-group' defined in these situations? What is the history of this situation and these groupings? What identities can people take up as a consequence? Social identity theorists would relate the strategies different groups and individuals adopt to the maximizing of positive group identity and self-esteem. They would also be interested in the cognitive consequences of categorization. Again it would be assumed that the analyst can take a neutral position in identifying and describing these intergroup strategies.

Social constructionists and discursive psychologists would want to examine the structure and organization of people's accounts, sense-making, rationalizations and justifications and the emotional logic contained in different versions of events. A particular interest would be in how these accounts might act as ideology, to maintain the position of powerful groups. It would be assumed that such discourse is central in any intergroup conflict, in structuring what happened and in defining realities for participants. This approach and social identity theory would also share the Sherifs' concern with the way the goal relationship is understood by different groups. Is this a 'zero sum' situation in which only one group can get what they want? Are groups in competition for a scarce resource? Discursive psychologists would be interested in how these different possibilities are constructed by the participants as part of the rhetoric of the situation.

Psychodynamic researchers, in contrast, while sharing the interest in categorization and identification would argue that all three of these approaches, and realistic conflict theory, ignore the passion and emotion in situations of conflict, along with the individual differences. Why do some people become activists, while others remain on the side-lines? What is the personal meaning of the group situation for them? Why are some people apparently open to different points of view while others quickly take up a dogmatic stance? How do the kind of internal group dynamics discussed in Chapter 2 operate in these situations? In response, social constructionists, realistic group conflict theorists and social identity theorists are likely to point to the 'normality' of group conflict as evidenced by the Sherifs' Summer Camp Experiments. Social constructionists might ask if we need a psychodynamic concept of self filled with defence mechanisms and unconscious processes to explain people's variable involvement in racism and the presence of strong emotions.

In any group situation there is always scope for a multi-layered analysis. There is room for research on individual differences as well as on cognition, ideological fields, the goal relationships of groups as well as on the consequences of group identification. But, as we have seen, these approaches do not agree on everything. There are also some strong points of disagreement. What are these decision points in your view? And which theory, or combination of theories, do you think holds the most potential for future development?

ACTIVITY 4.10

The following questions might be useful in considering these issues.

- What strategies would each theory propose for improving 'race relations'?

- Which theory gives the most optimistic picture of intergroup conflict and why?

- Which of these theories places most emphasis on the psychological causes of racism?

I argued in section 2.4 that one of the most contested areas in work on the social psychology of racism, the area where there is most disagreement, concerns the role of human nature. As we saw, the most extreme form of claims of this kind would place the origins of intergroup conflict in biology, claiming that we are driven in some way by our genetic heritage to discriminate and compete. A version of this argument is evident in the hypothesis that categorization and prejudice are inevitable because such strategies are an adaptive way of coping with the information overload involved in treating each individual as an individual. Social identity theory also could be understood as proposing an invariant psychological process at the heart of group relations which interacts with the social context, although it is unclear whether these theorists see this process as due to biology or to socialization. Other approaches, however, work on the premise that human nature is a product of human history and culture. It is the organization of this culture and social and material conditions which mould human reactions. From this disagreement about the role of human nature arise other points of disagreement that you may have thought of in Activity 4.10, such as the 'ordinary' versus the 'exceptional' nature of racism and the extent of pessimism and optimism about group conflict different theories display.

It may seem as if social psychological investigations into racism have raised more questions than they have answered. To some extent this is true. We do not have, for example, fool-proof ways of predicting when racist ideas will take hold of people or when individuals will discriminate against others on the grounds of 'race'. Such knowledge may be a chimera. But we do know a great deal about the ideological, material and group circumstances in which racism and intergroup hostility flourish. We also have a good understanding of the psychological effects of group membership in our types of cultures and the cognitive and emotional consequences of group conflict. Research on the causes of social conflicts framed at the individual, group and ideological levels has led in different directions and to competing accounts but this disagreement is no bad thing *per se*. For it is through this debate, rehearsed in this chapter, that theories have become honed, tried and tested, and their various claims, strengths and limitations have become clear.

Acknowledgement

I would like to thank Richard Skellington for giving me pre-publication access to material from his revised edition of *'Race' in Britain Today* for use in section 2.1 and Ali Rattansi for access to his Study Guide written for the Open University course *'Race', Education and Society* (ED356) which informed section 2.2.

Further reading

Some of the most revealing material can be found in detailed life histories which explore people's reasons for racist actions or the effects of a racist social climate in depth. Even if one doesn't agree with the researcher's theoretical perspective, such studies are a source of provocative data for the social psychologist. For example, Adorno et al. (1950) *The Authoritarian Personality*, New York, Harper Row, and the two case studies of Larry and Mack; the case studies in Frankenberg (1993) 'Growing up white: feminism, racism and the social geography of childhood', *Feminist Review*, 45, pp. 51–85; Billig's (1978) analyses of 'the classic authoritarian' and 'the man of violence' in *Fascists: A Social Psychological Investigation of the National Front*, London, Harcourt, Brace and Jovanovich; bell hooks' (1989) autobiographical account in *Talking Back: Thinking Feminist – Thinking Black*, London, Sheba; and Wellman's (1977) *Portraits of White Racism*, Cambridge, Cambridge University Press.

For a general account of the contribution of psychodynamic theory to understanding the relationship between 'race', culture and identity see Pajaczkowska and Young (1992) 'Racism, representation and psychoanalysis', in J. Donald and A. Rattansi (eds.) *'Race', Culture and Difference*, London, Sage.

Henri Tajfel's (1981) *Human Groups and Social Categories*, Cambridge, Cambridge University Press, is a dense but useful collection of important writings on social identity theory.

For a broader view of a social constructionist perspective, it is worth reading Stuart Hall's various writings on 'race' and identity. Hall is one of the best known advocates of this approach in sociology and cultural studies, for example, 'New ethnicities', in J. Donald and A. Rattansi (eds.) (1992) *'Race', Culture and Difference*, London, Sage; 'The West and the rest: discourse and power', in S. Hall and B. Gieben (eds.) (1992) *Formations of Modernity*, Cambridge, Polity and Open University; 'Cultural identity and diaspora', in J. Rutherford (ed.) *Identity: Community, Culture and Difference*, London, Lawrence and Wishart.

References

Adorno, T.W., Frenkel-Brunswik, E., Levinson, D.J. and Sanford, R.N. (1950) *The Authoritarian Personality*, New York, Harper and Row.

Allport, G.W. (1954) *The Nature of Prejudice*, Reading; Mass., Addison Wesley.

Banton, M. (1987) *Racial Theories*, Cambridge, Cambridge University Press.

Billig, M. (1978) *Fascists: A Social Psychological Investigation of the National Front*, London, Harcourt, Brace and Jovanovich.

Billig, M. (1985) 'Prejudice, categorization and particularization: from a perceptual to a rhetorical approach', *European Journal of Social Psychology*, 15, pp. 79–103.

Billig, M. (1987) *Arguing and Thinking: A Rhetorical Approach to Social Psychology*, Cambridge, Cambridge University Press.

Brown, C. (1992) 'Same difference: the persistence of social disadvantage in the British employment market', in Braham, P., Rattansi, A. and Skellington, R. (eds.) *Racism and Anti-racism: Inequalities, Opportunities and Policies*, London, Sage and Open University.

Brown, C. and Gay, P. (1985) *Racial Discrimination: 17 Years after the Act*, London, Policy Studies Institute.

Brown, R. (1988) 'Intergroup Relations', in Hewstone, M., Stroebe, W., Codol, J-P. and Stephenson, G. (eds.) *Introduction to Social Psychology: A European Perspective*, Oxford, Blackwell.

Bruegel, I. (1989) 'Sex and race in the labour market', *Feminist Review*, 32, pp. 49–68.

Bryan, B., Dadzie, S. and Scafe, S. (1985) *The Heart of the Race: Black Women's Lives in Britain*, London, Virago.

Campbell, D.T. (1965) 'Ethnocentric and other altruistic motives', in Levine, D. (ed.) *Nebraska Symposium on Motivation*, Vol. 13, Lincoln, University of Nebraska Press.

Cashmore, E. (1987) *The Logic of Racism*, London, Allen and Unwin.

Centre for Contemporary Cultural Studies (1982) *The Empire Strikes Back*, London, Hutchinson.

Clark, K.B. and Clark, M.P. (1947) 'Racial identification and preference in Negro children', in Newcomb, T.M. and Hartley, E.L. (eds.) *Readings in Social Psychology*, New York, Holt.

Condor, S. (1988) '"Race stereotypes" and racist discourse', *Text, 8*, pp. 69–91.

Duncan, B.L. (1976) 'Differential social perception and attributions of intergroup violence: Testing the lower limits of stereotyping of Blacks', *Journal of Personality and Social Psychology*, 34, pp. 590–8.

Elliot, A. (1992) *Social Theory and Psychoanalysis in Transition*, Oxford, Blackwell.

Fanon, F. (1967) *Black Skin, White Masks,* New York, Grove Press.

Frankenberg, R. (1993) 'Growing up white: feminism, racism and the social geography of childhood', *Feminist Review*, 45, pp. 51–85.

Fromm, E. (1942) *Fear of Freedom*, London, Routledge and Kegan Paul.

Frosh, S. (1989) *Psychoanalysis and Psychology: Minding the Gap,* London, Macmillan.

Fryer, P. (1984) *Staying Power: The History of Black People in Britain*, London, Pluto Press.

Gilroy, P. (1987) *There Ain't No Black in the Union Jack*, London, Hutchinson.

Hall, S. (1990) 'Cultural identity and diaspora', in Rutherford, J. (ed.) *Identity: Community, Culture and Difference*, London, Lawrence and Wishart.

Hamilton D.L. and Gifford R.K. (1976) 'Illusory correlations and the maintenance of stereotypic beliefs', *Journal of Personality and Social Psychology*, 39, pp. 832–45.

Hamilton, D. (1981) 'Illusory correlation as a basis for stereotyping', in Hamilton, D. (ed.) *Cognitive Processes in Stereotyping and Intergroup Behaviour*, Hillsdale, Erlbaum.

Hamilton, W. (1975) 'Innate social aptitudes of man', in Fox, R. (ed.) *Biosocial Anthropology*, London, Malaby Press.

Henriques, J. (1984) 'Social psychology and the politics of racism', in Henriques, J., Hollway, W., Urwin, C., Venn, C. and Walkerdine, V. *Changing the Subject: Psychology, Social Regulation and Subjectivity*, London, Methuen.

Katz, D. and Braly, K. (1933) 'Social stereotypes of one hundred college students', *Journal of Abnormal and Social Psychology*, 28, pp. 280–90.

Lalljee, M. (1996) 'The interpreting self', in Stevens, R. (ed.).

Lave, J. (1988) *Cognition in Practice*, Cambridge, Cambridge University Press.

Lewontin, R. (1987) 'Are the races different?', in Gill, D. and Levidos, L. (eds.) *Anti-Racist Science Teaching*, London, Free Association Books.

Lippman, W. (1922) *Public Opinion*, New York, Harcourt Brace.

Miles, R. (1989) *Racism,* London, Routledge.

Milner, D. (1981) 'Racial prejudice', in Turner, J.C. and Giles, H. (eds.) *Intergroup Behaviour*, Oxford, Basil Blackwell.

Oakes, P.J., Haslam, S.A. and Turner, J.C. (1994) *Stereotyping and Social Reality*, Oxford, Blackwell.

Pagden, A. and Lawrance, J. (1991) *Francisco de Vitoria: Political Writings*, Cambridge, Cambridge University Press.

Pettigrew, T.F. (1958) 'Personality and socio-cultural factors in intergroup attitudes: A cross-national comparison', *Journal of Conflict Resolution*, Vol. 2, pp. 29–42.

Rattansi, A. (1995) ED356 *'Race', Education and Society*, Study Guide, Milton Keynes, The Open University.

Reynolds, V. (1986) 'Biology and race relations', *Ethnic and Racial Studies*, 9, 373–81.

Rosch , E. (1978) 'Principles of categorization', in Rosch, E. and Lloyd, B.B. (eds.) *Cognition and Categorization*, Hillsdale; N.J., Erlbaum.

Rothbart, M. (1981) 'Memory processes and social beliefs', in Hamilton, D. (ed.).

Rustin, M. (1991) *The Good Society and the Inner World: Psychoanalysis, Politics and Culture*, London, Verso.

Said, E. (1981) *Covering Islam*, London, Routledge.

Sherif, M. and Sherif, C. (1969) *Social Psychology*, New York, Harper and Row.

Skellington, R. (1995) *'Race' in Britain Today*, (2nd edition), London, Sage.

Smith, D.J. (1977) *Racial Disadvantage in Britain: The PEP Report*, Harmondsworth, Penguin.

Stevens, R. (ed.) (1996) *Understanding the Self*, London, Sage/The Open University, (Book 1 in this series).

Synder, M. and Uranowitz, S.W. (1978) 'Reconstructing the past: some cognitive consequences of person perception', *Journal of Personality and Social Psychology*, 36, pp. 941–50.

Tajfel, H. (1969) 'Cognitive aspects of prejudice', *Journal of Biosocial Science*, Supp. No. 1, pp. 173–91.

Tajfel, H. (1981) *Human Groups and Social Categories,* Cambridge, Cambridge University Press.

Tajfel, H. (ed.) (1982) *Social Identity and Intergroup Relations*, Cambridge, Cambridge University Press.

Tajfel, H. and Turner, J.C. (1979) 'An integrative theory of intergroup conflict', in Austin, W.G. and Worchel, S. (eds.) *The Social Psychology of Intergroup Relations*, Monterey; California, Brooks/Cole.

Tajfel, H. and Wilkes, A. (1963) 'Classification and quantitative judgement', *British Journal of Psychology*, 54, pp. 101–14.

Taylor, S.E. (1981) 'The interface of cognitive and social psychology', in Hamilton, D.L. (ed.).

Turner, J.C. (1982) 'Towards a cognitive re-definition of the social group', in Tajfel, H. (ed.).

Van den Berghe, P. L. (1981) *The Ethnic Phenomenon*, Oxford, Elsevier.

Van Dijk, T.A. (1984) *Prejudice and Discourse*, Amsterdam, Benjamins.

Wetherell, M. (1982) 'Cross-cultural studies of minimal groups: Implications for the social identity theory of intergroup relations', in Tajfel, H. (ed.).

Wetherell, M. and Maybin, J. (1996) 'The distributed self', in Stevens, R. (ed.).

Wetherell, M. and Potter, J. (1992). *Mapping the Language of Racism: Discourse and the Legitimation of Exploitation,* London and New York, Harvester Wheatsheaf and Columbia University Press.

Reading A
The Phenomenology of Oppression

Frantz Fanon

Source: Fanon, F. (1967) *Black Skin, White Masks*, New York: Grove Press
(Chapter 5, pp. 109–15)

'Dirty nigger!' Or simply, 'Look, a Negro!'

I came into the world imbued with the will to find a meaning in things, my spirit filled with the desire to attain to the source of the world, and then I found that I was an object in the midst of the other objects.

Sealed into that crushing objecthood, I turned beseechingly to others. Their attention was a liberation, running over my body suddenly abraded into non-being, endowing me once more with the agility that I had thought lost, and by taking me out of the world, restoring me to it. But just as I reached the other side, I stumbled, and the movements, the attitudes, the glances of the others fixed me there, in the sense in which a chemical solution is fixed by a dye. I was indignant; I demanded an explanation. Nothing happened. I burst apart. Now the fragments have been put together again by another self.

As long as the black man is among his own, he will have no occasion, except in minor internal conflicts, to experience his being through others. … In the *weltanschanung* of a colonized people there is an impurity, a flaw that outlaws any ontological explanation. Someone may object that this is the case with every individual, but such an objection merely conceals a basic problem. Ontology – once it is finally admitted as leaving existence by the wayside – does not permit us to understand the being of the black man. For not only must the black man be black; he must be black in relation to the white man. Some critics will take it on themselves to remind us that this proposition has a converse. I say that this is false. The black man has no ontological resistance in the eyes of the white man. Overnight the Negro has been given two frames of reference within which he has had to place himself. His metaphysics, or, less pretentiously, his customs and the sources on which they were based, were wiped out because they were in conflict with a civilization that he did not know and that imposed itself on him.

The black man among his own in the twentieth century does not know at what moment his inferiority comes into being through the other. Of course I have talked about the black problem with friends, or, more rarely, with American Negroes. Together we protested, we asserted the equality of all men in the world. In the Antilles there was also that little gulf that exists among the almost-white, the mulatto, and the nigger. But I was satisfied with an intellectual understanding of these differences. It was not really dramatic.

[…]

And then the occasion arose when I had to meet the white man's eyes. An unfamiliar weight burdened me. The real world challenged my claims. In the white world the man of colour encounters difficulties in the development of his bodily schema. Consciousness of the body is solely a negating activity. It is a third-person consciousness. The body is surrounded by an atmosphere of certain uncertainty. I know that if I want to smoke, I shall have to reach out my right arm and take the pack of cigarettes lying at the other end of the table. The matches, however, are in the drawer on the left, and I shall have to lean back slightly. And all these movements are made not out of habit but out of implicit knowledge. A slow composition of my *self* as a body in the middle of the spatial and temporal world – such seems to be the schema. It does not impose itself on me; it is, rather, a definitive structuring of the self and of the world – definitive because it creates a real dialectic between my body and the world.

For several years certain laboratories have been trying to produce a serum for 'denegrification'; with all the earnestness in the world, laboratories have sterilized their test tubes, checked their scales, and embarked on researches that might make it possible for the miserable Negro to whiten himself and thus to throw off the burden of that corporeal malediction. Below the corporeal schema I had sketched a historico-racial schema. The elements that I used had been provided for me not by 'residual sensations and perceptions primarily on a tactile, vestibular, kinesthetic, and visual character,' but by the other, the white man, who had woven me out of a thousand details, anecdotes, stories. I thought that what I had in hand was to construct a physiological self, to balance space, to localize sensations, and here I was called on for more.

'Look, a Negro!' It was an external stimulus that flicked over me as I passed by. I made a tight smile.

'Look, a Negro!' It was true. It amused me.

'Look, a Negro!' The circle was drawing a bit tighter. I made no secret of my amusement.

'Mama, see the Negro! I'm frightened!' Frightened! Frightened! Now they were beginning to be afraid of me. I made up my mind to laugh myself to tears, but laughter had become impossible.

I could no longer laugh, because I already knew that there were legends, stories, history, and above all *historicity*, which I had learned about from Jaspers. Then, assailed at various points, the corporal schema crumbled, its place taken by a racial epidermal schema. In the train it was no longer a question of being aware of my body in the third person but in a triple person. In the train I was given not one but two, three places. I had already stopped being amused. It was not that I was finding febrile coordinates in the world. I existed triply: I occupied space. I moved towards the other ... and the evanescent other, hostile but not opaque, transparent, not there, disappeared. Nausea ...

I was responsible at the same time for my body, for my race, for my ancestors. I subjected myself to an objective examination, I discovered my blackness, my ethnic characteristics; and I was battered down by tom-toms, cannibalism, intellectual deficiency, fetishism, racial defects, slave-ships, and above all else, above all: 'Sho' good eatin'.

On that day, completely dislocated, unable to be abroad with the other, the white man, who unmercifully imprisoned me, I took myself far off from my own presence, far indeed, and made myself an object. What else could it be for me but an amputation, an excision, a haemorrhage that spattered my whole body with black blood? But I did not want this revision, this thematization. All I wanted was to be a man among other men. I wanted to come lithe and young into a world that was ours and to help to build it together.

But I rejected all immunization of the emotions. I wanted to be a man, nothing but a man. Some identified me with ancestors of mine who had been enslaved or lynched: I decided to accept this. It was on the universal level of the intellect that I understood this inner kinship – I was the grandson of slaves in exactly the same way in which President Lebrun was the grandson of tax-paying, hard-working peasants. In the main, the panic soon vanished.

In America, Negroes are segregated. In South America, Negroes are whipped in the streets, and Negro strikers are cut down by machine-guns. In West Africa, the Negro is an animal. And there beside me, my neighbour in the university, who was born in Algeria, told me: 'As long as the Arab is treated like a man, no solution is possible'.

'Understand, my dear boy, colour prejudice is something I find utterly foreign … But of course, come in, sir, there is no colour prejudice among us … Quite, the Negro is a man like ourselves … It is not because he is black that he is less intelligent than we are … I had a Senegalese buddy in the army who was really clever …'

Where am I to be classified? Or, if you prefer, tucked away? 'A Martinican, a native of "our" old colonies.'

Where shall I hide?

'Look at the nigger! … Mama, a Negro! … Hell, he's getting mad … Take no notice, sir, he does not know that you are as civilized as we.'

[…]

My body was given back to me sprawled out, distorted, recoloured, clad in mourning in that white winter day. The Negro is an animal, the Negro is bad, the Negro is mean, the Negro is ugly; look, a nigger, it's cold, the nigger is shivering, the nigger is shivering because he is cold, the little boy is trembling because he is afraid of the nigger, the nigger is shivering with cold, that cold that goes through your bones, the handsome little boy is trembling because he thinks that the nigger is quivering with rage, the little white boy throws himself into his mother's arms: 'Mama, the nigger's going to eat me up'.

All around me the white man, above the sky tears at its navel, the earth rasps under my feet, and there is a white song, a white song. All this whiteness that burns me.

[...]

I sit down at the fire and I become aware of my uniform. I had not seen it. It is indeed ugly. I stop there, for who can tell me what beauty is?

Where shall I find shelter from now on? I felt an easily identifiable flood mounting out of the countless facets of my being. I was about to be angry. The fire was long since out, and once more the nigger was trembling.

'Look how handsome that Negro is!'...

'Kiss the handsome Negro's ass, madame!'

Shame flooded her face. At last I was set free from my rumination. At the same time I accomplished two things: I identified my enemies and I made a scene. A grand slam. Now one would be able to laugh.

The field of battle having been marked out, I entered the lists.

What? While I was forgetting, forgiving, and wanting only to love, my message was flung back in my face like a slap. The white world, the only honourable one, barred me from all participation. A man was expected to behave like a man. I was expected to behave like a black man – or at least like a nigger. I shouted a greeting to the world and the world slashed away my joy. I was told to stay within bounds, to go back where I belonged.

They would see, then! I had warned them, anyway, Slavery? It was no longer even mentioned, that unpleasant memory. My supposed inferiority? A hoax that it was better to laugh at. I forgot it all, but only on condition that the world not protect itself against me any longer. I had incisors to test. I was sure they were strong.

[...]

What! When it was I who had every reason to hate, to despise, I was rejected? When I should have been begged, implored, I was denied the slightest recognition? I resolved, since it was impossible for me to get away from an *inborn complex*, to assert myself as a BLACK MAN. Since the other hesitated to recognize me, there remained only one solution: to make myself known.

CHAPTER 5
INDIVIDUALS AND INSTITUTIONS: THE CASE OF WORK AND EMPLOYMENT

by Diane Watson

Contents

1 Introduction

In this chapter we move beyond the study of small groups, attitudes and intergroup relations to explore aspects of the *institutional* level of society from a broadly *social constructionist* standpoint. The main focus of this chapter will be on *work*, the cultural meanings of employment and unemployment, and the personal significance for the individual of the institutions and organizations of work in modern society. We shall be exploring occupational choice and how people make sense of their employment patterns or periods of unemployment. We shall be looking at the experience of work, at motivation and at the process of managing and being managed. This chapter will complement the social psychological research on work groups and work organizations and the psychodynamic perspective which you met in Chapters 1 and 2 of this volume and bring another perspective to understanding the role which work plays in the psychology of the individual.

The core issue of social psychology has been defined as the nature of the relationship between the person and the social world. However, conceptions of the 'person' and of the 'social world' are contested, as is the nature of the relationship between them. Social psychologists have disagreed about the extent to which the individual may be seen as a fully centred, unified and defined entity, with a stable inner core which is amenable to observation and analysis, or the extent to which individuals may be perceived as fragmented and decentred, consisting of competing and contradictory identities which are socially constructed and formed through language and discourse (Gergen, 1992; Harré and Gillett, 1994; Layder, 1990, 1994; Potter and Wetherell, 1987).

In taking a social constructionist perspective, this chapter will side with the more fragmented view of self. The focus of this chapter will not primarily be on the individual but on the *forms of life* and *activities* which make up the social context. The starting point for analysis, therefore, will be the nature and influence of the wider social context in which the individual lives and creates meaning. This focus has important consequences for how we understand the 'working individual'. If, for example, we see individuals as having a unified and stable 'inner core', we would tend to think in terms of either 'fitting a person to a job' or 'fitting a job to a person'. But if we see people as developing their sense of identity and 'being' as they go about relating to and shaping the world around them, we are likely to take a different view of the relationship between individuals and their work. In this case, we would tend to see a two-way constructive process going on between individuals and the work that they do. Thus, the experience of doing social work influences the 'sort of person' a particular social worker is and, at the same time, the predispositions which that person takes into his or her job will, in part, define what that job is. The person is shaping the work and the work is shaping the person.

When we begin to consider work in terms of such things as occupational roles, as we are with this example of social work, we are moving into the sphere of sociology – the social science discipline especially concerned with the *institutional level*. And sociology has had its own set of debates which are equivalent to those within psychology. Here, disagreement has focused on the relationship between social and institutional structures on the one hand and the capacity for human agency and initiative on the other. Some forms of sociological analysis have emphasized the constraining and determining nature of social structures and institutions at the expense of human agency. Others have chosen to focus on the role of human beings and their capacity to construct meanings and actively create the social structures through which they live. And many have recognized that the relationship is complex and multifaceted, involving elements of both *structure* and *agency*, the *internal* and the *external*, in some form of dynamic or dialectical (back and forth) relationship (Berger and Luckmann, 1971; Giddens, 1984; Layder, 1990). In this view, human beings both shape the institutions within which they live and are at the same time shaped by them. Sociology, however, typically concerns itself a great deal with issues of *power* and notes that some people find themselves having a more significant 'shaping' role than others. Ordinary soldiers, for example, are both shaped by the military institutions within which they work and have some role in making those institutions what they are. Field marshals and generals are also both shapers and shaped, but they play a much bigger role in constructing military institutions than do the soldiers in the ranks.

Traditionally, if sociology has been concerned with the structure and functioning of whole societies and psychology with the study of individual and mental processes, then *social psychology* has operated at the interface between the two. Indeed, the examples of people working in the military and in social work involve consideration of both psychological and sociological issues. Given the fact that these two mainstream disciplines have areas of potential overlap and mutual reinforcement – which gives social psychology much of its rationale – it is not surprising that social psychologists have struggled with many of the same issues which have confronted psychologists and sociologists, and that the discipline has similarly confronted the problematic nature of the person and the relationship of the human subject with the social world. As we shall now see, in the same way that there have been rival conceptions of the person at the more psychological end of the social sciences, there are different ways of thinking about the relationship between the individual and the social at the more sociological, or institutional, end.

Aims of Chapter 5

The aims of this chapter are:

- To use a broadly *social constructionist* framework to explore the ways in which individuals both make and are made by the *social institutions* which surround them.

242

- To take, as a particular focus, the key *institutions* of *work* in modern societies – *capitalism, employment, bureaucracy and the work ethic* – and consider the relevance of these institutional patterns to the experience of work and the emergence of social identities.

- To consider the relationship between *human agency* and *social structure* – and elaborate their *mutual interdependence*.

- To complement the study of *micro* forms of collectivity such as the small face-to-face group with a consideration of more *macro* aspects of human organization and experience.

2   Institutions and persons

Previous chapters in this book have examined the psychological significance of social groups and how individual behaviour is altered and influenced as a consequence of group membership. Chapter 2, for instance, examined Bion's claim that the group as an *entity* exerts an influence on the actions of individual members, irrespective of their conscious intentions (see Chapter 2, section 5), while the experimental studies of Sherif, Tajfel and Asch discussed in Chapters 1 and 4 also explored the ways in which the group is more than the sum of its individual constituent parts. We have seen many examples in the course of this volume where groups assume their own dynamics which in turn constrain and structure the behaviour of individuals who make up the group.

This notion that the whole may in some ways be greater than the sum of the parts has been the focus of much debate in sociology and social psychology. It brings into focus the extent to which human agency might be constrained by social structures which are experienced, consciously or unconsciously, as in some way 'external' to the individual, even though individuals were also instrumental in their creation. We can illustrate this with the example of a family group. Those of us who live as adult members of family groups will all recognize that, to some extent, our family group is the *product* of our own efforts. Nevertheless, there will inevitably be times – especially if we have children or other dependants in the family – when we feel that the family, as a unit, amounts to more than just the individuals in it. The family seems to be *influencing* what we can and cannot do more than we are influencing it. This tension or contradiction applies similarly to our social contexts at the broader levels of *organization, institution* and *society*. Groups form a key part of the social context of each of us. But we need concepts to enable us to operate with a domain of analysis which is broader than that of the social group. The concept of *institution* is a key one here.

ACTIVITY 5.1   Pause for a moment and consider what the word *institution* means for you.

Do you use the word in your everyday conversation?

What does it suggest? A building or some other physical place?

Perhaps you think of something social rather than physical? A set of relationships perhaps?

Does the word have positive or negative connotations for you?

Why might the word have such connotations?

Before reading on, make a few notes of your ideas and any difficulties you might have with the idea of *institution*.

The concept of institution is widely used in social scientific analysis but often without precise definition. Like many other social science concepts, the word is derived from everyday and common-sense uses of the term but it has been changed and adapted for the more theoretical and technical requirements of the disciplines of sociology and social psychology. There are two main uses of the term which are relevant here and it is the *second* of these which we shall be using in this chapter.

First, the term is used to refer to organizations, such as prisons or mental hospitals, which *contain* people, often against their consent. In this sense, institution refers to a particular place – both a building and a location – and it may very well possess negative or positive connotations for you according to impressions or experiences you might have of such places. It is this notion of *institution* which the sociologist Goffman, for example, used in his work on *total institutions* (Goffman, 1961). Goffman explored the ways in which an individual's identity may be deliberately altered and changed when normal and taken-for-granted social support frameworks are undermined (the same processes were evident in the research on thought reform considered in Chapter 1).

Secondly, the term is used, as it will be here, to refer to any *organized* element of society. This gives us the sociological definition of institutions as those regularly occurring and continuously repeated patterns of activity or social practice which are of major significance in the social structure and which are sanctioned and supported by social norms (Abercrombie et al., 1994). Institutions in this sense include the family, marriage, the law or the state. And you might observe that this concept of institution is equivalent, at a higher level, to the concept of *role* (cf. Radley, 1996) and to the notion of institutionalized defence mechanisms (explored in Chapter 2, section 4). Roles, like institutions, involve regular and established patterns of behaviour, but the concept of role is applied at a more localized and specific level than the broader concept of institution. Institutions, often referred to as 'social institutions', entail higher-level patterns of activity which incorporate a range and a variety of roles.

Increasingly within sociology, the dominance of conceptions of role and institution as *structures* which integrate society, serve 'social needs', and into which individuals 'fit' or are incorporated, has been challenged by more *process-oriented* approaches. These approaches are more consistent with those perspectives which see *identity* and the *person* not as fixed entities, but as creations which are actively and endlessly in the making. Institutions, by this account, are created through the process of *institutionalization* and are 'simply patterns of behaviour which persist and crystallize in the course of time and to which people become attached as a result of their role in the formation of identity, or through investments of energy or social interests' (Wallis, 1985). Thus, institutions are more like processes than structures and are more amenable to construction and reconstruction through the actions of the individuals who live and work within them.

There are several *key institutions* associated with the sphere of work in modern societies. Work is too broad a category to be regarded as an institution in its own right. Work is a category of activity which we see taking an enormous variety of shapes and as being incorporated into a vast range of institutional patterns across human societies and human history. In modern societies we see work activities incorporated into the institutions of *capitalism*, for example. This institutional pattern involves a key role for the profit motive, for competition and for market relations in the organization of work activities. Central to it, also, is a further institution – that of *employment* in the sense of employees selling their capacity to work (their 'labour') to employers for a wage or a salary. This typically occurs within work organizations which follow the principles of *bureaucracy* – itself a key institution of modern societies (Weber, 1968). Bureaucracies involve a control structure based on a hierarchy of offices occupied by individuals with pertinent expertise. All of this is supported by the modern *work ethic*; an institutionally supported set of values and beliefs which define a strong commitment to work by individual persons as central to their basic social worthiness and notion of self-worth. Whenever we consider the *institutional context* of an individual's involvement in work in a modern society, we are likely to note the relevance in different ways of this set of institutional patterns. They are humanly created patterns but they are patterns which also help *shape* the identities and activities of those who are caught up in them.

The concept of social institution, then, acts as a *link or bridge between the individual and the social levels of social activity*. It provides a tool to help us make connections between the psychological and the sociological. Work institutions shape some of the key *sites* where we take on more formalized roles and take part in groups and group processes, and they play a significant part in a person's biography or life career. At work, language and social interaction, the most basic social psychological activities take on meaning on a larger scale and in a more structured environment than is typically the case in our private lives. The work environment is one of the key locations where our private individuality (our personal identity) and the roles and characteristics attributed by others (our social identity) meet in the creation and recreation of our awareness of our sense of self.

Institutions create psychological issues for the individual. Our biographies, life-histories and identities, through language and social interaction, involve us in engaging with relatively structured aspects of the wider social world. Again, depending upon the perspective taken, there are fundamental differences and disagreements about whether these institutions and social structures may be seen to be in some way distinct from people, concrete and 'out there'. This is very important whenever we are examining issues of work and employment – issues which frequently involve examining the relationship between institutional pattern and personal uniqueness.

Review of section 2

- The concept of institution is a tool which social scientists use to make connections between the individual and the social, the psychological and the sociological. It helps us to focus on aspects of the social world which operate at a level above that of the individual and the small-scale social group.

- The term institution is used to conceptualize any *organized* element of society which has *continuity* and involves *regular* and *established* patterns of behaviour.

- Institutions are both created by individuals through human agency and at the same time present themselves as structures with the capacity to constrain individual action. The interaction between individuals and institutions is one of *mutual* construction.

- Work institutions and organizations are the key focus of this chapter. The institutions of *capitalism, employment, bureaucracy* and the *work ethic* play a significant part in an individual's experience, biography, life career and social identity.

3   Work and employment

People live their lives in the context of a number of social institutions. Why then choose work institutions as prime examples? What is it about the institutions associated with work in capitalist, industrial society that is especially helpful in developing a better understanding of the social psychology of individuals and their location in the broader social structures of society?

Well, in the first instance, the work which we do plays a major part in our *subjective experience* of the material world. It plays a significant role in the way we are perceived and evaluated by ourselves and by others and, as such, is a significant factor in the construction of *self* and *identity*. Secondly, it socially *locates* us so that it is possible for other people to categorize and define us and make sense of our situation. In short, work institutions *place* us in the social and cultural world. The work we do has implications for our access to physical, material and cultural resources and consequently it *positions* us in the power structures of society. In addition to all of this, the ways in which work is *organized* in society create formal structures in which we live some part of our lives and through which we experience relationships with others. Work thus provides an important context for social interaction and for the social construction of the wider world. Work is about personal experience and identity as well as about structured relations. It provides a window on the division of labour, social class, 'race', gender inequalities and access to power and resources. And, it is about agency and structure as well as about individual choice and the lack of it.

3.1 The meaning of work

At this point you might well feel that unwarranted assumptions about the nature of work are being made. With so many people unemployed or not in paid work, how can these assertions about the centrality of the role of work in identity formation and social positioning be justified?

The short answer to that question would be to argue that it is not necessary to talk about *paid employment* to talk about work in this way. Paid employment is but one form of work in modern society; not all work in modern society is remunerated and much work is undertaken in a variety of other settings. Having said that, however, there is no denying the *cultural significance* of this distinction between paid and unpaid work, or the significance which is attached to 'a job' in modern society. Comparison with pre-industrial times, when most work was done for and in the household, when the viability of the household was vital for all, and when there 'was no *a priori* assumption that wage labour was a superior form of work or that men were the natural wage earners' (Pahl, 1988, p. 12), demonstrates that the notion of work as paid employment is a *modern* notion. Only within such a historical perspective can ideas about the 'male breadwinner', 'going out to work', 'being unemployed', or being 'just a housewife' be socially located or understood.

The nature and distinctiveness of the institutions of industrial capitalist society and the social organization of work and employment in such societies have been a major focus of sociology. Taking a historical perspective on the 'meaning' of work in different societies clearly shows that the way in which work is defined and how people experience work have differed greatly from society to society and from one epoch to another. For example, in ancient Greek society, work and labour were not highly valued activities. On the contrary, work was regarded as an ignoble activity, undertaken by women and slaves. In Christian societies, work was originally seen in a negative light, as something 'imposed upon humanity as a direct result of original sin and a means, therefore, to avoid the temptations of the devil and the flesh, as well as a penance' (Grint, 1991, p. 17). Work in this context was 'this-worldly', mundane, 'dirty' and *negative* for personal identity. However, this definition of work changed significantly with the emergence of the modern work institutions of industrial capitalism. Initially, for Christians, the route to salvation was through prayer and spirituality, but this began to change as the ideas of Luther and Calvin took hold and the process of the Protestant Reformation began. In this context:

> work, rather than prayer, could either save your soul or at least be taken as confirmation that your soul was already saved. It was this transformative period that is crucial ... in the elevation of work itself, from a necessary chore to a moral duty ...

> (Grint, 1991, p. 18)

There have been two major assessments within social thought of the significance of this emergence of the modern *work ethic*. First, Weber, in *The Protestant Ethic and the Spirit of Capitalism* (1930), argued that the work ethic found in Protestantism served to foster a 'spirit of capitalism' and gave personal meaning to one's life on earth, rather than personal meaning coming from spiritual preparation for one's life in heaven. The modern work ethic – in a more secularized world – has evolved from this essentially religious influence on work motivation, and functions as an equivalent to it. Secondly, there is the view of Marx, whose ideas were founded on a belief that, through labour, people have the positive potential to achieve creative self-fulfilment and self-realization. Work, according to Marx, should be the key source of meaning and satisfaction for the human being but, under capitalism, it is a negative experience. Not only does the structure of capitalism involve workers in being exploited by employers; it also prevents workers from 'realizing themselves' in the sense of fulfilling their creative potential. Because they carry out work for the profit of their employer and work under conditions dictated by the employer, their creative potential is stunted and they are said to be *alienated*. Thus, while Weber emphasized the positive influence of the work ethic in capitalism, Marx focused on the negative consequences, for the individual, of work in a capitalist society.

A dominant theme of much modern social psychology of work and much applied psychology of work can be understood to be framed by a discourse which has been derived from the discussions of the work ethic and of alienation found in nineteenth- and twentieth-century writers. These concepts will be of relevance to later parts of this chapter, but for the moment let's turn to the role which employment plays in the lives of individuals.

Work ethic or alienation?

3.2 The meaning of employment

I argued in the previous section that the meaning which work has for people in contemporary society is derived in part from culture and history and in part from direct personal experience. The value which is placed upon unpaid work is intimately linked to ideas about the value of paid employment. Identity and self-esteem are attached to our position in the structures of work and paid employment. '*Work*' and '*not work*' are socially constructed definitions and they hold within them a moral dimension.

In the light of the preceding discussion, make a note of the role that 'going out to work' or 'having a job' might play in an individual's experience.

ACTIVITY 5.2

What purpose does paid employment have in a person's life?

Might it serve more than one purpose or function?

If so, are these functions all of the same order?

As you do this, bear in mind the points made at the beginning of section 3 about why work has been chosen as the focus for this chapter.

What sorts of thing did you note down? You will probably have noted that being employed:

- allows people to earn an *income* or make a living;

- creates the opportunity for *social contact* with people beyond the domestic environment;

- locates individuals within the *public domain* as well as within the private sphere and provides them with social *status*;

- enables people to place themselves in relation to others and provides them with an answer to the question, 'What do you do?' – it provides them with a public *identity*;

- helps the individual structure time and gives structure to the day.

If these are some of the functions of employment for the individual, then it follows that there are likely to be some negative consequences for people when they become unemployed. 'Work' and 'not work', 'employment' and 'unemployment' are inextricably linked together.

3.3   The meaning of unemployment

The notion of 'being unemployed' is particular to the institutional patterns of modern industrial capitalist societies. As we saw earlier, in section 3.1, working within the context of paid employment did not, in previous eras, carry the positive evaluations it tends to carry in modern societies. Indeed, in certain periods of European history the highest status went to the landed 'leisured class' whose high status was reflected in the fact that they did not need to work. In societies influenced by the work ethic, however, this has changed and such people have come to be regarded much more negatively as the 'idle rich'. Not to be engaged in some form of gainful employment has become, for men at least, a matter of disgrace. Such cultural notions as this have also influenced modern attitudes to the broader phenomenon of people finding themselves unable to secure paid employment.

One important contribution to understanding the meaning of work in modern societies through focusing on the impact of unemployment on the individual can be found in the work of Jahoda (1982). Jahoda developed what she called a 'latent functions model' of the psychological value to the individual of paid work. Earning a living is clearly a significant *manifest* function of paid work but Jahoda argued for other significant *latent* functions of employment. Five latent functions were identified by Jahoda as vital to the psychological well-being of the individual, and unemployment is said to be harmful because it reduces access to them. These latent functions are:

1   regularly shared contact with people other than family members;

2   links with a set of goals and purposes which are collective and wider than the individual;

3   access to social status and identity;

4   enforced activity;

5   a time-structuring to the day, the week and the year.

In employment, people are able to locate themselves in a wider scheme of things, have a focused sense of purpose, experience the opportunity to direct and organize their activity, and experience security and structure in their lives. So, whatever the hardships people may experience as a consequence of the type of employment they have, the experience of *unemployment* generates significant psychological distress for the unemployed.

Whilst it would be unfortunate if Jahoda's influential formulation led us to overlook the significant *economic* deprivations associated with the loss of income, as a model it has generated much helpful debate about the role of employment in a person's social and psychological well-being. It has also helped us acquire a greater understanding of the subjective experiences of people who are not in paid employment even though they do *work*.

In an overview of the experience of unemployment, Gallie and Marsh (1994) examined some of the complexities associated with this experience and suggested that Jahoda *did* significantly underestimate the financial deprivations associated with unemployment. Her emphasis was on the need for individuals to have a *life structure* and *community ties* and she came to imply that it is only through *employment* in advanced capitalist societies that such a need can be met. More recent researchers, however, have emphasized other key factors. Kelvin and Jarrett (1985), for example, see the most significant issue for the individual as the undermining of identity and the concept of self – something which is accompanied by an increased psychological dependency on others. Burchell (1994) and Gallie and Vogler (1994), on the other hand, stress the role of *insecurity* as a significant component in the psychological ill-health associated with unemployment. However, they go on to point out that labour market insecurity exists in a range of circumstances far wider than unemployment. Unemployment is merely an extreme form of economic and work-related insecurity. Fryer and McKenna (1987), in fact, found similarities between the unemployed and those who were temporarily 'laid off' from their jobs, suggesting that Jahoda failed to take account of individuals' orientations to the future and the role of planning in helping diminish insecurity and anxiety.

One of the most systematic attempts to examine the effects of unemployment on the psychological well-being of workers was undertaken by Warr (1987) at the Social and Applied Psychology Unit in Sheffield. Warr, like these other researchers, suggests, in effect, that Jahoda's emphasis on the *latent* functions of work resulted in a neglect of the functions which are *manifest*. Loss of income is usually the most harmful effect. Furthermore, the social environments of the unemployed, as well as individual differences, need to be evaluated. Warr argues that the unemployed are likely to suffer by comparison with the employed along a complex range of dimensions. They are likely to have:

- less opportunity for control;

- less opportunity for skill use;

- less opportunity for purposeful, goal-directed behaviour;

- less variety in life;

- less certainty about the future;

- less available income;

- less physical security through loss of accommodation and home comforts;

- less opportunity for interpersonal contact;

- less social esteem and lower social prestige.

The Sheffield research supports the view that the unemployed suffer a significant deterioration in psychological health and well-being and that this experience undermines self-esteem and self-confidence as well as increasing anxiety and depression. Warr warns, however, that individuals vary in their responses to unemployment and that factors such as age, social class and gender all mediate. Overall, then, it would appear that the effects of unemployment 'depend not upon inherent features of personality, but upon the specific social conditions under which it occurs' (Roberts et al., 1985, p. 300). Individual characteristics and environmental conditions are both key factors in the experience of unemployment.

How far does this research and theorizing help us reach any broader conclusions about the meaning of work? Clearly, work and employment, in addition to their economic implications for individuals and families, significantly impact on the subjective experience of individuals and affect their sense of self and identity. This is something we shall continue to explore in this chapter. Furthermore, it is also clear that work and employment are *socially constructed* and indeed are *gendered categories* without universal meaning across time and place:

> That individuals come to be recognized as 'unemployed' rather than as 'mothers' or 'graduates' or 'gardeners' conveys a great deal about the significance allocated to formal employment as *the* distinguishing category of social life by the state. Similarly, the notion that domestic duties do not constitute conventional work or that certain people are 'just housewives', or that universal orientations to work can be derived from the experiences of male workers, connotes a culture shot through with patriarchal mores of work. The conventional adage may be 'one man's work is another man's leisure' but it might be more appropriately written as 'one man's leisure is another woman's work' … the meaning of work is not immanent to the activities; meanings are socially constructed and maintained, they are contingently present and permanently fragile.
>
> *(Grint, 1991, pp. 46–7)*

Review of section 3

- The study of the institutions of work tells us something about our personal experience and identity as well as about roles and structured relationships. The work we do locates us in the social and cultural world, positions us in relation to the power structures of society, and provides a context for social interaction.

- The *meaning* work has for people is derived from culture and history as well as from personal experience. The distinction between paid and unpaid work is of major cultural significance and plays a key role in the way people define themselves and others. Identity and self-esteem are closely related to our positions in the structures of work and paid employment.

- The concept of 'being unemployed' is peculiar to the institutional patterns of modern industrial capitalist societies. Research into unemployment indicates that the experience of unemployment generates psychological distress and a deterioration in psychological health and well-being. Work and employment are socially constructed and gendered categories.

4   Entering employment

As the preceding discussion suggests, the institutions associated with work in modern capitalist industrial society have a significance for all individuals, whether or not they are themselves formally in employment. The predominance of work, its cultural and 'moral' value and its links with access to material resources, pervades all our experiences and plays a significant part in how we value ourselves in relation to others. However, as our discussion of the implications of unemployment indicates, it is problematic to assume that there is a common process which affects all individuals in the same way. Our experience of work and unemployment is influenced by our past biographies and expectations as well as by our age, class, 'race', gender and educational achievement (Banks et al., 1992).

This is particularly so when we examine the range of factors which influence a person's *entry* into employment.

What factors generally influence people in taking up a job?

Do you think that people *choose* the work they do?

Do they have little by way of choice at all?

4.1   Entry into work: choices and circumstantial pressures

Psychological and sociological research on entry into employment has traditionally emphasized *either* individual *choice* or the *constraints* on individuals imposed by circumstances. Within the predominately psychological *occupational choice model* there have been two major approaches to 'choice': the 'personality-matching' and the 'developmental' approach (Moir, 1993, p. 17). 'Personality-matching' assumes that individuals possess relatively stable personalities and certain capacities which can be revealed through psychometric testing. Occupational choice is then predicted on the basis of these psychological assessments. A notable example is Holland's personality typology which identifies six types of personality delineated according to work-related preferences and aversions (Holland, 1959, 1985). On the other hand, the 'developmental' approach (Ginzberg et al., 1951; Super, 1957) uses interview responses to identify developmental stages in 'the maturation of vocational thinking' (Moir, 1993, p. 18). In this perspective, occupational choice is the conclusion of a number of stages. Individuals gradually develop and refine their ambitions, attitudes and abilities to a point where they make a 'realistic' choice of occupation in line with self-image and capable of providing them with satisfaction.

In addition to there being difficulties with this psychological notion of the fixed and stable personality, there have also been criticisms of these models of occupational choice from a sociological point of view because of the failure to attend sufficiently to the constraints of social circumstance. For many people, the notion of *choosing* an occupation would be an empty formality rather than a realistic possibility. Roberts's (1975) 'structure-opportunity' model, for example, recognizes that, to a very considerable extent, social class is the main influence on the occupations people enter. Consequently, it is not ambition which influences career choice but the available careers which shape ambitions. Social class and educational background place people in 'varying degrees of proximity with different ease of access' to various kinds of occupation and employment (Roberts, 1975, p. 140).

This debate between 'choice' or 'constraint' mirrors the broader social science debate about the relationship between the individual and society, and discussions about the influence of structure and the role of agency noted in section 1 of this chapter. In turning away from models which emphasize choice we could be in danger of adopting an equally one-sided and over-deterministic approach favouring the role of structural constraints. Recent debates in social theory have attempted to take analysis beyond the assertion of the primacy of structure over agency or the primacy of agency over structure (Giddens, 1984). Giddens's 'structuration theory', for instance, rejects the reductionism of both structure and action accounts, arguing that structure and agency are related through the 'duality of structure' and that each should be given equal weighting in analysis.

Layder et al. (1991) have attempted to link Giddens's theoretical ideas with an empirical analysis of the ways in which individual and structural variables combine to determine movement into the labour market. They argue that the 'transition from school represents a crucial point of intersection between major life domains, namely the educational system and the labour market'. The level at which young people enter the labour force plays a major part in influencing their future occupational security, income levels and status. Consequently, their attempts to control outcomes and 'ensure continuity in their life course' are vital at this point in their lives (ibid., p. 453).

Layder et al.'s findings indicate that structural variables such as social class, sex and local opportunity structures are of greater significance for people entering lower- and middle-level jobs in the youth labour market than for those entering higher levels. In the upper segments, individual variables such as attitudes and levels of educational achievement were of far more influence than for individuals entering the lower segments. They suggest that, at the higher levels, 'the factors which individuals perceive as being a product of their own efforts and achievements are indeed the most significant factors in determining the level at which they enter the labour market' (ibid., p. 459). At these higher levels, individuals have a greater capacity to control their job situation by the use of strategic activities such as job search and goal-directed behaviour informed by their social representations, attitudes and values. Consequently, the determining nature of social structure varies according to the social context. Furthermore, the influence of the 'strategic conduct' of young people at all the levels is indicative of the active agency of individuals in the creation of the segmented labour market.

Layder and his colleagues use empirical analysis to examine the theoretical notion proposed in structuration theory that 'agency and structure are implicated in each other'. Their research adds to our knowledge of the ways in which individuals are active agents who do not simply 'unreflectively reconstruct structural arrangements' (ibid., p. 460), and it throws light on some of the sociological and psychological processes

involved in entry into paid employment. As the results for young people from different social classes indicate, the psychological processes in which individuals engage when approaching work careers clearly cannot be appreciated without their being set within the institutional context in which they occur. However, further insights into this interaction have been developed by researchers looking at the role of social construction processes in the area of career 'choice'.

4.2   Making sense of our occupational choices

I now want to extend this analysis of agency and structure, choice and constraint, further by turning to a very different type of social psychological research on occupational choice. The social constructionist perspective, as we saw in Chapters 3 and 4 of this volume, has emphasized the key role of language and power in the process of constructing 'what we are'. For social constructionists, the boundaries between the person and the social context are blurred (cf. Wetherell and Maybin, 1996). The person is not an integrated, bounded 'object' to be described, and there is no one true self or consistent personality to be identified and measured. This perspective argues that our identities are in part the products of language and interaction and that language is a practical activity – a form of action in its own right. From this standpoint, as Chapter 3, Section 4 argued, *discourse analysis* is one approach to understanding the ways in which people use language as action to construct and reconstruct their social world. It is an approach which can give us a different kind of insight into entry into the labour market.

Traditional approaches to occupational entry attempted to reveal the inner psychological structures which govern occupational choice. As section 4.1 noted, the aim was to reveal appropriate 'personality types' or people at the right level of 'vocational maturity' (Super, 1957) and identify those individuals best suited to 'fit' into certain jobs or occupational structures. 'Personality matching' and 'developmental' approaches have influenced careers guidance and personnel selection procedures. By contrast, Moir (1993) advocates the application of discourse analysis to 'occupational choice accounts'. In this perspective, instead of 'studying the mind as if it were outside language, we study the spoken and written texts (and other types of text) – the conversations, debates, discussions where images of the mind are reproduced and transformed' (Burman and Parker, 1993, p. 2). Using interviews with undergraduates concerning their university courses and occupational choices, Moir demonstrated the influence of the *interactive context* on the construction of interviewee responses, the ways in which candidates work out what it is that the interviewer is interested in, and the processes by which individuals account for their decisions and behaviour retrospectively. Approaching the subject in this way involves rejecting the use of interviewee responses as indicative of a particular 'personality' or level of 'vocational maturity' and examining how it is that respondents use language to produce credible *narratives* around their occupational choices: what Potter and Wetherell (1987) call the 'linguistic repertoires' (broad types of account) which individuals draw upon when explaining their choice of course and career. From this perspective, the responses which candidates give should not be seen as indicating the 'real' reasons why they have chosen a given occupation. Rather, they are evidence of the ability of the candidate to give a realistic and convincing account of their decision after the decision has already been made.

Moir studied the transcripts of interviews with forty undergraduate vocational students on mechanical engineering and nursing courses, chosen for comparative purposes because these careers are conventionally regarded as attracting very different types of individual. In his detailed analysis he found some support for the view that 'personality' directs occupational choice, in that the mechanical engineering group consistently emphasized a preference for working with machines and an interest in mathematics whilst the nursing students tended to state a preference for working with people and helping them. It might therefore be argued that these interviews do indeed identify different *personality traits* which underlie occupational choice.

However, the position is more complex than this. If we approach these transcripts as *accounts* with an interactive function, then a different perspective emerges. By highlighting their possession of those characteristics conventionally associated with the chosen occupation, some respondents repeatedly emphasized what Moir calls the 'standard membership category repertoire' in *justifying* their occupational choice. This is demonstrated by frequent references, such as 'an interest in Meccano kits', or 'an interest in mechanical subjects at school', or 'I enjoyed the physics and maths side' (for engineering), or (for nursing) 'a well worth job … a lot of job satisfaction … helping them …'. So, for example, on a number of separate occasions the candidate quoted below used his knowledge of what is conventionally seen as the appropriate set of characteristics for an engineer in order to establish that he was suitable for such work:

> 'I'd always been interested in engineering, cars and motorbikes and stuff like that so it was just there wasn't any other option and I went straight into it. I wasn't really thinking career-wise what particular area I wanted to go into, it was more or less it was engineering or nothing else.'

(Moir, 1993, pp. 24–5)

Close examination of the interview transcript shows that, although this candidate refers to other reasons for choosing engineering, including the influence of brothers, he is consistent in returning to the 'standard membership category repertoire' to establish his suitability for this kind of work.

Other respondents, however, made far greater use of what Moir called the 'family influence repertoire' to justify their choice. This 'repertoire' is illustrated by the following candidate:

> 'My mum had been a nurse and I have lots of relatives who are nurses and they all sort of, not influenced, but I was always interested in what they had to say about their work. ... And, I just wanted to be a nurse 'cause I like people, that's the main reason.'
>
> *(Moir, 1993, pp. 26–7)*

Unlike the earlier respondent, this candidate does not consistently refer to her relevant interests or to the possession of attributes characteristic of nursing. The family influence is repeated as the key factor and this leaves the interviewer in doubt as to her suitability for the chosen career. Consequently, she is less successful in engaging the interest of the interviewer and convincing the interviewer that she has made a rational and appropriate career choice. Detailed analysis of the interview transcripts reveals the interactive processes involved in the interview and the ways in which the appeal to some 'linguistic repertoires' is more successful in helping candidates 'bring off' a convincing account of their occupational choice (Moir, 1993, pp. 28–9).

The application of discourse analysis to accounts of occupational choice provides the social scientist with a different kind of understanding from that produced by traditional approaches. Furthermore, the knowledge gained has the potential better to inform those involved in careers guidance and selection interviewing. Traditional approaches have utilized psychometric testing and vocational counselling techniques to find the 'appropriate personality' to 'fit' the job. What might be more effective in the light of this discursive analysis is an approach which trains interviewees in the linguistic skills required to accomplish a successful occupational choice account. Understanding the techniques which successful candidates use to produce convincing accounts can yield valuable insights into practices which play a major part in most modern work organizations and which influence the jobs into which people are subsequently channelled by selection and recruitment specialists. A key role in the interplay between personal choices and institutional pressures is clearly played by the discourses and linguistic repertoires which are available to individuals as they make sense, to themselves and to others, of the processes of work or occupational entry.

4.3   Narrating the self

Before concluding this section on entry to work, I want you to consider a little further the process of 'narrating the self' which is central to discursive analyses. You will find outlined in Chapter 6 (section 2.2) the view that '[a]s people live their lives they are continually making themselves as characters or personalities through the ways in which they reconcile and work with the raw materials of their social situation'. You will be reminded there also that social identity is not an *entity* but is a *project* which is continually in the making.

Personal accounts about occupational choice involve people accounting for their decisions *retrospectively* (Garfinkel, 1967). People do not necessarily 'know' and reveal the 'real' reasons for their choices and actions but they construct justifications and explanations as to why they come to be how they are. In short, they produce stories or narratives about themselves and work out who they are in the process of telling. These narratives connect human agency and activity to the social and institutional context, and come to constitute the kind of person we are.

ACTIVITY 5.3

At this point, you should turn to Reading A, 'Significant others and significant events', which you will find at the end of this chapter.

In this extract, you will find a number of brief accounts which were produced by full-time trade union officers when asked about their 'choice' of occupation. They are part of a study of the occupation of full-time trade union officers which was conducted using 'depth' interviewing of a type close to that which has been termed the 'ethnographic interview' (Spradley, 1979).

As you read, make a note of your responses to the following questions:

- What accounts do these interviewees offer to explain their choice of occupation?

- Do some accounts emphasize structural constraints and others human choice and agency?

- Are the accounts themselves constructed at different levels? In other words, do they combine elements of choice and determinism?

- To what extent can you apply the notion of 'linguistic repertoire' as used by Moir?

First, it is important to note that these accounts have been extracted by the author from the wider 'stories' produced by officers about their lives and experiences. It is the author who has drawn together these separate accounts to place them in the symbolic interactionist framework of 'significant others' and 'significant events'. So the accounts have, in part, been detached from their original context and from wider narratives. However, with this caution in mind we can proceed to identify several different types of account.

A number of officers clearly told the 'story 'of their route into full-time officer work in terms of personal choice and human agency. They actively 'chose' to become officers because they saw working people exploited and suffering injustice and wanted to change things (mining disasters; men being 'robbed blind'; fighting for the position of craftsmen; people needing protection). Whilst it is clear that these officers remembered these as significant events in their lives, it is also likely that they are telling a story about the importance in trade union work of fighting to protect the interests of the working class. The language of injustice and exploitation is used by the interviewees to make sense of their situation to themselves and to the listener.

Similarly, in talking about significant others, officers create an image of the trade union household, where parents are committed and use every means to educate and encourage their offspring (trade union family; family teaching; very working class; the encyclopaedia; taken-for-granted way of life). Note the point that some of the officers appeared to feel uneasy about their working-class 'credentials' and placed more emphasis on the influence of family background than those officers who felt more secure in their working-class status. They had to work at this aspect of identity when reviewing their life histories.

All the accounts, even where choice is acknowledged, suggest a recognition of structural constraints. For example, the mining officers had to have gone into mining to have become a member of the union in the first place. Others talk of lack of opportunity, being bored or blocked in their jobs and turning to (not necessarily choosing) trade union work as a diversion or alternative.

Finally, using the notion of 'linguistic repertoire', it is possible to identify something like the 'standard membership category repertoire' (possessing the characteristics required to be able to fight for and represent others; having the appropriate personality to do the job) and the 'family influence repertoire' (the influence of family members and significant others in going into this type of work).

What this brief discussion illustrates is that the study of 'whole life biographies' can give us greater insight into 'the meaning of social events as seen through the eye of the self observer', and this point will be developed in more detail in Chapter 6. Individuals reconstruct their 'self-images and personal histories in the light of recent and current happenings and strive to keep them in "good repair"' (Johnson, 1983, pp. 252–3). Whenever we wish to understand 'what actually happened' in the lives of people we are studying (or of people we know socially), we have little to go on other than the words that are spoken to us by these people themselves or by people who know them. To reach our own interpretation of 'what happened', it is therefore vital to recognize the importance of the interpretative work which the individuals themselves have engaged in when constructing their accounts. Part of what each of us is, as a unique individual with a distinctive self-identity, is the outcome of the stories which we construct to make sense to ourselves and others of who we are and where we have come from. These stories emerge out of culturally constructed meanings but they also help us to reconstruct and change these meanings. We are most likely to become conscious of this when we present ourselves to potential employers when entering work or trying to achieve a job change. But the need to make sense to ourselves and others of who we are and what we are doing continues as we become involved in whatever kind of work we enter.

Review of section 4

- Entry into paid employment is a key stage in a person's whole life career which is influenced by past biography and expectations as well as by structural variables such as age, class, 'race', gender and educational achievement.

- The study of occupational entry usefully highlights debates about the extent to which the individual is a unified and defined entity or may be conceived of as flexible and changing, constructed through language and interaction. Social constructionism brings a different perspective to bear on entry into the labour market and helps move the focus away from identifiable personality types to the interpretative processes which take place when human beings use language and action to construct and project their identities in the social context.

- Historically, the study of occupational entry has mirrored the general social science debate about the relative influence of social structure and human agency. Recent studies of occupational entry highlight the ways in which agency and structure are implicated in one another and the extent to which the determining nature of social structure varies according to social context.

- Interpretations of historical events and an understanding of 'what happened' need to take account of the interpretative work which individuals engage in when they construct and reconstruct their own self-images and life histories.

5   Experience and identity at work

Let us now turn to the experiences of individuals at work and the ways in which people act to control their environment and manage their identities. People undertake paid work in a whole range of contexts. They may:

- be 'home-workers', producing items at home on a 'piece work' basis;

- be 'self-employed' and receiving payments according to the completion of contracts or provision of professional services;

- follow occupational routes through public and private sector bureaucracies and organizations;

- undertake professional work within large-scale organizations;

- be service workers or engaged in manufacturing;

- be full-time or part-time, temporary or permanent;

- regard themselves as following a career, fulfilling a vocation, or merely 'having a job'.

In this section I intend to focus on aspects of the relationship between individuals and their work which have relevance to their conceptions of self and their social identities, particularly in work organizations. The notions of orientation to work and of the psychological contract are helpful in this.

5.1   Work orientations and psychological contracts

One facet of a working person's self-identity is their *orientation to work*. This has been defined as 'the meaning attached by individuals to their work ... which predisposes them both to think and act in particular ways with regard to that work' (Watson, 1995, p. 118). The nature of the job, and the individual's orientation to work, will affect the way in which they respond to experiences at work and the extent to which work is regarded primarily as a means to an end or as an end in itself. As we saw in the discussion of the *work ethic* and *alienation*, at a cultural level there are dominant ideas which permeate our experience and influence our expectations. Notions that work should be fulfilling, be intrinsically satisfying or be a valued thing in itself are cultural constructions. As such, they are material to be actively worked and reworked by individuals in the context of their own social location and experience in the social world. What our explorations of approaches like social constructionism and discourse analysis tell us is that explanations in terms of psychological needs or individual attitudes are too limited. Sociological studies of work and organization, and particularly of manual work, have indicated that many people find work stressful, unrewarding, physically damaging, boring and unfulfilling. On the other hand, sociological research also indicates that individuals do not necessarily expect work to offer intrinsic satisfaction. As the influential study of 'affluent workers' in the 1960s demonstrated, workers may deliberately choose to take work which provides them with a good standard of living rather than intrinsic job satisfaction. Whilst their work provided the workers in the study with little intrinsic satisfaction, they did not say that they were *dissatisfied* with the jobs they were doing. They had adopted an 'instrumental' attitude towards their work and had consciously chosen to regard it in that light (Goldthorpe et al., 1968).

When individuals enter paid employment, they bring with them a whole range of meanings and expectations (their 'prior orientations to work') which predispose them to act and think in particular ways once they are in the work environment. However, this orientation to work is not fixed but is dynamic (Watson, 1995). An individual's perceptions and expectations may change according to social circumstance, inside and outside of work. This can be illustrated with a hypothetical example of a young married woman whose orientation to work led her to be satisfied with a relatively low level of intrinsic satisfaction in a routine clerical job. Her priorities concerned building a home, and her wage was sufficient to help her meet her domestic aspirations. However, after her marriage ran into trouble she reassessed her life and decided to seek opportunities for promotion in her employment. She also decided to do a part-time degree by distance learning. Her work career and her personal life became re-defined and her employer provided opportunities for her to progress in the organizational hierarchy. She is now in a managerial position and says that she finds both her work life and her social life more fulfilling. A key part of her account of her recent life is the claim that she is a 'different person' from what she was several years previously. Her orientation to work changed radically, we can say, as she began to treat her employment as a major route towards building what she actually referred to as a 'new identity'. She deliberately changed her life, and her employment circumstances were such that she was able to train for a different job from the one she had originally entered. In effect, a new contractual relationship emerged between this woman and her employment.

In entering employment, the individual enters into a formal agreement to undertake specific tasks in return for agreed payment and specified terms and conditions. This is the basic employment contract which is explicitly drawn up between employer and employee. However, this contract of employment does not formally determine the behaviour and perceptions of the person at work. Employees also enter into a *psychological contract*. This is an implicit set of expectations about the nature of the relationship between the person and the organization. The psychological contract is 'an agreement between the individual and the organization, through a process of mutual bargaining, as to what is given and received, together with subsequent honouring of this agreement' (Blackler and Shimmin, 1984, p. 17). This tacit agreement about how much effort the employee will expend, and how much control they will have, in return for their rewards, is also known as the 'implicit contract' (Watson, 1995) and the 'effort bargain' (Baldamus, 1961). The psychological contract is clearly not a contract between equals, and the bargaining power of individuals will reflect their position within the organizational structure. Furthermore, the implicit contract is never fixed or stable. It will shift as employees, individually and collectively, seek to minimize effort and increase rewards, and as the employer pushes towards increasing efficiency and productivity. Economic behaviour of this type is frequently accompanied by a range of informal activities which also help people 'cope' with their working circumstances.

5.2   Coping and laughing

As section 2 of this chapter outlined, the nature of work organizations in capitalist society is that they are formally designed by owners and managers to achieve certain ends. Formal organizations are hierarchical and are founded on an imbalance of power between parties. Whilst employer and employee are tied into a framework of mutual dependency (employees needing the employer for their living and the employers needing to ensure the workers' continued willingness to work), the employment relationship also involves management and workers in a battle of conflicting interests. In the light of the uncertain and indeterminate nature of the employment contract, management attempts to develop control structures (technological and organizational) which may actively be contested by the workforce rather than simply being imposed on them by management. Employees develop their own strategies for coping and their own strategies for control and these may be both overt and collective or covert and personal.

At this point, I would like you to read Reading B, 'Managing a joke', by David   ACTIVITY 5.4
Collinson. This extract is taken from Collinson's (1992) study *Managing the Shopfloor.*

As you read, make a note of your answers to the following questions:

- What are the functions of humour in the workplace as outlined in this reading?

- What evidence is there here to suggest that workers do not passively respond to their circumstances but are active agents in their experience?

- What effect do the joking practices appear to have on the relationships between workers and between management and workers?

In Reading B, Collinson suggests that workplace humour in this factory fulfils a number of functions and contributes to the shaping of work *relationships* as well as *personal meanings*. Humour:

- allows the expression of frustration and conflict;

- may reduce hostility;

- maintains social order;

- works to produce consensus;

- allows active resistance to a controlled environment;

- reduces boredom;

- strengthens collective self-identity;

- differentiates the working group from other groups in the hierarchy;

- reinforces the 'us and them' and reinforces polarization.

In discussing the role of humour, Collinson argues that workers actively search for meaning and enjoyment at work, and collective humour is one of the ways in which they do this. This 'living culture' is a source of meaning and identity for workers who generally experience work as controlling and alienating. It is through these collective joking practices that 'workers hope to achieve a positive meaning, sense of personal power and validation of identity' (Collinson, 1992, p. 103). The study shows us yet again how the ways in which people experience work and work institutions have an important influence on their self-image and their social identity.

Where people spend a significant part of their time in work organizations or occupational activities it is inevitable that the institutional practices they experience (and contribute to) will have an effect on their formation of self. They also have to protect themselves psychologically from potentially damaging circumstances.

5.3   Anxiety and defence mechanisms

We have seen in the preceding section some of the informal social activities which assist people in coping with challenges to their autonomy and their sense of self at work. Chapter 2 of this volume described a classic study of unconscious defences operating in the workplace – a study of trainee nurses in a general teaching hospital in London in the 1950s. Whilst the psychodynamic approach, focusing on individual and collective unconscious anxieties, is clearly very different from the social constructionist framework adopted in this chapter (which emphasizes language and meaning), it is worth reflecting on the connections with the anxiety and defensive mechanisms explored in Chapter 2. For the purposes of the present discussion, my focus is on the 'defence mechanisms' which appeared to operate in the hospital to protect the nursing staff from the anxiety which was inherent in their work. A number of *institutional practices* had developed to help the nursing staff cope with the stressful nature of their work (see Chapter 2, section 4). These involved:

- splitting up the relationship of nurse and patient;

- depersonalizing the patient;

- an ethos of detachment and denial of feelings;

- the standardization of tasks to minimize the taking of life-and-death decisions;

- a system of checks and cross-checks to ensure that no one person has the responsibility of making a given decision;

- the apportioning of responsibility and irresponsibility to those senior and junior to oneself respectively;

- sticking to existing structure and procedures, even when they are no longer appropriate.

The author of this research, Menzies Lyth, argued that these institutional mechanisms are engendered by the unconscious anxieties brought about in the individual by the nature of the task and by the nature of involvement in a work organization (Menzies Lyth, 1988). Furthermore, she asserted that all organizations develop such mechanisms but that they are most often detrimental to the main task – in this case, caring for patients. From the social constructionist perspective this study illustrates, for the purpose of my discussion, that in any institutional structure individuals act, consciously or unconsciously, to protect themselves and find mechanisms of coping in situations of stress. These mechanisms are not just individual but become collective and part of the structured environment which any new member of the work team must confront.

Review of section 5

- One aspect of individuals' identity is their *orientation to work* – the range of meanings and expectations they bring with them to the work environment.

- As active social agents, individuals find ways, individually or collectively, of controlling their environments and managing their identities.

- When individuals enter work they enter into a *psychological contract* which is an implicit agreement about how much effort will be expended for negotiated rewards. Within this context, people develop individual and collective ways of coping with the work environment and protecting their notions of self, especially in alienating and stressful environments.

- Social constructionist accounts examine the ways in which individuals use language to produce 'accounts' and create personal meaning. Psychodynamic approaches analyse the ways in which unconscious fears and anxieties are amplified by stresses at work and have implications for institutional practices. Whilst very different in emphasis, both approaches can help our understanding of coping strategies in work organizations.

6   Being managed

Most of paid work takes place in work *organizations* where working practices and management approaches have been influenced in a number of ways by some pieces of psychological research and theorizing. Organizations are made up of individuals, work roles and groups. Managing people involves addressing such things as work design and technology, commitment and motivation, work satisfaction and conflict management, leadership and culture, stress and mental health. Employers and managers have derived elements of their models of the person and the organization from psychology and social psychology.

These models cover the impact of the person on the organization and the impact of the organization on the person, and some of the most influential research of this kind was discussed in Chapter 1. At the centre of much of this research has been the concept of *work motivation* and a whole discourse which has been jointly developed by psychologists and management experts around this notion. In considering this concept of motivation, this section will return to some of the themes of Chapter 1 concerning work groups and will place these in a broader content.

6.1   Motivating people at work

The discourse of 'work motivation' does not emphasize the task of managers as one of *managing work* – which might seem a fairly obvious way of looking at the functions of those holding directing roles within work organizations. Instead, it tends to stress the centrality to managerial work of *managing people.* And central to the task of 'managing people' is the process of motivating them. What this means is something quite simple (even though it is frequently stressed how difficult a thing this is to achieve) – it is a matter of identifying the needs which employees have and then meeting those needs in such a way that the employees will reciprocate by doing whatever it is that their managers require of them.

In the late nineteenth and the early twentieth centuries, as work organizations began to grow in size and as the nature of managerial work began to be addressed for the first time, the 'experts' who tried to generalize about how to induce workers to carry out the tasks designed by managers tended to be engineers like F.W. Taylor, the very influential, but controversial, proponent of 'scientific management'. Taylor (1911) advocated the restriction of practically all discretionary judgements and decisions in the industrial workplace to the scientifically trained managers. Work should be made as unskilled as possible so that workers could be directly rewarded with money simply for carrying out the tasks prescribed in the finest detail by managers. Taylor was concerned more with managing work than managing people and consequently he did not propose anything as elaborate as an explicit 'theory of motivation'. He did, however, lay down a set of principles against which, in one way or another, the range of social and organizational psychologists concerned with work motivation theory have since seen themselves as reacting. Taylor's concept of rewarding people with money for carrying out managerially prescribed tasks is one which clearly continues to play a central role in employment practices in all capitalist societies. Indeed, it has been argued that the basic logic of all work design in capitalist societies is one in which employers prefer to simplify or 'deskill' tasks so as to make the task of managing the 'labour process' a more straightforward one in which the cash nexus is the main motivational focus (Braverman, 1974).

Early questioning by psychologists of the assumptions of this engineering-influenced conception of human beings ('fuel up the human machine with cash and drive it wherever you wish' might crudely sum up the approach) came during the First World War as its limits came to be recognized in the munitions factories. A key figure in this work was C.S. Myers (1920). Myers emphasized the importance of what he called the 'psychological factor' in industry and commerce and tried to tackle what he saw as a series of barriers to the carrying out of effective work: these included 'mental and nervous fatigue, monotony, want of interest, suspicion, hostility' and so on. There is clearly a more sophisticated notion of the human being in this early occupational psychology than there was in the folk psychology of Taylor and his fellow scientific managers. And, as Chapter 1 noted, this new emphasis on the needs of workers was sustained through interpretations of the famous Hawthorne experiments in America (Mayo, 1933, 1949; Roethlisberger and Dickson, 1939). The key emphasis of this work, for present purposes, is the model of the human being which it encouraged. This was one of a creature who would come to work seeking to satisfy, not just economic rewards, but also a need to belong. Employers were thus encouraged to adopt a psychological model of employees as predominantly social animals who were more likely to do what was required of them if their social needs were met. Thus, attention had to be given by employers to locating people in meaningful work groups, to showing an interest in them as people rather than just as hired hands, and to making workers feel that they 'belonged' as employees of the organization. Such ideas were clearly not novel and had played some part in paternalist managerial practices in the earliest factories. However, the ideas of the 'human relations' social psychologists who were associated with the Hawthorne experiments have had a continuing influence on managerial practices and on attempts to win employee compliance through fostering a sense of belonging.

Social psychologists' contributions to managerial thinking were then added to these human relations concerns, further helping to shape the institutional patterns within which the modern employee works. Much influenced by the ideas of the humanistic psychologist Maslow (1943), who argued that human beings seek to satisfy ever higher 'levels' of need (culminating in the achievement of *self-actualization*) once they have satisfied 'lower level needs' like physical, social and esteem fulfilment, a whole managerial and psychological discourse has developed which sees employees as only being effectively 'motivated' in the long run if they are given as much responsibility or discretion as possible in the way they carry out their work roles. These principles were manifested early on in such practices as the redesign of jobs to achieve 'job enrichment' (Herzberg, 1966), and more recently in attempts to 'empower' employees and encourage them to work cooperatively and take initiatives in the context of team-working.

You may well have experienced, or attempted to implement, some of these innovations in your own work setting. If you have, you might reflect on the extent to which the rationale which is given to these practices by the employer makes explicit the social psychological principles behind them.

These practices have been influenced not only by the work of social psychologists and their claim to demonstrate through research what kinds of motivational practice 'will work' but also by the models of the human person which underpin their theorizing. The motivational practices which have come more fully into fashion than ever before in many modern work organizations, and which make particular use of the notions of team-working and empowerment, are based on a view of the human being which has clear roots in the modern work ethic which we identified earlier on as playing a key role in the institutional patterns of industrial capitalist societies. The human being at work is seen as someone who, whether initially conscious of it or not, *needs* to achieve self-fulfilment at work. One has to realize one's full potential in the workplace before one will readily yield to the employer the highest degree of active compliance – of 'motivation'.

Work motivation theories, as they exist within social psychology, and as they have influenced modern management practice, do not exist outside the human world which they attempt to explain. They are not the product of a lofty science which is in some sense outside and above the social world studied by social science. As much as they may have been developed by rigorous social scientific analysis (and this could be debated at length), they are still a product, in part, of a wider institutional or cultural pattern. They are the manifestations, in a 'rational' age, of cultural notions which go back to the religious roots of ideas about the relationship between work activity and the worthiness and identity of the human being. They are, however, ideas which tend to be focused on the human being as an *individual*. Although work motivation theories often recognize a social dimension to motivational influences, this is typically regarded as a matter of the 'social needs' of individuals rather than as a matter of institutional requirements of the work organization itself – conditions which need to be met for the organization to function successfully as something whereby the whole is greater than the parts. This latter concern has entered managerial ideas in the last decade and a half, however, with the very fashionable interest in managing the organization through shaping, or changing, its *culture*.

6.2 Managing and being managed through culture

It now a commonplace in work organizations of all types in Britain and America to find managers, and others, talking of the organization's culture and, especially, speaking of the need to change that culture. This is a type of managerial and organizational discourse which one would not have come across before the early to mid 1980s. At that time, business leaders (later followed by those in charge of public sector organizations), first in the USA, and then in Britain, saw a need to rethink in a fairly fundamental way how their enterprises were going to be managed if they were to be successful in a changing competitive environment. There was a growing recognition that further restructuring of businesses and a dependence on the analytical skills of more and more graduates of business schools were not going to be enough. Somehow, organizational leaders had to find a way of combining an increased capacity on their own part to exert leadership and give direction and inspiration to their workforces with a more effective approach to 'releasing' the skills and potential of the whole workforce. There was an increasing recognition that such claims as 'the people who work here are the most important assets we have' might not just be matters of public relations rhetoric or ritualistic attempts in the 'human relations' tradition to 'make workers feel important'. New ideas were needed.

The notion of organizations having cultures was one which had existed prior to this time within the literature of the social sciences, but little notice had been taken of it by those with a practical interest in work organizations. The 1980s, however, were a time when it could come into its own. Among the vehicles which brought this concept into managerial discourse and organizational practices was a series of books written by management consultants who had looked to the social sciences for ideas which would help managers rethink their practices. The most influential of these were the consultants Peters and Waterman whose book *In Search of Excellence* (1982) persuaded its massive readership that what gave the highest qualities of 'excellence' to enterprises was their possessing a 'strong culture'. At the core of this was a set of 'shared' values which would influence each and every member of the organization to focus attention on pleasing customers in a way which would benefit the enterprise's business position. People in such 'strong culture' organizations, it is claimed, do not need to be closely supervised by managers, directed by rule books and procedure manuals, or monitored by tight control and surveillance systems. People do what is beneficial to the organization as a whole and they do it, not because they are told to, but *because they want to*.

If we look at this influential book we can see that it mixed ideas from both sociological and psychological traditions together with an anthropological element (anthropology being a discipline in which the notion of 'culture' has always been central). At the psychological level, Peters and Waterman refer to what they call 'man [*sic*] waiting for motivation' and claim that excellent companies appear to take advantage of the 'very human need – the need one has to control one's destiny' (1982, p. 55). This might seem very similar to some of the principles we saw stressed by the motivation theorists we considered earlier. However, there is a move away here from the notion of 'needs' being fulfilled in a sequential or hierarchical way to a claim that people 'simultaneously seek self-determination and security' so that '[a]t the same time that we are almost too willing to yield to institutions that give us meaning and thus a sense of security, we also want self-determination' (ibid., p. 80). With the use of the word 'institution' here, a bridge is being built to the more sociological tradition of looking at organizations. Peters and Waterman draw on the classic industrial sociology of Selznick (1949) and his analysis of the way in which managers can 'mould' the 'character' of their organization, taking it beyond being simply an *organization,* in the sense of a set of pragmatic 'tools' designed to get jobs done, towards becoming an *institution.* Through a process of institutionalization, the organization comes to have its own identity and a set of values which mean that it can have a significance in the lives of employees which goes well beyond simply carrying out tasks and getting paid.

Numerous writers, some with an academic emphasis and some with a more prescriptive managerial intent, have used this notion of organizational culture – with its powerful characteristic of bringing together the individual or psychological level of the human tendency to 'seek meaning' with the social level of there being something in the institutional domain which functions both to help people 'find meaning' and to shape their behaviours. It is the potential of 'culture' to shape behaviour, of course, which makes it appeal to managers. But what is this phenomenon of 'culture' which has this double potential? The characteristics of organizational culture brought out by the range of writers on the topic have been summarized by Ott (1989, p. 50):

- Organizational culture is the culture that exists in an organization, something akin to a societal culture.

- It is made up of such things as values, beliefs, assumptions, perceptions, behavioural norms, artefacts, and patterns of behaviour.

- It is a socially constructed, unseen, and unobservable force behind organizational activities.

- It is a social energy that moves organization members to act.

- It is a unifying theme that provides meaning, direction, and mobilization for organization members.

- It functions as an organizational control mechanism, informally approving or prohibiting behaviours.

It is clear from this that the notion of organizational culture is a very broad one. It covers practically every aspect of life in an organization. It brings together such matters as the technologies that are used, the words that are spoken, the priorities which influence behaviour, and the structures that place people and activities. In effect, it is that which converts the work organization from being just a set of task-related activities into something 'institutionalized' which exists for those within it as more than the sum of its parts. However, all of this can become very vague. To see what happens in practice, when the managers of an organization set about 'changing a culture', we can look at the following report.

ACTIVITY 5.5

Read Extract 5.1 carefully and note all the various innovations which have been introduced by this company as part of what is presented as an attempt to 'change the culture' of the organization.

Extract 5.1 *New company culture gets off the ground*

It takes a long time to change the attitudes of a workforce and create a new company culture. So when Dowty Aerospace propellers (DAP) split off from a large engineering group to become an independent business, its management team designed a training programme that would last for two to three years.

'The attitudes of the directors was that we would become a single-status company with a much more empowered workforce, and you can't do that overnight,' says HR manager Fred Reed.

Before going through a major restructuring programme in 1991, the parent group, Dowty Aerospace Gloucester Ltd, had been organized along traditional lines, with eight layers of management and rigid demarcation lines.

DAP has a flatter structure with directors, managers and team leaders occupying three management levels and an employee council giving the workforce a say in running the company. Open-plan working areas where managers sit with their teams signal open communication and the removal of departmental barriers.

But having set up these new structures, the company needed to ensure that its employees could operate effectively within them. Employees also needed to understand their role in achieving business targets. The four-stage training programme launched almost three years ago has helped DAP rise to these challenges, as well as winning it a National Training Award.

Involving all 300 or so employees, the programme began with a half-day briefing in which senior managers outlined the company's structure and business objectives. This was followed by two large-scale conferences which continued to develop employees' understanding of the need for change. These were also occasions for two-way communications between participants and conference leaders. After presentations from directors, groups of employees held brainstorming sessions and voted on ideas from the conference floor. One of these – that the managing director should hold quarterly briefing meetings for the entire workforce – is now well established.

The third stage involved customer care training workshops, in which the focus was on internal as well as external customer service. These have improved internal communication and helped blur a distinction between white and blue-collar workers.

In the final stage of the training programme, now nearing completion, the company has looked at individual employees' needs and provided training tailored to specific groups or individuals. Employees have been encouraged to study for external awards and the company is piloting an NVQ in composite blade manufacture – not previously covered by a nationally recognized qualification.

Reed has no doubts about the benefits the training programme has brought the business. The company recently won a contract to supply composite propeller blades for the new Hercules aircraft against stiff competition, he says. The programme and the culture it has helped create have played a major part in this commercial success story.

Source: Anat Arkin, *Personnel Management,*
June 1994, p. 62

You will probably have noted some of the following managerial innovations – all of which can be seen in work organizations across the economy:

- a move to a 'single-status' workforce (i.e. where distinctions such as that between 'works' and 'staff' are removed);

- a concern to 'empower' the workforce (i.e. to give people much more discretion about how they carry out their work tasks);

- a flatter organizational structure (i.e. with fewer levels of authority than previously);

- open-plan offices and the removal of departmental barriers (i.e. both physical and behavioural divisions are broken down);

- employee briefings and participatory 'conferences';

- customer care training workshops.

To what extent have you come across any of these innovations in your own experience or heard about them from people you know?

To what extent have you, or others, seen these as part of attempts to 'change culture'?

It is very important when reading extracts such as Extract 5.1 to recognize that this is an account which has been given to a journalist by a senior manager of the organization which is being described. To point this out is not necessarily to raise doubts about the veracity of the account, or to suggest that the reality of life in the organization is not as comfortable and exciting as this account might imply. We cannot really know how much we are hearing of managerial aspirations and how much we are hearing about significantly changed practices. What we do know is that in some organizations the types of change which are being introduced by managers are spoken about in quite different terms by those who are on the 'receiving end' of the innovations. The account which I want you to look at in the next activity is also one presented to a journalist, and it is clearly being expressed by an aggrieved employee. The interview was carried out to illustrate a news story about a bank's union having successfully balloted members on taking industrial action over a pay claim.

Read Extract 5.2 from an interview with a bank employee — who, you will notice, uses the concept of 'culture' himself — and make a note of the following:

ACTIVITY 5.6

- How, on this evidence, would you characterize the old culture of this bank?

- How, on this evidence, would you characterize the new culture of the bank?

- Referring back to section 5.1 of this chapter, identify the key ways in which you think Mike Davison's *orientation to work* or his *psychological contract* with the bank have changed in recent times.

Extract 5.2 *A worker's lament*

Mike Davison, aged 29, works at Barclay's Kensington branch in central London:

When I joined Barclays almost eight years ago it had a family atmosphere. I was in a small branch where everybody knew each other and managers had a paternalistic approach.

On my first day I was taken aside for a pep talk and my boss told me: 'there's a marshal's baton in every private's knapsack'. I took that to mean that if I put my head down, I would become a manager in time.

For several years I enjoyed the work, and rose from a bank clerk to my present position as mortgage consultant. But recently the culture of the company has changed.

Barclays has become increasingly decentralized. My bank was merged with five other offices and it no longer feels like a family concern.

The company is also being driven by snowballing targets which mean that we have to work much harder just to stand still. Four years ago when I began in mortgages I was in a team of six that had to attain an annual business target of £2.4 million. Now we are down to two and we are expected to process £9.5 million.

We met that target last year – just. But last year they made 432 Barclays staff redundant across the Southeast, with three going from my bank.

That has left less time for those of us remaining to spend with customers. Clients have become numbers to push through the system rather than faces or names.

Job security has gone out of the window. It used to be said that a job at Barclays would see you through from 16 to 60. Not any more. Short-term contracts of less than 12 months are becoming common.

I wouldn't feel so bad if I was properly rewarded. I'm paid a basic wage of £12,400 with London weighting bringing it up to £15,000.

Six months ago a senior director for this area told us that we could look forward to an excellent profit share. After tax it came to £650, which was a good one-off payment but it all went on bills. I reckon I bring in about £130,000 for the branch in commissions but I don't see a penny of that.

What irritates me most is not that many of us work unpaid overtime, or that they have extended the opening hours of the bank by an hour from 9am to 5pm without taking on any more staff. It is that the bank does not practise what it preaches.

Its own mission statement says that employees should treat each others as they would like to be treated, with integrity and as a team player. Yet management imposes on us a pay rise that is below inflation for the third year running, while the chairman, Andrew Buxton, is awarded 18.6 per cent.

Morale in my branch has hit rock bottom. I'm no militant. But the way they treat us has made me very angry.

Source: Interview by Edward Pilkington,
The Guardian, 4 May, 1995

In this brief account, we can see the interplay of the personal and the institutional in one person's work experience. Insofar as his working life contributes to his notion of who and what he is, Mike Davison is having to cope with the pressures of considerable shifts in what his employer expects of him and, equally, with shifts in what he can expect from the bank. A lot of changes are taking place in the work he does, in the rewards he receives (actual rewards and potential ones such as long-term career expectations), and in the feelings he has about his work. There is a lot with which he has to cope. And this notion of 'coping' is central to the final reading for this chapter.

Please turn to Reading C, 'Managing work – managing self', which has been especially written for this book by Tony Watson on the basis of his close study of managerial work in an organization going through a culture change process (Watson, 1994). The focus here is on managers not just as 'agents' of their employer but also as private individuals and as employees themselves. Managers have to cope with the changes in which they are involved as much as do those to whom I referred earlier in this section as on the 'receiving end' of the changes. When reading this article ask yourself:

ACTIVITY 5.7

- Are there any parallels between what is happening in this company and the aerospace company (DAP) which featured in Extract 5.1?

- Are there any parallels between what is happening in this company and the bank which featured in Extract 5.2?

- How, conceptually, does the author relate the institutional level of 'human culture' to the individual level of personal identity?

- How, theoretically, does the author relate the institutional level of culture to the individual level of 'thinking'?

- How is the concept of *discourse* used to make a link between the cultural dimension of the organization and the processes whereby individuals manage their sense of identity – what the managers in this study seem to think of in terms of 'the sort of person I am'?

You will probably have noticed that ZTC were making a number of specific changes which were similar to those coming about in DAP – among them are the use of briefings, the stress on teamwork and the moves towards single-status or 'harmonized' terms of employment. In each case, there is an expressed interest in 'empowering' people as well as making them belong. Thus, an attempt to meet employees' simultaneous needs for security and for self-direction, which Peters and Waterman saw as a key feature of excellent 'strong culture' organizations, is being made in each case. However, in the ZTC case we can see that this is not the whole story. There are rival principles at work and the soft and caring tones of the cultural management discourse clash with the hard and harsh ones of economizing and working to strict targets.

In the ears of at least one employee of Barclays Bank, the latter tune is the loudest. Davison's criticism of the bank, in Extract 5.2, that it does not practise what it preaches, is one which could well have been uttered by employees of ZTC. There is perhaps an irony in the fact that the concept of 'culture' which is used so often by managers with positive and constructive overtones is used – against the bank's managers – by this critic who illustrates his claim that the culture has changed with the negative and critical observation that it 'no longer feels like a family concern'. Davison is here drawing on what Watson's paper calls 'discursive resources' – in this case the notion of culture itself – to shape and express his thinking about what is going on in the bank. In working out and expressing his position in relationship to his employer, he is weighing up a range of arguments in the 'rhetorical' fashion referred to by Watson (this being an aspect of the way Watson relates the 'individual' phenomenon of thinking to the institutional level of culture). We can also look at Davison's account to help us answer the final question asked in Activity 5.7. We can see in the final words of his account a statement which is explicitly about himself – about the 'sort of person' he is. He wishes us to know that he is angry but, to emphasize that this is not an unreasonable anger, he stresses that he is 'no militant'. Here, of course, he is drawing on a notion from a particular discourse which the press and public often utilize when discussing industrial disputes – a discourse in which 'militancy' is associated with unreasonableness. To analyse these words in this way is precisely to illustrate how the concept of *discourse* can be used to make a link between the cultural dimension of human or organizational life and the processes whereby individuals manage their sense of identity.

Review of section 6

- The notion of *work motivation* has been a central theme in the work of psychologists and management 'experts' and has been influential in elements of 'models of the person' adopted by managers and employers. Social psychological thinking has contributed to managerial practice and helped shape the institutional patterns at work. 'Human relations' psychology and the work of Maslow and Herzberg are examples of this influence.

- Work motivation theories have tended to focus on the human being as an *individual* with *social needs*. Recent managerial thinking, however, has turned to consider the institutional requirements of the work organization itself, recognizing that the organization is something greater than the sum of its parts. The notion of *organizational culture* is central to this perspective.

- Through the process of *institutionalization,* a work organization is transformed from a set of task-related activities to something with its own identity and set of values which becomes expressed as the *organizational culture.* This organizational culture has the potential to help people create meaning at work and to shape their behaviour.

- Managers and, to a lesser extent, employees use the notion of organizational culture as a 'discursive resource'. It provides them with a set of 'interpretative repertoires' to make sense of their situations, to cope with their own lives, to persuade others and construct realities for them. The 'empowerment skills and growth' and 'control, jobs and costs' discourses explored in Reading C are examples of this interactive process in practice.

7   Conclusion

In the final set of 'real-life' illustrations from three different organizations in section 6.2, we have looked at a number of ways in which a distinctive set of trends in the relationship between the institutional and the personal, the social and the psychological, are visible in the contemporary world of work in the UK. We must nevertheless remember that these changes are ones which relate to shifting patterns of economic, political and technological activity worldwide. These changing patterns are ones in which an increased level of competitiveness, between economies and between business enterprises, is putting pressures on practically every work organization and labour market across the globe. The three organizations considered in the last section were pressured to make the changes they are undergoing by these factors – which is not to say that any of the three organizations had to follow the particular route chosen by their managements. Incidentally, you may have noted the absence of 'gender' as an element in these discussions. This theme will be taken up in the final chapter of this book. The social construction of work and work identities in different historical periods has some obvious consequences, for example, for conceptions of what it means 'to be a real man' or a 'real woman'.

As you have read this chapter and engaged with the readings and the activities, I hope that you will have found some of these ideas insightful and, indeed, useful and will be able to apply them to your own changing circumstances – whatever your personal relationship is to work and employment. Each of us is a creature of the institutions in which we are born and brought up and in which we both work and play. But these institutions are, in the final analysis, human creations. A central theme of this chapter has been the ways in which we both make and are made by the social institutions which surround us. I trust that you have found the ideas in this chapter relevant to your own efforts in managing the institutional circumstances in which you find yourself.

Further reading

To follow up the arguments, issues and any topic from this chapter which particularly interests you, you might look at some of the following works, which have been cited in the text, as well as one or two additional texts.

Most of the matters looked at in the chapter – from theoretical issues to substantive topics such as the meaning of work, organizational cultures, employment, humour and so on – are covered in Watson (1995).

Grint (1991) covers some of these issues in a helpful way, as do contributors to the volume edited by Pahl (1988). The study by Banks and others (1992) will be of interest to those especially concerned with processes of entry into work and careers, whilst the collection of papers edited by Fineman (Fineman, S. (ed.) (1987) *Unemployment: Personal and Social Consequences*, London, Tavistock) and the studies in Gallie, Marsh and Vogler (1994) have a great deal to say about how we can better understand issues of employment and unemployment. The Collinson (1992) study is not only insightful on the role of humour in the workplace but on a range of other issues which arise in the contemporary factory. To look at detailed cases of organizations undergoing significant changes which have implications not just for the experience but also the sense of identity of employees at all levels, you might well look further at the study, *In Search of Management*, which Tony Watson's reading discusses (Watson, 1994) and compare this with similarly ethnographic accounts given by Casey (Casey, C. (1995) *Work, Self and Society: After Industralism,* London, Routledge) and Kunda (Kunda, G. (1992) *Engineering Culture: Control and Commitment in a High-tech Corporation,* Philadelphia, Temple University Press). For a helpful and critically astute overview of the growing academic and managerial interest in cultural aspects of organizations, see Anthony, P. (1994) *Managing Culture*, Milton Keynes, Open University Press.

References

Abercrombie, N. Hill, S. and Turner, B.S. (1994) *Dictionary of Sociology* (3rd edn), Harmondsworth, Penguin Books.

Baldamus, W. (1961) *Efficiency and Effort*, London, Tavistock.

Banks, M., Bates, I., Breakwell, G., Bynner, J., Elmer, N., Jamieson, L. and Roberts, K. (1992) *Careers and Identities*, Milton Keynes, Open University Press.

Berger, P.L. and Luckmann, T. (1971) *The Social Construction of Reality*, Harmondsworth, Penguin Books.

Blackler, F. and Shimmin, S. (1984) *Applying Psychology in Organizations*, London, Methuen.

Braverman, H. (1974) *Labor and Monopoly Capital*, New York, Monthly Review Press.

Burchell, B. (1994) 'The psychological consequences of unemployment: assessment of the Jahoda thesis', in Gallie et al. (eds) (1994).

Burman, E. and Parker, I. (1993) 'Introduction – discourse analysis: the turn to the text', in Burman, E. and Parker. I. (eds) *Discourse Analytic Research*, London, Routledge.

Collinson, D.L. (1992) *Managing the Shopfloor: Subjectivity, Masculinity and Workplace Culture,* Berlin, Walter de Gruyter.

Fryer, D. and McKenna, S. (1987) 'The laying off of hand – unemployment and the experience of time', in Fineman, S. (ed.) *Unemployment: Personal and Social Consequences*, London, Tavistock.

Gallie, D. and Marsh, C. (1994) 'The experience of unemployment', in Gallie et al. (eds) (1994).

Gallie, D., Marsh, C. and Vogler, C. (eds) (1994) *Social Change and the Experience of Unemployment*, Oxford, Oxford University Press.

Gallie, D. and Vogler, C. (1994) 'Unemployment and attitudes to work', in Gallie et al. (eds) (1994).

Garfinkel, H. (1967) *Studies in Ethnomethodology*, Englewood Cliffs, Prentice-Hall.

Gergen, K.J. (1992) 'Organization theory in a postmodern era', in Reed, M. and Hughes, M. (eds) *Rethinking Organization*, London, Sage.

Giddens, A. (1984) *The Constitution of Society: Outline of the Theory of Structuration*, Cambridge, Polity.

Ginzberg, E.J., Ginzberg, S.W., Axelrad, S. and Herma, J.L. (1951) *Occupational Choice*, New York, Columbia University Press.

Goffman, E. (1961) *Asylums,* Harmondsworth, Penguin Books.

Goldthorpe, J.H., Lockwood, D., Bechhofer, F. and Platt, J. (1968) *The Affluent Worker: Industrial Attitudes and Behaviour*, Cambridge, Cambridge University Press.

Grint, K. (1991) *The Sociology of Work: An Introduction,* Cambridge, Polity.

Harré, R. and Gillet, G. (1994) *The Discursive Mind,* London, Sage.

Herzberg, F. (1966) *Work and the Nature of Man*, Cleveland, Ohio, World Publishing Company.

Holland, J.L. (1959) 'A theory of vocational choice', *Journal of Counselling Psychology*, vol. 6, pp. 35–45.

Holland, J.L. (1985) *Making Vocational Choices: A Theory of Vocational Personality and Work Environments* (2nd edn), Englewood Cliffs, Prentice-Hall.

Jahoda, M. (1982) *Employment and Unemployment: A Social Psychological Analysis*, Cambridge, Cambridge University Press.

Johnson, M. (1983) 'Professional careers and biographies', in Dingwall, R. and Lewis, P. (eds) *The Sociology of the Professions*, London, Macmillan.

Kelvin, P. and Jarrett, J.E. (1985) *Unemployment: Its Social Psychological Effects*, Cambridge, Cambridge University Press.

Layder, D. (1990) *The Realist Image in Social Science*, London, Macmillan.

Layder, D. (1994) *Understanding Social Theory,* London, Sage.

Layder, D., Ashton, D. and Sung, J. (1991) 'The empirical correlates of action and structure: the transition from school to work', *Sociology*, vol. 25, no. 3, pp. 447–64.

Maslow, M. (1943) 'A theory of human motivation', *Psychological Development*, vol. 50, pp. 370–96.

Mayo, E. (1933) *The Human Problems of an Industrial Civilization*, New York, Macmillan.

Mayo, E. (1949) *The Social Problems of an Industrial Civilization*, London, Routledge and Kegan Paul.

Menzies Lyth, I. (1988) *Containing Anxiety in Institutions, Selected Essays*, Volume 1, London, Free Association Books.

Moir, J. (1993) 'Occupational career choice: accounts and contradictions', in Burman, E. and Parker, I. (eds) *Discourse Analytic Research*, London, Routledge.

Myers, C.S. (1920) *The Psychological Factor in Industry and Commerce*, London, University of London Press.

Ott, J.S. (1989) *The Organizational Culture Perspective*, Pacific Grove, Brooks/Cole.

Pahl, R. (ed.) (1988) *On Work: Historical, Comparative and Theoretical Approaches*, Oxford, Blackwell.

Peters, T.J. and Waterman, R.H. Jnr (1982) *In Search of Excellence*, New York, Harper and Row.

Potter, J. and Wetherell, M. (1987) *Discourse and Social Psychology: Beyond Attitudes and Behaviour,* London, Sage

Radley, A. (1996) 'Relationships in detail: the study of social interaction', in Miell, D. and Dallos, R. (eds) *Social Interaction and Personal Relationships*, London, Sage/The Open University (Book 2 in this series).

Roberts, B., Finnegan, R. and Gallie, D. (1985) *New Approaches to Economic Life – Economic Restructuring: Unemployment and the Social Division of Labour*, Manchester, Manchester University Press.

Roberts, K. (1975) 'The developmental theory of occupational choice', in Esland, G., Salaman, G. and Speakman, M. (eds) *People and Work*, Edinburgh, Holmes McDougall.

Roethlisberger, F.J. and Dickson, W.J. (1939) *Management and the Worker*, Cambridge, Mass., Harvard University Press.

Selznick, P. (1949) *TVA and the Grassroots*, Berkeley, University of California Press.

Spradley, J.P. (1979) *The Ethnographic Interview*, New York, Holt, Rinehart and Winston.

Super, D.E. (1957) *The Psychology of Careers*, New York, Harper and Row.

Taylor, F.W. (1911) *The Principles of Scientific Management*, New York, Harper.

Wallis, R. (1985) 'Institutions', in Kuper, A. and Kuper, J. (eds) *The Social Science Encyclopaedia*, London, Routledge.

Warr, P.B. (1987) 'Worker without a job', in Warr, P.B. (ed.) *Psychology at Work*, Harmondsworth, Penguin Books.

Watson, D.H. (1988) *Managers of Discontent: Trade Union Officers and Industrial Relations Managers*, London, Routledge.

Watson, T.J. (1994) *In Search of Management: Culture, Chaos and Control in Managerial Work*, London, Routledge.

Watson, T.J. (1995) *Sociology, Work and Industry* (3rd edn), London, Routledge.

Weber, M. (1930) *The Protestant Ethic and the Spirit of Capitalism* (trans. by T. Parsons), London, George Allen & Unwin.

Weber, M. (1968) *Economy and Society*, New York, Bedminster Press.

Wetherell, M. and Maybin, J. (1996) 'The distributed self: a social constructionist perspective', in Stevens, R. (ed.) *Understanding the Self*, London, Sage/The Open University (Book 1 in this series).

Reading A
Significant others and significant events

Diane H. Watson

Source: Watson, D. H. (1988) *Managers of Discontent: Trade Union Officers and Industrial Relations Managers*, London, Routledge, pp. 65–8.

Full-time trade union officers

In examining the route of becoming full-time union officers, all of my interviewees reflected upon the reasons why they had become actively involved in the union in the first place. These reasons were typically narrated in the form of 'significant events' which they regarded as having had a major impact on their view of the world. Sometimes these events were linked up with their awareness of the structural constraints on occupational choice [...].

One of the most striking accounts was given by an NUM officer who had started work at the pit on a Monday morning and on the following night shift had experienced a major disaster which killed eighty miners:

> When I went to work on Tuesday morning the pit was afire. On the next shift I was filling sandbags and on the third and fourth shifts I was helping to dig a mass grave. It struck me then that there was something wrong with the industry and there was a long way to go before things would be right for miners.

As a member of the colliery surveying staff, this man was involved in 'working out contracts and measuring up' and he became 'convinced that the men were being robbed blind'. This, combined with the disaster, which had 'a terrific impact' on him, 'really got me going in the union'.

The engineering officer who had been prevented from going to the high school by his financial circumstances explained how he came from a family with 'a long history of fighting for the working class'. He had become an active trade unionist at fifteen, when he became 'doorkeeper at the local branch because that was the only position that didn't have an age restriction'. His mother had 'educated him in trade union militancy' and he remembers well his 'first militant action'. This was in 1946, when he locked himself in the stores and wouldn't come out until the manager, rate-fixer, convenor and shop steward had been pressured to negotiate a 'bonus for stores-boys which has been paid ever since'.

One of the older mining officers explained how he had become involved in the union because of the injustices experienced by craftsmen in the industry in the early 1950s. Although highly-trained and crucial to the running of the pit, craftsmen were on a fixed payment without bonus. Along with other craftsmen, he tried to form a 'craftsmen's union in the area but they couldn't get recognition from the board. So then I thought the best thing, if I can't fight from outside, is to join the NUM and try to get elected as a union official.' After a series of lay posts, this person became the first craftsman to be elected as a full-time officer in the area.

Another officer in mining was struck by the fact that:

> father was fifty-one and could hardly read or write. When it came to reckoning his wages he'd say, 'Son, will you check that I'm right here. Am I on the right wages?' That's when I realized that people were exploited and need someone to help them. They have less ability than yourself and need advice or they lose out financially. That's when I took this line of career.

One NACODS officer had been on the 'managerial ladder' but began to consider a union career when the Board prevented him from following a particular course because it was argued that he was needed at his pit, which was experiencing an absenteeism problem. This, he felt, was an injustice and it hardened his attitude to the Board. Another officer, in COHSE, had been told by a senior nursing officer that he would not be likely to get any further in his nursing career because of his militancy in the 1979 'winter of discontent' disputes.

Two officers (in NUHKW and COHSE) had found themselves 'pushed into a prominent role as a consequence of lack of interest on the part of overall membership.' For example, the NUHKW officer had never been a union member but joined a non-union factory and found himself engaged in a battle to organize and get recognition. He was the only person willing to take on the shop steward role and felt obligated to do so. This was the beginning of a major interest in his life and his eventual appointment as a full-time officer. The COHSE officer took a job as a hospital porter having had no real experience of trade unions. He described how he had returned from his holiday one year to be informed by his colleagues that 'OK – while you were away we voted you in as a shop steward.' He 'got interested' and found the work 'addictive' – it 'seemed to fulfil some kind of need in me'.

Finally, two officers working in the large general unions commented on what one termed a 'rather inglorious start' to their trade union careers. Both were working in routine clerical jobs which were 'so boring' that they looked to union work as a form of diversion. One related the problems of white collar women to the fact that they were not organized and proceeded to take a major part in bringing organization about. The other found that being a shop steward added 'variety' to his work. He could 'take a day off from the desk' and enjoy the excitement of negotiating at a London hotel, or 'something similar'.

These are some examples of 'significant events' which, in looking back and reflecting on their work histories, officers felt had had a major impact on their perceptions of the world and their active involvement in trade unions. Officers also made reference to the influence of certain 'signficant others' (to use a key term in symbolic interactionist theory) who had played an important part in raising the awareness of trade union work and their ensuing commitment to it. *Significant events* were most often referred to in the mining group. This is perhaps to be expected, in view of their own and their families' experience of hard and dangerous work and the difficult and limiting circumstances of the 'times' in which they were growing up. The reference to *significant others* was much more widespread across all groups. Public service sector officers especially gave a major place to the influence of parents in developing their trade union awareness. Five out of the ten public sector officers talked in some detail about their own parents' involvement in the labour movement, either in local politics, as lay officials or, in one case, as a full-time trade union officer.

One father had been a 'full-time shop steward' and 'at an early age he would take me along with him to meetings at the very large factory where he worked.' Another had a father who was branch secretary in COHSE and felt that he had been 'brought up in a very trade union type family: I remember my very first holiday when I was six years old and we went with him to a union conference.' Both these officers had developed an awareness of the more public side of trade unions – addressing public meetings, organizing strikes, local negotiations and picket lines and one felt that this 'colourful side' is what appealed to him 'in the first instance'.

Others talked of the debates and discussions at home and the ways in which mothers and fathers had influenced their thinking. One of the graduates appointed directly to a post talked of his mother being a NUPE steward and how his awareness and commitment to socialism and trade unions had been stimulated by 'family teaching'. Another had a father who had founded a union branch in a textile firm and who encouraged her 'always to be helpful to the underdog' and to 'think of the various ways [she] might be able to do this'.

Among the mining officers, it was only the BACM officer who talked in a similar way, emphasizing that his parents were 'very working class', working in the Potteries. His father had helped form the first potters' union and led the first strike ever in this union. As a consequence, he had been sacked by his firm and no one stood by him. These events had assumed an important place in the growing child's awareness and had helped form his subsequent attitudes to trade unions.

In manufacturing/engineering, [there was] the account of the officer whose mother had compensated him for his disappointment at not being able to go to the high school by buying him an encyclopedia. From this, she taught him 'labour history and about trade unions'. He described at some length the 'very working-class background' of his immediate family and grandparents. The TASS officer, who attended university, explained that he felt he had the 'right sort of affinity with working-class movements of one sort or another' as a consequence of his 'political father's' background in the mining industry. Both of the officers from Scotland in this group emphasized how, there, the union is very much a taken-for-granted part of the way of life.

The father of one public sector service officer was the general secretary of one of the major unions in this sector. Although this was a stimulus to her interest and her determination to become a full-time officer, it also caused her problems and reservations. She was only too well aware of the stresses and strains imposed upon family life, for example, because she had experienced them at first hand. Furthermore, for a long time she had felt that knowledge of her relationship with this eminent officer led to people developing 'pre-conceived ideas about me and about what a General Secretary's daughter should be like – in some ways I haven't been able to be anonymous or develop myself without that feeling of there always being someone there behind you.'

Looking back over these accounts, it does seem that, in making sense of their work histories, public service sector officers in particular are not able to take for granted their 'credentials' as officers of the trade union movement. Their emphasis upon their families, their links with the 'working class' and their adoption of trade union values contrasts especially with the mining officers' emphasis on significant events. Where mining officers tend to talk in terms of significant events within a taken-for-granted framework of a working class environment, public sector service (and to a lesser extent manufacturing/engineering officers) have to work at this aspect of their identity when reviewing their 'biographies'. The notable exception in mining was the BACM officer who had gone into NCB industrial relations management. This factor makes his case consistent with this general interpretation.

Where all three groups did display a common emphasis on 'significant others' was in their recollections of the ways in which they had been 'sponsored' by certain individuals in their unions. Most officers stressed their lack of confidence about their abilities and the need to be encouraged to take on tasks that involved standing up and speaking in public or negotiating with managements on issues vital to their members' interests. Once they had become involved in the trade union movement and taken on lay offices of one kind or another, almost without exception officers referred to one particular person who had nurtured and encouraged them in their early years. This was most often an existing full-time officer with whom they were in close contact but also mentioned were members of management and academic tutors on courses which they had attended. These significant others did appear to have provided an important source of support and point of reference which supported officers when the 'going was rough' either at home or at work.

Reading B
Managing a joke

David L. Collinson

Source: Collinson, D.L. (1992) *Managing the Shopfloor: Subjectivity, Masculinity and Workplace Culture*, Berlin, New York, Walter de Gruyter, pp. 105–10.

[... W]orkplace humour can also be the means by which social frustration and conflict can be expressed in ways that may either reduce hostility and maintain social order (Emerson, 1969, 1970) or constitute resistance and a challenge to the status quo. Burawoy (1979) discovered that racial prejudice between blacks and whites was articulated in jokes on the shopfloor. Since the production process demanded a degree of worker co-operation, overt racial hostility had to be minimized and was therefore diluted in humour. For functionalists such as Radcliffe-Brown (1940), joking relationships enable the articulation of 'a mutually permitted form of disrespect' in an otherwise potentially conflictual social situation. This view is confirmed by Burns (1953, p. 657) who argues that joking is 'the short cut to consensus'. Wilson (1979) has suggested that joking constitutes a 'safety-valve', which has the conservative function of channelling hostility and thus sustaining social order.

The relationship between humour and social stability is highlighted by other studies that emphasize how those in positions of power can use the 'pacificatory' qualities of joking. Both Coser (1959) and Goffman (1961) have argued that humour tends to be the prerogative of those in charge.[1] Zijderveld (1968, p. 297) has noted that 'joking down' is a 'paternalistic device' which may provide subordinates with a feeling of 'belonging to the family'. Similarly, Pollert (1981) discovered that the sexual banter of a female dominated shopfloor can be incorporated into the language of managerial control. Male supervisors were able to disguise discipline within sexual innuendos, jokes and flattery. At Slavs [the factory studied], humour was used by managers in the subtle processes of discipline that were mediated through the corporate culture campaign. Hence humour can be used as a 'managerial resource to mask the authoritarian content of a message' (Dwyer, 1991, p. 5).

Yet, joking does not always constitute a shortcut to consensus and social harmony. Giddens (1979) highlights that joking can be deadly serious and inherently oppositional.

> Scepticism about 'official' views of society often is expressed in various forms of distancing – and in humour. Wit is deflationary. Humour is used socially both to attack and to defend against the influence of outside forces that cannot otherwise easily be coped with.
>
> *(1979, p. 72)*

---

[1]Goffman (1961) argues, 'The right to make a joke of something is often restricted to the ranking person present' (1961, p. 58).

Freud (1976) distinguished between jokes that are 'innocent' and those which are 'aimed'. Fletcher (1974, p. 158) has differentiated between 'wit' and 'satire'. He argues that wit is concerned to ridicule those who 'take themselves too seriously' and are 'too big for their boots'. It is a 'great leveller' which accepts the status quo. By contrast, satire is more disturbing since it seeks to see through and challenge the world taken for granted, turning it upside down through the medium of humour. Satire thereby generates a critical questioning of social conditions. Green (1978) and Pitt (1979) both assert that humour is an important element in the collective oppositional culture and group solidarity of the miners.

This point is elaborated by Linstead (1985) who argues that organizational humour is often closely related to particular practices of resistance and sabotage. His research highlights the way that joking helps to establish an informal world outside the strictures of organizational control and management. He shows how the canteen, toilets and workbreaks can be colonized by workers seeking to regain a degree of personal autonomy and control. By reversing the normal taken-for-granted order, joking contributes to this process of subversion.

Willis (1977) makes a closer link between humour, masculinity and resistance and is therefore a valuable development of many of the studies previously mentioned. Sufficient to repeat here, that he tends to romanticize this joking culture and to impute too strong a sense of solidarity between the lads. Seeking to deconstruct the joking culture at Slavs and to avoid romanticism, the following analysis examines these practices through an interrelated focus on power and subjectivity. This reveals how joking practices are a medium and outcome of interrelated cultural practices of resistance, conformity, control and self-differentiation on the shopfloor.

Humour as resistance

Practices of shopfloor humour can be seen, at least in part, as an expression of workers' resistance against both their highly controlled tasks and elite control within the company. The spontaneous and cutting creativity of shopfloor banter is indeed conditioned by a desire to make the best of the situation and to enjoy the company of others. Many of the workers themselves see the humorous repartee as a way of dealing with their monotonous work, as one told me,

> Some days it feels like a fortnight. A few years ago I got into a rut. I had to stop myself getting bored so I increased the number of pranks at work.

'Having a laff' allows the men to resist their mundane circumstances, providing the illusion of separation from an otherwise alienating situation. Their subjective investments in frivolity and absurdity also reflect and reinforce a shared sense of group identity and self differentiation. This is illustrated by the following comment,

> He's writing a book about this place, it'll be a best seller, bigger than Peyton Place with all the characters in here!

Concerned to show that they are 'big enough' to laugh at themselves, the men insist that joking reflects the essential nature of the person.

This collective self identity as a community of comedians is strengthened by the reputation of its members. These reputations are often sustained through nicknames. Based on exaggerated and stereotyped personal characteristics, their daily usage in shopfloor interaction helps to create a mythical, imaginary and even charismatic world that sustains a distance from boredom and routine. 'Fat Rat', 'Bastard Jack', 'Big Lemon', and 'The Snake' are names conjured up daily in the Components Division. 'Electric Lips' is unable to keep secrets. 'Pot Harry' is so nicknamed because, as a teaboy, thirty years before, he had dropped and broken all the drinking 'pots'. 'Tom Pepper' is reputed to have never spoken the truth in his life. Another man is known as 'Yoyo' because of his habit of walking away and then returning during a conversation and even in mid-sentence. His 'Yoyo' record has been calculated as fifteen returns in one conversation. Although exaggerated, these cultural identities contribute to shopfloor cohesion by developing a shared sense of masculinity. Only 'real men' would be able to laugh at themselves by accepting highly insulting nicknames (see also Lyman, 1987).

Joking facilitates manual workers' self-differentiation from, and antagonism to, white collar staff and managers. 'Taking the piss' is a defensive mode of managing their subordinated shopfloor status. Shopfloor workers perceive their own joking culture to be a symbol of freedom and autonomy that contrasts with the more reserved work conditions of the office staff. Permeated by uninhibited swearing, mutual ridicule, displays of men's sexuality and 'pranks', the uncompromising banter of the shopfloor is contrasted, exaggerated and elevated above the middle class politeness, cleanliness and more restrained demeanour of the offices. Ironically, when compared with others, the subordinated world of the shopfloor comes to be defined by the men as a free space in which the 'true self' can be expressed, as one machinist elaborated,

> You can have a load of fun on the shopfloor, but in the offices, they're not the type to have a laff and a joke. You can't say 'you fucking twat!' in the offices.

In a similar way, the joking culture reflects and reinforces the sense of 'us and them' in relations with the management. The perceived conformism of managers and their reputed inability to make decisions is reflected in their being nicknamed 'the yes men', and being ridiculed as effeminate. On one occasion, as a result of a workforce 'go-slow', a significant shortfall occurred on management's projected production levels. This stimulated Tom, the axle shop steward, to joke,

> (The production manager) will have a baby when he sees these figures.

Shopfloor humour directed at managers is usually concerned to negate and distance them, as Figure 6 illustrates. The irony that three foremen had not been informed of a course in communication skills, to which they had been assigned, was not lost on many shopfloor workers. Similarly, after one worker was reprimanded for being late for work, he responded by clocking on for work two hours early the following morning.[2] The same man also had a reputation for writing sarcastic poems about particular foremen and managers. In general, however, shopfloor humour tends to remain within and seeks to define the boundaries of the collective culture of the group.

Figure 6   Supervisors and bums

When the body was first made all parts wanted to be SUPERVISORS.

The Brain insisted. 'Since I control everything and do all the thinking, I should be Supervisor.' The Feet said, 'Since we carry man where he wants to go, we should be Supervisors.' The Hands said, 'Since we do all the work and earn all the money to keep the rest of you going, we should be Supervisors.' The Eyes too staked their claim, 'Since we must watch out for all of you, we should be Supervisors.'

And so it went on: the Heart; the Ears and finally … the BUM! How all the other parts laughed to think the Bum should be Supervisor!!!

Thus the Bum became mad and refused to function. The Brain became feverish: the Eyes crossed and ached: the Legs got wobbly and the Stomach went sick.

ALL pleaded with the Brain to relent and let the Bum be Supervisor. And so it came to be. That all the other parts did their work and the Bum simply Supervised and passed a load of CRAP.

…

MORAL: You don't have to be a Brain to be a Supervisor – only a Bum.

Source: Trade Union Noticeboard

---

[2]One story embedded in shopfloor folklore concerned the flowline production department. On one occasion, only after a lorry chassis had been assembled was it realized by the workforce that in the middle stood a stanchion of the building. 'Management went mad', I was told with delight by different manual workers on several occasions.

By contrast, management repeatedly try to engage shop stewards in humorous interaction. Yet the stewards are aware that this managerial humour is part of a wider strategy intended to obscure conflict and the hierarchical structure of status and power behind personalized relations. Hence they avoid participating, for as Eric, the AUEW convener explains,

> You've always got to retain a difference from management because they try to draw you in. At first they tried to come on a bit, but we didn't think much of their jokes.

Aware that the house magazine was widely dismissed and nicknamed 'Goebbel's Gazette' on the shopfloor, its editors published a 'jokey' response,

> Did you know that 'X' is being called Goebbel's Gazette in some quarters?
>
> No I didn't, but thank you for bring it to my Achtung.
>
> Don't get me wrong, but it is propaganda isn't it?
>
> If propaganda is informing everyone on topics which previously were known to only a handful of people, the answer is 'Yes'. We do concentrate on the plus points of the company but so what? Our performance compares favourably with the company's plants anywhere in the world, so why present any other picture?

The intention of managerial joking practices, to reduce conflict and emphasize organizational harmony, had the opposite effect of merely reinforcing the polarization between management and shopfloor. Indeed elements of this corporate culture are often converted into and thereby become part of shopfloor workers' resistance.

References

Burawoy, M. (1979) *Manufacturing Consent,* Chicago, Chicago University Press.

Burns, T. (1953) 'Friends, enemies and the polite function', *American Sociological Review*, vol. 18, pp. 654–62.

Coser, R.L. (1959) 'Some social functions of laughter: a study of humour in a hospital setting', *Human Relations*, vol. 12, pp. 171–82.

Dwyer, T. (1991) 'Humour, power and change in organizations', *Human Relations,* vol. 44, no. 1, pp. 1–19.

Emerson, J. (1969) 'Nogotiating the serious import of humour', *Sociometry*, vol. 32, pp. 169–81.

Emerson, J. (1970) 'Behaviour in private places', in Dreitzel, H.P. (ed.) *Recent Sociology, 2, Patterns in Communicative Behaviour*, New York, Macmillan.

Fletcher, C. (1974) *Beneath the Surface*, London, Routledge.

Freud, S. (1976) *Jokes and Their Relation to the Unconscious*, Harmondsworth, Penguin Books.

Giddens, A. (1979) *Central Problems in Social Theory,* London, Macmillan.

Goffman, E. (1961) *Encounters,* Harmondsworth, Penguin Books.

Green, A.E. (1978) 'Only kidding: joking among coal miners', paper presented at the Conference of the *British Sociological Association,* University of Sussex.

Linstead, S. (1985) 'Breaking the "purity rule": industrial sabotage and the symbolic process', *Personnel Review,* vol. 14, no. 3, pp. 12–19.

Lyman, P. (1987) 'The fraternal bond as a joking relation: a case study of the role of sexist jokes in the male group bonding', in Kimmel, M. (ed.) *Changing Men: New Directions in Research on Men and Masculinity,* London, Sage.

Pitt, M. (1979) *The World On Our Backs,* London, Lawrence and Wishart.

Pollert, A. (1981) *Girls, Wives, Factory Lives,* London, Macmillan.

Radcliffe-Brown, A. (1940) 'On joking relationships', *Africa,* vol. 19, pp. 133–40.

Willis, P.E. (1977) *Learning to Labour,* London, Saxon House.

Wilson, C.P. (1979) *Jokes: Form, Content, Use and Function,* London, Academic Press.

Zijderveld, A.C. (1968) 'Jokes and their relation to social reality', *Social Research,* vol. 35, pp. 286–311.

Reading C
Managing work – managing self

Tony J. Watson

Increasingly, those in charge of work organizations in both the business and the non-commercial sectors of western economies are attempting to 'change the culture' of their organization. ZTC, a telecommunications development and manufacturing company, is one such organization and I went to work for a year as a participant observer within its management with a view to writing the book which became *In Search of Management* (Watson, 1994a). I was particularly interested to learn about what it means to work as a manager in an organization which is entering what I felt to be such 'deep and dangerous waters'.

Culture, in the broad sense of the term, is something which human beings have developed to handle the most challenging and profound problems of existence and to make sense of who and what they are. To make sense of our lives, each one of us needs the help of other people. In fact, so challenging is the task of constantly maintaining our sense of who we are that we need the help of a far greater number of human beings than we could ever turn to face-to-face. We therefore have to turn to that massive and constantly growing fund of human experience, reflection and guidance which is human culture. We are constantly constructing and reconstructing our sense of self through telling ourselves and others about what we 'are at'. Our unfolding sense of self can be seen as the life story or autobiography that we are drafting and redrafting throughout our lives. And through listening to accounts of what others 'are at' – in news reports and in fiction, in the past and in the present, in the private and in the public domains – we are supplied with cues, with models, with ideas and with interpretive possibilities which help us construct our biography. In this way we make sense of ourselves through a constant dialogue with our culture.

Organizations engaging in culture change are, in effect, trying to change their employees' behaviour by manipulating the work-related cues, models and ideas which help shape behaviour in the organization. However, the managers whom I was working with and studying, as well as being involved in a corporate attempt to change the company's culture, were themselves as dependent as any other person on the general cultural supports available to them when it came to coping with their own lives. Note here that I have just used the word 'coping' – a notion very similar to that of 'managing'. Managers, like all other human beings, have to manage their own lives; to cope with whatever circumstances they meet. But, at the same time, they have to manage the activities of other people. Whether or not they directly supervise the work efforts of others, they are involved in the shaping of the way other people think and act – whether these other people be subordinates, customers, bankers, suppliers or fellow managers. There is thus a *double-control* aspect to all managerial work. Because managers are employed as members of the control apparatus of a work organization, they have to direct activities and people's thinking towards the performance of the organization as a whole. At the same time, however, they have to control their own lives and their identities; they have to make sense of the work they are doing in the light of both organizational or business imperatives and their own personal values, goals and desires.

All of us, in making sense of our lives, are involved in a dialogue with our culture. To make sense of being a parent, for example, one draws on cultural norms learned directly in one's own upbringing as well as taking up a thousand cues and suggestions from fiction, advertisements, magazines, gossip, hearsay and child-rearing manuals. A possible internal dialogue – which can be interpreted as a dialogue with culture – might involve debating with oneself along the following lines: 'My parents always said that it was a good thing to let a child cry itself to sleep if it wanted to. So perhaps I should do this. Yet my granny always used to say ... And wasn't I horrified by what happened in that story I read in the paper at the weekend. Then there was what they said about that family down the street who ... and all the books I've read say ... But on the other hand. OK, but the sort of parent I want to be is ...'.

This is an account of a parent's thinking process which I have made up. But it illustrates an idea I found very powerful in helping me make sense of how the managers in my study tended to think about how to act and how to decide what sort of personal and managerial identity they wished to take on; the idea that thinking processes are *rhetorical* and involve us in 'debating with ourselves' (Billig, 1987). We put up *arguments* derived from our experience and from our cultures against other arguments in order to come to decisions about how to act. This is not to suggest that all human actions are formally thought out in this way. Much human action is intuitive or habitual and this has been shown in studies of managers (Mintzberg, 1973; Kotter, 1982). But all of the managers I studied had been forced to think out how they should go about managing in ZTC Ryland. The company's directors had invested much time and effort into getting its managers to change the way they managed as part of a 'culture change' programme. This in itself had encouraged many of them to work out what the new management ideas which were presented to them should mean for their conception of 'being a manager' and for their managerial behaviour. But the degree of debate which went on within managers' minds as well as between managers was greatly increased by the fact the top management of ZTC, as the company came under increasing pressure from the larger corporation which controlled it to 'reduce costs', was increasingly placing them in a position where they were given conflicting signals about appropriate ways of managing.

To work among managers in ZTC was not to feel that one was part of a clear and consistent organizational culture. It felt increasingly as if one was living in a land in which a variety of *languages* was spoken and that people were often confused about which language to speak to each other.

This was a feeling which I heard managers themselves speak of. Indeed it was hearing one manager ask the question 'Which language are we really speaking these days?' that initially led me away from trying to characterize 'the ZTC Ryland culture' as part of my research and towards an analysis of the interplay between the managerial languages spoken in the plant.

Conventional management thinking encourages us to view work organizations as rationally designed systems into which employees are recruited and motivated to carry out tasks which fulfil certain organizational 'goals'. However, scholars are increasingly pointing to the advantages of an alternative perspective. This regards organizations as ongoing and ever changing patterns of human interactions, meanings, negotiations, conflicts and ambiguities. The organization is not so much a 'thing' which we can see or touch as sets of stories or practical fictions which help shape relationships within which work tasks get done. As Paul Bate puts it, 'When people get together they "make things up". This is what organization is: a "made up" or constructed world; a profusion of theories, explanations and interpretations that people devise in order to cope with the exigencies of their everyday lives' (1994, p. 15). He follows the anthropologist Clifford Geertz (1973) in speaking of fiction as 'something made', 'something fashioned'. Thus when the managers of organizations attempt to 'change culture' they are trying, in my terms, to 'change the story' or, as Bate puts it, 'decisions to move from a "production facing" to a "customer facing" culture, for example, or from a "volume" to a "quality" culture are all made up – fictions designed for a purpose' (1994, p. 15).

Working within this view of the organization as something which is continually being socially constructed and reconstructed, I came to the view that there were, operating in ZTC, two major management *discourses*. A discourse, in this sense, is 'a connected set of statements, concepts, terms and expressions which constitutes a way of talking or writing about a particular issue, thus framing the way people understand and act with respect to that issue' (Watson, 1994a, p. 113). ZTC's top management had initiated a major programme of training its whole workforce in the principles of culture change, teamwork, flexible working and a style of employee relations in which employees would be rewarded with security, 'personal growth' and 'performance related pay' in return for continually acquiring new skills and responsibilities and for actively contributing to innovations. The currently dominant figures at the corporate centre of ZTC were, however, increasingly applying to ZTC Ryland tight short-term financial controls and regular cost-cutting measures which repeatedly involved employee redundancies. The managers in the Ryland plant of ZTC consequently found themselves having to operate simultaneously within what almost seemed like two contradictory logics, a short-term cost-control one and a longer-term human investment one.

To be a manager in Ryland ZTC was not just to be under two sets of rather contradictory pressures, it was to find available to one, when working out issues of the sort of manager one wanted to be or when deciding how to act in a particular circumstance, two discourses or two sets of *discursive resources*. I labelled the first discourse an *empowerment, skills and growth* one and this spoke of all employees of the company committing themselves to helping *grow the business* through providing an excellent *service to customers*, be they external customers for products and services or other departments within the business. *Continuous improvement* would be sought in all activities and everyone would be *empowered* through receiving whatever skill training the employee felt would help them increase their contribution. This is also a discourse of *winning culture, team-working, flexibility, team-briefing, performance-related pay, skill* grade (*not* 'job') and terms and conditions which would be fully *harmonized* to give a *classless society*.

The rival *control, jobs and costs discourse* speaks of a company whose employees are simply there to do the *job* for which they are recruited and trained – as long as they are needed. Departments are managed in line with the direction established by the corporate directors and costs are carefully *monitored and controlled* so that the *accounting ratios* of the main controlling company are adhered to. If costs rise too much for the *return* being obtained, *savings* are rapidly achieved and this can include *losing heads*. Production managers give primary emphasis to meeting *month-end targets* and only train people to the level necessary for basic *efficiency*.

Implicit in each of these discourses is a conception of how a manager should think and behave and a set of values with regard to human relationships which managers should adopt. But each manager is a person with their own values, priorities and preferred ways of working with others which are as much shaped by elements in their biographies which are external and prior to their involvement with ZTC as by the 'cultural shapers' within the company. Their involvement in ZTC and their constant exposure to these two discourses is bound, however, to challenge each of them to take account of these influences in shaping the way they go about their day-to-day managerial work. This can be conceptualized in terms of the way they *utilize* the various *discursive resources* made available to them in the organizational context. The two sets of discursive resources identified above provide the manager with what Potter and Wetherell call *interpretive repertoires* – 'systems of terms used for characterizing and evaluating actions, events and other phenomena' (1987, p. 149).

The participant research study in Ryland ZTC allowed one to get much closer to the people being researched than is often the case in social science investigations. As I worked alongside managers, interviewed them, chatted with them, argued and commiserated with them I found them frequently talking of themselves in terms such as 'the sort of person I am'. They frequently related their considerations of how they should work as a manager to this ever-emergent concept of self-identity by drawing on the rival sets of discursive resources or interpretive repertoires current in the organization.

To illustrate this type of process we can look at words spoken by just one manager in ZTC. Colin Keyworth explained

I don't think I am a different sort of person from what I was when I came here. I always treated people as people, you know; I mean the people who worked for me. But perhaps I am more like that now that I know about empowering people and getting them to see that by increasing their skills they can get more out of working here – as well as helping us continually improve the quality of what we give to our customers. But what are my people going to think of me if they think that all this appraisal stuff I've been doing is going to be used to select people for redundancy. I know we've got a cost problem. It's all very well losing heads. But what sort of prat will I look like when I start yelling about month-end when I've lost half my team. It's just not me to have to keep coming down on people. And I thought it wasn't meant to be what we did any more; that was the old culture.

This manager is telling us something of his identity, of his biography and of the part played in his emergent concept of self by learning how to 'empower people'. He draws on the *empowerment, skills and growth* discourse to make sense of and to express what he 'is like' and how he has possibly changed. It would appear that the principles associated with that discourse 'fit' his personal values. And to express his worries about his current situation, he utilizes the terms of the alternative *control, jobs and costs* discourse – something he associates with an 'old culture'. He envisages himself 'yelling about month-end [targets]' and behaving in a way which is 'not me'. He is talking here about the way he is going to shape his 'self' and his practices in the coming months. The discourses with which he is operating are central to that shaping. He appears to prefer the values and practices associated with one of the discourses but cannot speak without drawing on the other. He accepts that there is a 'cost problem' (which not all managers did) and he seems not to wish to rule out redundancies as a legitimate practice (along with most ZTC managers), even if the tone with which he draws on some of the control-discourse ('It's all very well losing heads') reveals a degree of equivocality.

Colin Keyworth's dilemmas with regard to his notion of self and with regard to decisions about how he is going to behave in the future are framed within the language and rhetorics of the social context within which he works. As with all human situations, there cannot be identity or action outside of language. The words used by Keyworth do not simply report who he is and what he is doing. They are essential elements in the shaping of what he is and what he does. And the words he uses are drawn from the various 'stories' which are told about the nature of life and about managing within the culture that is ZTC. The stories do not come out of the blue or simply 'evolve', however. Organizations are political arenas and the stories influencing middle managers like Colin Keyworth have been disseminated by people above him in the hierarchy. Power has been deployed in the process through which Keyworth comes to shape himself. And by the same token Keyworth will tell stories to the people working in his department. He will attempt to construct realities for them. He will tap the interpretive repertoires available to him in a search for discursive resources which will help him persuade people.

He might talk primarily of 'empowerment' or he might talk primarily in terms of 'costs'. But what is more likely is that he will judiciously and creatively mould arguments and interpretations from whatever sources he judges helpful – helpful both in getting done the job he is paid for and in maintaining his own sense of personal worth, consistency and integrity. In doing this he is doing something essentially similar to what I have been doing in writing this chapter. My working and researching among managers convinced me of a similarity between what one did as an academic researcher and as a manager. Managers and researchers alike were 'playing with words, concepts, information and our imaginations to make sense of our own lives and our work tasks so that we could both shape our own identities and shape the understandings and actions of others with whom we work and whom we wish to persuade' (Watson, 1994b, p. 86). I hope you are persuaded!

References

Bate, P. (1994) *Strategies for Cultural Change*, Oxford, Butterworth-Heinemann.

Billig, M. (1987) *Arguing and Thinking: A Rhetorical Approach to Social Psychology*, Cambridge, Cambridge University Press.

Geertz, C. (1973) *The Interpretation of Cultures*, New York, Basic Books.

Kotter, J.P. (1982) *The General Managers*, New York, Free Press.

Mintzberg, H. (1973) *The Nature of Managerial Work*, New York, Harper and Row.

Potter, J. and Wetherell, M. (1987) *Discourse and Social Psychology: Beyond Attitudes and Behaviour*, London, Sage.

Watson, T.J. (1994a) *In Search of Management: Culture, Chaos and Control in Managerial Work*, London, Routledge.

Watson, T.J. (1994b) 'Managing, crafting and researching: words, skill and imagination in shaping management research', *British Journal of Management*, vol. 5, special issue, pp. 77–87.

CHAPTER 6
LIFE HISTORIES/SOCIAL HISTORIES

by Margaret Wetherell

Contents

1   Introduction

This book (along with the second volume in this series, Miell and Dallos (eds), 1996) has tried to describe some of the central features of the social contexts in which individuals are embedded – patterns of interaction, relationships, families, social networks, groups, collective sense-making, intergroup relations and institutions. Throughout, a major theme has been the reciprocal relationship between the person and the social field. We have looked at the ways in which people's identities are actively constructed in these contexts. The previous chapter argued, for instance, that 'individuals both make, and are made by, the social institutions which surround them' (section 1). In this chapter, the *making of identity* will continue to take centre stage along with the processes involved in the broad formation of social identities.

We shall be considering the relationship between life history (the narratives of an individual life) and social history (the cumulative effects of group processes, institutions, social structures and social divisions over time). We shall be asking how, precisely, 'all that has made my society' might connect with 'all that has made me'. As with the last chapter, the answers this chapter finds will be broadly social constructionist in emphasis. By now, this term 'social constructionist' is becoming familiar. It implies that there will be a focus on the multiple and plural nature of the individual (we don't have one true essence but are a mix of voices and accounts which are closely related to our social and cultural contexts). Social constructionism implies an emphasis on language and discourse and I have already defined life history as 'the *narratives* of an individual life'. Finally, social constructionism focuses on the organization of the very different forms of life found in society and the way in which diverse meanings and identities are built within these.

This is all very well in the abstract, but one of the aims of this chapter, as in the last chapter, is to look at the concrete details involved in 'the making of identity'. In section 2, our reference points will be two powerful and moving autobiographical accounts from two eminent social scientists. I chose these accounts because they exemplify some important theoretical points (and indeed the two social scientists are well-known advocates of the kind of social constructionist principles described above). This doesn't mean, however, that we shall be dealing with foregone conclusions. Each account presents the *particularities* of a life. Each account, like autobiographies in general, challenges us to explain personality, the choice to go one way rather than another, and presents a set of puzzles about the way the social influences considered in this volume and in Miell and Dallos (eds) (1996) work on the individual.

Section 3 will then try to apply the general picture emerging from this discussion to a social identity so far absent in this volume – gender and gendered identities. I want to focus this discussion, however, mainly on *men* and *forms of masculinity*. It is only recently that men have been studied as men, as people with a gender which gives them a certain place in society. This part of the chapter will look at some interesting developments in social scientific research on the 'making' of masculinities.

As a third focus, you will be asked, at the end of section 2, to read a paper on the disabled self prepared for this volume by Susan Gregory. This reading is a useful reminder that one's status as an able-bodied or disabled person, seemingly a physical or biological characteristic, is also a *social* identity. It is a marker of social position in much the same way as membership of other social categories considered in previous chapters (such as 'race').

Aims of Chapter 6

The aims of this chapter are:

- To develop a perspective on the relationship between life history and social history which can focus on how people's social identities are 'made' and constructed.

- To look at the detail of how this happens through the ways in which people are positioned as they develop.

- To investigate forms of masculinity and the process of 'becoming a man' in modern society.

2   The making of a life

At this point, you should read Readings A and B at the end of the chapter. Reading A, 'Leaving home', comes from the sociologist Stuart Hall and concerns growing up in pre-independence Jamaica in the 1930s and 1940s, while Reading B, 'The weaver's daughter', comes from the social historian Carolyn Steedman and looks back at a childhood in South London in the 1950s. As you read, make brief notes on:

ACTIVITY 6.1

1 . The social influences which were important in each life history.

2   The message these autobiographical accounts provide about the relationship between the individual and society. To what extent are people free to make their own history, for instance?

3   The specific ways in which aspects of the broader social context (gender relations, 'racial' divisions in society, social class) affected the relationships and interpersonal dynamics within Hall and Steedman's families of origin.

Hall and Steedman's stories are their independent attempts to 'explain how they got to the place they currently inhabit' (Steedman, 1986, p. 6). Like all autobiographies, these accounts are reconstructions of memories where the reconstructions are actively woven into a pattern and made to tell a story. The remainder of section 2 will try to disentangle the elements in these narratives and their import for the social psychology of identity.

2.1   The weight of social history

One thing which emerges strongly in the accounts from Steedman and Hall is a sense of society as a 'thing in itself' over and above any one individual. Yet what is the nature of this 'thing' which constrains individual choice? Society is not given or unchanging but is continually evolving and brought into being as people create their own life histories. This point was made in the previous chapter in relation to the study of institutions. Institutions were seen there not as fixed and unchanging structures but as patterns of activity endlessly in the process of being made and remade. These 'makings', as we saw, however, acquire a logic and density so that every new generation confronts and must deal with a set of already-organized practices from the past.

Both Hall and Steedman's accounts suggest that people's current identities strongly depend on their past and present social positions – the place of their families in the class systems of the societies in which they grew up, the significance of 'race' in those societies, and the accepted sexual division of labour which regulates what is expected of men and women inside and outside the home. Hall and Steedman concentrate particularly on class, 'race' and gender but other autobiographical writers might well have picked up on other features of organized social life, such as religion, for example, taboos on homosexuality, inequalities due to age, and so on.

> Try to construct a narrative about your life history which makes no reference to your gender, social class, 'race', age, sexuality, religion and other aspects of your social position. What parts of your life would become incomprehensible if these features were not part of the story?

Steedman states in her book that her family belonged somewhere within those gradations of manual labour which sociologists label social classes III, IV and V, part of what she calls the 'ordinary working class'. This group, she says, was never seriously deprived enough to warrant much social attention and so the stories of her mother and people like her are in large measure still waiting to be told. Class and the material circumstances entailed in belonging to the working class rather than the middle class were beyond either Steedman or her mother's control. These aspects embody the sense mentioned earlier of society as a 'thing' above and beyond the individual, a thing which paradoxically is also nothing but a human creation.

Similarly, Hall describes the complex 'racial' stratification of Jamaican colonial society before independence and the social significance of being 'mixed-race'. 'Race' is presented here as both material and symbolic. It directly affected the economic position of Hall's family. Light skin was desirable since skin-colour was closely tied to cultural understandings of status and place in hierarchies constructed in relation to 'white'. This, in some sense accidental or trivial, mark of the body thus came to significantly determine people's life chances.

These accounts suggest that society has a set of effects which cannot be 'wished away', and that to understand someone's life history their social position must be part of the equation. Yet, on the other hand, it also seems too simple to say that society determines individual life history. To what extent can people be 'read off' from their social positions? Can we say that we know a person or that we fully understand them when we know their class, 'race' and gender or the history of their particular society?

Hall and Steedman's accounts imply that what seems to be crucial, from a social psychological point of view, is how the large organizing principles of societies become translated *on the ground* into constraints on choices, opportunities, advantages and disadvantages, fantasies, desires, dreams, longings, everyday habits and rituals. The makings of past generations directly affect at a material level the kind of person one can be, and they enter into the narratives, internal voices and dialogues which constitute the subjectivity and consciousness of current generations. Class, 'race', gender and other social divisions are enacted as forms of activity and it is this enacting which seems to make them psychologically powerful.

Let us look at this in a bit more detail. Steedman argues that one thing which had a strong impact on her own personality was her mother's bitterness about her lot and her sense of the terrible unfairness of life as a result of the poverty and deprivation experienced by generations of the family which was described and re-described in family stories. Steedman reports in her book an often-repeated phrase of her mother's which seems to sum up some of the ways in which she understood her social position – 'Never have children, dear', she said, 'they ruin your life' (1986, p. 17). Here Steedman's mother was recognizing a material circumstance – she saw her children as a barrier between herself and the good life – and developing a response to it. It is possible that she also expressed pleasure and delight in her children but Steedman sees it as significant that her memories are to do with being a burden.

Again, it seems too simple to say that the social class position of Steedman's mother and the restrictions placed on women in the 1950s caused her bitterness and the particular narratives about life she passed on to her children. Yet, as Steedman points out, this material does have something to do with class. It reflects a certain kind of post-war class consciousness. Steedman describes her mother's story as one of unfulfilled wants. Compared to some social groups, she was part of a culture of longing and envy. Her bitterness was to do with her particular sense of deprivation and exclusion in a time of rising living standards.

Steedman argues that some of the classic theorists of working-class consciousness such as Seabrook (1982) and Hoggart (1959) ignore the extent to which class consciousness is also a complicated *psychological* consciousness, a matter of ambivalent desires, longings, impulses, and a set of emotional responses to the everyday. Class consciousness, she suggests, is not just a rather distanced matter of beliefs, opinions and ideologies about society. It is not just the political perspective or angle on society which a person gains from their particular position in the division of labour. Rather, such consciousness exists in the details and is a structure of feelings as well as a narrative structure learnt in childhood as a girl listens to her mother's stories about unfulfilled desires.

The significance given to material objects and what Hall calls the 'culture of aspirations' in a family provide other examples of how broader patterns of social and economic organization are acted out in everyday experience. For Hall's mother, the 'culture of aspirations' concerned England, as a source of standards, ideals and norms, the maintenance of middle-class respectability, and the 'country estate ways' of her childhood. In both accounts, objects such as the 'twenty yards of cloth' and 'the country estate' become multi-layered emblems of social position in family stories and crucial influences on self-understanding.

Freud identified a process occurring in dreams called condensation whereby one event or image becomes a symbol which combines in shorthand many different wishes and impulses. Consumer objects such as the 'New Look' skirt can also acquire this symbolic status. Condensation is evident, too, in the fantasy Steedman reports of walking over polished wooden floors in clicking high heels while 'tending the machines'. She states that she could apply this image to primary school teaching as she walked between the desks – seeing the children as like little looms working away but needing her constant adjustment. The image was based on childhood memories of seeing women working as weavers (a group Steedman later understood as exploited when she came to explore the history of women factory workers in Lancashire). However, this exploitation was also transformed into an image of feminine power combining conventional signs of femininity (the high heels and lipstick) with feelings of authority, competence and control.

ACTIVITY 6.2   Hall and Steedman's accounts could be used as a stimulus for conducting 'memory work' about your own life history. A good starting point might be this notion of 'cultures of aspirations' and/or the remembered sayings and philosophies of parents. What material objects were significant when you were growing up? What do the emotions they carry reveal about the way the narratives, stories and constructions which make up your sense of identity have intertwined with social history? Is there any equivalent in your childhood to the 'New Look skirt' or the 'country estate'?

To summarize – the first point to make in relation to Steedman and Hall's life histories is that any account of a person's identity is incomplete without an understanding of circumstances directly encountered, given and transmitted from the past. However, I also want to suggest that, from a social psychological point of view, we need to study the way these abstract structuring principles become real for people in the everyday. Class, 'race', and the sexual division of labour are sociological concepts for understanding social organization, yet, in psychological terms, when we talk about class, 'race' or gender we are investigating not only the effects of material constraints but also memories, fantasies, desires, dreams and constructions of oneself. These, at the psychological level (but not the economic or the political), seem to make up the substance and experience of social organization.

2.2   Personality and social practices

> … personality has to be seen as social practice and not as an entity distinct from 'society'. Personality is what people do, just as social relations are what people do, and the doings are the same.
>
> *(Connell, 1987, p. 220)*

As people live their lives they are continually making themselves as characters or personalities through the ways in which they reconcile and work with the raw materials of their social situation. Stuart Hall describes, for example, how his mother came to express herself through her aspirations for her family, through her understanding of the complicated class and 'racial' categorizations of pre-independence Jamaican society, and through the relations she established with those who worked for her. In doing so she was living out her personality and her sense of herself (her 'indomitable spirit'), but she was also reproducing a certain colonial and middle-class Jamaican way of life. In terms of the quotation from Connell (1987) which introduces this section, Hall's mother was both 'doing society' and 'doing personality' at the same time. The making of oneself as an individual also makes and reproduces a society.

Connell suggests that it helps to understand the formation of individual social identities if we see these as *projects* which people develop from a number of sources, including collective understandings in local and global communities about what it means to be black or white, male or female, working-class or middle-class (see also Stevens and Wetherell, 1996). This emphasis on projection through time, and the constructing of self, suggests that identity is something actively and continually *made* rather than a preordained pattern which simply unfolds in the course of a life: 'What is made, specifically, is the coherence, intelligibility, and liveability of one's social relationships through time' (Connell, 1987, p. 221). According to this view, when people 'make' their identities they are attempting to develop positions which might relate their current lives to what has gone before, rendering the past, the present and the future plausible and meaningful. Personality, identity or character are, in this way, attempts at unification. People try to develop unified narratives about all the diverse relationships and activities which comprise their lives.

In this sense we could describe Hall or Steedman's accounts as accomplished acts of self-unification, a working through and reconciliation of many of the threads of social relationships which they have experienced. To *be* a black middle-class man or a white working-class woman of a certain age, an able-bodied or perhaps disabled person – to have these social identities – is exactly this process of self-construction and narrative unification within the constraints established by one's social and material situation. Sometimes the disjuncture between people's old and new social circumstances becomes so great that they must start again and re-invent themselves. But the process of constructing an identity is a never-ending process of telling stories and discovering narratives which 'make sense' in terms of the internal 'conversations' we hold inside our heads, in our dialogues with others, and which work pragmatically in terms of our social positions.

Connell argues that the attempt to unify or to make sense may involve considerable struggle, repression and internal conflict. This point is also emphasized by psychodynamic social psychologists (cf. Thomas, 1996). Some of the threads which make up the raw materials for an identity project may not be easy to knit together. Connell argues that a level of contradiction is inevitable in every personality because the child and adult are weaving 'a path through a field of practices which are following a range of collective logics' (1987, p. 222). And these collective logics, such as the requirements of different institutions (e.g. family and work), often contradict and may be in extreme tension.

> What 'collective logics' might conflict in the following cases: the situation of a black manager of white employees in a colonial society; a bright girl in a Victorian home; an unemployed male head of a household; a female prime minister; a male secretary?

Connell notes that for some people the contradictions might be so great as to be irreconcilable, in which case no coherent or reasonably unified set of narratives about oneself may emerge. He considers the case presented by one of Freud's patients – the 'Wolf Man' – as an example of this possibility:

> The 'Wolf Man' is a howling mass of contradictions, and his personality is contradictory because the elements of an emotional life offered him were impossible to work into a smooth and consistent whole. Obviously enough the class relations between peasants and landowners in pre-revolutionary Russia were in tension. The case history shows how these relations intersected with gender dynamics – ambivalences between husband and wife, divisions of labour among servants in childcare and housework, rivalries between girls and boys – to construct a household that was an emotional minefield for the small boy.
>
> (Connell, 1987, p. 222)

This point about contradictions is an important one to stress. Social identity is often assumed to be homogeneous – one is black or white, a woman or a man, homosexual or heterosexual, working-class or middle-class. However, social identity is not necessarily evenly distributed in this way. It is a mix of positions. And some combinations may simply be untenable places for people to live.

To summarize – in this section we have seen that people are both active and passive when it comes to the construction of a life history, and that the balance between the two is difficult to judge. On the one hand, people 'make themselves'. As Connell stresses, every social identity can be seen as a 'project', an active attempt to unify diverse and contradictory themes. On the other hand, people also seem to be 'made' or 'produced'. People, particularly children, often have little choice or control over the constructions of others such as family members, or over the collective ways in which gender, for instance, is understood in a society. Connell argues that we need to analyse 'personality' and 'society' not as static objects but as streams of activities. And, he suggests, those streams of activity come to the same thing. Society is reproduced through people's activities and those activities projected through time are how we know a person and recognize them as having a certain kind of character.

Connell's formulation of the nature of social identity has been strongly influenced by the ideas of the French existential philosopher Jean-Paul Sartre. From Sartre comes the concept of identity as a project and the idea of people trying for unification. Sartre, in his life histories of Jean Genet and the novelist Flaubert, for example, aimed to discover the truth of someone's life by describing the elements from which the life was constructed, and the unique ways in which the person had worked with these elements to produce a unified and idiosyncratic personality. Social constructionists, in contrast, would prefer to speak of 'unifications' rather than 'unification'. They would agree with the criticisms of Sartre's work presented by other French theorists such as Barthes.

In his own attempts at biography and autobiography, Barthes (1977) argued that one can never discover a final, ultimate truth about anyone. Indeed, he suggested that the attempt to define the individual's project in a coherent life history or biography be replaced instead by an assemblage of 'biographemes': 'random scraps of biographical debris: bits of knowledge, images and observations which are likely to have aesthetic rather than tendentious value' (Collins, 1980, p. 23). From this viewpoint, there is no one essence to the person, one identity, one enduring unification, or just one story to be told. Rather, there are a multiplicity of angles on personality, fitting a multiplicity of relationships. People move variably in and out of narratives of identity as the conversations shift and change. Identity may thus be more fragmented than the notion of one 'unification' might imply. Psychodynamic researchers, too, of course, emphasize the contradictory and fragmented nature of the self and claim that any one consistent truth about the self may be hard to come by (Thomas, 1996).

2.3   Family life and subject positions

The notion of people as both making and made points to the importance of the constructive processes which occur in family life (and other small groups which socialize the individual, such as peer groups and work groups). What seems to have been decisive for the 'Wolf Man', for example, was the way in which contradictory social conventions and social structures combined in disordered family relationships. The theory of social identity developing here suggests that small groups, particularly families, will play a decisive role in channelling social practices, making them real and vivid for the individual, as well as being the place where identity projects are formed and acted out. Some of the ways in which this happens in small and larger groups through the development of group norms, the construction of roles and the psychodynamics of group process were discussed in Chapters 1, 2 and 4 of this volume (and see also Miell and Dallos (eds), 1996).

Both Hall and Steedman describe family processes which were important in their own development. Hall talks, for example, about the construction of him as 'a coolie baby', different in colour from the rest of the family. He describes how this early family image of 'not belonging' became a useful hook in his identity narratives, compounded as a full-blown working through of difference, rebellion and escape in later years. Similarly, Steedman refers to the family secret of her illegitimacy and the way a half-understood atmosphere around 'the other woman and her family' structured her sense of who she herself might be. She describes, in her book, the way her identity had to be constructed from two contradictory fragments – awareness of being 'a burden', but also awareness that she and her sister were a valued weapon in their mother's conflict with their father. From such positions and from such family processes, ambivalent identities emerge (Thomas, 1996).

These types of family constructs, rules and dynamics are strongly bound up with social conventions, social class, economics, the position of women, and so on. Yet, as family researchers have demonstrated (Dallos, 1996), we can see how these things become psychologically powerful when created and lived *as relationships*. Family interactions as they shift together, combining and clashing over time, provide a kaleidoscope of potential patterns. The child and the adult work with these patterns, with the voices of others and with their identity projects, and from this 'working out' identities coalesce in the form of some characteristic stances or positions in relation to the world and other people.

In the 1960s, this point was developed forcefully by the British psychiatrist Laing and his colleagues (Laing, 1971; Laing and Esterson, 1970). Their main concern was with the experience and origins of mental illness. Laing and Esterson (1970) argued that schizophrenia and other disorders were best seen as intelligible responses to difficult social circumstances. Behaviour, thought patterns and delusions which may seem bizarre, grotesque or wildly inappropriate to the outsider will make sense if one considers the person's existential position and the social situation in which they have tried to realize themselves, in particular their family situation.

Schizophrenia is not our concern in this chapter and Laing's contentions about the family roots of mental illness have been hotly contested. Looking back now from the perspective of the 1990s, Laing's work has a 'mother-blaming' and 'family-blaming' quality which doesn't do justice to the complexity of women's positions in family life and to the multiple determinants of schizophrenia. What is worth pursuing, however, is Laing and Esterson's analysis of how patterns of 'mystification' arise in families. Laing and Esterson argued that it was necessary to look at how families create a web of meaning, relationships and negotiations such that paranoia or ideas of persecution are a sensible response as the child struggles to unify and construct an identity from the fragments available (see Box 6.1).

BOX 6.1   Sanity, madness and the family

In their classic work *Sanity, Madness and the Family* (1970), Laing and Esterson examined eleven case histories, trying in each case to identify the family logic surrounding the family member who had become the patient. The excerpt below comes from a case history of the 'Churches' and is the transcript of a conversation between Mrs Church and her daughter Claire who had been diagnosed as paranoid schizophrenic:

Mother: I used to think at times you were sensitive about certain things, about different things. I sometimes think you see I was very like you – an only daughter, and when you haven't any sisters to mix with, I do think one is inclined to be a little sensitive in those directions.

Daughter: I don't think with me –

Mother: No?

Daughter: – it was a case of not having any sisters – it was the case of having a brother very much younger than myself.

Mother: Of course I had two brothers, but I didn't have very much to do with my eldest brother, but my younger brother – I was in a very similar position again.

Daughter: Of course the more you mix in your own home, the more people you're among in your own home, the easier it is to mix in the outside world.

Mother: Maybe. I should think that is very true. I have noticed myself now, and Aunt Cissie and Aunt Elsie, the three of us, we've all been only, and we have had very similar ways, and we often used to say, 'Oh, we're really three odd ones out, we're only daughters,' and we often used to feel a little bit out at times – used to see other girls go off with perhaps sisters, and we did have one but unfortunately lost her. But you mixed well with them socially didn't you?

Daughter: No.

Mother: No? Oh what about the tennis club, with Betty and that little crowd?

(Laing and Esterson, 1970, pp. 80–1)

In this rather banal and ordinary-seeming conversation the mother is trying to construct a claim of similarity between her daughter, Claire, and herself on the basis that both are 'only daughters'. Laing and Esterson argue that in fact what is going on here is typical of many interactions between this mother and daughter where the mother attributes to her daughter memories, experiences and actions which do not match Claire's own self-attributions. Laing and Esterson claim that the mother is by and large impervious to any of her daughter's statements which disagree with the mother's point of view. Typically, in this relationship, such disagreement or assertion became seen as the illness. The constantly repeated sequence in this relationship, state Laing and Esterson, is one where the daughter makes a statement and her mother invalidates it by concluding (i) she does not really mean what she says, or (ii) she is saying this because she is ill, or (iii) she cannot remember or know what she feels or felt, or (iv) she is not justified in saying this (1970, p. 88).

We can get another angle on the way in which identities emerge from this constructive process within family life if we combine Laing and Esterson's approach with the social constructionist concept of 'identity positions', sometimes also called 'subject positions' (Hollway, 1984; Harré and Davies, 1990).

Harré (1983) argues that the best way of understanding a person is to see them as a set of possible and actual locations which emerge out of conversations and social acts. The person is a changing location in an interaction rather than an object with a predefined essential character. The activities and practices associated with teaching and learning provide a good example of what Harré means by this notion of a location or position in a set of social practices. Classroom teaching, for example, has a story-line or set of conventional expectations associated with it and this story-line places the participants. To speak 'as a teacher' is to take up a certain position of authority in relation to the pupil. We could say that identity positions are rather like acting out social roles except, as Harré and Van Langenhove (1991) argue, positions are much more dynamic and are a way of understanding how small-scale interactions build together to make up the large-scale of social life.

Harré and Van Langenhove distinguish three possible orders of positioning – first order, second order and third order. The first order is evident in a conversational exchange such as this, when A says to B: 'Please iron my shirts.' As Harré and Van Langenhove note, both B and A are positioned by this utterance: A as someone with the moral right to command and B as a person commanded. However, Harré and Van Langenhove ask us to consider the case where B objects, 'Why should I do your ironing, I'm not your maid?' In these kinds of exchange, the first order positioning has become the subject of discussion and a second order of positioning is emerging from the negotiation as B attempts to position A as someone claiming an illegitimate right. Finally, Harré and Van Langenhove point to a third possible layer of conversation where A might tell a friend about the whole exchange with B and in the process reposition B as someone who is such a radical feminist that she refused even to do his ironing!

Look back now at the exchange between mother and daughter in Box 6.1. Try to use the concept of positionings to describe what is occurring on a line-by-line basis. Since there is dispute between mother and daughter, there is both first and second order positioning to be found. Laing and Esterson's conclusions about this particular mother can be seen as an example of the third order of positioning identified by Harré and Van Langenhove. ACTIVITY 6.3

These detailed negotiations may seem to have little to do with the emergence of the kinds of pattern Steedman and Hall were concerned with in their autobiographies. But if we assume the kind of repetition and regularity in positioning over time which Laing and Esterson identified in Box 6.1, we can see how people might become, in Hollway's (1984) terms, 'invested' in certain positions as they have the same kinds of interactions over and over again, and where, in psychodynamic terms, these positions key into prevalent defense mechanisms adopted by the person. Also, although there is no reason why A needs to be a man and B a woman, this reading tends to dominate our interpretation of Harré and Van Langenhove's A and B example. We could argue that these are also *gendered positions*. Positioning can have a social history, in other words, and a social regularity, as well as being an activity which reinforces the flexible and dynamic nature of social action and the scope for change.

Once again, the history of family positionings is both individual and social. The kinds of positions available in families follow both the logic of the particular family as well as the collective logics in which the family is embedded. Steedman's position as 'burden' and Hall's position as 'coolie baby' indicate this complex and simultaneous determination. In conclusion, we can see how family groups, like the individual, are both creative and reflective, producing and produced. Families rework various social materials and this process of reworking creates new forms of relationship between husbands and wives, parents and children, brothers and sisters, and new unifications of diverse social positions. An individual's social identity describes their position in patterns of social organization, yet the *psychology* of that social identity, the way it is personally experienced, has a great deal to do with the logics of those creative family reworkings.

2.4   Power and the production of identity

In this section I want to consider the relationship between power and social identity before we go on to look at one social identity (forms of masculinity) in detail. How do power relations in society become involved in the 'making' of identity?

ACTIVITY 6.4
Before reading on, look back through the life histories from Steedman and Hall in Readings A and B. Who could be described as powerful in these histories? What are the signs of their power and what are its origins?

The identities Steedman and Hall construct are marked by power at many different levels. Broad power relations in society between men and women, between black and white, have an effect. Within the family, there is also a 'micro-politics' of power. Hall portrays his mother, for example, as dominant within the narrow domestic circle. (Her gender and 'race' would have circumscribed that power outside the household.) He suggests that his life is, in an important sense, a response to that power, made by it. Within family life, therefore, power seems to be *relational*. To a certain extent, family members seem to be powerful because they are constructed as such by other family members, and this construction is often strongly endorsed by patterns in the broader social world; for example, the authority given to parents.

How is power evident, and how is it practiced? On the one hand, power is guaranteed by violence and by the capacity to use force successfully against another, even if this force is potential rather than actual. In parent-child relationships, this kind of power is often deployed and, as the prevalence of domestic violence cases suggests, this 'ultimate sanction' is also a fairly regular feature of relationships between men and women. Power also depends on access to resources and on equity or inequity in the division of those resources. Thus, the ability to pay others to do one's work, financial dependence and independence within marriage, and confinement to certain places in the labour market as a result of discrimination against ethnic minorities are all markers of power. But, power also depends on ideologies and collective constructions, on the network of beliefs, assumptions and ideas people have about their place in life. Managers of factories, for example, may regulate the lives of their workforce, or a husband may determine where the family lives, without any use of force whatsoever. In these cases, power works partly through the tacit consent that the husband or the manager has the right to command in this way. Ideologies are networks of discourses and practices which justify the actions of the powerful and which make these actions seem entirely reasonable, appropriate, natural and unquestionable.

One way of understanding the relationship between power and social identity is to see power as a *possession* of the individual or group, a possession by virtue of one's social position. Power could be seen as a property of agents where those agents could be individuals or entire social classes. It is the capacity to influence others, to command resources, to have one's rights and wishes respected and enacted. Power is about independence, self-determination and a certain immunity from the actions and desires of others. Power is a form of authority, something which A does to B. And, certainly, in the case of force, power is often seen as something negative and intermittent.

But is this all there is to power and identity – a distinction between those who can wield power and those who cannot? Previous sections have discussed the 'making of identity' as a continuous project of 'making sense' in terms of the narratives and subject positions available in one's family and broader social situation. What does this concept of 'making' suggest about the relationship between power and identity? Feminist research suggests that the connection between power and identity is a subtle one. Power relations in society, as we have seen, can be manifest through being ordered to do something, where power is experienced as something outside oneself, imposed from above. But, perhaps more commonly, the consequences of power can also be welcomed, accepted and seen as an inseparable part of one's identity – something which feels right or natural, the appropriate way to behave, part of one's most intimate self-understanding, rather than something negative and external to the self.

Obsessions with body shape and dieting, for example, often seem, from a feminist point of view, to be harmful for women, yet they engage much of the time and energies of many women because of the kinds of feminine bodies which are currently valued in Euro-American societies. As feminist theorists have pointed out, power can be involved just as much in what is seen as pleasurable (feeling good about oneself) as what is seen as painful (conforming to the wishes of others). It may be evident in what may feel like positive and life-affirming choices, and in what may feel like acts of self-expression (such as dieting). Power may operate as a subjection which feels like liberation. In such cases, ideology is obviously at work and it is no longer meaningful to see power in simple causal terms as one person compelling another.

The French social theorist Michel Foucault's work has also been very important in this development of a more complex view of power as 'positive', 'productive' and 'subjective', bound up with the very 'making of identity'. Foucault (1980) asks us to reconceive our common-sense view of power as a property of agents, whether those agents are individuals, groups, corporations or, as in Marxist social theory, entire social classes. If you remember, I discussed earlier in this section the idea of power seen not only as a negative force but as a *possession*. Foucault suggests we shift this angle of view. Instead of seeing power as *owned* in this way, as originating with people, he suggests that we see people (their identities) as the product, outcome, or *effect* of power. In other words, we make power the prior term.

This is a difficult point to grasp. One way of gaining more insight into Foucault's claim is to see it as a statement about how to study social history and the operation of power through time. When social history is recounted, it is often related as a story of who did what to whom. The main actors may be important individuals (American presidents, revolutionary figures) or they may be large groups (as in the Marxist conception of social classes as the agents of history). One of Foucault's main arguments is that this mode of telling history is misleading; we should focus instead on what he called in his later work 'power/knowledge complexes' moving through time and space.

Modern history (at least) is the story of these power/knowledge formations and the kinds of individuals, subjectivities, relationships and modes of understanding they create: '[Power] needs to be considered as a productive network which runs through the entire social body' (Foucault, 1980, p. 119). In other words, power can be regarded as a network in which identities and identity projects are made. One example of such a power/knowledge complex is the gradual development of the medical professions. Here we can see not only new types of social organizations, institutions and people emerging ('the consultant' and 'the patient', hospitals and clinics), but also that these are linked to new forms of knowledge, new ways of perceiving, interpreting and discussing the human body which empower newly defined categories of specialists.

In addition, Foucault argues that there is no vantage-point on history which is independent of power/knowledge complexes. The perspective of any teller of history, his or her understanding of truth and what counts as knowledge, will be formed from within these complexes. Indeed, what is taken to be the 'truth' of an age, as most natural and obvious, is the sign of the power/knowledge complexes in operation.

Foucault's point about power as a productive network has implications for understanding how social identities emerge from both the small-scale negotiations of everyday life and the large-scale events of social history. At the end of this section, I will ask you to look at Reading C prepared by Susan Gregory. This reading is concerned with the construction of social identities for disabled people and takes up Foucault's point about the large-scale creation of categories of people, particularly through the emergence of the medical and psychiatric professions (see also Miell and Croghan, 1996).

In terms of the small-scale, family life and the kind of 'positioning' discussed earlier (see Box 6.1) are good examples of how a local regime of power (found in one household, for example) 'produces' identity. If you think back through these examples, other features become clear. We can see that power is connected to narrative and discourse, to the kinds of 'story-lines' and forms of knowledge found in families. Sometimes it is useful to understand power as something that A can exert on B, but we also need to see how power emerges from a pattern of interaction in which both A and B become positioned.

Look back to Harré and Van Langenhove's example of A and B's domestic dispute and the first, second and third order positioning involved. Consider how the power shifts in each case. To what extent is power something that A does to B and to what extent are powerful identities (i) negotiated and (ii) emergent from the logic of the positionings and narratives associated with the power/knowledge complexes which produce different gender identities?

To summarize – power is intimately connected with social identity in the sense that people's place in a system of social organization has a large bearing on the resources they can command, and on whether attempts to secure power are seen as reasonable and appropriate or as disruptive and illegitimate. Such power, however, is relational in two senses. First, it is enacted through everyday relationships and, secondly, it is dependent on the positions others take up, not just one's own capacities. Powerful identities are also the product of social history in the sense that social processes (power/knowledge complexes) which emerge gradually over time create new categories of people and new modes of justifying and legitimating power. Finally, we are beginning to see that power is closely linked to the *formation* of subjectivity, to the very making of identity. As Foucault puts it, in a typical play on words, power is a form of 'subjectification'. People are caught in networks of power at precisely the moments when they come to recognize themselves as certain kinds of subjects, as active agents with certain identities.

Foucault and the social constructionist perspective in social psychology treat the concept of the independent actor with much more scepticism than many writers from other social psychological perspectives such as the experiential perspective (Stevens, 1996). Existentialists or experiential social psychologists tend to see human activity as demonstrating *autonomy* and see this capacity for free choice as a fundamental and prior aspect of human nature.

Foucault is suggesting that people are active, produce social life, can and do 'make' themselves, but his work contradicts the view that this activity indicates agency or autonomy in any strong sense of a fundamental human capacity for free choice and independent action. Foucault sees people's current understanding of agency, the modern view of people as in control of their lives, and indeed the very terms in which the debate about determination and free-will is couched, as an effect of power/knowledge complexes. This sense of people as free to choose is not a given, it is a historical product. Foucault, therefore, makes the operation of power primary in conceptualizing how identities emerge from social history, while experiential writers make agency primary.

ACTIVITY 6.6 You should now read Reading C, 'The disabled self', by Susan Gregory. In what ways does the experience of disabled people exemplify Foucault's points about power/knowledge complexes, such as the development of the medical professions, creating new kinds of identities?

Review of section 2

- The aim of this section was to outline a broadly social constructionist perspective on the relationship between life history and social history.

- This approach stresses the ways in which the individual and the social are blurred together so that the 'making of the individual' and the 'making of society' are seen as one stream of activity from which life history and social history emerge.

- Concrete ways in which this happens include the kinds of identity positions and narratives which develop in small groups such as the family. These groups act as a bridge between individuals and their society. Identity is seen as produced from relationships and social interaction in sites of this kind, which are in turn organized by wider power relations in society.

- A key debate concerns the active role of the individual in this process. The balance between the process of 'being made' and 'making ourselves' is often unclear since both are stressed in this approach.

3 The making of masculine identities

In the remainder of this chapter I now want to try to *apply* the perspective on life history and social history just developed to one type of social identity – to forms of masculinity. In line with the emphasis in section 2, I shall be arguing that men are not born but are 'made'. But what contributes to the making of masculinity? The sections which follow will look at the influence of men's occupations, at the relationship between masculinity and 'race', at how power relations between men and women in society structure masculine identity, and at the role of the body. Before this, however, there is the most basic question of all.

3.1 What is a man?

I want to explore this issue, first, through the words of ordinary men as they reflect on their sense of identity and what it means to be a man. The extracts below come from discussions conducted with male Open University students. These men, who have been given pseudonyms, volunteered to take part in a wider research project on masculinity and male identity (Wetherell and Edley, 1994). The men, who were interviewed in small groups, came from a wide range of social backgrounds and were of varied ages, from men in their twenties to men in their sixties.

As you read Extracts 6.1 to 6.5 below, make some notes on the ways in which these men define masculinity and on the factors which have been important for them in developing a sense of themselves as male.

ACTIVITY 6.7

In the first extract, Dave, a white man in his twenties, is describing to one of the other men in his group, Craig, and to the interviewer (Nigel Edley) how he behaves when he is at work. Dave works as a machinist in a large Midlands factory. A particular theme for Dave in his interview was how to reconcile his own views and values with the forms of masculinity prevalent in the working-class environment in which he had grown up and which dominated the factory in which he worked.

Extract 6.1

DAVE: I am aware that at work you will sort of *hide* certain characteristics more than if you were outside of work or in a more friendly situation.

CRAIG: Is that because you work within (DAVE: In, en, (.) yeah with a lot of men), a lot of males, so you've got to be assertive to …

DAVE: You have to be assertive in (.), otherwise you're just a wimp.

CRAIG: Just to sort of keep your head above …

DAVE: That's right, yeah. And I mean you wouldn't dream of, say, *crying* or anything, that's just *out*. I mean that's *taboo* almost, showing emotion in that way. (NIGEL: Right) Because that would like *demean* yourself in their eyes.

CRAIG: Yeah. But in certain situations that's (.) I mean that's allowed these days, isn't it? Like (DAVE: Yeah) at funerals or something like that men are allowed to be …

DAVE: But the sort of people I work with, they've got the sort of *old* attitude.

Transcription conventions:

(.) indicates pause
Italics indicates emphasis
… indicates overlap or interruption

The second extract also concerns showing emotion and whether it is appropriate for men to cry. In this discussion between Barry, Neal and the interviewer, Nigel Edley, the conversation turns, first, to the episode in the 1990 Football World Cup where the English player Paul Gascoigne ('Gazza') was booked. Neal and Barry then move on to discuss managing emotions at funerals.

Extract 6.2

NEAL: But it still, (.) it still wouldn't feel right to me if I was in a room with a load of men who are crying. To me that still wouldn't seem right. (NIGEL: Right) I still don't know whether that comes from the same (.) from the same thing and it's inbred in me.

BARRY: But don't (.) I accept what you're saying and I would concur with it. Except I'm (.) I'm *torn* by that image, what two years ago? When Gazza got booked (NIGEL: Hmm). And he cried. Now I don't (.) I mean there's been little digs at him here and there but there's not been a general, 'What a sissy!'. I mean, he was a hero. (NIGEL: Hmm) People were very struck by this. My goodness, here's somebody who really cares.

(Later in the interview)

NIGEL: Can any of you recall moments, maybe they'll be common ones, frequent ones for you, where you do that job of managing your emotions?

BARRY: At funerals.

NEAL: Oh yeah.

BARRY: Funerals I would say is a very good one (NIGEL: Hmm). Erm ...

NEAL: But, you know, I mean, you don't mind a tear trickling down your face but you wouldn't break down sobbing, you know, that sort of thing, but even if you feel like it, you wouldn't really want to.

One very common theme in all the group discussions was the *conflicting* nature of definitions of what it means to be a man. Extracts 6.3 and 6.4 take up this idea of conflicts, first in relation to being a breadwinner, and then in a discussion about what men should look like. Finally, in Extract 6.5, the discussion extends to what men should *smell* like, as Harry, a 64-year-old retired truck driver, discusses differences in attitudes across generations.

Extract 6.3

BEN: I think there is (.) there does seem to be more and more pressure these days to *be* more aggressive (NIGEL: Hmm) and more macho (.) and I think a lot of people ...

PAUL: I think there's pressure both ways which is why there's so many people that are screwed up and can't cope with things. (BEN: Yeah) There are pressures, erm, with the, erm, feminist movement (NIGEL: Mm) a man's got to pull his weight in the family. You can't go swanning off with the lads all the time, you've got to be a father (.) yes, you've got to be a breadwinner (.) they still expect a man to be a breadwinner but it's much more trying times (.) as well as, erm, (.) there's far more pressures from all different directions.

Extract 6.4

NIGEL: OK. Um, I mean are there any sort of ways, everyday ways, in which you feel yourself as a man, feel yourself to be masculine?

(pause)

PETER: Shaving, yeah, simple things like that, shaving, the way I dress, I think you're conscious of not trying to (.) I don't know. Yeah I would be conscious of trying not to look too effeminate with the way I dressed.

(later in the interview)

PETER: I think you can go too *far* that way. I mean, that tends to become unattractive, if you try to be too macho, the medallion man type image. You can go *too* far.

Extract 6.5

HARRY: When I was a young man if you used scented soap you were very, very funny! (laughs) Do you know what I mean?

NIGEL: Right, Yeah.

HARRY: It always used to be Fairy, you know Fairy Snow, you know, that doesn't smell but, you know, if you had brilliantine on, you know, the sweet smelling brilliantine or scented soap (NIGEL: Hmm) you was, you know, you were going that way to, you know, femininity (laughs).

NIGEL: So there was no such thing as, well, men didn't use, erm, under-arm deodorant?

HARRY: *No*, no *never*!

NIGEL: What about after-shave, did they use that?

HARRY: No, I never, not even to this day!

NIGEL: You don't?

HARRY: No!

NIGEL: There's so many adverts trying to flog this stuff (HARRY: Hmm) especially around Christmas, erm, why not, why don't you give in to that? (laughing).

HARRY: My son uses it and I keep saying, 'You smell like a ponce!' (laughter) You know what I mean? (NIGEL: Hmm) And, I've never, as I say I've been brought up, you know, not to be, you know, one of the big muscle men sort of thing. (NIGEL: Right) You don't, you know, smell like that sort of thing.

NIGEL: Do you think, I mean, do you think it would, make you seriously uncomfortable if you did smell perfumy?

HARRY: It would. I've, erm, well, my sister-in-law, they bought me Grecian 3000 and Old Spice after-shave and I always throw it away. I never use it. I say, 'Thank you, that's just what I wanted'. But it's never, it never gets used, talcum powder ...

NIGEL: Right, okay. So, you know, we talked about, I dunno, 20 minutes ago about, erm, learning some lessons about what it means to be masculine, yeah? Well it seems as though you've unsuccessfully tried to teach your son one, right? (laughing) Which is that you should avoid perfume. I mean my *dad* doesn't wear those things.

HARRY: I don't, I don't tell him, you know, he should avoid it. I'm saying, he is a person on his own now. He's 23, he pleases himself what he does. But I'm always, when he goes out, I say, 'Phew! No more of that son, you smell like a ponce.'

Of course, these extracts are only a small selection from much longer discussions and the influences on any particular man will range much more widely, but they can be used to make some broad conceptual points about the nature of masculine identities which develop themes from section 2.

Masculinity is an active project

Masculinity is often thought to be built in to men – something men know how to do naturally. Extracts 6.1 to 6.5 demonstrate that, whatever the biological basis of masculinity (and we shall consider the role of the body in the next section), male identity is also *actively created* by men. Masculinity is a set of choices about what to wear, what to look like, and about how to behave in different social situations. These choices or decisions may become automatic but, as we can see, also need to be negotiated by every individual man, and they involve dilemmas which require active resolution. The men in Extracts 6.1 to 6.5 conclude that a man should be able to cry, but not too much. He should dress in a way which is neither too macho nor too effeminate. He should be out earning the daily bread and yet spend time with the kids. As ordinary men go about their daily lives, they are constantly confronted by such dilemmas. In listening to the ways in which they talk about themselves and their lives as men, we can hear them constantly trying to make sense of it all.

Masculinity is both personal and social

If we apply the argument developed in section 2, masculinity can be seen as a personal trajectory that each man weaves through a web of social resources. Remember Connell's point that in 'doing personality' people are also 'doing society'? Masculinity is highly personal, private and individual and yet also collective, historical and social. Some of the ways in which identity is produced from social constructions are clear in the extracts above. Thus, in becoming unemotional, for example, and learning not to cry in certain situations, men train themselves to conform to social expectations. Social scripts about masculinity become part of the individual, defining what comes naturally or what feels right. In this way social history comes to organize individual life history.

It is difficult not to be struck in Extract 6.5, for instance, by a sense of how profoundly the physical lives of Harry and his son have been structured by existing cultural notions. Harry, cast as the 'unreconstructed man', is trying to assert a puritan ideal against the more liberal 'new man' version played by his son. Both are, of course, products of their different generations; constructed by the leading definitions of their day. For Harry, brought up in the 1930s and 1940s, smelling sweetly and being a real man do not go together. Yet for his son, a child of the more 'permissive' 1960s and 1970s, the wearing of after-shave and deodorant in no way threatens his masculine identity. Each is invested in his own ideal, and probably feels strongly about the correctness of his own position. Neither feels like an actor playing out a preordained scene, despite the fact that aristocratic fathers, more than 300 years before them, were entertaining precisely the same kinds of concerns as their cavalier sons returned from the court of Louis XIV at Versailles, still practising how to toss their periwigs back and forth in a special swoop called the 'French wallow' (see Edley and Wetherell, 1995, Chapter 5, for an account of changing cultural definitions of masculinity).

Masculinity is connected to other social institutions

Although gender can be treated as a separate type of identity, it is also obviously connected to other organized social processes and institutions. Work, for instance, seems to be very important in defining masculinity. In Extract 6.3, for example, Paul talks about not just economic pressures but the institution of the family and what is expected of men in that realm. Similarly, the organization of leisure in society has been central in defining masculinity, particularly in this century. Think, for instance, about the role of football, and sport in general. Extract 6.2 notes the importance of prominent sportsmen in constructing and reworking definitions of how men should behave on and off the pitch. The class backgrounds of the men speaking in Extracts 6.1 to 6.5 varied from working-class to middle-class. All shared the same ethnic background, however. As we shall see later in the chapter, 'race' and ethnicity are also crucial in forming masculine identities.

It is more meaningful to talk of masculinities in the plural rather than masculinity in the singular

Because men are embedded in different class relations, in different economic niches, differ in their 'race', their sexuality, their relationship to family life, and so on, it makes sense, as many commentators have noted (e.g. Segal, 1990), to talk of masculinities in the plural. The men in Extracts 6.1 to 6.5 seemed in some respects rather homogeneous. However, it is not difficult to illustrate the *diversity* in men's identity projects by simply adding a few more such discussions which include, for instance, gay men or men from different cultural backgrounds.

This diversity applies not just across groups of men but is also found *within* the individual man himself. Section 2.2 noted that identity can be fractured, multiple and contradictory because the different institutions in which someone is embedded may pull them in different directions. Any particular man's personality or character may represent a compromise between many different and contradictory influences. These tensions may become evident as he represents himself, either for others in the context of social interaction, or else for himself in the form of private voices, internalized dialogues or patterns of subjectivity (such as when he asks himself: 'What kind of man am I?' or 'What kind of man should I be?').

ACTIVITY 6.8　　Look through any popular magazines you have available or think back through a typical evening's television viewing or radio output and make notes on the range of masculinities on offer to men.

It seems that a man can be rough, tough and dangerous to know. He can be an intellectual, a family man, a 'ladies man', a loner, thoughtful and sensitive, streetwise, a 'new' man, an 'unreconstructed' man, a 'macho medallion man', chivalrous or go-getting. He can attempt to be some or all of these things. It doesn't take long to accumulate a dozen cultural possibilities. Any particular male identity can be seen as an attempt to unify or live out many contrasting threads and imperatives.

Masculinity is relational

It is also clear from Extracts 6.1 to 6.5 that masculinity (like power) is relational in form (Connell, 1995; Segal, 1990). In other words, any definition of what men are is always constructed in relation to other possible definitions. This is true in two senses. First, men tend to define their identity *in relation to other men*. Dave, for instance, in Extract 6.1 talks about the notion of 'the wimp'. Barry in Extract 6.2 draws on the notion of 'the sissy'. For Harry, in Extract 6.5, an important principle is that a man should not be 'a ponce'. Any definition constructs a sense of insiders and outsiders, self and other, what is acceptable and what is beyond the pale. It depends not just on what men assert they are but on what they say they are not. And, of course, it has very often been gay men who have provided the strongest sense of contrast or 'otherness' for straight men (Dollimore, 1991).

Crucially, however, masculinity is also defined *in relation to women*. Often, the simplest and most accurate way of describing forms of masculinity in a particular society is to say that masculinity is *not femininity*. Again, this contrast is very evident to Harry in Extract 6.5, but it is present tacitly in the other discussions as well.

Masculinities are constructed through power relations

Why is the contrast between femininity and masculinity so important? In many animal species, male and female are differentiated to an extraordinary extent by plumage and body shape. In comparison, humans are weakly sexually differentiated. Yet masculinity and femininity have assumed a huge *symbolic* importance, strongly accentuated in clothes, in non-verbal gestures, in speech styles, and in the cultural and social realm.

Feminist theorists suggest that being 'not feminine' has become so important for men because forms of masculinity are linked to power. Differences between men and women are so strongly emphasized, compared to the commonalities, because masculinities have tended to be the privileged identities and, as we shall see, this power has been central to the construction of male subjectivities and identities.

Connell (1995) notes that relationships between men are also imbued with power. He distinguishes between what he calls *hegemonic, marginal, complicit* and *subordinated* masculinities. Hegemonic masculinities are those that in a particular historical period or social situation have come to dominate or have come to be seen as the ideal masculine type. Connell suggests that hegemonic masculinities are usually those that best serve men's general interests in relation to women and which maintain male collective power, although few men may actually embody these masculine qualities. For instance, in many branches of popular culture hegemonic masculinity is currently the 'robocop' – invulnerable, tough, emotionally distant, assertive, aggressive, all-conquering, cool and big – although few men can actually emulate the on-screen identities of Arnold Schwarzeneggar, Bruce Willis or Sylvester Stallone.

Hegemonic forms of masculinity become a standard to which many men aspire and become important, for instance, in the fantasy lives of boys as they practise at 'being men'. These forms of masculinity can influence and infiltrate other forms of masculinity as well, even subordinated forms of masculinity such as gay identities. And, often, these dominant forms of masculinity become deliberately parodied, critiqued and undercut in the process. In Connell's typology, marginal masculinities are those which are not directly persecuted but which are not held up as ideal either. Complicit forms of masculinity are those which may reject the excesses of the macho men, and which may not even come close to

Marginal and subordinated masculinities meet hegemonic masculinity?

fulfilling the hegemonic ideal, but which do not challenge the hegemonic version either, and thus feed off dominant forms of masculinity. (For a fascinating study of the way these competing forms of masculinity develop among boys in UK secondary schools see Mac an Ghaill, 1994.)

The director Quentin Tarrantino's films, such as Reservoir Dogs *(from which this image comes) and* Pulp Fiction, *have been seen by some commentators as revising hegemonic images of masculinity to allow more reflexivity and ironic style while still celebrating extreme violence*

I have tried, in section 3.1, to establish a number of general features of masculine identities, and the remainder of section 3 will now develop and elaborate upon this picture.

3.2   Male bodies

Central to any man's experience will be his sense of embodiment – his sense of what his body can do, what he looks like, physical differences from women and from other men, sexual responsiveness, and so on. Does this mean that masculinity is biologically determined? How can we analyse this bodily experience from a social psychological perspective?

Although an enormous amount of research has been conducted on sex differences and on the biological bases of masculinity and femininity, the exact roles biology and culture play in the development of gender remain controversial, and no easy resolution of this debate seems likely in the near future (see Edley and Wetherell, 1995, Chapter 1, for a review of the evidence). Some writers on masculinity have attributed a crucial role to biology and have used this to argue for the inevitability of gender inequalities. Goldberg (1977), for example, has argued, from a sociobiological standpoint, that gender inequalities result from male hormones such as testosterone. These hormones give men, in his words, an 'aggressive advantage' over women. The roles of men and women in family life, and in the public domain of work, have been seen as a consequence of this 'aggressive advantage'.

Critics of this stance point out that this approach has difficulty explaining social change. In some parts of the UK, for instance, more women than men are now active in the labour market. In addition, the causal links postulated from the action of genes to the structure of the mind to social action have never been demonstrated but are simply assumed. It is often taken for granted that there must be some connection between chromosomal differences and behaviour, but as soon as we consider exactly how chromosomes or hormones might lead to the phenomena associated with masculinity – to football hooliganism and amazing football skills, for instance, or to male success in company boardrooms and to a disinclination to change nappies – then the influence of environmental and social factors quickly becomes evident.

Most commentators in this area posit a complex interrelationship between biology and society. This view can be seen, for instance, in Connell's claim that:

> The physical sense of maleness is not a simple thing. It involves size and shape, habits of posture and movement, particular physical skills and the lack of others, the image of one's own body, the way it is presented to other people and the ways they respond to it, the way it operates at work and in sexual relations. In no sense is all this a

consequence of XY chromosomes, or even of the possession on which discussions of masculinity have so lovingly dwelt, the penis. The physical sense of maleness grows through personal history of social practice, a life-history-in-society.

(Connell, 1987, p. 84)

Connell argues that, although bodily experience does seem 'natural' and rooted in biological foundations, it is also highly interpenetrated with social life. He refers to the 'personal history of social practice', and, 'life-history-in-society'. The effects of the social domain on men's bodies can be seen at a number of levels, from the way men cut their hair, to whether they wear make-up, to the size of their muscles. Bodily experience is not simply present. It involves a lot of interpretation, the recognizing and labelling of sensations, and developing a narrative around them. The acting out of the social signals of gender in dress, for instance, as transsexuals and transvestites discover, is a complicated process of learning quite subtle modes of self-presentation (Kessler and McKenna, 1978).

Caroline Eggerton (30) is a cross-dresser. During the day, he/she works for a merchant bank. As 'Caroline', however, she feels she is able to express her more sensitive feminine side. Cross-dressing demonstrates some of the complex training and work which goes into 'looking right' as a man or a woman

Connell argues that any natural differences are not suffered (or enjoyed) passively. Biological differences between men and women are not a physical given of the order of being subject to gravity. Rather, Connell argues, human beings are continually working with and transforming natural biological phenomena. Connell asks us to consider the human relationship to other aspects of nature and the material world. He suggests that human history is actually a story of the transcendence of the material world. Thus plants and animals become organized in systems of agriculture, metals and other raw materials become cars and a transport system. To some extent even gravity can be defied through rocket power. In each case, social and human practice creates *new* objects and new conditions from which the future must develop. Nature or material reality certainly constrain what can be done (a plant will not grow from a piece of metal planted in the ground, rockets sometimes fall back to earth), but the properties of objects are also changed in the process of transformation (when chemicals are combined to produce plastic, for instance).

Most men can grow beards, most women cannot; many women can bear children, men cannot. This is the natural material people work with and make the object of their practice. Yet, as I argued earlier, human practice produces an enormous diversity of gendered identities – drag queens, macho men, housewives, sissies, tomboys, soldiers, courtiers, husbands and career women. Men and women are thus more than the addition of society to biology. They represent the active interpenetration of nature and society.

3.3   Working-class and middle-class masculinities

In addition to bodily experiences and interpretations of these, a man's occupation is also likely to be decisive in his sense of masculinity. In the previous chapter, people's diverse experiences of work were considered and it was argued that work is one site where the individual encounters some of the more *organized* and *institutionalized* processes of a society. Several researchers have seen strong connections between the general economic organization of society (modern capitalism) and the broad psychology of masculinity (Tolson, 1977; Seidler, 1991).

These researchers suggest that one of the reasons why hegemonic forms of masculinity are often associated with competitiveness, aggressiveness and inarticulate and detached emotional responses is because capitalist forms of economic production encourage precisely these characteristics. It is argued that contradictions and tensions in the way paid work is organized condition what Tolson calls the 'deep structure' of masculine identities – self-esteem, a sense of creativity, and the forms of camaraderie men experience at work. The social conflicts of capitalism, it is claimed, become rooted in the bodies and energies of men, producing distinctive and entirely habitual sets of gestures, and even certain tones of voice and personalities.

One of the defining features of capitalism is its competitive basis and organization around a struggle for comparative advantage. There is competition between producers to sell goods and make profits and there is competition among workers within the employment market to sell their skills and labour. Competition is evident, too, within the hierarchical structure of modern corporations as the workforce attempt to gain qualifications and promotions. Capitalist production is also organized around a series of divisions between home and work, between work and leisure, private life and public life. Current working practices create basic divisions between people: for example, between those producing goods and those in management, and between paid and unpaid work.

Seidler (1991) argues that these working practices encourage men, since traditionally men have been most involved in paid work, to split their sense of identity between a 'real me' of private life and a work personality. Men became emotionally inarticulate, not just because the capitalist ethos tends to favour self-control, stoicism and self-discipline, but because, in Seidler's view, divisions in experience between the private and the public, along with the institutionalization of competitiveness, cause a process of 'depersonalization'. Men have little alternative, he argues, within these sets of social relations but to become 'working machines', closed and separate from others, fearful of intimacy and vulnerability, regulated, controlled and disciplined. Seidler talks of a pervasive sense of 'unreality' which he claims many men feel as a consequence of the structure and organization of their working lives.

> What is your initial reaction to these claims. To what extent is the psychology of masculinity influenced, in your view, by economic organization?

Although Seidler's assessment seems to fit Dave's experience in Extract 6.1 above, it also seems to me to be too negative. Many men enjoy their work and, indeed, may say that they feel most 'at home' when they are at work. A distinction between a 'real self' which is authentic and an inauthentic, unreal self when at work seems too arbitrary. As Foucault would suggest (see section 2.4), men who enjoy their work are no less 'positioned' by power relations, and their experience is no less constructed by capitalist social relations. In Foucault's view, it is through people's sense of their achievements and through their choices, through those moments when they feel most 'real', as well as through moments of constraint and discipline, that they are inserted into social structures and come to personalize these as their own identity projects.

Tolson and Seidler argue that what distinguishes working-class and middle-class men is the kinds of masculinity which are possible when a man has a wage versus a salary, works by the clock versus by appointments, has job security and a career structure versus job insecurity and fear of personal injury. There is, in Tolson's view, a major difference between the type of masculinity which can emerge in corridors with personal offices, meetings, telephones, and names on doors, compared with the masculinity which emerges through the fraternity of the factory floor and through confinement to local spaces and local communities.

Tolson argues that working-class men have a more instrumental and a less deluded attitude to work. Work becomes more obviously a matter of getting by, of making money. For working-class men, the structures of discipline within the workplace are usually imposed more externally. As a consequence, in Tolson's view, working-class men are more directly humiliated by capitalist practices, and more directly subordinated. He argues that they are more likely to adopt, as compensation, an exaggerated masculine culture within the workplace, a language of brotherhood, a chauvinistic sexuality, blatant machismo, and to invest in forms of resistance which involve direct confrontations with authority. Tolson talks about the drama of group interaction and self-presentation involved and the development of defensive masculine displays which, through talk of sport, sex, and practical joking, achieve what he describes as a highly stylized symbolic exchange of masculinity (cf. Chapter 5, Reading B).

Seidler also sees a strong difference between working-class and middle-class masculinities. Middle-class men, he argues, are more isolated than working-class men, more engaged in an individual struggle with themselves for success. Work is less containable and more engulfing of both time and identity. The development of a successful middle-class career, argues Seidler, demands that personality, character and social skills become commodities to be sold on the labour market along with knowledge and expertise.

The working lives of middle-class and working-class men are also thought to structure in profound but different ways their relations with women within the family. Tolson and Seidler argue that working-class men may become more 'patriarchal' in their outlook in the sense that, as subordination increases in the workplace, the desire to dominate and gain recognition at home becomes more pressing. Similarly, if work is instrumental, just a matter of breadwinning, then family life becomes more important since the financial support of family life becomes the main motive for men to continue their working lives.

Middle-class men are more powerful outside the family. They can thus afford, these commentators argue, to be more superficially egalitarian within the family and more involved in 'partnership'. Middle-class men's concepts of partnership and the 'companionate marriage' (Brannen and Collard, 1982), however, are often dependent on female partners acting as good 'career wives', on female identification with male goals and ambitions, rather than the reverse, and are highly dependent, too, on women's domestic labour which makes a male career feasible in the first place.

The ethnographic research Tolson based his conclusions upon was conducted in the 1970s. Make some notes on the changes which you think have taken place since then and on the effects these might have on forms of masculinity.

ACTIVITY 6.9

Tolson and Seidler write as socialist critics of capitalist working practices. Conservative theorists of masculinity (cf. Clatterbaugh, 1990, Chapter 2, for a review) identify similar patterns but many also see work regimes as a desirable way of containing male aggression and competitiveness. These theorists tend to argue that men are naturally competitive, and in recent years their concern has focused upon the breakdown of the family and what is seen as its civilizing influence, resulting in more extensive male violence and 'yob culture'. The solution in their view is to strengthen the traditional family, rather than change the forms of working practices.

The main changes, since the 1970s, lie in what has been called the 'feminization' of the workforce which has accompanied a shift from more traditional, heavy manufacturing industries to new service and technology-based industries. In 1973, only 53 per cent of women were in the labour market compared to 65 per cent in 1991, although many of these new jobs are part-time. During the same period, male involvement in the labour market dropped from 93 per cent to 86 per cent (Grant, 1994). Similarly, the unemployment rate increased disproportionately for men. The 10.3 per cent unemployment rate for February, 1994, for example, concealed a rate of 13.2 per cent for men and a rate of 5.4 per cent for women (Keegan, 1994).

Several commentators have argued that traditional masculinity is in crisis as a result of the increasing insecurity of the workplace and the broader changes in the demography of work:

> Feminism has given women confidence to move into masculine areas, combining work and motherhood, and even seeing opportunities in new work patterns. Men, on the other hand, are experiencing their work changes, the so-called feminization of labour, more like a smack in the eye.
>
> … Ray Pahl author of *After Success* … says, 'People are scared of not being seen as good workers although they are in a changing market, they are not clear what that means. The traditional male career has collapsed. One response is extreme competitiveness but the other is anxiety and even disillusionment about work altogether.' … Pahl claims that men, particularly, have been hit hard by the needs of the global market for job flexibility. The idea of the unilinear career was the basis of masculine identity. It involved sacrifices, either of the body to physical labour or of the soul to the company, to provide for the family. Now 'contracting out', 'down-sizing' and 'delayering' means the end to steady career paths.
>
> *(Coward, 1995, p. 11)*

There is a need for further research on masculinity and work which would update the early studies by Tolson and others. As Carrigan et al. (1985) argue, perhaps the notion of the 'new man', and the current popularity of writings on masculinity, simply reflect the most recent attempts to 'modernize' men, producing new types of working-class masculinity and corporate masculine identity more in tune with the contemporary demands of capitalism. The changes described above obviously also impact on the relationship between men and women, and section 3.5 will return to this topic.

3.4   Black masculinities

More attention needs to be paid, too, to the position of black men in this nexus of social and economic practices. 'Race' has independent dimensions which will interact with a man's class position. To be a black, middle-class man, for instance, in a society organized in terms of 'race', clearly introduces new dimensions to middle-class experience. In Hall's account in Reading A, for example, we can see that he experienced many of the privileges of masculinity in comparison to his sister, but this privilege was overlaid by his position in a 'racial' and ethnic hierarchy in a colonial society. The effects of 'race' and ethnicity are often thought to be important just for black people alone, but 'race' is also crucial for white identity. White masculinity, in a society where 'race' is salient, is always defined *in relation to* black masculinity, and vice versa.

Hall's experiences as a member of the Jamaican middle-classes differ from the economic and cultural contexts many black men in Britain and the USA experience. As Clatterbaugh (1990) notes, black men in general constitute the 'underclass' of the male working class. Clatterbaugh cites, for instance, Staples's estimate in the 1980s that in North America as many as 46 per cent of black men between the ages of 16 and 62 were not in the labour force. As Chapter 4 noted, racism is similarly built into the division of labour found in the UK, with systematic differences for white and black British citizens in terms of rates of pay and unemployment (Skellington, 1995).

The research, principally North American, which has focused on forms of black masculinity (Davis, 1982; Franklin, 1984; Staples, 1985; Wallace, 1979) has pointed to a contradiction black men face between patriarchal expectations of masculinity, and the possibilities offered by capitalism: 'The message to black men from patriarchy is to "be a man"; the message from capitalism is "no chance"' (Clatterbaugh, 1990, p. 143). In one of the few studies of black British men conducted to date, Westwood (1990) points to the importance for the young working-class black men she studied of being 'streetwise' in response to this contradiction. Being streetwise addressed several pressures. It was a way of acting out conventional masculine expectations for emotional control and independence while developing strategies for coping with racist violence, poverty and the police (see Box 6.2).

BOX 6.2   Streetwise strategies

What is called up in relation to being streetwise is the ability to handle the dangers of street life, and this links masculinity, defence and manly behaviour. Contrary to the popular views, however, that being streetwise privileges physical prowess and fighting acumen, it is essentially an intellectual, cerebral attribute. What is required as a context for being streetwise and being able to operate safely on the streets is an intimate knowledge of locality which all the men shared. ...

Faced with the power of the police the men would say that it was vital 'to know how to handle yourself' and this meant everything but a physical response. As Dev commented, 'You have to stay cool and let them heat up'. Staying cool is essentially about maintaining dignity and control in a situation which very often denies both. It means remaining calm, signalled through a quiet voice and reasonableness in the face of what the men considered to be provocation. The quietness covers the necessity of staying mentally alert and agile. ...

An intimate knowledge of locality allowed the men to disappear quickly if there was trouble on the streets and to reappear at some distance, usually, from the police. The speed of disappearance meant an ability to run and this was marked by the tracksuits and trainers that the men wore which were also a symbol of their commitment to sport. Tracksuits and trainers are not just about the whims of fashion, they express something about the nature of street life and the importance of physical fitness.

(Westwood, 1990, pp. 64–5)

Tolson in his research argued that one of the main characteristics of working-class men is their dependence on local territory and their local community for a sense of identity. This dependence is economic in origin and historically established. Westwood notes that this localism is even more intensely experienced by young, black, working-class men. When fear of racist attacks is a dominant experience, then 'our streets' become even more crucial territory. This sense of territory may also be linked to a pattern of informal economic activity based on barter of goods and services. Westwood notes that, for the men she interviewed, being able to get things done, or to get things on the cheap through people they knew, was an important source of masculine self-esteem and masculine activity. Again, however, as with white men, it is important to emphasize the diversity of experiences among black men.

3.5 The patriarchal dividend

We men are formed and broken by our own power.

(Hearn, 1987, p. 98)

Masculinity is constructed in a very complex and tense process of negotiation mostly with women right through adult life.

(Carrigan et al., 1985, p. 563)

When we look at men's experiences of work, and research on 'race', we become aware of men as 'top dogs' and as 'underdogs' at the bottom of the heap. We see the very different ways in which men's positions construct the psychology of masculinity. When we look at the relation between men and women as entire groups, however, the perspective shifts again and the *collective power* of men comes into view. Men are diverse and their relation to women is diverse too, but running through this is the set of social practices feminist theorists call 'patriarchy'. I want to suggest that any man's identity projects, the impressions he forms of himself as a man, and the subject positions available to him will reflect his negotiation or living out of these social practices.

Power and privilege are, of course, sometimes difficult to experience directly. When interviewed, many men say that they do not feel powerful or that they are not aware of being privileged (Griffin, 1991). What might be most salient to these men is their *lack* of power compared to other men (and some few women) who perhaps have more money, are higher up in status hierarchies, belong to more privileged social classes and 'races', or who are more physically forceful, aggressive or well-built. But, if power is not directly felt, if it is not absolute but only relative, does that mean it doesn't exist?

Connell argues that in sociological terms men can be treated as an interest group and that men regularly receive a 'dividend' from the patriarchal organization of society. He expands on these points as follows:

> … A gender order where men dominate women cannot avoid constituting men as an interest group concerned with defence, and women as an interest group concerned with change. This is a structural fact, independent of whether men as individuals love or hate women, or believe in equality or abjection, and independent of whether women are currently pursuing change.

> To speak of a patriarchal dividend is to raise exactly this question of interest. Men gain a dividend from patriarchy in terms of honour, prestige and the right to command. They also gain a material dividend. In the rich capitalist countries, men's average incomes are approximately *double* women's average incomes. (The more familiar comparisons of wage rates for full-time employment greatly understate gender differences in actual incomes.) Men are vastly more likely to control a major

block of capital as chief executive of a major corporation, or as direct owner. For instance, of 55 US fortunes above $1 billion in 1992, only five were mainly in the hands of women – and all but one of those as a result of inheritance from men.

Men are much more likely to hold state power: for instance, men are ten times more likely than women to hold office as a member of parliament (an average across all countries of the world). Perhaps men do most of the work? No: in the rich countries, time-budget studies show that women and men work on average about the same numbers of hours in the year. (The major difference is in how much of this work gets paid.)

Given these facts the 'battle of the sexes' is no joke. Social struggle must result from inequalities on such a scale. It follows that the politics of masculinity cannot only concern questions of personal life and identity. It must also concern questions of social justice.

(Connell, 1995, pp. 82–3)

In section 3.3, I described the increasing 'feminization' of the labour force. Does this invalidate Connell's analysis? Research suggests that it is still meaningful to talk of a 'patriachical dividend'. Of the 11,767,000 women in work in the UK in June 1995, 47 per cent were working part-time and, according to 1994 figures, these women earned on average only 30 per cent of the national average full-time wage, while women who worked full-time earned only 80 per cent of the national average full-time wage (Smith, 1995).

Does the increasing number of women at work mean that men are taking more responsibility for domestic tasks? The results here are mixed. On the one hand, men are spending more time with their children. There has been an increasing trend since the 1960s. In 1961, fathers of under-fives spent 12 minutes a day on average with their children, in the mid-1970s, that figure had increased to 17 minutes, while in the 1980s it was 43 minutes (Weale, 1995). However, the 1995 Mintel survey of leisure time in the UK demonstrated that a considerable disparity between men and women still exists. (Men claim 45 hours of leisure a week on average, compared to 40 hours for women). This disparity in leisure increases with the arrival of children, and the survey concluded that the main burden of domestic work still falls on women (Erlichman, 1995). Men's contribution to domestic work is still largely seen as optional, not a necessary part of their role.

Child-rearing, domestic work and caring for others (with the exception of paid child-minders, nurses, etc.) do not have the same 'exchange-value' as labour for money outside the home, but are none the less also vital to the reproduction of society. Hearn (1987) argues that, in relation to this kind of work, men as a group (if not all individual men) stand in an exploitative and thus antagonistic relation to women. Men appropriate what Hearn calls the 'human values' women produce. In Hearn's

description, men as a group extract 'human tithes' from women. These tithes can extend from trivial favours to major domestic commitments. As husbands and fathers, Hearn suggests, most men routinely receive privileges from women without recompense (1987, p. 69).

Connell's notion of a 'patriarchal dividend' refers also to men and women's differential access to honour and prestige. In relation to this, the psychoanalytic theorist Frosh (1994) has argued that masculinity is 'impossible': in the sense that no man is ever big, strong and tough enough to match the cultural fantasy of the 'real man'; but also because masculinity is continually defined *against* a devalued femininity. Forms of masculinity often represent a struggle to be different from women, a struggle not to 'collapse back' into femininity. But why a struggle of this order unless in some sense masculinity is the privileged identity?

The devaluation of women and the importance of this in the making of masculinity is evident in the concern expressed about feminine boys, in taunts heard on the football field ('you played just like a girl'), in many men's concerns to establish their heterosexuality ('I'm not one of those you know'), in routine expressions of homophobia, in the standard, but now changing, practice of using 'he' and 'man' to stand for humans in general, in the humour involved when male comedians dress in women's clothes, although there is no equivalent humour based on women dressing as men, and so on. This principle of cultural life which Spender (1980) calls the 'plus male, minus female' principle, and the demands placed on men to be 'real men', also indicate something of the power relation between men and women and the way in which this power might construct masculine identities.

3.6   The changing nature of patriarchy

It seems clear that many men (not all) have a collective, if unacknowledged, interest in the maintenance of disparities between women and men. It is important to stress, however, that this power is not maintained on a daily basis through active and self-conscious male conspiracies (although these do occur). I am not suggesting that most men wake up in the morning thinking – 'Today I'm going to extract my rightful tithes from the women around me', 'Today I'm going to continue making sure women are oppressed and men remain in a position of dominance in public and private life'.

As Connell (1990) points out, we are dealing with a set of continually changing *processes* which maintain power relations between women and men, along with a set of established but continually changing institutions through which power is exercised, such as the courts, the tax offices, welfare agencies, police and government bureaucracies. To some extent these are structures and circumstances beyond individual control. Connell wonders if we should embark on a search for 'Patriarch Headquarters' to try to find the coordinating centre from which men's collective interests are directed. He concludes, however, that, although there may be many localized 'Patriarch Headquarters', or groups of men using their power to protect their gendered interests, the general process of regulation which supports male power is likely to be much more complex, indirect and subtle. Often it is a matter of what seems reasonable and obvious to those in power, including those few women in power.

As forms of patriarchy change, and thus the basis for what Connell (1990) calls this 'aristocracy of sex', different possibilities for male and female identities emerge. Walby (1990) argues that we have moved, for example, in recent times from a situation of 'private patriarchy' where women were directly controlled by their husbands and fathers to a new and modernized form of 'public patriarchy'. As an example of 'private patriarchy', Walby asks us to consider the position of women in the mid-nineteenth century in relation to the legal procedures of the state:

> Before 1857 divorce was impossible (except by an Act of Parliament). At this time a woman had no legal rights as an independent person when married, since the law conceptualized the married couple as one, and that one was represented by the husband. The husband's rights over his wife were extensive. He had the right to insist that she lived with him; runaway wives could be returned by force and legally held in the husband's house against their will. He had the right to beat her. He legally owned all her goods, for instance, any wages she earned or property she inherited. He had the right to care and custody of the children and to determine their education. He had the right of sexual access to his wife's body. A wife could not engage in any financial or legal transaction except as the agent of her husband.
>
> *(1990, p. 163)*

Patriarchal control at this period was direct and personal, mediated through family relationships. The main patriarchal strategy here, particularly among the middle classes, was the exclusion of women from public life along with tight control on female sexuality.

What kind of masculine and feminine psychologies would you expect to see being produced by the social practices of private patriarchy?

Women, now, are free to divorce, they can obtain custody of their children, and they are freer to enter a range of sexual relationships, with 'serial monogamy' becoming a new norm. Women are now no longer actively excluded by law from public life. Does this mean that society is no longer patriarchal, and there has been substantial progress for women? Walby argues that there have certainly been changes, many of which both women and men have campaigned for, and which in some areas have improved the position of women. She also argues, however, that the main changes have been in the *mode* of patriarchy not in its existence.

Modern public patriarchy, she suggests, is much less personal in the sense that it is not so commonly experienced as administered by one man (husband or father) who is the direct beneficiary. This new public form of patriarchy, Walby argues, works not by the exclusion of women from public life but by the segregation of women within public life in certain areas of the economy and, as we saw earlier, in part-time work. Women enter paid work and public life but usually on a basis where women's jobs typically carry less pay and power. Within the family, women are free to divorce but, as we saw, they are still largely responsible for domestic labour and child-rearing, and in many cases are expected to provide domestic services for the men with whom they have relationships.

As an example of the changes associated with the emergence of 'public patriarchy', consider the way identities such as the 'single mother', 'absent father', 'female secretary', 'male corporate manager' have been constructed and recent debates about new forms of relationships and the decline of marriage.

Some women are certainly better off, but Walby argues that it is debatable whether the majority of women can be described as beneficiaries. Women's new freedom, for instance, and the 'feminization of the labour market' described earlier have been accompanied also by a massive 'feminization of poverty' as women lose the kinds of relative financial security private patriarchy offered and as the number of men fleeing the financial and other responsibilities of fatherhood has increased. And, 'while there have been many changes which facilitate women's entry to the public sphere there are not so many which improve the position of women within it' (Walby, 1990, p. 171).

In trying to make sense of the *psychological* effects of these changing patterns in social organization, there are many avenues to explore. There are differences, for example, between men and women's interactional and non-verbal styles which seem connected to the different status relationships in which men and women are embedded (Radley, 1996). Men tend to monopolize and dominate conversational space, for example, as well as other forms of personal space. Henley (1973) has suggested these findings demonstrate the 'micro-politics' of gender encounters. She, and other feminist social psychologists, have argued that the evidence suggests that, if power relations in society between women and men were reversed, then differences in non-verbal behaviour and conversational strategies would be likely to change rapidly in line with new status patterns. In other words, these non-verbal and interactional patterns seem to have social rather than biological origins.

Work of this kind (and see Miell and Dallos (eds), 1996, for other examples of how power operates in relationships) demonstrates how gender inequalities come to discipline the body, the smallest movement, and the most mundane practices of everyday life. In other words, as we have seen, patriarchy has a strongly material and economic dimension but it also has a phenomenology (Bartky, 1990). It organizes people's consciousness, their daily experience, and their sense of what is normal.

Review of section 3

- This section developed a feminist social constructionist analysis of masculine identities which argued that these are plural, personal *and* social, relational, actively constructed and imbued with broader power relations.

- Both nature and nurture combine to produce 'real men'. Masculinity depends on bodily experience but this experience is interpreted through 'life-history-in-society'.

- Institutionalized social processes such as capitalism, and the social divisions associated with class and 'race', play a crucial role in defining masculine identities.

- Male psychology is constructed under patriarchal circumstances and reflects the privileges most men enjoy as a group in relation to women.

4 Conclusion

One of the difficulties in studying masculinity, as with all social identities, is combining the broad-brush picture gained from statistics (such as information on the incidence of sexual violence, rates of pay, and participation in the workforce, for example) with an understanding of the life histories of *particular* men. More research is needed which focuses on the individual and which recognizes diversity, but which can also pay attention to the broad cultural patterns which men are negotiating, accepting or resisting, as well as the varied social contexts in which men come to find their place.

Traditionally, social psychology has been based on experimental research and the assumption that theories should (ideally) stand and fall on the experimental evidence. In this chapter a different notion of the role of social science has been evident, and the usual domain of social psychology has been extended to include cultural criticism. An analysis of social identity has been developed through a process of reasoning and argument. At various points in the chapter, this theory has been linked to interpretations of evidence such as statistics about rates of pay, research on family dynamics, ethnographic research on men's working lives, empirical investigations of non-verbal behaviour, and so on. The validity of these interpretations, as with any interpretation of data, is crucial in the evaluation of this approach to social identity. But, more broadly, in assessing this approach, you will need to ask questions about the plausibility of this account, about its internal coherence, whether it gives rise to new insights. Does it make sense in itself? Are there aspects of social identity and life history left unexplained? Theories developed by a process of reasoning and argument stand and fall on the degree of enlightenment they might offer and how useful they are in 'making sense'.

Further reading

In writing this chapter I was strongly influenced by the work of the Australian sociologist, Robert Connell. His work is well worth reading in the original; see the following:

Connell, R. (1987) *Gender and Power*, Cambridge, Polity.

Chapter 10 of this book develops the concept of personality as a project. It is worth looking, too, at the case histories of men's lives presented in:

Connell, R. (1995) *Masculinities*, Cambridge, Polity.

For general reviews of research on masculinity and differing perspectives on the development of male identities see:

Edley, N. and Wetherell, M. (1995) *Men in Perspective: Practice, Power and Identity*, London, Harvester Wheatsheaf.

Segal, L. (1990) *Slow Motion: Changing Men, Changing Masculinities*, London, Virago.

The question of how best to capture and describe someone's life remains a difficult problem for philosophers, biographers and psychologists alike. For two dense, but fascinating and contrasting, attempts at 'psychobiography', one from a largely existential and experiential point of view, the other from a more social constructionist perspective, see:

Sartre, J.P. (1988) *Saint Genet: Actor and Martyr*, London, Heinemann.

Rose, J. (1991) *The Haunting of Sylvia Plath*, London, Virago.

Acknowledgement

I would like to thank Nigel Edley for allowing me to draw on our joint research and writing on masculinity for section 3 of this chapter and on material and examples from Edley and Wetherell (1995). This research was funded by a grant from the UK Economic and Social Research Council and the Open University Research Committee.

References

Barthes, R. (1977) *Roland Barthes*, New York, Hill and Wang.

Bartky, S. (1990) *Femininity and Domination: Studies in the Phenomenology of Oppression*, New York, Routledge.

Brannen, J. and Collard, J. (1982) *Marriages in Trouble*, London, Tavistock.

Carrigan, T, Connell, R. and Lee, J. (1985) 'Towards a new sociology of masculinity', *Theory and Society,* vol. 14, pp. 551–604.

Clatterbaugh, K. (1990) *Contemporary Perspectives on Masculinity,* Boulder, Colorado, Westview Press.

Collins, D. (1980) *Sartre as Biographer*, Cambridge, Mass., Harvard University Press.

Connell, R. (1987) *Gender and Power,* Cambridge, Polity.

Connell, R. (1990) 'The state, gender, and sexual politics', *Theory and Society,* vol. 19, pp. 507–44.

Connell, R. (1995) *Masculinities,* Cambridge, Polity.

Coward, R. (1995) 'Men reeling from a kick in the job market', *The Guardian,* 2 October, p. 11.

Dallos, R. (1996) 'Creating relationships: patterns of actions and beliefs', in Miell, D. and Dallos, R. (eds) (1996).

Davis, A. (1982) *Women, Race and Class*, London, The Women's Press.

Dollimore, J. (1991) *Sexual Dissidence*, Oxford, Clarendon Press.

Edley, N. and Wetherell, M. (1995) *Men in Perspective: Practice, Power and Identity,* London, Harvester Wheatsheaf.

Erlichman, J. (1995) 'New man retreats on the home front', *The Guardian,* 24 May, p. 4.

Foucault, M. (1980) *Power/Knowledge: Selected Interviews and Other Writings 1972–1977,* New York, Harvester Wheatsheaf.

Franklin, C.W. (1984) *The Changing Definition of Masculinity* , New York, Plenum.

Frosh, S. (1994) *Sexual Difference: Masculinity and Psychoanalysis*, London, Routledge.

Goldberg, S. (1977) *Inevitability of Patriarchy*, London, Temple Smith.

Grant, L. (1994) 'First among equals', *The Guardian Weekend*, 22 October, pp. 36–46.

Griffin, C. (1991), 'Experiencing power: dimensions of gender, "race" and class', *British Psychological Society Psychology of Women Section Newsletter*, no. 8, pp. 43–58.

Harré, R. (1983) *Personal Being*, Oxford, Basil Blackwell.

Harré, R. and Davies, B. (1990) 'Positioning: the discursive production of selves', *Journal for the Theory of Social Behaviour*, vol. 20, pp. 43–63.

Harré, R. and Van Langenhove, L. (1991) 'Varieties of positioning', *Journal for the Theory of Social Behaviour*, vol. 21, pp. 393–407.

Hearn, J. (1987) *The Gender of Oppression: Men, Masculinity and the Critique of Marxism*, Brighton, Harvester Wheatsheaf.

Henley, N. (1973) 'Status and sex: some touching observations', *Bulletin of the Psychonomic Society*, vol. 2, pp. 91–3.

Hoggart, R. (1959) *The Uses of Literacy*, Harmondsworth, Penguin Books.

Hollway, W. (1984) 'Gender difference and the production of subjectivity', in Henriques, J., Hollway, W., Urwin, C., Venn, C. and Walkerdine, V. (eds) *Changing the Subject*, London, Methuen.

Keegan, W. (1994) 'Girls on top in jobs market', *The Guardian*, 9 April, p. 25.

Kessler, S. and McKenna, W. (1978) *Gender: An Ethnomethodological Approach,* New York, Wiley.

Laing, R.D. (1971) *Self and Others*, Harmondsworth, Penguin Books.

Laing, R.D. and Esterson, A. (1970) *Sanity, Madness and the Family,* Harmondsworth, Penguin Books.

Mac an Ghaill, M. (1994) *The Making of Men*, Buckingham, Open University Press.

Miell, D. and Dallos, R. (eds) (1996) *Social Interaction and Personal Relationships*, Sage/The Open University (Book 2 in this series).

Miell, D. and Croghan, R. (1996) 'Examining the wider context of social relationships', in Miell, D. and Dallos, R. (eds) (1996).

Pahl, R. (1995) *After Success*, Cambridge, Polity.

Radley, A. (1996) 'Relationships in detail: the study of social interaction', in Miell, D. and Dallos, R. (eds) (1996).

Seabrook, J. (1982) *Working Class Childhood*, London, Gollancz.

Segal, L. (1990) *Slow Motion: Changing Men, Changing Masculinities*, London, Virago.

Seidler, V. (1991) *Recreating Sexual Politics: Men, Feminism and Politics*, London, Routledge.

Skellington, R. (1995) *'Race' in Britain Today* (2nd edn), London, Sage.

Smith, T. (1995) 'Across the great divide', *The Guardian*, 27 September, pp. 6–7.

Spender, D. (1980) *Man Made Language*, London, Routledge and Kegan Paul.

Staples, R. (1985) *Black Masculinity: The Black Male's Role in American Society*, London, Black Scholar Press.

Steedman, C. (1986) *Landscape for a Good Woman: A Story of Two Lives*, London, Virago.

Stevens, R. (ed.) (1996) *Understanding the Self*, London, Sage/The Open University (Book 1 in this series).

Stevens, R. (1996) 'The reflexive self: an experiential perspective', in Stevens, R. (ed.) (1996).

Stevens, R. and Wetherell, M. (1996) 'The self in the modern world: drawing together the threads', in Stevens, R. (ed.)(1996).

Thomas, K. (1996) 'The defensive self: a psychodynamic perspective', in Stevens, R. (ed.) (1996).

Tolson, A. (1977) *The Limits of Masculinity*, London, Tavistock.

Walby, S. (1990) *Theorizing Patriarchy*, Oxford, Blackwell.

Wallace, M. (1979) *Black Macho and the Myth of the Superwoman*, New York, Dial Press.

Weale, S. (1995) 'Work ethic stunts the growth of new man', *The Guardian*, 17 June, p. 6.

Wetherell, M. and Edley, N. (1994) 'Men and masculinity: a socio-psychological analysis of discourse', End of Award Report, London, Economic and Social Research Council.

Westwood, S. (1990) 'Racism, black masculinity and the politics of space', in Hearn, J. and Morgan, D. (eds) *Men, Masculinities and Social Theory*, London, Unwin Hyman.

Reading A
Leaving home

Stuart Hall

In a world which changes so rapidly from one day to the next, we are often tempted to reconstruct our families in memory as one of the few, stable, supportive unchanging structures in our lives. Christopher Lasch called it 'a haven in a heartless world'. But memory can play funny tricks.

I was born in Jamaica in the 1930s, into what was then a middle-class and in the language of that time, 'coloured', that is, 'mixed-race', Jamaican family. We were 'mulattoes' – an old word for the offspring of that miscegenation between white European colonials and black African slaves which had been a feature of the exploitative social relations of the Caribbean plantations. As a consequence, the majority of middle- and lower-middle class Jamaican families were, to one degree or another, 'mixed' in this way. In my childhood, what mattered was not so much the 'pure' ends of this 'race'-colour spectrum, but the refined gradings and positions in between. In those days the middle classes used these distinctions of colour to mark themselves off, symbolically, from the mass of Jamaican people who – though many of them are also mixed – looked 'black' – a word, incidentally, which no-one, including blacks themselves, would ever at that time have dreamt of using.

Defining them in terms of skin-colour may seem an odd, and curiously impersonal, way to describe one's family. However, looking back, I am convinced that, for me at least, my family's place in the social landscape of pre-independence Jamaica, and above all its location in the complicated map of 'race', ethnic origin and colour that defined social status, were the coordinates that shaped our family culture.

My family consisted of my mother and father and three children – two boys and a girl – of whom I was the youngest. My father, a rather short, mahogany-skinned Jamaican, smoked stubby Cuban cigars and spent most of his working life with one of the big North American banana companies which, for many years, dominated the Caribbean and Central American economy. He had been to one of the 'good' boys' secondary schools, modelled on the English public school and had taken his accountancy exams by correspondence. But he entered United Fruit Company as a junior clerk and, when he retired as chief accountant, he had been the first native-born, coloured Jamaican to hold each of the jobs to which he was promoted. Since my mother never worked, the family income depended on the patronage of this foreign company and my father's social position depended on his symbolic proximity to, and his success in winning the approval and cultivating the approbation of, the local whites and expatriates from Boston head office who occupied the higher echelons of the company. Hard working, respectable, financially cautious as accountants often are, he was a rather self-effacing compliant person who evaded family squabbles – even at home, a good 'company man'. His income was secure but never ample – never enough to match the position in Kingston society to which he and my mother aspired. The tensions derived from this struggle to keep up a position to which he never properly belonged, except on the sufferance of others, became subtly intertwined with the culture of our family and formed one of the main parameters of the 'culture of aspirations' into which I grew.

My father's mixed European and African parentage was obvious from his colour and other physical features. His parents were poor but respectable people from the country lower-middle class. His father, my grandfather, kept a drugstore in Old Harbour, a small dusty county town on the plains of St Catherine outside Kingston. The house where my grand-mother and my father's many unmarried sisters – my aunts – lived was a modest, wooden house, with a front and side porch, set in a large but scrubby yard planted out with mango trees. It is the only 'family house' we have left in Jamaica. My aunt started keeping school in a tiny school room built to the side of the house at 19 and she still – aged 102 – teaches a staunchly Victorian form of English grammar to a few of the brightest local children from the salt flats of Old Harbour Bay in the mornings on the back verandah. I loved visiting this house as a child. It was small, overcrowded – I never understood where all the aunts slept – and filled with neighbours and friends. Though much less grand than our Kingston house, I always thought it much more friendly and wel-coming. Wonderful smells of Jamaican country cooking drifted through the house from the dark, outdoor kitchen, and over the multitude of visi-tors (including the Catholic priest and Anglican parson, for our family was divided in religious affiliation) the benevolent, loving, crenellated brown face of my grandmother presided. I still wear – and treasure – her gold wedding ring.

The dominant figure in *our* family was my mother: not a symbol of 'petticoat power', governing the family, as so many strong Jamaican mothers do, from the wings, but bang in the middle of the scene, com-manding everything and everyone, including my father. She was a hand-some, strong-willed woman, who should have had an active career outside the home. But, as befitted my father's rising position, she was obliged to make our family her 'career'. It absorbed all her powerful emotional energies, her creative vitality. It became the theatre for the exercise of her indomitable spirit. She managed us all with a passionate exercise in sheer willpower.

Like my father, her family also belonged to the mulatto middle class, but a very different part of the 'mix'. My father's family were clearly the product of an act of miscegenation – never referred to or acknowledged – between some English planter or overseer and an African slave woman. My mother's family, however, were only one generation away from their English and Scottish forbears; and thus much lighter in skin-colour than me or my father's family – though still, of course, to a practised

Jamaican eye, 'coloured'. They, too, were respectable but relatively poor. Her mother worked as a postmistress in the bustling town of Port Antonio; her father was a schoolmaster.

However, their light colour gave them a certain status in Port Antonio society. My mother had been adopted from an early age by her aunt and uncle, a prosperous lawyer and landowner, and taken to live on the medium-sized plantation they owned in a rather grand estate house – Norwich – which stood on a hill, at the end of a long driveway of majestic palm trees, overlooking the sea. In this setting, she was brought up to identify, not with her own parents' rather humble life-style in the town, but with the rather grand, privileged, 'country estate' ways of 'Uncle Charlie'. She worked briefly in his law office and would have made a formidable lawyer. Instead she married my father and moved to Kingston. But her image of 'the good life', her standards of decorum and style, and her ambitions for the family and for us, were indelibly shaped by that already dying estate world of her childhood. She tried to inject its 'old world' standards into the faster commercial world into which my father had moved. She employed a retinue of servants, as the Jamaican aspirant middle classes always did in those days. This was swelled by a vast collection of odd-job people and 'handymen' who cut the grass or trimmed the hedge or sharpened the knives, and became part of her extended patronage system. She paid them, not a wage, but a 'bounty' in recognition of the feudal dues she thought they owed her, rather than anything so vulgar as 'the rate for the job'.

I keep coming back to the question of colour and position in the 'racial' pecking order. Jamaican colonial society before independence was carefully, complexly, exquisitely graded according to an intricate matrix composed of skin colour, hair texture, physical features, wealth and education – in that order. The norm – to which, of course, only a small minority of white settlers belonged – was European: everyone else took their position in terms of their proximity to or distance from that norm. The vast majority, who were African slave stock, were thus the most distant. Among the middle classes, the closer in colour, feature, manners and behaviour to the white people, the higher the status. Personal success in this colonial system meant mobility along this colour-class graded spectrum, and far from this being an external matter of social attitudes only, it penetrated deeply and personally into the culture of families and into our individual self-images.

My father was more oriented, through his business contacts, toward the North American model of success. My mother, denying to the last the manifest evidence of her African heritage, identified with 'the Mother Country' – England; especially as England was symbolized through and realized in the near-white settler life-style of her plantation childhood. Both these models were already, even in those days, somewhat 'archaic', and destined rapidly to become more so. Ambitious middle-class Jamaicans like my father were already beginning to identify with the growing independence movement and looking forward to taking over from the colonials and starting local business careers. The small estates of my mother's childhood were already a fading dream from another world. Nevertheless, between them these two ideals defined the 'culture of aspirations' in our family. My parents' education had stopped at the secondary school level. We all did well at school and my brother and I – but, typically, not my sister – were encouraged to win scholarships, study abroad and return to an enhanced position that would bring the family reflected glory. But what mattered, much more, in our everyday family life, was how these competing models were relived by us as an intrinsic part of our family drama. Partly as a result, I have never been able to understand the sharp distinction people make between what in social science we may loosely call the 'structural' and the 'subjective' aspects. Our family was a microcosm – a translation to another register – of the tensions and contradictions of the colonial culture – a fact I recognized, however unconsciously, long before I became a social scientist. Each of us not only lived out, at a personal level, these tensions but invested them with all the psychic and emotional energy of the so-called 'family romance'.

There is often a family myth – a story which is told and retold on family occasions, which places each family member in some kind of symbolic narrative. It may or may not be literally true: it is certainly symbolically significant. The story which 'placed' me was about the occasion when my mother first brought me as a baby home from the hospital, and my sister – then about 7 years old – looked into the crib and is supposed to have exclaimed, 'Where did you get this coolie baby from?' The story was retold to gales of laughter. What she had registered, in her childish way, was the fact that I was the 'blackest' member of the family. And the term 'coolie' showed that she understood that this meant I was, socially, an outsider – for 'coolie' was the abusive slang term used by the Jamaican middle class for very poor itinerant East Indian market gardeners who, as far as my mother was concerned, were even lower in status than Jamaican black people.

The first time I consciously understood this story may have been the moment when I began to feel as if, in some subtle way, I didn't quite belong. In fact, like a self-fulfilling prophecy, I gradually became what my sister, in jest, had named me: the 'coolie' of the family. When I look now at early family photographs of myself as a small boy, I look cross, sullenly rebellious – and above all, depressed. As I grew up I realized I could identify who I was and who I wanted to become with *neither* of my family's images of success. Long before I could analyse it properly, I felt estranged from the way our family strove to be something we manifestly were not. I hated the way poor, black folk were constantly distanced from us and made the objects of derision in casual family talk; I squirmed with embarrassment at the way my father was patronized by the men at the cricket club he aspired to, but could never really join. I reacted strongly against the whole collective family project to 'keep up' in the colour/class game. My schoolfriends were Jamaicans of all shades and colours, reflecting the new 'black' Jamaica that was to emerge in the 1960s; and when my parents barred many of them entry to our home on the euphemistic grounds that 'they weren't the sort of people I should be fraternizing with' – I knew exactly what *that* code meant – I simply opted out, and began to spend more and more time with them elsewhere.

My family's obsession with these distinctions went far beyond the usual kind of social snobbery. When my sister – then in her early twenties – began a relationship with a black medical student, who later came to be a prominent member of the Jamaican medical fraternity, my parents forbade it, and intervened to prevent it. The emotional and mental breakdown which that triggered was prolonged and traumatic, and one from which she has never fully recovered. That was the moment, on the threshold of my scholarship to study in England, when I realized that she had become a kind of family victim, not just of the illusions sustained at such cost within my family, but of the whole colonial cultural drama we were living out in our daily lives. Looking back to that experience, it may well have been the moment when I first unconsciously realized that, if ever I had the good fortune to escape that world, I would be well advised never to return to it. Winning my chance to study abroad and leaving for Europe – accompanied, of course, by my mother who personally delivered me and a gigantic steamer trunk direct to Merton College, Oxford – I was regarded by my family as representing the triumph and justification of the way they had brought me up. But already, in my hearts of hearts, I knew it was the beginning of a long escape attempt.

Of course, our families shape us one way or another – positively because of what in them we identify with, negatively because of how we react against them; and whichever it is, because they are the place where powerful, often unconscious but primordial feelings are invested and attachments made. As a student, I became a passionate anti-imperialist – in part because my family seemed so 'colonialist' in outlook. I felt intensely 'Jamaican' because I came to experience so much of my early family life as a kind of collective denial of that identification. Having been warned by my mother against it, I instantly – once I reached London – grew a beard, which I have never symbolically abandoned, and frequented the London haunts of radical West Indian students. I'm not seeking to offer some psychological, family-determined explanation for the sort of person I became or for the beliefs and attitudes I hold. But I am aware that, in so far as one, consciously or unconsciously, invents oneself, I invented a set of identities in resistance against the ideal self-image, the ego ideal, which my family invited me to become.

I don't for a moment imagine you will find my family experience at all representative! Most people remember their families in much more posi-tive terms – though sometimes I wonder whether our memories don't screen out the tensions and difficulties which seem to me endemic in the close-knit, intense world of familial, parent/child or sibling relationships. My experience may have been extreme. If so, the extremities arose almost entirely from the way our family – as a collective system of emotionally-charged relationships – first internalized – then acted out day by day in the family theatre – the larger contradictions and anxieties of a colonial culture.

Whatever your own family experience, I do think voyages of recovery – whether real returns to one's family and home, or voyages in the memory to that imaginary place we think of as 'home' – are a traumatic process. They awaken feelings and fears, which never quite disappear, longings and desires which can never be satisfied or assuaged; they bring back hopes and aspirations – particularly those which others have for and about us – which cannot be met, because – fortunately in my case – we go on inventing ourselves anew and we take turnings which move us in different directions from the scripts which families write for us. But the feelings of restlessness which the encounter with these unfulfilled selves awakens to life leave us disturbed. My father and mother are long since dead. But, long before they died, I had internalized my quarrel with them, with their picture of what Jamaica was and should become and of the sort of 'me' they saw reflected in the mirror of our family culture. With that 'family of the mind' I will never be at peace, though I may one day strike a sort of uneasy truce.

Reading B
The weaver's daughter

Carolyn Steedman

Source: Steedman, C. (1986) *Landscape for a Good Woman: A Story of Two Lives*, London, Virago, pp. 27–40.

When I was three, before my sister was born, I had a dream. It remains quite clear across the years, the topography absolutely plain, so precise in details of dress that I can use them to place the dream in historical time. We were in a street, the street so wide and the houses so distant across the road that it might not have been a street at all; and the houses lay low with gaps between them, so that the sky filled a large part of the picture. Here, at the front, on this side of the wide road, a woman hurried along, having crossed from the houses behind. [...]

She wore the New Look, a coat of beige gaberdine which fell in two swaying, graceful pleats from her waist at the back (the swaying must have come from very high heels, but I didn't notice her shoes), a hat tipped forward from hair swept up at the back. She hurried, something jerky about her movements, a nervous, agitated walk, glancing round at me as she moved across the foreground. Several times she turned and came some way back towards me, admonishing, shaking her finger.

Encouraging me to follow in this way perhaps, but moving too fast for me to believe that this was what she wanted, she entered a revolving door of dark, polished wood, mahogany and glass, and she started to go round and round, looking out at me as she turned. I wish I knew what she was doing, and what she wanted me to do.

[...] That dream is the past that lies at the heart of my present: it is my interpretative device, the means by which I can tell a story. My understanding of the dream built up in layers over a long period of time. [...] I understood what I had seen in the dream when I learned the words 'gaberdine' and 'mahogany'; and I was born in the year of the New Look, and understood by 1951 and the birth of my sister, that dresses needing twenty yards for a skirt were items as expensive as children – more expensive really, because after 1948 babies came relatively cheap, on tides of free milk and orange juice, but good cloth in any quantity was hard to find for a very long time.

[...]

Now, later, I see the time of my childhood as a point between two worlds: an older 'during the War', 'before the War', 'in the Depression', 'then'; and the place we inhabit now. The War was so palpable a presence in the first five years of my life that I still find it hard to believe that I didn't live through it. There were bomb-sites everywhere, prefabs on waste land, most things still on points, my mother tearing up the ration book when meat came off points, over my sister's pram, outside the library in the High Street in the summer of 1951, a gesture that still fills me with the desire to do something so defiant and final; and then looking across the street at a woman wearing a full-skirted dress, and then down at the forties straight-skirted navy blue suit she was still wearing, and longing, irritatedly, for the New Look; and then at us, the two living barriers to twenty yards of cloth. Back home, she said she'd be able to get it at the side door of the mill; but not here; not with you two ...

My mother's story was told to me early on, in bits and pieces throughout the fifties, and it wasn't delivered to entertain, like my father's much later stories were, but rather to teach me lessons. There was a child, an eleven-year-old from a farm seven miles south of Coventry, sent off to be a maid-of-all-work in a parsonage in Burnley. She had her tin trunk, and she cried, waiting on the platform with her family seeing her off, for the through train to Manchester. They'd sent her fare, the people in Burnley; 'But think how she felt, such a little girl, she was only eleven, with nothing but her little tin box. Oh, she did cry.' [...] The lesson was, of course, that I must never, ever, cry for myself, for I was a lucky little girl: my tears should be for all the strong, brave women who gave me life. This story, which embodied fierce resentment against the unfairness of things, was carried through seventy years and three generations, and all of them, all the good women, dissolved into the figure of my mother, who was, as she told us, *a good mother*. She didn't go out dancing or drinking (gin, mother's ruin, was often specified. 'Your mother drank gin once,' my father told me years later, with nostalgic regret). She didn't go, as one mother she'd known, in a story of maternal neglect that I remember thinking was over the top at the time, and tie a piece of string round my big toe, dangle it through the window and down the front of the house, so that the drunken mother, returning from her carousing, she could tug at it, wake the child, get the front door open and send it down the shop for a basin of pie and peas. I still put myself to sleep by thinking about *not* lying on a cold pavement covered with newspapers.

The eleven-year-old who cried on Coventry station hated being a servant. She got out as soon as she could and found work in the weaving sheds – 'she was a good weaver; six looms under her by the time she was sixteen' – married, produced nine children, eight of whom emigrated to the cotton mills of Massachusetts before the First World War, managed, 'never went before the Guardians'[1]. It was much, much later that I learned from *One Hand Tied Behind Us* that four was the usual number of looms in Lancashire weaving towns.[2] Burnley weavers were badly organized over the question of loom supervision, and my great-grandmother had six not because she was a good weaver, but because she was exploited. In 1916, when her daughter Carrie's husband was killed at the

[1] That is, never applied to the parish authorities for financial assistance under the Poor Law.

[2] Jill Liddington and Jill Norris, *One Hand Tied Behind Us: The Rise of the Women's Suffrage Movement*, Virago, 1978.

Somme, she managed that too, looking after the three-year-old, my mother, so that Carrie could go on working at the mill.

But long before the narrative fell into place, before I could dress the eleven-year-old of my imagination in the clothing of the 1870s, I knew perfectly well what that child had done, and how she had felt. She cried, because tears are cheap; and then she stopped, and got by, because no one gives you anything in this world. What was given to her, passed on to all of us, was a powerful and terrible endurance, the self-destructive defiance of those doing the best they can with what life hands out to them.

[...]

Sometime during 1950, [...] I was taken north to Burnley and into the sheds, where one afternoon my mother visited someone she used to know as a child, now working there. The woman smiled and nodded at me, through the noise that made a surrounding silence. Afterwards, my mother told me that they had to lip-read: they couldn't hear each other speak for the noise of the looms. But I didn't notice the noise. The woman wore high platform-soled black shoes that I still believe I heard click on the bright polished floor as she walked between her looms. Whenever I hear the word 'tending' I always think of that confident attentiveness to the needs of the machines, the control over work that was unceasing, with half a mind and hands engaged, but the looms always demanding attention. When I worked as a primary-school teacher I sometimes retrieved that feeling with a particular clarity, walking between the tables on the hard floor, all the little looms working, but needing my constant adjustment. [...] I wanted to walk like that, a short skirt, high heels, bright red lipstick, in charge of all that machinery.

[...]

As a teenage worker my mother had broken with a recently established tradition and on leaving school in 1927 didn't go into the sheds. [...] [S]ometime, it must have been 1934, [she] came South, worked in Woolworth's on the Edgware Road, spent the War years in Roehampton, a ward-maid again, in the hospital where they mended fighter pilots' ruined faces. Now I can feel the deliberate vagueness in her accounts of those years: 'When did you meet daddy?' – 'Oh, at a dance, at home.' There were no photographs. Who came to London first? I wish now that I'd asked that question. He worked on the buses when he arrived, showed me a canopy in front of a hotel once, that he'd pulled down on his first solo drive. He was too old to be called up (a lost generation of men who were too young for the first War, too old for the second). There's a photograph of him standing in front of the cabbages he'd grown for victory, wearing his Home Guard uniform. But what did he *do* after his time on the buses, and during the War years? Too late now to find out.

During the post-War housing shortage my father got an office job with a property company, and the flat to go with it. I was born in March 1947, at the peak of the Bulge, more babies born that month than ever before or after, and carried through the terrible winter of 1946–7. We moved to Streatham Hill in June 1951, to an estate owned by the same company (later to be taken over by Lambeth Council), and a few years after the move my father got what he wanted, which was to be in charge of the company's boiler maintenance. On his death certificate it says 'heating engineer'.

[...]

Now, thirty years later, I feel a great regret for the father of my first four years, who took me out and who probably loved me, irresponsibly ('It's alright for him; he doesn't have to look after you'), and I wish I could tell him now, even though he really was a sod, that I'm sorry for the years of rejection and dislike. But we were forced to choose, early on, which side we belonged to, and children have to come down on the side that brings the food home and gets it on the table. By 1955 I was beginning to hate him – because *he* was to blame, for the lack of money, for my mother's terrible dissatisfaction at the way things were working out.

Changes in the market place, the growth of real income and the proliferation of consumer goods that marked the mid-1950s, were used by my mother to measure out her discontent: there existed a newly expanding and richly endowed material world in which she was denied a place. The new consumer goods came into the house slowly, and we were taught to understand that our material deprivations were due entirely to my father's meanness. We had the first fridge in our section of the street (which he'd got cheap, off the back of a lorry, contacts in the trade) but were very late to acquire a television. I liked the new vacuum cleaner at first, because it meant no longer having to do the stairs with a stiff brush. But in fact it added to my Saturday work because I was expected to clean more with the new machine. Now I enjoy shocking people by telling them how goods were introduced into households under the guise of gifts for children: the fridge in the house of the children we played with over the road was given to the youngest as a birthday present – the last thing an eight-year-old wants. My mother laughed at this, scornfully: the clothes and shoes she gave us as birthday presents were conventional gifts for all post-War children, but the record player also came into the house in this way, as my eleventh birthday present. I wasn't allowed to take it with me when I left, though: it really wasn't mine at all.

[...]

We weren't, I now realize by doing the sums, badly off. My father paid the rent, all the bills, gave us our pocket money, and a fixed sum of seven pounds a week housekeeping money, quite a lot in the late 1950s[3] went on being handed over every Friday until his death, even when estrangement was obvious, and he was living most of the time with somebody else. My mother must have made quite big money in tips, for

---

[3]Richard Hoggart mentions the sum of £8 a week as an extravagant amount to spend on housekeeping in 1956/7. *Uses of Literacy*, p. 43.

the records of her savings, no longer a secret, show quite fabulous sums being stored away in the early 1960s. When she died there was over £40,000 in building-society accounts. Poverty hovered as a belief. It existed in stories of the thirties, in a family history. Even now when a bank statement comes in that shows I'm overdrawn or when the gas bill for the central heating seems enormous, my mind turns to quite inappropriate strategies, like boiling down the ends of soap, and lighting fires with candle ends and spills of screwed up newspaper to save buying wood. I think about these things because they were domestic economies that we practised in the 1950s. We believed we were badly off because we children were expensive items, and all these arrangements had been made for us. 'If it wasn't for you two,' my mother told us, 'I could be off somewhere else.' After going out manicuring she started spending Sunday afternoons in bed, and we couldn't stay in the house or play on the doorstep for fear of disturbing her. The house was full of her terrible tiredness and her terrible resentment; and I knew it was all my fault.

Later, in 1977, after my father's death, we found out that they were never married, that we were illegitimate. In 1934 my father left his wife and two-year-old daughter in the North, and came to London. He and my mother had been together for at least ten years when I was born, and we think now that I was her hostage to fortune, the factor that might persuade him to get a divorce and marry her. But the ploy failed.

Just before my mother's death, playing about with the photographs on the front bedroom mantelpiece, my niece discovered an old photograph under one of me at three. A woman holds a tiny baby. It's the early 1930s, a picture of the half sister left behind. But I think I knew about her and her mother long before I looked them both in the face, or heard about their existence, knew that the half-understood adult conversations around me, the two trips to Burnley in 1951, the quarrels about 'her', the litany of 'she', 'she', 'she' from behind closed doors, made up the figure in the New Look coat, hurrying away, wearing the clothes that my mother wanted to wear, angry with me yet nervously inviting me to follow, caught finally in the revolving door.

Reading C
The disabled self

Susan Gregory

To be categorized as a disabled person is to be described in terms of what you cannot do. The very term 'disabled' carries the meaning 'not able'. The World Health Organization offers the following definitions:

Impairment: any loss or abnormality of psychological, physiological or anatomical structure or function.

Disability: any restrictions or lack (resulting from an impairment) of ability to perform an activity in the manner or within the range considered normal for a human being.

(WHO, 1980)

Disability is a relational term. It defines a person in relation to others according to a criterion of difference. A disability only has meaning in terms of an ability which is lacking. People are visually impaired, not blind impaired. It is those with sight, not those who are blind, who are the norm. Formal definitions, including those used in legislation and the way the term is used in general, reinforce and maintain a view of disability as biologically determined. According to this perspective, blind people and deaf people, for example, are unable to function effectively in society without help, because of their sensory impairment. In this reading, I wish to argue that, for disabled people, their identity is not essentially physically or biologically determined but arises within their social context which translates the medical model of disability as pathology into social action and interaction.

Much of our understanding and representation of disability is from the able-bodied perspective. This emphasizes notions of deficiency, impairment, lack, and absence. By common convention, the tragedy of blindness is not to be able to see the beauty of a sunset, and that of deafness not to hear the birds sing, conceptions that differ dramatically from accounts of deaf and blind people themselves. For example, Hull, a blind man writes vividly of the meaning that wind and rain have for him, in ways which differ from the meanings for sighted people. Of his blindness, he says:

There is still much I do not know, but the conviction has deepened in me that blindness is a paradoxical world because it is both independent and dependent. It is independent in the sense that it is an authentic and autonomous world, a place of its own. Increasingly, I do not think of myself so much as a blind person, which would define me with reference to sighted people and as lacking something, but as a whole-body-seer (WBS). A blind person is simply someone in whom the specialist function of sight is now devolved upon the whole body, and no longer specialized in a particular organ. Being a WBS is to be in one of the concentrated human conditions. It is a state, like the state of being young, or of being old, of being male or female, it is one of the orders of human being.

(Hull, 1991, p. 164)

The perception of disability simply in terms of impairment shows more than a lack of empathy. Together with accounts which emphasize disability as personal tragedy, or which present disability plus achievement as a triumph over adversity, such a view indicates how disability is defined by 'outsiders'. Jenny Morris, herself a disabled woman, describes the impact of the portrayal of disability by some charities working for disabled people, a major source of such representations:

Disabled people object to the way we are portrayed in charity advertisements. We object to words like suffer, condemned, confined, victim, and to negative images portraying disability. It is common for a wheelchair to be used as a symbol of imprisonment. This creates two stereotypes. First it translates the meaning of disability into a mobility impairment and makes it less likely that non-disabled people will recognize and understand other forms of disability. Second it creates an image of an intolerable life – of confinement, passivity, frustration and victimization (all of which can be 'overcome' by plucky little cripples) instead of portraying a wheelchair for what it actually is, namely a means of mobility, a means of movement, a potential for freedom rather than imprisonment.

(Morris, 1991, p. 110)

To be born with a disability is not to have an inherent sense of oneself as deficient, though maybe a gradual sense of difference will emerge. How then do disabled people come to understand themselves as disabled? The way in which notions of disability may be acquired by individuals and how these may impinge upon the development of their self-identity is suggested in the following quotations:

When I was small I thought I was only deaf when I was at school. The only people at school were deaf people and there were no deaf people outside of school. I just thought – and this is awful – that school made people deaf, because only deaf people were there. I don't know why I thought this but that also everyone outside school was hearing.

(Deaf Asian man, 28 years old, quoted in Moorhouse, 1994, p. 87)

I remember being told 'You don't hear things, you're deaf' and I thought my brother and sister were deaf, I thought they couldn't hear either. And they said 'No they can hear'. And I said 'What does it mean?' as I really did not know what it meant. I did not think that deafness means you don't hear, but it was just a word for me. I didn't know what it meant.

(Josie, 24 years old, quoted in Gregory et al., 1995, p. 193)

Padden and Humphries (1988) describe the experience of a number of deaf people. Sam, who had deaf parents, played with the hearing girl who lived next door. It was only after some time that he observed her communicating with her mother and was surprised to see they did it by moving their mouths. Jim, who had hearing parents, says that he assumed for a long time that everyone lip-read and he was amazed that everyone could do it better that he could. Padden and Humphries suggest that, for the deaf child in the hearing family, there may be few clues as to their difference – they could notice that whenever an adult goes to the door there is someone there, which is not the case for themselves, having not heard the bell ring, but they could attribute this to a general difference between adults and children. They suggest that it is only through time that the person becomes aware of themselves as deaf, and its implications. They describe this process as 'learning to be deaf'.

One part of coming to realize one is disabled is to recognize oneself as significantly different. Yet difference alone is not enough. To be red-headed is to be a minority but not to be disabled. It is how the difference is evaluated that is significant. This evaluation may be related to efficiency in performing particular tasks, but the significance attached to particular skills is socially defined. Neither can the inability to perform particular tasks be the only relevant criterion, as skills that are essential in one society may be irrelevant in another. In this society, lack of hearing or sight is a disability while lack of smell or taste is not. The extent to which disabled people assimilate the dominant negative view of disability may depend on whether they have a viable or alternative group with which to identify: people who either share their disability or for whom the difference which defines their disability is irrelevant.

Finkelstein (1981) writes of an imaginary community in which everyone was a wheelchair user. He describes what happened for a few able-bodied people who were part of the community. Able-bodied people were marked by bruises from constantly knocking their heads on door lintels, and backache from walking about bent double. They had to be supplied with special equipment – helmets and back-braces. Amputation was suggested to make them the right height. Money was collected for them in upturned helmets with 'help the able-bodied disabled' written on them.

Connors and Donnellan (1993) describe the Navajos living in Northern Arizona. Disability was not an issue in Navajo society and evoked no social evaluation. As they say: 'Terms such as blindness, paralysis, seizures, running away, temper tantrums, thinking slow or with difficulty, therefore do not carry the negative connotations or value judgements associated with Western culture. Rather they are descriptive terms as neutral as terms describing height, weight, colour of hair, and other personal characteristics that define the personal self. Historically, the Navajo had no words for handicap, disabilities or mental or physical impairments beyond such descriptive terms' (1993, p. 275). Connors and Donnellan suggest this is because, firstly, within Navajo culture the demands on a person reflect their particular competence and, secondly, because the Navajo tend to define all individuals in terms of their unique traits.

The notion of disability arises from a situation where a norm is established and then deviations from it are defined as abnormal. This is perhaps most clearly articulated within medical and psychological discourse. In order to understand the power of the concept of disability within disabled people's lives, it is perhaps useful to explore its historical and sociopolitical roots. Finkelstein (1991) argues that definitions of disability achieved their status and power as a result of the Industrial Revolution. During this period, manufacture shifted from individualized, home-working environments to large-scale factory production, and the new machinery was designed to be operated by a workforce of 'average people'. It became necessary to categorize unemployed people into those who could not work and were deserving of charity and support and those who would not work; that is, to separate the infirm from the indolent. Doctors became the experts for identifying the infirm and Finkelstein claims that this marked the beginning of a process of classifying disabled people and interpreting disability in medical terms. He further suggests that this period also saw the development of a medical focus on normalization – on making disabled people as much like 'normal' people as possible to facilitate their rehabilitation and assimilation into the workforce.

The concept of 'normal', however, has a much earlier history, which is important in understanding its current status within psychological discourse and its tenacious hold on the way disability is perceived both by professionals working in the field of disability and by the general population. The conceptual framework within which normalization operates reflects a social construction of disability which has its roots in the eighteenth century. Foucault (1977) describes how, during this time, the idea of the body as discrete, objective, passive and analysable developed. People came to be conceived of as individuals and were objectified in a particular way as the result of particular forms of disciplinary surveillance. The essential feature of this form of surveillance was that it allowed an observer to watch a number of individual people without them knowing whether or not they were being observed. Thus, in a prison, a central watch-tower provided an ideal vantage-point for observing individual prisoners, allowing an unseen person to monitor the behaviour of individuals.

Foucault argues that disciplinary surveillance combined with techniques of examination in hospitals, prisons, schools and barracks led to the extraction and recording of information about individuals from which the notions of normality (and consequently normalization) emerged:

> The judges of normality are present everywhere. We are in the society of the teacher-judge, the doctor-judge, the educator-judge; it is on them that the universal reign of the normative is based: and each individual, wherever he [sic] may find himself subjects to it his body, his gesture, his behaviour, his aptitudes, his achievements.
>
> *(Foucault, 1977, p. 304)*

Consequent upon the establishment and definition of the 'normal' came surveys which further categorized and refined notions of deviance. At the end of the nineteenth century and the beginning of the twentieth, large-scale surveys were introduced to identify children with disabilities. In 1851, the Census in England and Wales made an attempt to count the 'blind and deaf and dumb' in the community, and 'lunatics in asylums'. The 1913 Mental Deficiency Act required Local Authorities to identify all mentally defective children in their areas between the ages of 7 and 16. Such observations and categorizations have been further refined throughout the twentieth century. Thus, these groups became the subject of control.

Having constructed particular individuals as different, Euro-American societies currently espouse the view of normalization. Establishing the normal as desirable legitimated an approach to disabled people which was to demand that they appear and behave as normally as possible. Goffman suggests that, 'Society establishes the means of categorizing persons and the complement of attributes felt to be ordinary and natural for members of each of these categories' (1963, p. 2). In the absence of these 'ordinary and natural' attributes, the usual flow of behaviour is disrupted and interactions have to be managed in some way. The subtitle of Goffman's book *Stigma* is *Notes on the Management of Spoiled Identity*. One of the strategies he describes is 'passing' where the stigmatized person, to avoid disruption and to maintain the status quo, will preserve a semblance of normality.

Sally French, who is visually impaired, describes how this can come about:

> Some of my earliest memories are of anxious relatives trying to get me to see things. I did not understand why it was important that I should do so, but was acutely aware of their intense anxiety if I could not. It was aesthetic things like rainbows that bothered them most. They would position me with great precision, tilting my head to precisely the right angle, and then point to the sky saying, 'Look there it is: look, there, there ... THERE!'. As far as I was concerned there was nothing there, but if I said as much their anxiety grew even more intense; they would rearrange my position and the whole scenario would be repeated. In the end, despite a near total lack of colour vision and a complete indifference to the rainbow's whereabouts, I would say I could see it. I thus was able to release the mounting tension and escape to pursue more interesting tasks. It did not take long to learn that in order to avert episodes such as these and protect the feelings of people around me I had to deny my disability.

> (French, 1993, p. 69)

Ostensibly with the goal that individuals should not be unnecessarily marginalized, emphasis has been placed by professionals on such normalization. The work of the Peto Institute of Hungary has been endorsed in this country, for instance, whereby children with cerebral palsy are encouraged to walk, sometimes being put through rigid programmes to achieve this, when mobility may well have been more easily achieved by other means. Hari, the director of the Peto Institute, describes it thus:

> The duty of the pedagogue is to promote the discovery of conditions which enable the spinal cord injury patient to learn how to walk etc. and enter everyday life without any special mechanism. [...] In order to make a spinal cord injury patient walk, teaching must restore the will of the individual to do so.
>
> *(Hari, 1975, quoted in Sutton, 1986, p. 162)*

People with disabilities have described the impact of such polices on their lives:

> The aim of returning the individual to normality is the central foundation stone upon which the whole rehabilitation machine is constructed. If, as happened to me following my spinal injury, the disability cannot be cured, normative assumptions are not abandoned. On the contrary, they are reformulated so that they not only dominate the treatment phase, searching for a cure, but also totally colour the helper's perception of that person's life. The rehabilitation aim now becomes to assist the individual to be as 'normal as possible'. The result for me was endless soul destroying hours at Stoke Mandeville Hospital trying to approximate to able-bodied standards by 'walking' with callipers and crutches. [...] Rehabilitation philosophy emphasizes physical normality and, with this, the attainment of skills that allow the individual to approximate as closely as possible the able-bodied behaviour (e.g. only using a wheelchair as a last resort, rather than seeing it as a disabled person's mobility aid like a pair of shoes is an able-bodied person's mobility aid).
>
> *(Finkelstein, 1988, quoted in Oliver, 1990, p. 54)*

Yet the idea of normality is socially constructed and a contested notion. For example, within the field of deaf education, there has long been a debate as to whether deaf children should be brought up to use sign language or spoken language as their first language. Many professionals feel it is better for a deaf child to be trained in speaking and lipreading, to use 'normal' language, whatever the impoverishment and delay this approach creates in their language development. Others express concern about such delay as the first words can be acquired as late as 5 years of age, or sometimes not at all. They suggest the child be introduced to sign language in the first instance to allow the development of age-appropriate communication ability. The following two excerpts indicate the ferocity of this debate:

> Oralists support the idea that attempts should be made *to overcome* the barrier to communication caused by deafness by exploiting the use of residual hearing to the maximum rather than by *circumventing* the problems of deafness and communication by, for example, substi-

tuting sign language for speech. [...]. We believe that the oral-auditory approach offers a feasible alternative to any form of total communication and furthermore facilitates the normal development of the child. [...] Oralists recognize that the development of the deaf child's vocal/verbal behaviour will undoubtedly be delayed in comparison with a normally hearing child.

(Lynas et al., 1988, excepts from pp. 5–23, their italics)

Language must be introduced and acquired as early as possible or its development may be permanently retarded and impaired. [...] Deaf children must first be exposed to fluent signers, whether these be their parents, or teachers, or whoever. Once signing is learned – and it may be fluent by three years of age – then all else may follow: a free intercourse of minds, a free flow of information, the acquisition of reading and writing, and that of speech. There is no evidence that signing inhibits the acquisition of speech. Indeed the reverse is probably so.

(Sacks, 1989, pp. 31–2)

But what is the normality that is being endorsed here, normal language (i.e. speech) or the attainment of normal competence in communication?

In this reading, I have tried to show the way in which disability, rather than being a biological given, can only be understood within particular social and cultural frameworks. In particular, physical and mental characteristics are not in themselves either necessary or sufficient causes for the attribution of the category 'disabled'. Disability is a social category, which legitimates, or at the very least condones, the disempowerment of people with particular mental or physical attributes. The desirability of the norm has consequences for the expectations of disabled people and, thus, such social and cultural understandings of disability are fundamental to the ways in which people who are labelled disabled come to understand themselves and their own identity.

References

Connors, J.L. and Donnellan, A.M. (1993) 'Citizenship and culture; the role of disabled people in Navajo society', *Disability, Handicap and Society*, vol. 8 , pp. 265–80.

Finkelstein, V. (1981) 'To deny or not to deny disabilities', in Brechin, A., Liddiard, P. and Swain, J. (eds) *Handicap in a Social World*, Sevenoaks, Hodder and Stoughton.

Finkelstein, V. (1991) '"We" are not disabled, "You" are', in Gregory, S. and Hartley, G.M. (eds) *Constructing Deafness*, London, Printer Press.

Foucault, M. (1977) *Discipline and Punish*, London, Allen Lane.

French, (1993) '"Can you see the rainbow?" The roots of denial', in Swain, J., Finkelstein, V., French, S. and Oliver, M. (eds) *Disabling Barriers – Enabling Environments*, London, Sage.

Goffman, E. (1963) *Stigma: Notes on the Management of Spoiled Identity*, New Jersey, Prentice Hall.

Gregory, S., Bishop, J. and Sheldon, L. (1995) *Deaf Young People and their Families: Developing Understanding*, Cambridge, Cambridge University Press.

Hull, J.M. (1991) *Touching the Rock: An Experience of Blindness*, London, Arrow Books.

Lynas, W., Huntington, A. and Tucker, I. (not dated, published 1988) *A Critical Examination of Different Approaches to Communication in the Education of Deaf Children*, Manchester, Ewing Foundation Publication.

Moorhouse, D. (1994) 'Knowing who I am', supplementary reading D251 *Issues in Deafness*, Unit 10, Milton Keynes, The Open University.

Morris, J. (1991) *Pride Against Prejudice,* London, The Women's Press.

Oliver, M. (1990) *The Politics of Disablement*, Macmillan, London.

Padden, C. and Humphries, T. (1988) *Deaf in America: Voices from a Culture*, London, Harvard University Press.

Sacks, O. (1989) *Seeing Voices*, London, Picador.

Sutton, A. (1986) 'Problems of Theory', in Cottam, P.J. and Sutton, A. (eds) *Conductive Education: A System for Overcoming Motor Disorder*, London, Croom Helm.

World Health Organization (1980) 'International classification of impairment', *Disability and Handicap*, WHO, Geneva.

Index

Acknowledgements

Grateful acknowledgement is made to the following sources for permission to reproduce material in this book:

INTRODUCTION: *Photograph:* p. 3: Popperfoto.

CHAPTER 1: *Figures:* Figure 1.2: Baron, R.A. and Byrne, D.E. (1981) *Social Psychology: Understanding Human Interaction,* 3rd edn., copyright © 1981, 1977, 1974 by Allyn and Bacon, Inc. *Photographs/Cartoons:* p. 16: Reproduced by kind permission of Professor Solomon E. Asch/Photo: William Vandivert; p. 22: copyright 1965 Stanley Milgram. Stills from the film *Obedience* distributed by the New York University Film Library; pp. 27 and 34: Copyright the Estate of Mel Calman p. 32: Vanessa Miles/Environmental Picture Library.

CHAPTER 2: *Text:* Hinshelwood, R.D. (1987) *What Happens in Groups?,* Free Association Books; Bion, W.R. (1961) *Experiences in Groups and Other Papers,* Tavistock Publications.

CHAPTER 3: *Text:* Brindle, D. (1994) 'Mental care risks isolation problem', *The Guardian,* 4 March 1994; Durham, M. (1994) 'Probe into killing by mental patient', *The Observer,* 26 June 1994; Jodelet D. (1991) *Madness and Social Representations,* Harvester Wheatsheaf; Solzhenitsyn, A. (1973) *The Gulag Archipelago,* © Aleksandr I. Solzhenitsyn 1973, © English language translation Harper & Row Publishers, Inc, 1973, 1974; 'Psychiatrist reveals the agony and the lunacy of great artists', *The Guardian,* 30 June 1994. *Figures:* Figure 3.1: Azjen, I. (1988) *Attitudes, Personality and Behaviour,* Open University Press; Figure 3.4: Jodelet, D. (1991) *Madness and Social Representations,* Harvester Wheatsheaf. *Photographs/Cartoons:* p. 127: Laurie Sparham/Network; p. 128: Copyright Evening Standard/SOLO; p. 141: The Advertising Archives; p. 159: Andrew Wiard/Network.

CHAPTER 4: *Text:* 'Anger as BNP chief walks free over race attack', *Independent,* 18 June 1994; Myers, P. (1994) 'BNP leader jailed for race attack', *The Guardian,* 18 June 1994; Bennetto, J. (1994) 'Anti-Jewish incidents rise by 20%', *Independent,* 22 June 1994; Fanon, F. (1967) *Black Skin, White Masks,* Grove Atlantic, Inc. Also by permission of HarperCollins Publishers Ltd. *Table:* Table 4.1: Tajfel, H. (1981) *Human Groups and Social Categories: Studies in Social Psychology,* Cambridge University Press; *Photographs/Cartoons:* pp. 180 and 199: Hulton Deutsch; p. 206: Figures 11.7(b), 11.10 (a,c,d) and 11.11 (a) from *Social Psychology* by Muzafer Sherif and Carolyn W. Sherif. Copyright © by Muzafer Sherif and Carolyn W. Sherif. Reprinted by permission of HarperCollins Publishers, Inc; p. 226: Gideon Mendel/Network.

CHAPTER 5: *Text:* Arkin, A. (1994) 'New company culture gets off the ground', *Personnel Management,* June 1994, Institute of Personnel Management; 'Interview by Edward Pilkington', *The Guardian,* 4 May 1995; Watson, D.H. (1988) *Managers of Discontent: Trade Union Officers and Industrial Relations Managers,* Routledge; Collinson, D.L. (1992) *Managing the Shopfloor: Subjectivity, Masculinity and Workplace Culture,* Walter de Gruyter. *Photographs/Cartoons:* p. 249: Reprinted by permission of the Peters, Fraser and Dunlop Group Ltd; pp. 250, 254, 256: Copyright the Estate of Mel Calman.

CHAPTER 6: *Text:* Steedman, C. (1986) *Landscape for a Good Woman: A Story of Two Lives,* Virago. *Cartoons/Photographs:* p. 324 (cartoon): reproduced by kind permission of the Peters, Fraser and Dunlop Group Limited; p. 324 (photo): Ronald Grant Archive; p. 326: Debbie Humphrey; p. 335: Steven Appleby/Assorted Images.

COVER ILLUSTRATION: Kasimir Malevich, *Sportsmen,* c.1928–32, oil on canvas, 142 × 164 cm., State Russian Museum, St Petersburg.